HOMICIDE

matt delisi

iowa state university

MW00562253

Kendall Hunt
publishing company

Cover image © Shutterstock, Inc.

Kendall Hunt
publishing company

www.kendallhunt.com
Send all inquiries to:
4050 Westmark Drive
Dubuque, IA 52004-1840

CONTENTS

Chapter 1   Types and Correlates of Homicide 1

SECTION 1   Criminological Perspectives **23**

Chapter 2   Homicide and the Interactionist Perspective 25

Chapter 3   Homicide and the Regional Perspective 39

Chapter 4   Homicide and the Code of the Street Perspective 51

Chapter 5   Homicide and the Lifestyle Perspective 65

Chapter 6   Homicide and the Self-Control Perspective 81

Chapter 7   Homicide and the Social Control Perspective 95

Chapter 8   Homicide and the Institutional Anomie
Perspective 109

Chapter 9   Homicide and the Social Learning Perspective 121

Chapter 10   Homicide and the General Strain Perspective 135

Chapter 11   Homicide and the Structural Perspective 145

Chapter 12   Homicide and the Social Disorganization
Perspective 159

**SECTION 2   Interdisciplinary and Psychiatric
Perspectives** **171**

Chapter 13   Homicide and the Personality Perspective 173

Chapter 14   Homicide and the Evolutionary Perspective 187

Chapter 15   Homicide and the Epidemiological Perspective 197

Chapter 16   Homicide and the Biosocial Perspective 211

Chapter 17   Homicide and the Victimology Perspective 223

Chapter 18   Homicide and the Criminal Career Perspective 233

Chapter 19   Homicide and the Psychopathy Perspective 247

Chapter 20   Homicide and the Substance Abuse Perspective 259

Chapter 21   Homicide and the Bipolar Disorder Perspective 267

Chapter 22   Homicide and the Schizophrenia Perspective 277

Chapter 23   Homicide and the Antisocial Personality Disorder
Perspective 291

Chapter 24   Homicide and the Neuropsychological Perspective ...301

Chapter 25   Critical Concepts 309

References *325*
Index *367*

CHAPTER 1

Types and Correlates of Homicide

© ruskpp/Shutterstock, Inc.

Since Cain murdered Abel, humanity has been plagued by and intrigued by homicide.

Introduction

A variety of complexities relate to homicide. It is the most serious criminal offense in all human societies, and it is the main offense that has historically and even today that is potentially punishable by death. It is also the rarest form of violent crime. Although homicide offenders tend to have serious antisocial histories compared to persons who never commit homicide, most criminal offenders do not have a homicide arrest in their criminal history, nor will they ever commit one. In fact, many of the most frequently used datasets in criminology, some of which have sample sizes in the thousands nevertheless have only a handful of participants who have been arrested for homicide (DeLisi, 2001a). Thus, even among serious criminals, homicide is the exception, not the norm.

Many times, the immediate "causes" or circumstances that give rise to homicides are extraordinarily ordinary: arguments gone too far, jealousy fueled by alcohol or drug usage, greed, or something as simple as bumping into another person at a bar or restaurant. As Daly and Wilson (1999, p. 58) quipped, many homicides are "Barroom interactions among unrelated men became heated contests concerning dominance, deference, and face, and escalated to lethality."

The normalcy of motivations for homicide is particularly true in the event of very young individuals committing homicide. In cases of homicide by children under age 10 years, for instance, mundane events such as simple arguments are self-reported by the murderer as the cause of the murder (see Bernstein, 1979). Yet the same "causes" are experienced by millions of other people who manage to never commit homicide, or even contemplate doing so. As Dietz (1986, p. 490) concluded:

> "Mass, serial, and sensational homicides share several common features. First, they occur with a frequency too low to permit the ordinary research habits of psychiatrists or criminologists to elucidate their characteristics. Second, they typically evoke a premature and sometimes erroneous conclusion that the offender must have been mad. Third, they generate an extreme degree of publicity, leading to unusual media influences, both beneficial and detrimental, on criminal investigation, the processing of cases through the criminal justice system and the behavior of offenders, would-be offenders, and others."

Even conventional wisdom about homicide offenders is seemingly contradictory and complex. Some view homicide offenders as monsters who are very different from other people, whereas others view homicide offenders as relatively normal individuals who unfortunately made a snap decision that changed the course of lives. On these latter points, there is evidence to support both perspectives. A study of 18 months of data on convicted homicide offenders in England and Wales found that 44 percent of convicted killers had a lifetime history or mental illness, but only 14 percent had symptoms of mental illness at the time of their murder. Only 14 percent ever reported contact with mental health services and just 8 percent did so in the year before their homicide (Shaw, Appleby, Amos, McDonnell, Harris, et al., 1999). Although persons convicted of homicide have substantial prevalence of personality disorders and substance use disorders, most do not have severe mental illness, and few have prior or current involvement with the mental health system to treat these problems. And although most homicide offenders have a range of biological, social, and psychological risk factors in their backgrounds (Heide & Solomon, 2009), it is often difficult to distinguish them from "normal" people who do not commit homicide. Indeed, the primary reason why friends, family, and neighbors often characterize their friend, son, or neighbor as a "normal guy" after his arrest for murder is that for all intents and purposes, he appeared normal.

There are also important and at times contentious scholarly and policy debates about the primary causes of homicide, and the explanations for its decline. For example, like many American cities, New York was once plagued by approximately 1,500 to nearly 2,000 homicides each year during the 1970s and 1980s. In 1984, when vigilante shooter Bernard Goetz shot four youths who he thought were going to rob him, there were 1,458 murders...nearly four per day. The violence peaked in 1990 with 2,262 killings then it began to drop sharply. By 1997, there were 767 homicides. Many attribute the homicide decline to more aggressive and strategically utilized policing. Others disagree. For example, Bowling (1999) suggested that the rise and fall of the crack cocaine problem corresponds to the rise and fall of homicide in New York and that credit to the police is overstated. Thus, even the experts cannot agree on reasons for fluctuations in murder.

Still another challenge is that it is challenging to predict who will commit homicide even when using a sample of serious offenders. For example, Berk and his colleagues (2009) attempted to forecast homicide offending using a population of over 60,000 cases from the Philadelphia Adult Probation and Parole Department. Using simulation models, they estimated that only one in 100 probationers will commit murder. And when the highest-risk offenders were considered, the forecast was still generally low at eight in 100 probationers (Berk, Sherman, Barnes, Kurtz, & Ahlman, 2009). Due to its low base rate, and the uncertainty and unpredictability with which offenders ultimately commit murder, it is no wonder homicide is such a controversial and complex phenomenon to explain.

Box 1.1   The Costs of Homicide

An important reason why there are so many theories of homicide and why there is such intellectual curiosity and practical concern about understanding its causes relates to the costs of homicide. On one hand, the costs of homicide are incalculable given the loss of human life and the extraordinary and often lifelong suffering which friends and family members of homicide victims endure. There is also the broader societal effect of the fear that the crime imposes. Alvarez and Bachman (2003, p. 204) captured this feeling well. "The high rates of murder that our society endures annually affect us all. Even those of us who have never been personally touched by lethal violence are aware of the widespread presence of this violence in our communities. The ever-present fear that we or someone we love may be killed is but another form of psychic violence that we must all endure."

Acknowledging the humanistic or spiritual reasons why homicide cannot be calculated, scholars have nevertheless provided cost-estimates for murder. Drawing on actuarial approaches that calculate the direct and indirect costs, several estimates of a price tag for murder exist. Miller, Fisher, and Cohen (2001) analyzed state-level data from Pennsylvania to produce estimates for homicides involving juveniles and adults. Considering medical care costs, lost future earnings, public program costs, property damage and losses, and quality of life losses, the average murder of a juvenile was approximately $4.2 million and the average cost of the murder of an adult was nearly $3.5 million. Other studies have estimated the costs of homicide at $163,000 (Cohen, 1998), $426,000 (DeLisi & Gatling, 2003), and $8.9 million (McCollister, French, & Fang, 2010). Estimates also exist for homicides occurring in other nations. For example, Mayhew (2003) calculated an individual cost for homicide of $1.6 million based on data from Australia. Based on data from England and Wales, Brand and Price (2000) estimated that each homicide costs £ 1.1 million.

In a study that focused exclusively on murder, DeLisi, Kosloski, Sween, Hachmeister, Moore, and Drury (2010) replicated the crime estimates of earlier researchers on a sample of convicted homicide offenders selected from eight states. They found that each murder cost more than $5.16 million in direct costs and over $12 million in willingness-to-pay costs for a combined cost of $17.25 million per murder. Willingness-to-pay is a concept that attempts to quantify the pain and suffering that crime creates even though pain and suffering is not a construct that can be readily bought and sold as opposed to tangible goods and services. Essentially, willingness-to-pay estimates capture public concern about crime and public willingness to assist in crime prevention. In addition, because murderers in their sample were also convicted of other crimes, the average murderer in their data produced costs of approximately $24 million. The most violent and chronic offenders in their data singly produced costs in the range of $150 million! The costs of other specific forms of homicide, such as workplace homicides are also in the billions (Hartley, Biddle, & Jenkins, 2005)

While it is true that one cannot truly monetize the pain, suffering, and loss of homicide, it is also true that the enormous fiscal toll of homicide is substantively comparable when the sheer monetary amount is considered.

Sources: Alvarez, A., & Bachman, R. (2003). *Murder: American style.* Belmont, CA: Thomson; Brand, S., & Price, R. (2000). *The economic and social costs of crime.* London, England: Home Office Economics and Resource Analysis Unit; Cohen, M. A. (1998). The monetary value of saving a high-risk youth. *Journal of Quantitative Criminology, 14,* 5–33; DeLisi, M., & Gatling, J. M. (2003). Who pays for a life of crime? An empirical assessment of the assorted victimization costs posed by career criminals. *Criminal Justice Studies, 16,* 283–293; DeLisi, M., Kosloski, A., Sween, M., Hachmeister, E., Moore, M., & Drury, A. (2010). Murder by numbers: Monetary costs imposed by a sample of homicide offenders. *The Journal of Forensic Psychiatry & Psychology, 21*(4), 501–513; Mayhew, P. (2003). *Counting the costs of crime in Australia.* Canberra, Australia: Australian Institute of Criminology; McCollister, K. E., French, M. T., & Fang, H. (2010). The cost of crime to society: New crime-specific estimates for policy and program evaluation. *Drug and Alcohol Dependence, 108*(1), 98–109; Miller, T. R., Fisher, D. A., & Cohen, M. A. (2001). Costs of juvenile violence: Policy implications. *Pediatrics, 107,* 1–7; Hartley, D., Biddle, E. A., & Jenkins, E. L. (2005). Societal cost of workplace homicides in the United States, 1992–2001. *American Journal of Industrial Medicine, 47*(6), 518–527.

Mass media outlets similarly present conflicting images of homicide and the characteristics of those who perpetrators and victims of the most severe crime. Television and film tend to exaggerate the prevalence of more sensationalistic forms of homicide, such as those involving multiple victims, and obscure the more mundane characteristics of what are sometimes called "normal" homicides. A study of homicide characteristics in popular culture in the United Kingdom is illustrative. Brown, Hughes, McGlen, and Crichton (2014) compared 217 fictional homicides committed by 105 perpetrators on the television show "Midsomer Murders" to 55 homicides committed by 53 perpetrators in the Lothian and Borders region of Scotland. Virtually all of the real homicides were unplanned, single offender crimes where the murderer used a kitchen knife to stab or fists and feet to pummel the victim. Usually, the murderer was intoxicated. In contrast, the fictional murders most frequently involved a serial killer, were planned, were more likely to have a female killer, and used guns or poison to perpetrate the crime. In addition, the television show dramatically underestimated the presence of mental disorder (11.4 percent of fictional murders compared to 47.2 percent of real murders). Fictional homicides were also more likely to involve women, whites, and older persons.

Irrespective of one's position on these issues, there is no question that homicide offenders also impose a considerable amount of fear on the community, and even motivate self-defense measures. For example, Lee and DeHart (2007) surveyed residents in the Baton Rouge, Louisiana area during the midst of a serial killer episode. They found that nearly 60 percent of residents reported significant personal fear while the homicide offender was at large, and nearly half took steps to increase the security of their home. After the apprehension of the suspect, resident fear declined considerably.

To be sure, it is likely there is so much disagreement about the nature of homicide offenders because there is considerable diversity or heterogeneity among homicide offenders, and, more fundamentally, types of homicide. This diversity is examined next.

Types of Homicide

Homicide is the killing of a human being by another human being. Although all homicides share the killing of another human, the legal ramifications of homicide depend sharply on contextual circumstances and the criminal mindset or *mens rea* of the perpetrator. *Mens rea* means guilty mind and reflects the offender's criminal intent. In the case of homicide, it reflects the degree to which an individual meant to cause the death of another person homicide. There are gradations of *mens rea*. In descending order of seriousness and culpability, *mens rea* ranges from purposely, knowingly, recklessly, and negligently. For example, the killing of another during armed conflict while on military service is not viewed by most as homicide, and it is not viewed by most as criminal behavior. A police officer who kills a felon during the commission of a serious crime has committed the act of homicide, but in this context, it is a **justifiable homicide**. Justifiable homicides are measured in two ways, the Supplementary Homicide Reports of the Uniform Crime Reporting program and the National Vital Statistics System mortality data. Over the last 40 years, between 250 and 500 persons are killed by police in the line of duty. Eight percent of those killed are in the crime-prone years between ages 10 and 39. The majority of those killed by police are white (between 56 and 62 percent) with blacks (between 35 to 41 percent) over-represented by population but comparable to their involvement in violent crime (Loftin, Wiersema, McDowall, & Dobrin, 2003).

A homicide that is criminal behavior is murder. According to federal law, **murder** is the unlawful killing of a human being with malice aforethought. This means that the individual planned, premeditated, or deliberated in a specific way to cause the death of another human being.

Homicides that meet this level of premeditation are known as first-degree murder. Lesser forms of homicide, such as second-degree murder lack the premeditation. States have created additional statutes that pertain to homicide committed with intention but in the immediate heat of passion (**voluntary manslaughter**), homicide committed due to accident or negligence (**involuntary manslaughter**), and unplanned homicide caused by motor vehicle/traffic violation (**vehicular homicide**). Cases involving accident and negligence essentially mean that *mens rea* was reduced from an individual purposely intending to cause another's death.

Homicides are also differentiated by the characteristics and/or relationship between the homicide perpetrator and victim. As shown in Figure 1.1, the age of the homicide offender and victim is associated with the type of homicide that is committed, the weapon that is used, and the nature of the relationship between offender and victim. These varieties of homicide are examined next.

Filicide

Filicide is the murder of a child by a parent. Although it is fortunately rare, filicide is nevertheless more prevalent than commonly believed. For example, a large-scale study in the United States utilized 32 years of data from the FBI Supplemental Homicide Reports (Mariano, Chan, & Myers, 2014). Filicides accounted for 15 percent of all homicides occurring during the study period and totaled 94,146 filicides. The modal age of a filicide victim was 1 year and one-third of all filicide victims were less than 1 year of age. More than two-thirds of filicide victims were age 6 years or less. African Americans were significantly likely to perpetrate filicide compared to whites. The manner of filicide involved beatings with hands or feet, strangulation, asphyxiation, drowning, and defenestration (throwing out a window). Although biological and stepparents were about equally likely to commit filicide, stepparents were two times more likely to kill with a firearm. Overall, the filicide prevalence has been estimated at 0.56 per 100,000 children per year (Makhlouf & Rambaud, 2014).

There is often psychiatric disturbance among parents who perpetrate filicide. For example, Liem and Koenraadt (2008) analyzed forensic psychiatric data from a hospital in Utrecht, Netherlands, for the period 1953 to 2004. They discovered 79 men and 82 women who had killed 132 children or attempted to kill 29 other children. More than half of women and one-third of men were mentally ill at the time of their filicide. About 25 percent of men who committed filicide did so after being separated or divorced by their spouse. A study of nearly 40 years of homicide data from Sweden found that major psychiatric disorder (nearly nine fold increased

	Victims					Offenders				
	Total	Under 18	18–34	35–49	50 or older	Total	Under 18	18–34	35–49	50 or older
All homicides	100%	10.0%	53.2%	22.8%	14.0%	100%	11.0%	65.5%	17.1%	6.5%
Victim/offender relationship										
Intimate	100%	1.3%	48.5%	33.6%	16.6%	100%	1.0%	47.0%	34.7%	17.2%
Family	100%	19.5	32.8	26.0	21.9	100%	6.1%	50.5	27.5	15.9
Infants	100%	100				100%	7.4	81.2	10.2	1.1
Elders	100%				100	100%	9.4	47.8	20.7	22.1
Circumstances										
Felony murder	100%	7.5%	48.2%	22.2%	22.1%	100%	14.6%	72.7%	10.7%	2.0%
Sex related	100%	18.4	45.3	18.2	18.1	100%	9.7	73.1	15.2	1.9
Drug related	100%	5.4	70.9	20.2	3.6	100%	10.8	76.4	11.5	1.3
Gang related	100%	23.7	68.8	6.2	1.3	100%	28.0	70.2	1.6	0.2
Argument	100%	5.7	56.2	26.3	11.8	100%	7.0	60.7	23.0	9.2
Workplace	100%	0.5	26.7	33.5	39.3	100%	2.8	53.6	28.0	15.6
Weapon										
Gun homicide	100%	8.1%	59.7%	22.0%	10.3%	100%	12.2%	65.9%	15.1%	6.9%
Arson	100%	27.9	26.4	20.4	25.2	100%	10.6	57.0	24.9	7.5
Poison	100%	28.6	20.8	16.8	33.8	100%	3.5	48.8	29.8	17.8
Multiple victims or offenders										
Multiple victims	100%	17.9%	47.0%	19.3%	15.8%	100%	9.5%	66.3%	18.3%	5.9%
Multiple offenders	100%	10.4	58.4	19.2	12.0	100%	17.9	73.1	7.7	1.3

Figure 1.1 Homicide types and the age structure of offenders and victims, 1980–2008.

Source: Modified from Cooper, A., & Smith, E. L. (2011). Homicide trends in the United States, 1980–2008. Annual rates for 2009–2010. Washington, DC: U.S. Department of Justice, Office of Justice Programs, Bureau of Justice Statistics.

likelihood) and prior suicide attempt (nearly 12 times increased likelihood) were significant predictors of a parent committing filicide (Lysell et al., 2014). Multiple births increased the likelihood of filicide nearly five times.

Given these risk profiles, typologies have been developed to describe filicidal individuals. These include altruistic filicides, where the parent kills the child to relieve the child of real, perceived, or imagined stress and suffering; extended suicides, where the child is killed as an extension of the parent's self during a suicide; and psychotic filicides where the murder is the result of psychotic symptoms of the parent (Bourget & Bradford, 1990; Liem & Koenraadt, 2008). Regardless of its causes, filicide creates great societal outrage. For instance, in January 2015, 22-year-old Hyphernkemberly Dorvilier was charged with stopping her car in the middle of a road in Pemberton Township, New Jersey, dousing her newborn child with an accelerant and then setting her child on fire. The attack was fatal. Witnesses indicate that Dorvilier had a calm demeanor after the incident, and told them that she had set fire to dog feces (Robinson, 2015). Although the case has not gone to trial yet, it has nevertheless generated international outrage.

Infanticide

The horrifying case just described is actually an alleged infanticide. **Infanticide** is the murder of a child in the first year of life. The incidence of infanticide is estimated at 8 per 100,000 in the United States, and in the majority of cases, the perpetrator is the infant's biological mother. It is important to note, however, that the incidence of infanticide is difficult given that many of these are not classified as homicides. The usual methods of infanticide are smothering, suffocation, and drowning, and about 55–60 percent of infanticide victims are male. In their review of 40 years of research on the topic, Porter and Gavin (2010, p. 108) summarized that infanticides "are generally committed by more mature women who use a variety of violent methods, may premeditate the crime, and engage in infanticide for reasons ranging from retaliation against another adult to child abuse or neglect to removal of an unwanted child."

Overpeck and her colleagues (1998) conducted one of the most impressive studies of infanticide using data from 2,776 infanticides in the United States between 1983 and 1991. They produced several key findings. Half of the infanticides occurred by the infant's fourth month of life. The age and educational attainment of the mother (the primary perpetrator of infanticide) was strongly associated with risk for infanticide. Women who had their second child by age 17 were 10.9 times more likely to commit infanticide and women with two children by age 19 were 9.3 times more likely. Women who had no prenatal care were greater than 10 times more likely to murder their infant. Mothers with less than 12 years of education were eight times more likely to kill their infant than mothers with 16 or more years of education.

Neonaticide

A still more specific form of filicide is neonaticide. **Neonaticide** is the killing of a child in the infant's first 24 hours of life. Women who commit neonaticide are often characterized by a troubled psychiatric profile. Most women who commit neonaticide engaged in denial of their pregnancy, had dissociative thoughts, and/or were experiencing psychosis. The prevalence of sexual abuse victimization among women who commit neonaticide is also high (Spinelli, 2001).

Neonatcides are rare. An 18-year study of homicide data in France revealed a neonaticide prevalence of 0.12 per 100,000 births (Makhlouf & Rambaud, 2014). They are usually perpetrated by the child's mother and involve head trauma or passive neglect (e.g., leaving the child outside to be exposed to the weather elements). The most common apparent motives for neonaticide are altruism (the parent's belief that the killing will spare the child from real or perceived suffering), psychosis, revenge against the spouse or father of the child, accident, or simply the killing of an unwanted child (Resnick, 1969, 1970).

The profile of neonaticide offenders differs from infanticide offenders. According to Porter and Gavin (2010, p. 108), "Neonaticide is generally committed by women who often conceal the pregnancy, give birth away from a hospital and then suffocate, strangle, or drown the unwanted newborn before hiding the corpse. Neotnaticidal women generally do not have an incapacitating mental illness." Overall, persons who commit various forms of filicide, usually women, and usually the victim's mother present with a troubling profile that renders these cases controversial in the public's view.

Fatal Child Assault

Fatal child assault is the death of a child from acts of violence perpetrated by another person. Unlike other forms of homicide of children that mostly focus on the relationship between the child and their murderer, fatal child assault is primarily focused on the basic fact that the child's death was caused by violence (Lawrence, 2004). For a look at infanticides of children under the age of 5 years from 1980 to 2008, see Figure 1.2.

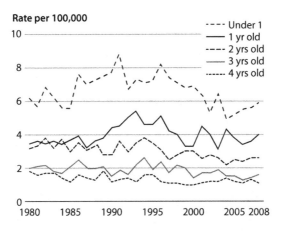

Figure 1.2   Infanticides of children age 5 years and younger, 1980–2008.

Source: Modified from Cooper, A., & Smith, E. L. (2011). *Homicide trends in the United States, 1980–2008. Annual rates for 2009–2010.* Washington, DC: U.S. Department of Justice, Office of Justice Programs, Bureau of Justice Statistics.

Parricide, Patricide, and Matricide

Parricide is the killing of one's father, mother, or another close relative. Two major types of parricide are **patricide**, the killing of one's father, and **matricide**, the killing of one's mother. A common theme among parricide offenders is one of abuse and highly dysfunctional family relationships in which the abuse often serves as the catalyst for the homicidal behavior. I this way, a patricide is seen as the child's way of atoning for abuses endured from one's father and a matricide is seen as the child's way of retaliating against the mother for her abuses. As Palermo (2014, p. 1260) recently summarized, "Some of these children store within themselves feelings of anger, resentment, and hostility beyond childhood and adolescence into adulthood. At times, they explode into acts of patricide or step-patricide. They are the human faces of the statistics."

Although themes of revenge and retaliation are common in parricide, there is heterogeneity among parricide offenders. One of the most influential researchers of parricide is Kathleen Heide. In a series of works, Heide (1993a,b, 1994, 1995) developed a typology that captures the three general types of children who murder their parents. These include severely abused children who ultimately kill a parent or parents to end the abuse, severely mentally ill children who kill a parent or parents due to deficits resulting from the disorder, and dangerously antisocial children who kill a parent or parents in conduct that is part and parcel of a general involvement in conduct problems and violence.

It is important to note that despite these severe risk profiles, sometimes matricide occurs in the absence of any apparent risk factors. For instance, Erik Mouridsen and Tolstrup (1988) reported of a 9-year old boy who murdered his mother despite no family history of discord or severe family conflicts. The child had no clinical problems; however, one year later began displaying psychotic symptoms and evidence of schizophrenia.

Fratricide

Fratricide is the killing of one's brother or sister. Children who murder their siblings commonly have a multitude of family, environmental, and psychological problems in early life including psychopathic traits, cruelty to other children, adverse and negative relationships with parents, unstable residency or home environment, and various forms of abuse (Shumaker & Prinz, 2000; Sorrells, 1977). There are documented cases of children as young as age 6 years who have killed their siblings, such as a case study of Maggie who murdered her 4-year old brother (Paluszny & McNabb, 1975). In the Book of Genesis, the first murder is the fratricide in which Cain murdered Abel.

Uxoricide

Uxoricide, commonly known as intimate partner homicide, domestic homicide, or spousal homicide, is the killing of an individual by their intimate partner usually a spouse. Technically, uxoricide is the murder of a wife by her husband, and meriticide is the murder of a husband by his wife. Adinkrah (2008) studied 72 spousal killings in Ghana and found that males were five times more likely to murder their wife than women were to murder them. The most common motives for spousal killings in Ghana were sexual jealousy, alleged or real infidelity, and an instrumental need to replace one's spouse with a new intimate partner. Intimate partner homicide is significantly more likely to occur when couples are estranged and separated compared to when they are living in the same domicile. For example, Wilson and Daly (1993) examined spousal homicides occurring across several decades in the United States, Canada, and Australia and found similarities across these settings.

A recent worldwide meta-analysis of 492,340 homicides in 66 nations found that intimate partner homicides account for 13.5 percent of all homicides in the world (Stöckl, Devries, Rotstein, Abrahams, Campbell, Watts, & Moreno, 2013). This equates to one in seven homicides and nearly 40 percent of female homicides. Worldwide, the proportion of women killed by an intimate partner is six times higher than the proportion of men killed by an intimate partner. Fortunately, like most forms of homicide, intimate partner homicide has declined over the past decades. A study of intimate partner homicide in 1,341 U.S. counties from 1980 to 1999 found that it has declined significantly with the exception of very rural counties which had a low base rate of homicide (Jennings & Piquero, 2008).

Another important feature of uxoricide is its effects on children because a single act of homicide produces the loss of both parents. Children who lose one parent to murder and the other to the criminal justice system have their lives changed in terms of how becomes their guardian, where they live, the school they attend, and other logistical issues. Even into adulthood, child survivors of uxoricide are prone to greater psychiatric problems, intimate partner abuse in their own relationships, and generally greater psychopathology (Parker, Steeves, Anderson, & Moran, 2004).

Eldercide

Eldercide is the homicide of a person age 65 years or older. The rate of eldercide is more than three times lower than the homicide rate of persons age 64 years or younger, and eldercides account for about 4 percent of homicides annually (Roberts & Willits, 2011).

Homicide-Suicide

Also known as murder-suicide or dyadic death, **homicide-suicide** is the killing of one or more individuals followed by the suicide of the perpetrator. Homicide-suicide is rare with an annual incidence of 0.2–0.3 events per 100,000 person-years and accounts for approximately 1,000–1,500 deaths per year in the United States (Marzuk, Tardiff, & Hirsch, 1992). By comparison, there are approximately 15,000 homicides and 33,000 suicides each year in the United States (Manning, 2014). The incidence of homicide-suicide is higher in the United States than in peer western nations. A comparative study reported a homicide-suicide rate of 0.22 per 100,000 in the United States, 0.09 per 100,000 in Switzerland, and 0.05 per 100,000 in the Netherlands (Liem, Barber, Markwalder, Killias, & Nieuwbeerta, 2011).

This form of homicide is more commonly perpetrated by whites, males, and older adults and the primary motivation or causal force is sexual proprietariness, depression, and prior suicide attempts. Indeed, cross-nationally homicide-suicide is usually committed by men with a firearm in a residence (Liem et al., 2011). When female-perpetrated, the motivation is usually a maternal salvation fantasy where the mother believes that killing her family will spare her children a life of misery. This is sometimes referred to as altruistic homicide or mercy-killing suicide (Manning, 2014).

Persons who commit homicide-suicide are generally older males who are married to or separated from their spouse and other victims (commonly the children of the perpetrator and victim). A recent large-scale systematic review and meta-analysis reported important differences between persons who commit homicide-suicide, those who commit homicide, and those who commit suicide. For example, homicide-suicide perpetrators are five times more likely than homicide offenders to use a firearm and 12 times more likely than suicide perpetrators to use a gun. They are two to three times more likely to be male than homicide and suicide perpetrators, and less likely to be under the influence of alcohol (Panczak, Geissbühler, Zwalen, Killas, Tal, & Egger, 2013). Interestingly, serial homicide offenders are not likely to commit suicide. Lester and White (2012) analyzed a sample of 483 serial killers and found that just 6.2 percent were documented to have committed suicide.

Sexual Homicide

Sexual homicide is a homicide in which some form of sexual activity occurs with the victim prior to, during, or after the death of the victim. According to Ressler, Burgess, and Douglas (1988), several criteria comprise sexual homicide. These include attempted or completed sexual intercourse (oral, anal, and/or vaginal), exposure of the sexual parts of the victim's body, victim being left naked or partially naked, sexual positioning of the body, insertion of foreign objects into the victim's body cavities, substitute sexual activity, such as masturbation, exhibitionistic or voyeuristic behavior, sexual interest of the offender, and admitted sexual fantasies of the offender.

Sexual homicide is rarely perpetrated by females. For instance, Chan, Frei, and Myers (2013) analyzed 32 years of FBI Supplemental Homicide Reports data which included 632,017 individuals who were arrested for homicide. From this massive sample, 3,977—just 0.6 percent of the total—were sexual homicides. And of these nearly 4,000 cases of sexual homicide, only 204 (5 percent) were female-perpetrated. A major difference between men and women who commit sexual homicide is that women are significantly more likely than men to kill with a firearm (Chan & Frei, 2013) whereas men usually kill with their hands.

Serial Murder/Homicide

Sexual homicide is often repeated over a period of years or even decades. This is known as **serial murder**. Holmes and DeBurger (1988) developed one of the most popular typologies of serial killers, defined as offenders that murder at least three victims with stoppages or "cooling-off" periods between the homicides. The typology centers on the motive of four distinct types. *Visionary murderers* are believed to be actively psychotic at the time of their killing and are motivated by either good or evil hallucinatory voices or visions. *Mission-oriented killers* are motivated to remove certain groups of people from society, such as prostitutes. *Power/control-oriented killers* are motivated by the feeling of life-or-death control over their victims. *Hedonistic killers* are theorized to derive psychological satisfaction or thrill from the act of killing (hedonistic killers were further classified into two subgroups called *lust killers* and *thrill killers*).

Mass Murder/Homicide or Multicide

Mass murder or multicide is the killing of multiple victims during a single event with roughly the same location or place and occurring at the same time. It has various definitions including:

- The killing of four or more victims at a single location during a single criminal episode (Holmes & Holmes, 2001).
- "offenses in which multiple victims are intentionally killed by a single offender in a single incident" (Dietz, 1986, p. 479). The time duration is specified as within a 24-hour period.
- "the antisocial and non-state sponsored killing of multiple victims during a single episode at one or more closely related locations" (Levin & Madfis, 2009, p. 1227).

Spree Murder/Homicide

Spree homicide is a type of homicide that lies between mass murder and serial murder in terms of its temporal unfolding. Spree homicides involve homicides at multiple locations over a relatively short period of time that can be hours, days, or weeks. Spree killing also has been defined variously:

- "[offenders] who kill repeatedly during a series of crimes motivated by the search for excitement, money, and valuables" (Dietz, 1986, p. 487).
- "killing at two or more locations with no emotional cooling-off period between murders. The killings are all the result of a single event, which can be of short or long duration" (Douglas, Burgess, Burgess, & Ressler, 1992, p. 12).

Other researchers indicate that the brief, frenetic nature of spree killings is what is important, not necessarily a requirement of multiple homicide victims. For instance, DeLisi and colleagues (2008, p. 40) defined spree murderers as "homicide offenders who committed their crimes in a time span that was greater than one day and less than 14 days inclusive."

Given the frenzied nature of spree murder, it is believed that spree murderers commit a greater array of offenses during their homicide event. A comparative study found that spree murderers committed more murders, attempted murders, rapes, robberies, assaults, incidents of child molestation, kidnapping, burglary, and weapons violations during the course of their instant homicide offense(s) than non-spree homicide offenders (DeLisi, Hochstetler, Scherer, Purhmann, & Berg, 2008). Overall, the prior criminal careers of both types of murderers were similar.

Multiple-Homicide Offenders

Recently, criminologists have attempted to develop more integrated conceptual schemes that transcend earlier typologies of homicide offenders. For instance, DeLisi and Scherer (2006) suggested that the case study approach and fixation on characterizing as serial, spree, or mass murderers has hindered the broader scientific understanding of individuals who commit multiple murders. For example, on July 22, 2011, Anders Behring Breivik detonated a car bomb in Oslo that killed eight people and injured nearly 100. About 2 hours later, Breivik killed an additional 77 victims, most of whom were adolescents and young adults, at a summer youth camp located on an island near Oslo. The case attracted international attention for the horrifyingly high death toll and is generally characterized as a mass murder. However, given that two separate acts of violence occurred at two settings, the event could perhaps more accurately be characterized as a spree murder. Due to uncertainties such as this, DeLisi and Scherer suggested that combining these typologies into **multiple-homicide offenders** facilitates a criminal career approach with the hope of identifying risk factors for the perpetration of multiple homicides before the event occurs. In their empirical work, DeLisi and Scherer (2006) found that 30 percent of multiple-homicide offenders were severe career criminals long before their homicide events. However, they also found that 40 percent of multiple-homicide offenders had zero prior arrests suggesting that more research is needed on the antisocial histories of these offenders.

Correlates of Homicide

There is sharp sociodemographic variance in homicide victimization and homicide offending as shown in Figures 1.3 and 1.4 and Figures 1.5 and 1.6, respectively. Across societies, homicides follow rather similar patterns in terms of who kills whom. About 65 percent of homicides involve males killing other males and 22 percent involve males killing females. Approximately

10 percent of homicides involve females killing males, and just 3 percent of homicides involve females killing other females (Duntley, 2012).

In the United States, African Americans are significantly more likely than whites to not only commit homicide, but also be the victim of homicide. Other than heart disease, homicide is the main reason for life expectancy differences between whites and blacks, and blacks are between 5 and 10 times more likely than whites to kill or be killed (O'Flaherty & Sethi, 2010). Much of the race differential in homicide relates to other involvement in antisocial behavior. For instance, the black to white ratio for homicide involving other felonies, such as robbery is more than 10 to 1. For drug crimes, the ratio is nearly 8 to 1, and for other arguments and assaults the ratio is between 4–1 and 9–1 (O'Flaherty & Sethi, 2010).

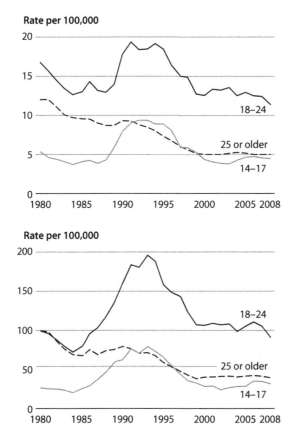

Figure 1.3   White and black male homicide victimization by age, 1980–2008.

Source: Modified from Cooper, A., & Smith, E. L. (2011). *Homicide trends in the United States, 1980–2008. Annual rates for 2009–2010.* Washington, DC: U.S. Department of Justice, Office of Justice Programs, Bureau of Justice Statistics.

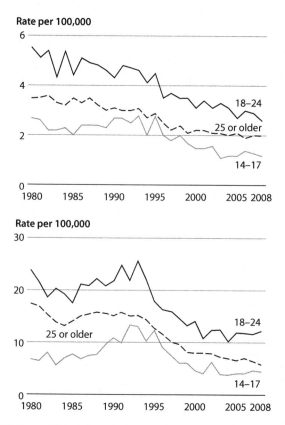

Figure 1.4 White and black female homicide victimization by age, 1980–2008.

Source: Modified from Cooper, A., & Smith, E. L. (2011). *Homicide trends in the United States, 1980–2008. Annual rates for 2009–2010.* Washington, DC: U.S. Department of Justice, Office of Justice Programs, Bureau of Justice Statistics.

One explanation for black-white homicide differentials is the **adversary effect**, defined as an offender's tactical response to the threat posed by an adversary. Using national data from the National Incident-Based Reporting System (NIBRS), Felson and Painter-Davis (2012) found that offenders are more likely to use firearms against black victims, especially young, black, male victims. Black offenders respond more strongly to their victim's race than white offenders. In addition, a violent incident between two black males is six times more likely to involve a firearm (and be more likely to be a homicide) than a violent incident between two white males.

Homicide is the leading cause of death for blacks between the ages of 10 and 24 and is the second leading cause of death for Hispanics of those ages (Herrenkohl, 2013). Among juvenile offenders, being male (Stoddard-Dare, Tedor, Quinn, & Mallett, 2014) and being African American are the

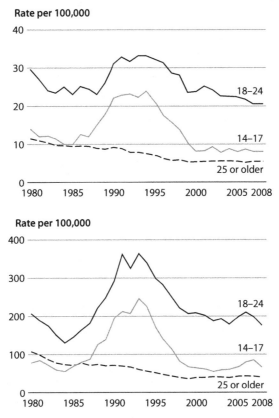

Figure 1.5   White and black male homicide offending by age, 1980–2008.

Source: Modified from Cooper, A., & Smith, E. L. (2011). *Homicide trends in the United States, 1980–2008. Annual rates for 2009–2010.* Washington, DC: U.S. Department of Justice, Office of Justice Programs, Bureau of Justice Statistics.

strongest predictors of subsequently being murdered (Chassin, Piquero, Losoya, Mansion, & Schubert, 2013). Although there are drastic race differences in homicide offending and victimization, similar processes, such as exposure to severe poverty are associated with murder among both whites and blacks (Lee, 2000).

Race differences in homicide are large; sex differences in homicide are immense. There are dramatic sex differences in various forms of homicide. According to the most recent data from the Uniform Crime Reports, females accounted for 7.7 percent of homicides in the United States. Sex differences are even more pronounced for multiple-homicide. For example, a 9-year survey of newspaper coverage of multiple murders found just 32 cases of women committing multicide in a domestic context (Messing &

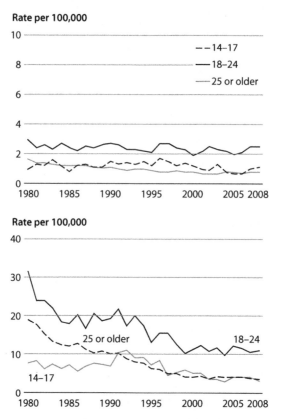

Figure 1.6   White and black female homicide offending by age, 1980–2008.

Source: Modified from Cooper, A., & Smith, E. L. (2011). *Homicide trends in the United States, 1980–2008. Annual rates for 2009–2010.* Washington, DC: U.S. Department of Justice, Office of Justice Programs, Bureau of Justice Statistics.

Heeren, 2004). Most studies of multiple-homicide rely on samples that are exclusively male since the prevalence is so low among females.

When women do murder, it is often domestic-oriented. As Messing and Heeren (2004, p. 125) suggested, "[t]he domestic scene is the quintessential setting for gaining insight into women's homicidal activity." Given the sheer sex differences in homicide, some scholars have developed specific theories to account for homicidal behavior among women. For example, Ogle, Maier-Katkin, and Bernard (1995) articulated several propositions based on their reading of the literature. These are (1) stress is higher among women, on average, than for men, (2) women with lower social status experience higher stress, on average, than women with higher social status, (3) women, on average, have more blockages on coping mechanisms for dealing with anger than men, (4) women with lower social status, on average, have more blockages on their coping mechanisms for dealing with anger than women with higher social status, (5) women are more likely to develop overcontrolled personalities than men, (6) women, on average, are less likely than men to have developed regulative rules for the experience and expression of anger, (7) women experiencing peaks of stress are more likely than men to explode with episodes of extreme undercontrolled violence, and (8) targets of this violence are most likely to be those in the immediate environment, whether or not those targets represent the actual source of stress.

The overall picture of female perpetrator is generally consistent with these theoretical propositions. In the United States and other nations, women are most likely to kill intimates in a domestic context, and their murders often occur at home (Eckhardt & Pridemore, 2009). Fox and Allen (2014) recently examined thirty years of data from the Federal Bureau of Investigation's Supplementary Homicide Reports to examine sex differences in homicide and the relationship of the homicide offender and victim. As shown in Table 1.1, the sheer sex differences in homicide are striking for all forms.

Substantively similar results were shown in a study of 40,000 homicides perpetrated by juveniles in the United States between 1976 and 2005. Heide, Roe-Sepowitz, Solomon, and Chan (2012) reported significant gender differences among juvenile homicide offenders. The typical male juvenile homicide offender was a 16- or 17-year old from a large city and kill one victim either with our without codefendants. The typical female juvenile homicide offender was under the age of 16 and twice as likely as males to be under the age of 14. Girls were more likely to act alone and murder

Table 1.1   Sex Differences and the Victim Offender Relationship in Homicides, 1980–2009

Sex Dyad	Relationship	Number of Homicides
Male kills male	Family	13,631
Male kills male	Acquaintance	87,943
Male kills male	Stranger	30,950
Male kills female	Family	20,064
Male kills female	Acquaintance	25,098
Male kills female	Stranger	4,607
Female kills male	Family	9,641
Female kills male	Acquaintance	10,555
Female kills male	Stranger	667
Female kills female	Family	2,078
Female kills female	Acquaintance	2,691
Female kills female	Stranger	294

Source: Modified from Fox, K. A., & Allen, T. (2014). Examining the instrumental–expressive continuum of homicides: Incorporating the effects of gender, victim–offender relationships, and weapon choice. *Homicide Studies, 18*(3), 298–317.

one victim. Females were significantly more likely to kill younger victims, females, family members, intimate partners, and their children. Males were more likely to kill strangers, to use accomplices, and to be involved in gang-related homicides.

Age is another strong correlate of homicide with younger individuals significantly more likely than older adults to both perpetrate homicide and be the victim of homicide. Homicide is a leading cause of death of adolescents and young adults, and persons ages 15–34 account for half of the homicide victims in the United States (Centers for Disease Control and Prevention, 1994) from the 1960s to early 1990s. More recently, young people under age 25 years accounted for 34 percent of murder victims and 49 percent of offenders (Cooper & Smith, 2011).

Understanding the youthful nature of homicide is placed in context when considering the relative rarity of homicide among older adults. For example, in a large-scale study of homicide patterns among persons ages 55–74 spanning the years 1985–2009, Feldmeyer and Steffensmeier (2013) examined trends in elderly homicide. They found that elderly homicide rates have remained stable over this period and that overall, elderly homicides account for a fraction of total homicides. These findings suggest that a homicide involving a person in the latter decades of life is quite rare.

Research Purpose

Because homicide is such an extraordinary, horrible, and rare behavior, it has understandably generated tremendous lay and scientific attention. Theories of homicide are legion. A mistake that criminal justice students sometimes make; however, is feeling that one must be forced to accept a specific theory or cause of homicide. Few phenomena have a single cause especially in the study of crime. Instead, it is more realistic to acknowledge that homicide can be understood from multiple explanatory frameworks that span the social and behavioral sciences.

With this in mind, the structure of *Homicide* is to examine homicide from a specific theoretical or disciplinary perspective. Because so many scholars have researched homicide, the 25 chapters in this text are relatively brief and contain an overview of the perspective as it relates to homicide, the research support for the perspective, and also research that challenges the perspective. The final chapter contains critical concepts from the chapters to facilitate classroom activities that help students critically analyze homicide from all of the perspectives. Section I contains criminological explanations of homicide. Section II contains interdisciplinary and psychiatric explanations of homicide from across the social and behavioral sciences.

Section I

Criminological Perspectives

CHAPTER 2

Homicide and the Interactionist Perspective

The interactionist perspective points to the dynamic relationship between the homicide offender and the homicide victim in producing a homicide event.

Conceptual Background

Popular in sociology, the **interactionist perspective** is a soft theory of human behavior that asserts that behavior emerges from social interaction and the subjective states relating to that interaction and is not caused by objective characteristics of individuals. There are three fundamental principles to interactionist theory. The first is that behavior is driven by the symbolic meanings that other people, interactions, and other objects have for the individual. The second point is that symbolic meanings are created by social interaction that an individual has with other people, groups, and organizations. Situations do not have "meaning" until the person experiences the event and the ways that others are interacting with him or her. Third, behavior is changed based on how individuals adjust the meaning of the behavior based on the responses they receive from ongoing interactions. It is sometimes suggested that the motto of symbolic interactionist theory is that there is no objective reality—everything is "made up" from its symbolic meaning.

In terms of understanding homicide, the interactionist perspective is applied by considering the relationship and the interaction between the offender and victim, and how that interaction produces homicidal outcomes. An important point, and one that many of the empirical works in this chapter have shown, is that homicide victims often set into motion their demise in part because homicide offenders and victims commonly share life circumstances and behaviors. In other words, both homicide offender and victim are often involved in risky lifestyles (e.g., drug use, drug selling, party lifestyle) and engaged in generalized criminal behavior. The duality between homicide offender and victim is explored extensively in this chapter.

There are not specific interactionist theories of homicide per se, but there are several important criminological perspectives that have clear relevance to the study of homicide. One is Kaplan's **self-derogation theory.** In a variety of works, Kaplan developed a theory of self-derogation to understand antisocial development (Kaplan, 1967, 1970; Kaplan & Pokorny, 1969) particularly during adolescence. Kaplan noted that individuals have a fundamental desire to feel good about their life and sense of self and are distressed by negative self-evaluations. Self-derogation pertains to the set of negative feelings and low self-esteem regarding one's abilities, personal qualities, and behavior. Self-derogation is theorized to be the negative emotions that result from rejection by others. Kaplan particular focused on adolescent delinquency development and the role of peer rejection in cultivating self-derogation among delinquents. Individuals who have high self-derogation link these negative feelings to conventional peers and behaviors—peers and behaviors from which they feel excluded. As a result, persons with high self-derogation seek delinquent associations and delinquent behavior as a way to thwart the conventionality of their peers and improve their self-esteem and self-worth.

Kaplan did not conceptualize his theory for homicide, but did theorize that its principles were responsible for aggressive and violent behavior. According to the theory, the negative self-feelings inspire antisocial persons to replace them by adopting a deviant lifestyle. Because conventional standards have not worked well for antisocial people, they seek to avoid additional failure and negative evaluations. To do this, they adopt new deviant standards and avoid evaluating themselves by the standards of conventional society. Indeed, the back story and childhood experiences of many homicide offenders are consistent with self-derogation theory. Homicide offenders display significantly more psychopathology than those who do not commit homicide, and certainly more compared to those who do not commit crime. Homicide offenders often experience considerable anxiety, depression, and adjustment problems and learn early in their school career that they are unlike their peers. Over time, these adjustment problems fester and contribute to additional psychiatric distress, and often, attendant behavioral problems.

Self-derogation also occurs at home. Most pronounced among those who commit multiple homicides, the childhoods of homicide offenders are often appalling depressing and characterized by neglect, abuse, and exposure to a host of deprivations. These negative home environments weigh heavily on the developing homicide offender's mind, and also contribute to his or her general feelings of unease, insecurity, and worthlessness. Indeed, the motivation to "get back" at society or the people who homicide offenders feel are persecuting them is a common theme among adolescent school shooters.

Self-derogation and the rejection of the conventional self in favor of an antisocial self are also seen among homicide offenders who are engaged in a generalized criminal lifestyle. Many homicide offenders have extensive criminal history (see Chapter 18 for their criminal careers), and the various failures that a life of crime brings—unemployment, school dropout, drug abuse, higher mortality, and others—"protects" them from failing to meet the standards of conventional society, such as completing high school, furthering their education, being gainfully employed, maintaining a home, being responsible for a family, etc. For example, a large-scale population study found that nearly 43 percent of homicide offenders have a prior felony conviction compared to just 3.9 percent of the general population (Cook, Ludwig, & Braga, 2005). Another common feature among antisocial individuals is pathological narcissism which is an exaggerated sense of self-worth or even feelings of omnipotence that develops in response to rejection and humiliating events. A case study (Schlesinger, 1998) of an individual who murdered six victims revealed an exaggerated façade of narcissism that was constructed to compensate for the offender's various shortcomings and failures in life.

A different approach but still an interactionist-oriented theory of crime is Cohen and Felson's (1979) routine activities theory. **Routine activities theory** suggests that criminal behavior is produced by the coming together in time and space of three basic elements. The first is a motivated offender, the second is a suitable target, or potential victim, and the third is the absence of capable guardians, or simply, there are not police or others who could stop the crime. When these three parties coincide, crime occurs. Unlike the general approach of symbolic interactionism, routine activities theory does not consider the self, perceptions, and interpersonal interaction as the causes of crime. Instead, the interactionist component is meant in an ecological sense where the social interaction of parties renders them available or unavailable for offending and victimization.

A unique feature of routine activities theory is that it boils crime and victimization down to its basic elements. In terms of homicide, the empirical scenarios of normal, reactive homicides are consistent with motivated offenders, suitable targets, and absence of capable guardians. Many homicides occur as the result of heated exchanges, arguments, or quarrels in places where people are intoxicated (e.g., bars, nightclubs, or domiciles) and largely safe from police presence, especially in private homes. In the case of proactive homicides, routine activities theory is also applicable. Serial killers prey on often specific victims or types of victims, and attack their victims when the right opportunity structures are present. Most of these homicides occur at night, in secluded places, and far from the reach of the general public or police.

Finally, the interactionist perspective is unlike other criminological theories in that it is generally critical of the notion that specific criteria "cause" crime, or for the current book, homicide. Instead, it points to the essential nature of human interaction, and how our thoughts, beliefs, and behaviors are often not static but depend widely on who is around, and in what context. The following quotation by Katz captures this sentiment well:

"The statistical and correlational findings of positivist criminology provide the following irritations to inquiry: (1) whatever the validity of the hereditary, psychological, and social-ecological conditions of crime, many of those in the supposedly causal categories do not commit the crime at issue, (2) many who do commit the crime do not fit the causal categories, and (3) what is most provocative, many who do fit the background categories and later commit the predicted crime go for long stretches without committing the crimes to which theory directs them. Why are people who were not determined to commit a crime one moment determined to do so the next?" (2010, p. 351).

Indeed, and as discussed in Chapter 1, the apparent "causes" of homicide (e.g., lust, wrath, envy, and other basic emotions) are often universally experienced, but almost no one engages in violence let alone homicidal violence. This supports Katz' critique and offers promise for interactionist explanations of homicide.

Recently, Lee (2011) advanced a cultural explanation of homicide that encompasses the interactionist and regional traditions (see Chapter 3). According to Lee, violence in the deep-south among rural whites and in large inner cities among African Americans share cultural features that make homicide more likely. In these settings, defensive or honor-based violence norms emerge in part because the law is viewed as unavailable or unresponsive, and in part where widespread institutional breakdown and poverty have engendered predatory violence. From these environments, five interactionist processes guide the creation of homicide.

First, homicide is *intersubjective* and constructed through the process of social interaction. Homicide offenders and victims often share sociodemographic characteristics and thus are similar in their attitudes and beliefs. How they respond to one another directly influences whether violence use will be escalated to a lethal level.

Second, behavior is *performative* in the sense that individuals behave in certain ways to maintain public face or aura. For example, a person who is disrespected in public might commit homicide to reinforce his or her image as a "badass," to do otherwise would risk losing that reputation.

Third, many homicides reflect habituated *affective-cognitive* processes where the homicidal behavior is perpetrated out of habitual or impulsive reactions to common situations, not necessarily because the actor feels the homicide reflects a particular culture.

Fourth, homicide can reflect *relational position* that is where one is located in social space relative to other individuals. In this way, homicide is an important way to control those who are in an inferior position or who potentially threaten the homicide offender's social status.

The fifth part of Lee's (2011) theory is *world making* where behavior produces and reinforces structural realities. This is similar to a self-fulfilling prophecy where expectations of serious violence, including potentially the commission of a homicide, contribute to environments where these behaviors are common. These interactionist themes are commonly seen in film portrayals of the inner city and in autobiographical accounts of gang life and homicidal behavior.

Box 2.1   Interactions and Hot Spots of Homicide

The interactionist perspective makes clear that certain contexts, situations, and routines are more conducive for a homicide to occur than others. Interactionist perspectives are very micro-oriented in that the focus is on the individual and his or her engagement with another person or small group. But do these effects aggregate? A related area of study is **hot spots theory** popularized by Lawrence Sherman. In a series of studies and quasi-experiments, Sherman (1995) noted that criminal behavior generally and violent criminal behavior specifically was tremendously concentrated in specific areas of a geographic area. These areas of crime and violence are known as hot spots. For example, a study of police calls in Minneapolis found that only 3 percent of places accounted for more than 50 percent of the approximately 323,000 calls for service in the city. For predatory crimes, just 5 percent of the 115,000 street addresses produced all—100 percent—of the calls for service. Armed robberies, which can and often do result in gun assaults and homicides, are particularly concentrated. In Minneapolis, 90 percent of armed robberies occurred on just eight streets all of which were busy boulevards with many bars (Sherman, 1995).

Sherman and Rogan (1995) conducted a quasi-experiment of intensive police patrol and gun seizures in a hot spot of crime in Kansas City, Missouri. The area of focus was an eight by ten block of the city that had a homicide rate that was a staggering 20 times higher than the national average. Over a 6-month period of the policy, gun crimes in the target area were significantly reduced. There was a 65 percent increase in gun seizures by the police and a commensurate 49 percent decline in gun crimes which included homicides and attempted homicides. Moreover, there was a not significant displacement effect which means that gun crimes did not spillover into blocks not covered by the program. The saturation patrol underscores the notion that gun control need not be widespread to reduce firearm violence. Instead, seizing guns from active gun-using criminals who routinely shoot others is a focused way to reduce the homicide rate.

Similarly, Ratcliffe and Rengert (2008) found that once a shooting occurred in hot spots in Philadelphia, there was a 33 percent increased likelihood of a repeated shooting within 2 weeks, and within one city block of the prior incident. Substantively similar findings have also been found in Houston (Wells, Wu, & Le, 2012). As mentioned above, police behavior certainly affects gun availability and shootings. Another study of 5,687 gun arrests and 5,870 shootings in Philadelphia found that shootings declined between 28 and 47 percent after a firearm arrest; however, these suppression effects only lasted a few days (Wyant, Taylor, Ratcliffe, &

Wood, 2012). Afterward, normal interactionist dynamics resumed, and the somewhat predictable homicidal violence found in hot spots appeared shortly thereafter.

Sources: Sherman, L. W. (1995). Hot spots of crime and criminal careers of places. *Crime and Place, 4,* 35–52; Sherman, L. W., & Rogan, D. P. (1995). Effects of gun seizures on gun violence: "Hot spots" patrol in Kansas City. *Justice Quarterly, 12*(4), 673–693; Ratcliffe, J. H., & Rengert, G. F. (2008). Near-repeat patterns in Philadelphia shootings. *Security Journal, 21,* 58–76; Wells, W., Wu, L., & Ye, X. (2012). Patterns of near-repeat gun assaults in Houston. *Journal of Research in Crime and Delinquency, 49*(2), 186–212; Wyant, B. R., Taylor, R. B., Ratcliffe, J. H., & Wood, J. (2012). Deterrence, firearm arrests, and subsequent shootings: A micro-level spatio-temporal analysis. *Justice Quarterly, 29*(4), 524–545.

A similar cognitive approach is seen in Brookman's (2014, 2015) work. Heavily rooted in an interactionist perspective, Brookman theorizes that homicide offenders ultimately commit homicide based on how they are thinking and feeling at the moment of the murderous event. She cites research which indicates that homicide offenders often do not plan to commit a murder and that the conditions for the homicide materialize immediately before the event. In large part, the conditions that make a homicide more likely pertain to the behavior of the victim, and his or her interaction with the offender.

Additionally, Brookman noted that homicide offenders and their victims are often immersed and engage in an antisocial world where substance use, criminal offending, and nonproductive behaviors are common. In these environments, offenders develop cognitive schemas which are essentially minirecipes for how to behave in certain situations. These cognitive schemes are refined over time from repeated exposure to criminal and often dangerous situations. In a perverse way, the antisocial cognitive schemas that develop form a sort of expertise where offenders know how to respond in uncertain, dangerous situations. These cognitive and affective templates are often the context in which homicide offenders and victims find themselves immediately prior to their homicide event.

Empirical Linkages to Homicide

One of the first criminologists to empirically note the emergent, interactionist, and interactional dynamics of homicide was Marvin Wolfgang. In a seminal paper, Wolfgang (1957, p. 1) expressed, "In many crimes, especially in criminal homicide, the victim is often a major contributor to the criminal act. Except in cases in which the victim is an innocent bystander and is killed in lieu of an intended victim, or in cases in which a pure accident is involved, the victim may be one of the major precipitating causes of his own demise." Although it could be viewed as controversial because of a sense of blaming the victim, Wolfgang's work was seminal because it directed attention to the relationship between killer and killed, and how their interactions set into motion the homicide event. This is known as **victim-precipitated homicide**.

To substantiate his account of homicide, Wolfgang studied 588 consecutive cases of homicide occurring in Philadelphia between January 1, 1948, and December 31, 1952. Of these, 150 or 26 percent of cases were victim precipitated. He found that victim-precipitated homicides were significantly more likely to involve African Americans as offenders and victims, to involve female offenders and male victims, to be domestic in context (e.g., spousal killing), to involve alcohol use, and for both offenders and victims to have a prior arrest history often for assault. In other words, the most common type of homicide during this era involved a domestic dispute between partners who were intoxicated and who had a contentious relationship evidenced by prior arrests among both parties. Moreover, homicide offenders and victims often matched each other demographically, a finding that is matched by national data (see Figure 2.1).

The trends that Wolfgang documented are not limited to Philadelphia. A study of the relationships between homicide offenders and victims produced similar results. Loftin, Kindley, Norris, and Wiersema (1987) reviewed studies of the victim-offender relationship including Wolfgang's work in Philadelphia in the 1940s and 1950s along with research of Detroit homicides from the 1920s to 1960s, Houston in the late 1950s and early

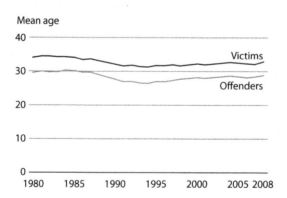

Figure 2.1   Age of homicide offenders and victims, 1980–2008.

Source: Modified from Cooper, A., & Smith, E. L. (2011). *Homicide trends in the United States, 1980–2008. Annual rates for 2009–2010.* Washington, DC: U.S. Department of Justice, Office of Justice Programs, Bureau of Justice Statistics.

1960s, and the United States overall. They found that between 15 percent and 42 percent of murders involved friends and acquaintances as the offender and victim. Between 1 and 18 percent of murders in these locations and eras involved strangers. Thus, basic relationships and interaction patterns accounted for far more murders than those involving strangers. These commonly included domestic disputes, parricides, jilted lovers, arguments over money or property, and other drunken disputes.

The interactionist perspective is a prominent sociological viewpoint where individuals understand and attribute meaning to themselves, others, and behavior based on the dynamics of their interaction. Almost by definition, most homicides can be understood as a social interaction that goes horribly wrong. Another influential interactionist study of homicide identified several steps in an interactionist process that can culminate in homicide. Based on analyses of 70 murder cases, Luckenbill (1977) found that homicides were essentially confrontations where the offender and victim attempted to save face in the midst of an interpersonal dispute. Like Wolfgang's seminal research, Luckenbill found that victims commonly initiated the confrontation with some interpersonal affront. In turn, the homicide offender retaliated with a verbal and/or physical challenge. According to Luckenbill, the offender and victim created a working agreement that violence would be appropriate to resolve the dispute. In the course of their battle, the offender fatally wounded the victim.

In a six-city examination of women who kill during domestic disputes, Richey Mann (1988) found clear evidence of interactionist dynamics. Most of the killings involved highly abusive male spouses or partners who initiated another violent dispute immediately prior to being killed. The women's homicidal behavior was indicative of self-defense whereby lethal violence via a firearm was used to counteract physical strength differences between men and women.

In court, self-defense outcomes were often found even in contexts where they potentially were not relevant. For example, one woman fatally shot her abuser six times in the back of the head and claimed the act was self-defense. The charges were dismissed. This means that even the criminal courts recognize the interactionist dynamics of homicides, and that at times the "victim" of a homicide might actually appear more villainous than the offender. This viewpoint would explain the dismissal of charges in Mann's work, and in many cases like it.

Drawing on data from 102 homicides occurring in Baltimore, Maryland from 1987 to 1989, Cheatwood (1996) explored the interactional dynamics of homicides involving multiple offenders. Compared to single offender homicides, which Cheatwood found were often caused by character disputes between the offender and victim were one or both felt the need to save face, multiple-offender homicides had different dynamics. First, they tended to be unplanned and involved little to no communication among offenders about whether a homicide would even be committed. Instead the main point of the attack was to perpetrate some other felony often a burglary or robbery and the homicide resulted from the initial felony "going bad." Second, multiple-offender homicides that do not involve another felony tend to be planned events that are intended to resolve a long-running dispute or grievance, such as retaliation for a drug debt. In these murders, the multiple assailants clearly premeditate and perpetrate the homicide.

Felson and Messner (1996) suggested that the decision to commit homicide is part of an emergent process that unfolds as the potential murderer and potential victim interact usually in a criminal context. They argue that homicides can arise from an offender having concern that the victim will seek retaliation, will report the offender to the police, or will otherwise identify him. In this way, the victim poses too much of a threat to the offender, and to avoid that threat and forestall the potential retaliation of legal consequences, the victim is killed.

The role of third parties, witnesses, or audiences is very important for understanding homicide from an interactionist perspective. Drawing on ethnographic insights of homicides among street offenders in Saint Louis, Missouri, Decker (1995) suggested that audiences to homicide assume five types of identities: victim or offender surrogates, facilitators, precipitators, bystanders, and incapable guardians. The role is largely determined by protective stakes, which is the intensity, duration, and priority of the prior relationship among the audience, homicide offender, and homicide victim. The following vignette captures how audiences can affect a homicide:

"The victim and suspect (friends) had been drinking with 8 or 9 men in front of a lounge. The suspect purchased a bottle of liquor which the victim snatched from him. They argued and then fought. The group of men (witnesses) broke it up, and the victim and suspect both left the area. Each retrieved a weapon and returned to the lounge. They shot at each other several times before the suspect killed the victim" (Decker, 1995, p. 447).

Gang dynamics are generally consistent with the interactionist perspective. Several studies drawing on gang data from various cities indicated that gang members often victimize members from their own gang rather than a rival gang. In their study of gang homicides in Saint Louis, Missouri, Decker and Curry (2002) found that most gang members were murdered by nongang affiliated offenders. Moreover, when gang members were the homicide perpetrator, the offender and victim were often from the same gang. Based on data from homicides in Newark, New Jersey, Pizarro and McGloin (2006) found that approximately 60 percent of gang homicides involved an offender/victim relationship characterized as acquaintance, friend, or significant other.

Others have similarly produced support for an interactionist explanation for homicide using data outside of the United States. Ganpat, van der Leun, and Nieuwbeerta (2013) compared 126 homicides to 141 attempted homicides using court data from The Netherlands. They found several factors that escalated nonlethal to lethal violence including alcohol use by the victim, victim precipitation, not having bystanders, and firearm use by the offender. They found that homicide victims were greater than three times more likely than the homicide offender to initiate the confrontation with an insult. In half of the homicides, the incident was started by the victim or jointly by the offender and victim. The more threatening and insulting the victim, the greater and more severe the response was from the offender—and the interactional dynamic largely explained aggravated assaults from homicides.

Rountree (2012) examined the rationales that convicted murderers who have been sentenced to death use to waive their appeals and elect or volunteer to be executed. She found that the most common logic that murderers used was that their sentence was fair, lawfully applied, and just and second, that life on death row was so miserable that death was a better alternative. Thus, in an interesting way, the interactionist dynamics of life as a condemned prisoner drove these men to waive their legal appeals, and simply accept their sentence. To put it another way, the travails of prison life constitute the interaction that motivates their ultimate death by execution.

The interactionist perspective has also been applied to those who work in homicide, namely homicide detectives. In a qualitative study of homicide investigators in a major U.S. city, Hawk and Dabney (2014) found that a variety of factors affect how homicide detectives approach a case that they are investigating. An important issue centered on the perceived deservedness of the victim and the circumstances that lead to the homicide event. Detectives generally distinguished between true victims and persons whom seemed to invite their victimization based on their involvement in criminal activity, their drug activity, or other factors that encouraged the confrontation that resulted in their death. All the while, detectives pledged to investigate each case equally and not use the victim's characteristics in their decision making. The following quotation illustrates the interactionist dynamics of their work:

"I'd say 70% of our homicide victims played some part in their homicide. Whether it's that they're out committing a crime, or whether they're just doing something silly that's putting them in harm's way, you know. But for the real victims who were just minding their business and doing what…they've been brought up to do or trying to live a decent, honest life, yeah...I can honestly say I do a little bit more in those particular cases. I might go above and beyond" (Hawk & Dabney, 2014, p. 1138).

Ample empirical support for routine activities theory has also been furnished by criminologists in a range of cities including Houston (Pokorny, 1965), Milwaukee (Caywood, 1998), Pittsburgh (Berg & Loeber, 2011), and New York (Messner & Tardiff, 1985). Drawing on Chicago homicide data, Nelsen and Huff-Corzine (1998) examined homicide victimization among the elderly. Consistent with the theory, they found generally lower levels of homicide among older residents due to their safer daily routines. However, because the elderly are less capable guardians and more suitable victims, they also found that older persons were more at risk for theft-oriented homicides.

Lundrigan and Canter (2001) examined the geographic distribution of victim disposal sites of serial killers. Using data from 126 U.S. serial murderers and 29 U.K. serial murders who had killed between 2 and 24 victims, they explored the role of routine interaction patterns in the course of their killings. They found that most serial killers leave the bodies of their victims in places familiar to them because of the routine activities in which they are engaged. Many of the disposal sites where near the home or work location of the offender suggesting that their familiarity with the landscape and places where there would not be capable guardians drove the decision of where to dump the bodies. In other words, murder and the disposal of murder victims were "opportunities taken within the awareness space of day-to-day life" (Lundrigan & Canter, 2001, p. 597).

Dobash, Dobash, Cavanaugh, and Lewis (2004) compared the interactionist dynamics among male who murdered other men and males who murdered an intimate partner as part of the Murder in Britain Study. Men who killed their intimate partner were significantly more likely to be employed and to have an ongoing dispute with their spouse. In about three-fourths of murders, there was a confrontation immediately preceding the murder. In nearly 60 percent of intimate partner murders, there was a prior history of violence. Other interactionist factors and routine behavioral activities were seen in the event of men killing other men. These cases were more likely to involve the offender drinking, more likely to involve the offender using drugs, more likely to involve the victim drinking, more likely to involve the victim using drugs, more likely for the offender to be intoxicated, and more likely for the victim to be intoxicated. Male on male murders usually did not occur in the home but instead in a bar or other venue.

Drawing on homicide data from Newark, New Jersey, a city with one of the highest homicide rates in the United States, Pizarro, Corsaro, and Yu (2007) examined the reason for homicide victims and offenders travel and how those routine activities corresponded to the motive for their homicide event. They found that nearly 78 percent of domestic homicide victims were killed at home, which was expected and that nearly 18 percent were killed while hanging out or at work. For dispute homicides, nearly 80 percent of victims were murdered at home, work, or while hanging out. For drug homicides, most were killed while hanging out, during consensual crime, or while shopping or running errands. Most gang homicides occurred while victims were hanging out or running errands. Victims of robbery homicides were killed in a variety of contexts including at home, while running errands, while hanging out, or while engaging in consensual crime. These trends were similar for homicide offenders; however, large proportions of domestic, dispute, drug, gang, and robbery homicides were perpetrated while offenders were actively engaged in other predatory crimes against person, property, or both.

An interactionist-routine activities approach has also been applied to the study of mass murder. Drawing on data from 165 mass murders in China, Hilal, Densley, Li, and Ma (2014) recently reported that mass murders in China can be directly related to the routine daily activities of offenders and victims. Most mass murders occur in rural areas where offenders are motivated by revenge and or profit and perpetrate their crimes most commonly with knives. Victims live in isolated areas far from the reach of urban police. These conditions meet the three concepts articulated by Cohen and Felson (1979).

In his research on **focused deterrence programs** in policing, which are targeted enforcement efforts to reduce gun homicides, Braga (2003) has shown the deadly consequences of motivated offenders. For example, in Boston, Massachusetts, during the 1980s and early 1990s, about 1 percent of the juvenile population was responsible for 60 percent of the youth homicides occurring in the city. Overwhelmingly, these homicides were the result of gang-involved, serious offenders who settled their disputes with rival gang members by shooting them. To echo Cohen and Felson (1979), most of these homicides reflected motivated offenders and suitable targets...and often, no police around.

To counteract this, cities began employing focused deterrence strategies such as Operation Ceasefire and Operation Peacekeeper to reduce juvenile homicide. In Operation Peacekeeper in Stockton, California, special enforcement teams were freed from regular patrol duties and instead practiced strict law enforcement of known gang members. This included seemingly minor offenses such as traffic violations and drinking in public (Braga, 2008). In addition, these programs involve the use of a working group of juvenile justice and social service providers to encourage gun-using gang members to desist from violence and engage in conventional activities. By dramatically increasing the presence of capable guardians (as opposed to the absence of them), these programs are very effective at reducing juvenile homicide.

By targeting small numbers of gang members, focused deterrence strategies have yielded large reductions in homicide. For instance, Operation Ceasefire in Boston produced a 63 percent reduction in youth homicides, the Indianapolis Violence Reduction Partnership produced a 34 percent reduction in total homicides, Operation Peacekeeper in Stockton, California, yielded a 42 percent reduction in gun homicides, Project Safe Neighborhoods in Lowell, Massachusetts, contributed to a 44 percent reduction in gun assaults, and the Cincinnati Initiative to Reduce Violence produced a 35 percent reduction in homicides (Braga & Weisburd, 2012).

Focused deterrence strategies have yielded large reductions in homicide. For instance, Operation Ceasefire in Boston produced a 63 percent reduction in youth homicides, the Indianapolis Violence Reduction Partnership produced a 34 percent reduction in total homicides, Operation Peacekeeper in Stockton, California yielded a 42 percent reduction in gun homicides, Project Safe Neighborhoods in Lowell, Massachusetts contributed to a 44 percent reduction in gun assaults, and the Cincinnati Initiative to Reduce Violence produced a 35 percent reduction in homicides (Braga & Weisburd, 2012).

Finally, there is interesting negative evidence for the interactionist perspective particularly the role of victim precipitation in homicide. Green and Wakefield (1979) conducted a study of 119 cases of homicide that were perpetrated by 121 upper-class individuals as reported in the New York Times between 1955 and 1975. First, it should be noted that upper-class persons rarely commit murder. The defendants in the current sample represent just 0.05 percent of all the homicides committing during the study period. Thus, it is not just a stereotype: wealthy people really rarely commit murder. Green and Wakefield (1979) also found no evidence of victim precipitation in these upper-class murders. Instead the most common motivation for the crimes was for financial gain, such as to gain an inheritance. In addition, more than 98 percent of the killers were white.

The next chapter somewhat extends the interactionist perspective by looking at how regional differences shape not only the prevalence of homicide, but how and why individuals living in certain regions are differentially likely to kill or be killed.

CHAPTER 3

Homicide and the Regional Perspective

Many nations, including the United States, have experienced greater homicide rates in the Southern region suggesting a cultural adaptation that is unique to the South.

Conceptual Background

In the nineteenth century, several European scholars particularly in France and Italy noted that homicide appeared to be more prevalent in southern parts of those respective nations compared to other regions. Given the consistency of this "southern effect," a variety of explanations were advanced. These explanations included the idea that more temperate weather in southern regions enabled greater social interaction, and thus more opportunities for conflict and violence. In this way, the southern effect and homicide would just reflect weather, climate, and social interaction opportunities, similarly to how there is less crime during extreme or highly inclement weather. Other explanations were structural and socioeconomic and focused on the living conditions of these regions as the prime cause of homicide.

Others pointed to types of people arguments and suggested that ethnic enclaves in specific regions of the country were associated with homicide because the people in those enclaves were inherently more violent. (An example of these various explanations in the case of nineteenth century French serial killer Joseph Vacher can be seen in the excellent book *The Killer of Little Shepherds* [Starr, 2010].) One of the most enduring explanations is a separate cultural ethic exists in the southern parts of nations that is more disputatious in nature and thus lends itself to conflict and the use of violence to resolve conflict.

In the United States, Redfield (1880 [2000]) was the first to study regional differences in homicide with his landmark book *Homicide, North and South: Being a Comparative View of Crime Against Person in Several Parts of the United States*. He systematically used available crime data to compare homicide rates of the states and noted the disproportionately high number of murders in the southern states. Redfield reviewed the usual explanations for southern violence that were similar to those advanced by European scholars and found them to be lacking in explanatory power. Instead, Redfield noted that distinct role of subcultural honor beliefs in the south that seemed to correspond to the reasons why homicides often occurred. For instance, Redfield suggested (1880/2000, p. 108), "The fearful aggregate is made up of individual cases of man shooting or stabbing his fellow-man, generally about some trivial matter or so-called insult." This refusal of southerners to let minor affronts go without some violent reaction led to an idea called the southern subculture of violence.

The **southern subculture of violence** thesis advances that an honor-based culture exists in the southern United States that is potentially conducive to violent provocation and retaliation. In this subculture, slight affronts are viewed as challenges and other forms of provocation, such as arguments, bumping into someone inadvertently, or staring at another, are viewed as direct threats that must be responded to with aggression. To not respond aggressively is to lose face. From this perspective, homicide is more likely to occur among individuals embedded in a subculture where violence is a preferred or even expected way to respond to interpersonal disputes, no matter how minor. It appears frequently in southern history and country music. Andrew Jacksons' mother was told him that law (or avoiding violence), "affords no remedy that can satisfy the feelings of a true man" (cited in Friedman, 1993, p. 178). Many country/western songs, particularly Kenny Rogers' song *Coward of the County* contain lyrics that embody a regional honor code that advocates the use of violence. In this way, the use of violence even potentially homicidal violence is perceived to be more acceptable than responding to an insult with non-violence. To respond nonviolently or to not respond at all to a direct challenge from another, is viewed in this culture as cowardice. And cowardice brings tremendous feelings of shame, regret, and low self-esteem. These negative self-emotions could not and should not be tolerated even if the violent response carries with it severe consequences such as an arrest for murder. The same logic pertains to homicides by African Americans in large cities as part of the street code which is explored in Chapter 4.

From Redfield's basic idea, other variations have been developed. A variety of conceptualizations of the south exist beginning with mapping its geographic boundaries. Some approaches used the Confederate south from the Civil War era as the official map of the southern United States. Others used smaller maps that generally omitted Texas and included what is today known as the deep-south states such as Alabama, Arkansas, Mississippi, Tennessee, Georgia, Louisiana, Florida, North Carolina, South Carolina, and Virginia. Some included the southwestern United States whereas others omitted it (for a review of different conceptualizations and different maps of the south, see Corzine, Huff-Corzine, & Whitt, 1999). Scholars have geographically defined the south in disparate ways which points to the difficulty of trying to operationalize and study homicide in this region when the region itself has not been consistently defined.

A common way to understand southern homicide is to point to the disproportionately large black population that resides in the south. As examined in Chapter 1 and throughout this book, African Americans have historically and currently had dramatically higher involvement in homicide as both offenders and victims. Thus, the southern homicide effect could just be a race effect. Indeed, this is generally the logic of Wolfgang and Ferracuti's (1967; Ferracuti & Wolfgang, 1962) **black subculture of violence thesis**. Their thesis serves as a bridge between regional theories of homicide (particularly with a focus on the south) and race-specific theories of homicide like the street code examined in the next chapter.

However, Gastil (1971) noted that southern whites also have significantly higher involvement in homicide especially compared to whites living in other regions of the country. Similarly, Messner (1983) analyzed data from 204 Standard Metropolitan Areas or SMSAs and found that southern region was significantly associated with homicide even when controlling for socioeconomic and demographic factors. In addition, no linkage was found between race and homicide in the south but was found in other regions of the United States. Thus, the southern effect is not just a proxy for race or percentage of African Americas, but instead reflects a distinct subcultural adaptation that transcends race.

An intriguing theory is Nisbett and Cohen's work on herding economies and the culture of honor. In a variety of works, (e.g., Nisbett, 1993;
Nisbett & Cohen, 1996), these authors theorize that the southern United
States was populated with Celtic people from Scotland and Ireland who
had a long history of animal herding. Herders are vulnerable economi-
cally and invest considerable resources in their herds, thus the loss of any
of their animals, such as from theft, would result in financial difficulty.
As a result, herders first in the United Kingdom and then in the United
States cultivated a swift, violent response to anyone who attempted to steal
their animals or otherwise jeopardized their livelihood. From this herding mentality emerged a broader honor culture where one's reputation and
self were built upon the steadfast use of violence to prove one's worth. In a
way, the honor culture was an internalized and to outside observers, somewhat exaggerated form of self-defense. Overall, this type of explanation is
known as the **herding/honor culture.**

In advancing their approach, Nisbett and Cohen (Cohen & Nisbett, 1994;
Nisbett, 1993; Nisbett & Cohen, 1996) conducted empirical analyses and
closely examined other explanations for southern homicide. Like Redfield
had more than a century earlier, they arrived at several conclusions. First,
there is negative evidence for a temperature explanation and they found
that the warmest areas of the south had the lowest homicide rates. Second,
they critiqued the argument that the lineage of slavery in the United States
accounts for the southern homicide effect because areas that historically had
the highest concentration of slavery have the lowest homicide concentra-
tions today. They also critiqued the idea that a nineteenth century phenomenon would continue to explain homicide today. Moreover, it is unclear why
the vestiges of slavery would similarly affect southern blacks and whites.
They similarly reported negative evidence for poverty-based explanations
by noting that many affluent southern towns have much higher homicide
rates than comparable yet impoverished southern towns. Nisbett and Cohen
also clarified what specifically about southern views of violence makes them
more involved in homicide. There are not strong regional differences in general endorsements of violence; however, southerners are significantly more
likely to use violence as a socialization tool for children, to connect the use
of violence with the protection of self, and to connect the honor culture with
specific forms of murder such as those relating to arguments.

Finally, as described in the prior chapter, Lee (2011) theorized that
violence in the deep-south among rural whites and in large inner cities
among African Americans shared cultural features that make homicide
more likely. In these settings, defensive or honor-based violence norms
emerge in part because the law is viewed as unavailable or unresponsive,
and in part where widespread institutional breakdown and poverty have

engendered predatory violence. From these environments, five interactionist processes were theorized to guide the creation of homicide.

First, homicide is intersubjective and constructed through the process of social interaction. Homicide offenders and victims often share sociodemographic characteristics and thus are similar in their attitudes and beliefs. How they respond to one another directly influences whether violence use will be escalated to a lethal level. This means there is extraordinary variation in how one defines what is disrespectful and how to respond to that disrespect.

Second, behavior is performative in the sense that individuals behave in certain ways to maintain public face or aura. For example, a person who is disrespected in public might commit homicide to reinforce his or her image as a "badass," to do otherwise would risk losing that reputation. Traffic behavior provides another example. A person who is cut off in traffic while others are in the car likely feels compelled to respond in an aggressive manner otherwise he appears "soft" because of an unwillingness to escalate the situation.

Third, many homicides reflect habituated affective-cognitive processes where the homicidal behavior is perpetrated out of habitual or impulsive reactions to common situations, not necessarily because the actor feels the homicide reflects a particular culture.

Fourth, homicide can reflect relational position that is where one is located in social space relative to other individuals. In this way, homicide is an important way to control those who are in an inferior position or who potentially threaten the homicide offender's social status.

The fifth part of Lee's (2011) theory is world making where behavior produces and reinforces structural realities. This is similar to a self-fulfilling prophecy where expectations of serious violence, including potentially the commission of a homicide, contribute to environments where these behaviors are common. These interactionist themes are commonly seen in film portrayals of the inner city and in autobiographical accounts of gang life and homicidal behavior.

Taken together, there is a long history of theoretical explanations for the southern violence trends that have characterized the United States but also European nations including France and Italy. Empirical studies of regional arguments for homicide are examined next.

Empirical Linkages to Homicide

Overall, a variety of research studies using diverse sources of data have provided general support for a southern subculture of violence both in the United States and using data from other nations. In an early study, Pettigrew and Spier (1962) noted that states with the highest homicide rates tended to be southern states. They also noted that ecological cultures of violence were particularly pronounced among African Americans. According to Pettigrew and Spier (1962, p. 629) black homicide offenders, "turn to homicide because he is often a product of a region with a violent tradition, and because he is often a migrant in a new and threatening environment that makes it difficult for him to throw off this cultural predilection for homicide." In this way, they suggested that data support a southern regional effect for murder, and that migrants from the south bring a homicidal propensity to use in other regions.

Gastil (1971) found that the degree of "southernness" in a population explained more of the homicide rate than income, education, age, and percent urban. Moreover, southernness continued to exert an effect on homicide even when these demographic and socioeconomic explanations were considered. Southern white males, for instance, are more likely than other white males to advocate the use of violence (potentially culminating in a homicide) for self-protection, to defend one's honor, and to discipline children (Cohen & Nisbett, 1994). Other research has similarly pitted the southern subculture thesis against competing arguments, such as greater poverty in the American south, and still found that homicide rates were associated with the southern subculture (Huff-Corzine, Corzine, & Moore,

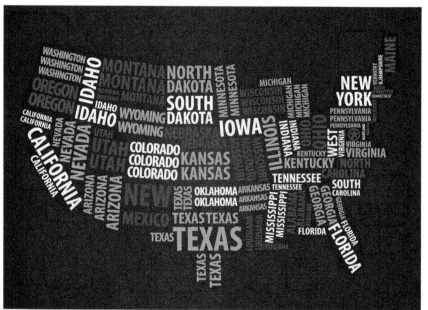

© Alan Uster/Shutterstock, Inc.

There is compelling evidence for a southern effect for homicide, particularly argument-based homicides that relate to the defense of status and honor.

1986; Nisbett, 1993). Others have found that southern culture is associated with more homicide in part because of conservative Protestant cultural traditions (Ellison, Burr, & McCall, 2003).

Ellison (1991) analyzed data from the General Social Survey and found that southerners were significantly more likely to condone violence for defensive purposes and for retaliatory purposes. There was also evidence that religious views moderated these views in the south thus contributing to greater advocacy for violence. Drawing on a sample of more than 35,000 participants in the General Social Survey, DeLisi (2001b) found that persons from the south were significantly more likely to advocate the use of violence against persons accused of child abuse, against persons accused of domestic abuse, and to generally advocate the use of violence. Moreover, southerners were more favorable of capital punishment and the use of police violence against various criminal offenders. In other words, southerners advocated the use of violence against disreputable people.

Using national-level data from the Federal Bureau of Investigation, Rice and Goldman (1994) found that Southerners were more likely than those from other regions to not only commit homicide in argumentative situations, but also more likely than non-Southerners to murder people with whom they were acquainted. The notion that "southern blood runs hot" was applicable to their findings.

Brown, Osterman, and Barnes (2009) analyzed two decades of data derived from the U.S. Centers for Disease Control and Prevention as part of the Youth Risk Behavior Surveillance System and tabulated by the National Center for Education Statistics. They examined whether a culture of honor was associated with school shootings, one of the most visible forms of homicide in recent decades. Controlling for temperature, proportion of state that was rural, economic insecurity, social insecurity, and social composition, they found that culture of honor was associated with a higher percentage of high school students bringing a weapon to school. In addition, culture of honor was significantly associated with the prevalence of school shooting over a 20-year period.

In a study of U.S. counties in 2000, Lee and Shihadeh (2009) found strong evidence that argument-based homicides among whites are higher in counties where white Southerners are more spatially concentrated. This effect was also only found in southern counties. They concluded, "As an historical legacy, the Southern culture of violence has undoubtedly declined over time as the U.S. population has intermingled, and as our social world has become larger and less circumscribed. However, within the South itself there remains a high degree of traditional *Southernness* that intensifies with the spatial concentration of Southern whites, and continues to make a modest contribution to their use of homicidal violence" (Lee & Shihadeh, 2009, p. 1688).

Although region has been shown to be a significant correlate of homicide, it is not immune from the palliative effects of other factors. For example, individuals in the South who participate in religious and other civic responsibilities are less likely to be involved in homicide than southerners who are not involved in these activities (Lee & Bartkowski, 2004). Other research also suggests that southern males might not be as approving of violence as believed. Hayes and Lee (2005) analyzed data from the General Social Survey and found that southerners had similar views on the use of violence and defensive violence as Americans from other regions especially in contexts where self-defense is involved. But, in contexts where the overall approval of use of violence was moderate to low, southerners were more likely to approve of the use of violence.

The regional perspective is not only pertinent to males. There is also research suggesting that females from the southern United States are also more likely to commit homicide. A recent study that examined female homicide rates among U.S. counties found that counties with more Southern-born women had higher murder rates even when taking other factors into account (Doucet, D'Antonio-Del Rio, & Chauvin, 2014). Doucet and her colleagues referred to girls raised in the south, and their putative involvement in homicide by the acronym G.R.I.T.S. (Girls Raised in the South). In another study of female homicide victimization based on data from 33 nations, Stamatel (2014) found significant evidence of regional effects in many disparate countries each reflecting unique historical and subcultural themes.

Lee and Ousey (2010) examined qualitative data and found that many types of people (e.g., men and women, white and blacks, young and old) occasionally view violence as an appropriate response to problems relating to self-defense and in cases where it is believed that the police will not be able to resolve the problem. In this way, the subculture of violence is perhaps not as brutish as it appears, but is more reasonable when understood in context.

The regional argument for southern violence is rooted in subcultural norms among both whites and blacks and the subculture of violence has been influenced by racial socialization and religious doctrine. The culture is mobile in the sense that former southerners who subscribe to the subculture take approval of violence with them when moving outside of the south. Research has shown support for argument-based homicides among both whites and blacks in and out of the American south (Lee, Thomas, & Ousey, 2009). Since research has shown the effects of a putative southern subculture on homicide outside of the south, it is perhaps important to view it more in subcultural as opposed to regional terms (Lee, Bankston, Hayes, & Thomas, 2007).

There is provocative evidence that people generally believe regional theories of violence, and thus view persons from the southern United States as more prone to use violence. A study by Felson and Pare (2010) is revealing. They utilized data from the National Crime Victimization Survey and Supplemental Homicide Reports to examine the relationship between region, race, and homicide. They found that offenders avoid assaulting blacks and southern whites unless they have guns because these victims are perceived as a greater threat. Moreover, southern whites were significantly more likely than whites from other regions of the United States to be involved in violent disputes such as homicide and gun assaults.

Box 3.1   Lynching and Southern Homicide

© Everett Historical/Shutterstock, Inc.

Lynching is the extra-legal homicide of alleged homicide offenders and other accused criminals.

Lynching is an extra-legal trial (meaning that the trial was not formally conducted by the criminal justice system) and punishment of an alleged wrongdoer. Historically, a lynching was a mob-based execution that usually involved hanging. Lynching was relatively common in earlier eras of the United States and had a distinctive purpose of racial intimidation against blacks especially in the southern United States during the Antebellum, Civil War, and Reconstruction eras. To some, the historically high homicide rates in the southern United States are directly attributable to slavery and the racialized use of violence that typified that era. To others, the notion that a historical event or era can continue to exert effects on contemporary homicides is far-fetched. However, criminologists have examined this issue empirically and produced some interesting findings.

In an intriguing study, Messner, Baller, and Zevenbergen (2005) hypothesized that the frequency of lynching in the past was positively associated with homicide in the present. They theorized that lynching created two violent adaptations that were segregated by race. Among whites, lynching had a brutalization effect whereby exposure to violence and capital punishment fueled the fire of continued lethal violence among whites. Among blacks, lynching imposed fear and homicide emerged as a form of self-help in which murder was a form of self-defense. These violent adaptations— one white and one black—contributed to a subculture of violence that when combined with other structural factors resulted in homicide. Drawing on data from the National Center for Health Statistics and Supplementary Homicide Reports from the Federal Bureau of Investigation, they found that lynching was associated with contemporary homicides across sources of data. They also found that historical lynching was predictive of white-on-black homicides that stemmed from arguments, disputes, or other interpersonal conflicts. A subsequent study reported associations between lynching that occurred between 1882 and 1930 and contemporary use of hate crime statutes (King, Messner, & Baller, 2009).

These are provocative and interesting findings. The conceptual model makes sense, but makes less sense when considering that homicides in the United States—irrespective of region—disproportionately involve a black male murdering a black male. If lynching was a driving causal force, it is unclear why this dyad would emerge. Moreover, white males are more involved in homicide than females even black females. And most commonly, white males murder other white males or white females. It is unclear how nineteenth century lynching explains these trends either. Nevertheless, lynching is an intriguing hypothesis for the enduring place of homicide in the southern United States.

Sources: Messner, S. F., Baller, R. D., & Zevenbergen, M. P. (2005). The legacy of lynching and southern homicide. *American Sociological Review, 70*(4), 633–655; King, R. D., Messner, S. F., & Baller, R. D. (2009). Contemporary hate crimes, law enforcement, and the legacy of racial violence. *American Sociological Review, 74*(2), 291–315.

Like any perspective, there is not universal support for the southern sub-culture of violence thesis and other covariates including temperature, eco-nomic factors, and population factors have reduced the apparent importance of region (cf., Anderson & Anderson, 1996; Corzine, Huff-Corzine, & Witt, 1999; Dixon & Lizotte, 1987; Huff-Corzine et al., 1986; Loftin & Hill, 1974). For instance, Dixon and Lizotte (1987) found that gun ownership among persons indicated that subcultural violent beliefs were not associated with region once other structural factors were considered. Using data from the National Self-Defense Survey, Copes, Kovandzic, Miller, and Williamson (2014) examined actual violent behaviors as opposed to attitudes about the usefulness of violence that potentially limited prior research. They found no evidence that southerners were more likely to use violence for self-defense.

It could be that southern areas have more homicides not because of cul-tural reasons, but structural reasons relating to health care. There is evidence that the rural social structure of the south compared to the more densely populated northeast for example, results in more sparsely available medical services that could treat gunshot wounds and other injuries. This means that in the south, stabbings and gun assaults are more likely to become homi-cides because of medical care that was provided too late (Doerner, 1983, 1988; Doerner & Speir, 1986). Conversely, stabbings and gun assaults in more urban and northern settings have greater opportunity to more quickly bring the victim to emergency medical services. In this example, there is nothing culturally violent about the south instead the homicide rate is more of a function of geography, resource availability, and timing.

Similarly, southern states could also simply be states with greater gun ownership and thus opportunities for homicide. Siegel, Ross, and King (2013) found evidence for this using data from the Centers for Disease Control and Prevention's Web-Based Injury Statistics Query and Reporting Systems database. They found that each percentage point increase in gun ownership was associated with a 0.9 percent increase in the firearm homi-cide rate irrespective of region.

A major weakness of regional theories of homicide is the variable ways that the south has been defined in terms of its geography and culture. It is likely there are many minisouthern subcultures in the southern United States that could differentially increase the prevalence of homicide. Corzine and his colleagues (1999) showed, for example, that the geographic area that encompasses the south is not uniform, and a variety of different maps have been used to capture what is meant by the south. In some cases, these maps are sharply different with some limited to the Confederate south included just the southeast while others include the southwest as far west as California. It is likely that such large geographic differences, even if consid-ered by some to reflect the south actually reflect sharp cultural differences that exist across and within states. In their study of the Appalachian area of Kentucky, Schwaner, and Keil (2003) reported linkages between mining, mining culture, economic distress, alcohol use, and homicide. These effects were not seen in other areas of the state that had a different economic background and history. In other words, there are pockets of homicide in the south but these underscore the considerable heterogeneity of homicide occurring across and within southern states (Doerner, 1975, 1978, 1979).

In addition, homicides in other areas of the United States, especially the western U.S., have surged in recent years and these changes are attributable to structural conditions, not regional subcultures (Parker & Pruitt, 2000a). Others have also shown that the western United States has much higher homicide rates once other explanations are controlled (Nisbett, 1993). Indeed, during the 1990s, a spate of high profile homicides in the rap music community was attributed in part to subcultural effects in the western United States especially localized to the gang culture of Los Angeles, California.

Similarly, a study of the Canadian General Social Surveys found that those in the western part of the country were more likely to own guns for self-protection in part to traditions relating to rurality and cultural differences compared to eastern Canada (Pare & Korosec, 2014). Thus, it appears that other regions beyond the south in the United States and Canada are now "known" for homicide. A general explanation for this would be increased mobility where individuals are more likely to relocate to other areas of the country for educational and employment opportunities or family reasons. It is more difficult for a regional subculture to become a part of the broader culture when the population changes more frequently.

Finally, a study of hidden homicide increases during the era of declining crime rates also shows that areas outside the south are responsible for many homicides. Using data from the Centers for Disease Control and Prevention, Hu, Webster, and Baker found that between 1999 and 2005, there were significant increases in firearm homicides. Among men between the ages of 25 to 44, the black increase was 31 percent and the white increase was 12 percent. Significant increases occurred in Alabama, California, Michigan, Minnesota, Nebraska, Nevada, New Jersey, Ohio, Pennsylvania, Texas, and Washington. In other words, only one true southern state—Alabama—was included in these homicide increases.

Regional arguments for homicide have historically been controversial and dogged by conflicting evidence. But the broader argument that there are subcultural differences across the United States that variously employ violence in day-to-day encounters still holds. A specific example of one of these subcultural theories—the code of the street—is examined in the next chapter.

CHAPTER 4

Homicide and the Code of the Street Perspective

Homicide is the leading cause of death of young African American males, and many of these homicides can be explained by the code of the street theory.

Conceptual Background

Readers of this book who are football fans will likely recognize the name Aaron Hernandez. Hernandez was a former tight end for the New England Patriots who was one of the best players at his position in the league, had played in the Super Bowl, and had just received a multimillion dollar contract from the National Football League. In August 2013, Hernandez was indicted for the murder of his friend and acquaintance Odin Lloyd who was an aspiring professional football player. As the public outcry and media frenzy about the event spread, it was revealed that Hernandez was also involved in a double homicide that occurred in 2012. In May 2014, Hernandez was indicted for that case also for the murders of Daniel de Abreu and Safiro Furtado. Cut from the NFL and without his lucrative contract, Hernandez was taken into custody and is awaiting trial for these cases. In 2015, Hernandez was convicted of the murder of Odin Lloyd and sentenced to life imprisonment.

As shocking as the case of Aaron Hernandez is, the apparent *cause* of the double homicide is even more shocking. According to the prosecutors account of the incident, while dancing at a nightclub, de Abreu accidentally bumped into Hernandez and spilled his drink. Not knowing that he had bumped into Hernandez, de Abreu continued dancing and enjoying himself at the club. The spilled drink and failure to apologize apparently enraged Hernandez who thought that the incident was an example of people trying to "test him." After leaving the club and going to another bar, Hernandez was convinced that de Abreu was following him. After leaving the club and driving around, Hernandez obtained a firearm from his vehicle and waited for de Abreu to leave. Around 2 AM, Hernandez drove beside de Abreu at a red light and opened fire into the car killing both de Abreu and Furtado (Hanna, 2014).

In other words, a minor incident was apparently internalized by Hernandez as a massive sign of disrespect, and one that needed to be redressed with violence. The regional approaches to explaining homicide assume that subcultural value structures that define violence in certain contexts as good or appropriate lend themselves to the use of violence to resolve problems. Once the use of violence becomes normalized, in part because it is culturally supported, then it is not unexpected that a homicide could occur. Another lingering issue from regional explanations of crime is the issue of homicide among blacks. The theory examined in the current chapter is an attempt to articulate a theory of black homicide that is conceptually similar to the regional approaches.

As discussed in several chapters in this text, there are startling race differences in homicide (see Figure 4.1). Compared to whites, African Americans are significantly overrepresented among those who attempt homicide, perpetrate homicide, and are victims of homicide. For example, based on national data from the National Center for Health Statistics, O'Flaherty and Sethi (2010) found that the homicide offending and victimization ratios (black to white) have ranged from 6.6 to 12.4 for men and 3.3 to 7.9 for women since 1950. Moreover, the overrepresentation of

	Percent of —			Rate per 100,000	
	Victims	Offenders	Population	Victims	Offenders
Total	100%	100%	100%	7.4	8.3
Age					
Under 14	4.8%	0.5%	20.0%	1.8	0.2
14–17	5.2	10.6	5.8	6.6	15.0
18–24	24.4	37.5	10.6	17.1	29.3
25–34	28.7	28.0	15.6	13.7	14.9
35–49	22.8	17.1	21.1	8.0	6.7
50–64	8.9	4.9	14.7	4.5	2.7
65 or older	5.1	1.6	12.3	3.1	1.1
Sex					
Male	76.8%	89.5%	48.9%	11.6	15.1
Female	23.2	10.5	51.1	3.4	1.7
Race					
White	50.3%	45.3%	82.9%	4.5	4.5
Black	47.4	52.5	12.6	27.8	34.4

Figure 4.1   The uneven distribution of homicide, 1980–2008.

Source: Modified from Cooper, A., & Smith, E. L. (2011). *Homicide trends in the United States, 1980–2008. Annual rates for 2009–2010*. Washington, DC: U.S. Department of Justice, Office of Justice Programs, Bureau of Justice Statistics.

African Americans in homicide data as offenders and victims is seen in all types of homicide, and usually at levels several times their proportion of the population (see Figure 4.2).

Similarly, Fox and Zawitz (2006) studied homicide offending and homicide victimization among white and black males ages 14–24 as a proportion of the total United States population, homicide victim population, and homicide offender population spanning 1976–2004. During this time period, young white males constituted about 10 percent of the total population in 1976 to about 6 percent in 2004. Across the time period, young white males comprised about 10 percent of homicide victims, and this rate was consistent. Young white males comprised about 18 percent of homicide offenders and this rate fluctuated between approximately 16 and 20 percent.

For African American males ages 14–24, the proportions are quite different. While young African American males comprised about 1 percent of the total population, they accounted for significant numbers of homicide victims and offenders. For victims, the rate hovered at 10 percent before escalating in 1985 to a peak of nearly 20 percent in 1995 and leveling off to about 15 percent in 2004. For offenders, a similar slope is observed albeit with about twice the magnitude. Young African American males ages 14–24 accounted for about 20 percent of homicide offenders—20 times their proportion of the population from 1976 to 1985. This rate peaked in

		Victims				Offenders		
	Total	**White**	**Black**	**Other**	**Total**	**White**	**Black**	**Other**
All homicides	100%	50.3%	47.4%	2.3%	100%	45.3%	52.5%	2.2%
Victim/offender relationship								
Intimate	100%	55.0%	42.7%	2.4%	100%	54.2%	43.5%	2.3%
Family	100%	59.2	38.2	2.0	100%	59.2	38.3	2.5
Infants	100%	56.2	41.0	2.81	100%	55.8	41.6	2.6
Elders	100%	69.6	28.6	1.8	100%	56.3	41.9	1.8
Circumstances								
Felony murder	100%	53.1%	44.1%	2.8%	100%	38.4%	59.9%	1.7%
Sex related	100%	66.8	30.4	2.8	100%	54.4	43.4	2.2
Drug related	100%	36.9	62.1	1.0	100%	33.2	65.6	1.2
Gang related	100%	56.5	40.0	3.5	100%	53.3	42.2	4.6
Argument	100%	49.5	48.1	2.4	100%	47.5	50.2	2.4
Workplace	100%	83.9	12.5	3.6	100%	70.8	25.8	3.3
Weapon								
Gun homicide	100%	46.5%	51.4%	2.0%	100%	41.2%	56.9%	1.9%
Arson	100%	57.9	38.8	3.3	100%	55.6	41.7	2.7
Poison	100%	80.5	16.8	2.8	100%	80.6	16.8	2.6
Multiple victims or offenders								
Multiple victims	100%	61.7%	34.7%	3.6%	100%	53.9%	42.4%	3.6%
Multiple offenders	100%	51.5	45.7	2.8	100%	43.2	54.3	2.5

Figure 4.2 Homicide and Race, 1980–2008.

Source: Modified from Cooper, A., & Smith, E. L. (2011). *Homicide trends in the United States, 1980–2008. Annual rates for 2009–2010.* Washington, DC: U.S. Department of Justice, Office of Justice Programs, Bureau of Justice Statistics.

about 1993 at nearly 35 percent—35 times their proportion in the population and leveled off to about 28 percent in 2004.

Data for firearm homicides similarly show distinct black-white differences in homicide mortality. This is important for the current chapter because firearms are the most common way that trivial street code disputes are "handled." Hu, Webster, and Baker (2008) analyzed trends from 1999 to 2005 using data from the Centers for Disease Control and Prevention. They disaggregated the firearm homicide mortality rate per 100,000 by race and age group. The results were striking:

- For 15-19-year olds, among whites, the highest rate was 7.0 and the lowest rate was 6.2. Among blacks, the highest rate was 56.4 and the lowest rate was 48.5. In other words, the *lowest* black rate was nearly seven times higher than the *highest* white rate.

- For 20-24-year olds, among whites, the highest rate was 10.7 and the lowest rate was 9.0. Among blacks, the highest black rate was 106.1 and the lowest rate was 94.2. In other words, the *lowest* black rate was nearly nine times higher than the *highest* white rate.
- For 25-29-year olds, among whites, the highest rate was 8.4 and the lowest rate was 6.7. Among blacks, the highest black rate was 93.1 and the lowest rate was 74.4. In other words, the *lowest* black rate was nearly nine times higher than the *highest* white rate.
- For 30-34-year olds, among whites, the highest rate was 6.3 and the lowest rate was 5.1. Among blacks, the highest black rate was 64.4 and the lowest rate was 44.0. In other words, the *lowest* black rate was nearly seven times higher than the *highest* white rate.
- For 35-39-year olds, among whites, the highest rate was 4.9 and the lowest rate was 4.1. Among blacks, the highest black rate was 35.8 and the lowest rate was 27.3. In other words, the *lowest* black rate was nearly six times higher than the *highest* white rate.
- For 40-44-year olds, among whites, the highest rate was 4.0 and the lowest rate was 3.4. Among blacks, the highest black rate was 26.2 and the lowest rate was 20.3. In other words, the *lowest* black rate was five times higher than the *highest* white rate.

Indeed, a variety of studies employing diverse data sources indicate that blacks are significantly more involved in homicide as offenders and victims than whites (Hawkins, 1983, 1985, 1999; Hu, Webster, & Baker, 2008; Sonderman, Munro, Blot, Tarone, & McLaughlin, 2014).

In *Code of the Street: Decency, Violence, and the Moral Life of the Inner City*, Anderson (1999) advanced a subcultural theory of African American violence specific to large urban centers in the United States. According to the theory, two basic types of persons reside in large cities. The largest group that Anderson referred to as **decent people** is generally prosocial and abides by the conventional norms of society. They value school, work, self-discipline, and do not view crime and violence as a reasonable course of action. During interpersonal disputes or conflicts, decent people utilize an array of skills to handle the situation including ignoring the other person, refusing to engage in an argument, using their verbal skills to facilitate a conversation to resolve the situation, and the like. These normative adaptations explain why the majority of people living in disadvantaged or impoverished environmental contexts do not resort to criminal behavior.

The other group that Anderson referred to as **street people** is antisocial and tacitly or explicitly rejects involvement in conventional social institutions. This group is extensively involved in crime and violence, and moreover, considers violence as the appropriate and necessary way to resolve interpersonal disputes. In this way, the use of violence is expected and culturally normative and this even extends to the use of homicidal violence. Even very minor affronts or inconveniences of daily life are interpreted by street people as threatening and direct attacks of their reputation. At all costs, street people vow to protect their self-image and anyone who disrespects them must be retaliated against. In short, street people observe the **street code**.

The main reason that street people so willingly advocate the use of violence is that their entire upbringing is generally characterized by antisociality and exposure to antisocial people. To Anderson, "These children of the street, growing up with little supervision, are said to 'come up hard.' They often learn to fight at an early age, using short-tempered adults around them as role models. The street-oriented home may be fraught with anger, verbal disputes, physical aggression, and mayhem. The children are victimized by these goings-on and quickly learn to hit those who cross them" (1999, p. 49). Due to relentless exposure to antisocial behavior and the use of violence to respond to even the slightest of aggravating circumstances, street people are inured to violence which only serves to increase the likelihood of it occurring again.

Fatalism and hopelessness are important emotions in the street code process. Adolescents who report greater feelings of hopelessness in their life are more likely to subsequently identify with street code attitudes. In turn, this contributes to higher involvement in violent delinquency. This is an important finding because it is compatible with the fatalism that is inherent in the "kill or be killed" culture that typifies crime-ridden neighborhoods. According to Anderson (1999), the feelings of hopelessness stem from a mostly structural interpretation where street people believe that conventional opportunities are not provided to them. They feel that "society" is designed against them from the start thus there is little point in playing by the conventional rules of society. There are also heavy racial overtones to this worldview whereby blacks see society as dictated by whites and that it is unfairly stacked against the interests of blacks.

Although the street code can be viewed by critics as a paranoid rationalization for antisocial behavior, Anderson does not agree. In the conclusion of the book, he suggested that "Any effort to place the blame solely on individuals in urban ghettos is seriously misguided" (1999, p. 315). Irrespective of whether one agrees with the theory, it does provide a specific theoretical context with which it interpret the dynamics of the thousands of homicides that occur in large cities and among African Americans in the United States. Empirical examinations of the theory are examined next.

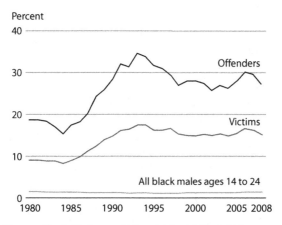

Figure 4.3   Young Black Males and Homicide, 1980–2008.

Source: Modified from Cooper, A., & Smith, E. L. (2011). *Homicide trends in the United States, 1980–2008. Annual rates for 2009–2010.* Washington, DC: U.S. Department of Justice, Office of Justice Programs, Bureau of Justice Statistics.

Empirical Linkages to Homicide

The code of the street provides a theoretical explanation that seems to comport with the reality of homicide offending in the United States. As a demographic group, young black males account for about 1 percent of the U.S. population but account for between 10 to 35 times that proportion of homicide offender and victims (see Figure 4.3). That empirical reality and the evening news seem to provide tremendous anecdotal support for Anderson's theory.

Many studies have tackled this issue empirically. Konstantin (1984) analyzed national FBI to examine the situations that resulted in the murder of law enforcement officers. Race and a general disposition toward and involvement in crime figures prominently. The most common incidents that result in the murder of a police officer are when the officer is attempting to make an arrest for some other crime, responding to an armed robbery, traffic pursuit, incident to an assault on an officer, the investigation of a suspicious person, and the traffic pursuit or car stop of a known offender. African Americans were overrepresented as the perpetrators of police killings, and black officers were disproportionately killed. Often, the racial dyads involved a black male offender murdering a black male officer.

Kubrin and Herting (2003) examined 15 years of homicide data from St. Louis, Missouri to explore the causes of **general altercation homicides**, which they defined as public killings that occur between acquaintances because of an argument or fight. Consistent with the code of the street, general altercation homicides reflect an offender and victim who are unwilling to back down from an argument or fight because to do so would risk the appearance of being weak. Between 1980 and 1994, there were 1,599 general altercation homicides in the city, which far exceeded others types of homicides relating to domestic violence and other felony offending. General altercation homicides were significantly more common in the most disadvantaged neighborhoods.

There is considerable evidence of the code of street in rap music, a genre that is disproportionately constituted by African American male artists from disadvantaged backgrounds. Based on analyses of 403 gangster (or gangsta) rap songs, Kubrin (2005) noted that rap artists commonly present images of themselves or characters in their songs that are related to being a violent person who will use homicide as a means to solve problems. These include the following depictions: "untamed guerilla," "3rd world nigga," "thuggish, ruggish, niggas," "the nigga with the big fat trigga," "no limit solder," "young head busta," "wig splitas," "cap peelers," "trigger man," and many others. Many song lyrics were found to similarly convey street code homicides. Art sometimes imitates life as several rappers have been arrested for homicide or been victims of homicide in the past few years. In fact, a Virginia man was arrested for a double homicide after bragging about the murders in one of his songs (Moran, 2013).

The salience of homicide to the African American community has become a pressing national issue in recent years.

In a related study, Kubrin (2006) examined rap music to see if elements of the street code were evident in its lyrical content. There was substantial evidence of street code themes in the 403 gansta rap songs. Issues centering on respect and the role of disrespect appeared in 68 percent of songs. Violent themes appeared in 65 percent of songs. One in four songs had explicit references to nihilism or hopelessness. Most tellingly, 35 percent of songs mentioned violent retaliation in contexts that were consistent with the theory. In addition, the song names were replete with words such as death, capital punishment, killing, being constantly in danger, and perceiving imminent death.

In their study of the effects of public housing policy changes in Chicago, Illinois, Hagedorn and Rauch (2007) interviewed gang members who engaged in street violence including homicide on the street of Chicago. The transition from notorious public housing projects to new facilities revealed how entrenched the street code is in their consciousness. Consider this quotation from one African American gang member:

> "…when all the projects get moved down, that gonna be a, I'm talkin' about, man, a real, I'm talkin' about, man, a war, a war that you've never seen before, man. 'Cause niggers from the projects gonna come try to take over niggers' lands and shit and, ain't nobody gonna let it, you know what I'm sayin'…'cause you came from the projects. It's gonna be a lot of people dyin' and getting shot and getting hurt, robbed…" (Hagedorn & Rauch (2007, pp. 450–451))

In a quantitative study of repeat shootings in Philadelphia, Ratcliffe and Rengert (2008) found that there is a 33 percent increased likelihood of a shooting within 2 weeks and one city block of a prior shooting. Generally, the original and subsequent shootings were driven by street offenders who committed gun assaults or homicides to maintain their street credibility and antisocial reputation followed predictably by a similarly antisocial person seeking to do the same. In other words, specific locations in the city reflect an ebb and flow of shootings driven by the street code.

Hall and Pizarro (2011) examined the role of cool pose in black homicides. They defined cool pose as a subcultural tradition that requires violent resolutions in defense of manhood. Drawing on data from more than 700 homicides from Newark, New Jersey, they found that many murders involved cool pose issues, and that these types of defenses of manhood were more common among younger and unemployed African Americans.

Drawing on data from the Mobile Youth Survey, Drummond, Bolland, and Ann Harris (2011) explored the role of hopelessness and the street code in various forms of violent delinquency. They measures street code at both the individual level and the neighborhood level. The internal street code included items such as "When I get made, I usually don't care who gets hurt," "If someone starts a fight with me, I am going to finish it," "Hitting someone really knocks some sense into them," and "When you are in an argument, you should stand your ground to get what you want." Neighborhood items included "It is not possible to avoid fights in my neighborhood," "If you don't carry a knife or gun in my neighborhood, something bad might happen to you," "Kids who are in a gang get respect from other kids in my neighborhood," and "Carrying a weapon lets other kids know they shouldn't mess with you." They found that youth who had adopted the internal street code were more likely to fight, carry weapons, use weapons, and to engage in potentially homicidal violence by stabbing. Those with more hopelessness were also more likely to brandish weapons and to stab others.

Qualitative research also provides support for the code of the street interestingly even among non-African American offenders in the United Kingdom. Brookman, Bennett, Hochstetler, and Copes (2011) interviewed 118 offenders who were imprisoned for a variety of street crimes and found substantial evidence of attitudes and behaviors that were fully consistent with the street code. Offenders used violence even potentially homicidal violence in order to punish others for their disrespectful behavior, to preclude possible victimization through fearsome acts of violence, to resolve disputes, and to maintain a formidable reputation to preserve one's status as a street offender (also see, Brookman, Copes, & Hochstetler, 2011).

Although the study was not framed as an examination of the code of the street, Cunningham, Sorensen, Vigen, and Woods (2010) examined the situational dynamics surrounding homicides among prison inmates. Drawing on data from 35 inmate homicides in the Texas Department of Criminal Justice prison system spanning 2000–2008, they found that the seriously antisocial histories and personalities of both homicide perpetrators and victims were responsible for their homicide events. Most of the inmate killers (and killed) had extensive and violent criminal criminals and were generally noncompliant and disruptive while in confinement. About 43 percent of inmates killings related to gang issues, 34 percent were associated with racial animosity, more than 54 percent involved an altercation or argument, and 17 percent of the killings were acts of revenge. In other words, a generally contentious and negative interpersonal style and an unwillingness to let slight affronts go is what precedes inmate homicides. This is fully consistent with the code of the street thesis.

Box 4.1   Murder and the Street Code Contagion

The code of the street presents a subcultural ethic that is greater than the sum of its part, that is, it is a sociological entity that exists beyond the traits and behaviors of individuals. Papachristos and his colleagues have studied the network structure of gang murder in Chicago and have generally found that murders are overwhelmingly consistent with Anderson's thesis. Using a network approach, Papachristos (2009) found that murders in Chicago spread through an epidemic-like process as gang members commit murder and retaliate in kind in order to save face and preserve their criminal reputation as a violent person. Almost all gang homicides in the city reflect expressive reactions of perceived disrespectful actions and its attendant retaliation. Indeed, being a member of the densest network of gang members in Chicago increased one's chances of being a homicide victim by an astonishing 3,080 percent (Papachristos & Wildeman, 2014).

In addition to the prevalence of the code of the street, there is another issue of legal cynicism. Legal cynicism is the idea that the criminal justice system is generally unresponsive, indifferent, and ill-equipped to respond to crime and disorder. Legal cynicism is more prevalent in high-crime areas and among minorities especially African Americans. Kirk and Papachristos (2011) also found that legal cynicism is endemic to Chicago disorganized neighborhoods. Moreover, one way that the code of the street is perpetuated is that gang members perceive that since police cannot or will not resolve their disputes, they must. In this way, gang homicide can be seen as a form of "self-help" that is driven in part by a lack of faith in the police.

The contagious nature of gang murders in large cities is consistent with the code of the street and also overwhelmingly concentrated among blacks, again, the group about whom the theory was developed. In a similar analysis, Papachristos, Hureau, and Braga (2013) reported similar findings for gang homicides in Boston and Chicago. In their concluding remarks, they advised:

> "In both cities, the majority of violent acts created a single large network that linked the majority of gangs either directly or indirectly. In this sense, gang violence is a highly connected and structured phenomenon. Gangs—and the violence they engage in—tend to cluster along racial and ethnic cleavages, with a higher density of interaction among black gangs." (Papachristos et al., 2013, p. 438)

Indeed, 85 percent of gunshot injuries, both fatal and nonfatal, occurred within one network (Papachristos, Braga, & Hureau, 2012). Using different methods and data, very similar effects were also found in Philadelphia in a study of shootings and repeat shootings (Ratcliffe & Rengert, 2008). In sum, gang homicides in large cities in the United States are strongly consistent with the code of the street. They represent cluster of highly antisocial persons collected in gangs and are driven by insults, affronts, and being "dissed," along with the subcultural-mandated retaliation.

Sources: Papachristos, A. V. (2009). Murder by structure: Dominance relations and the social structure of gang homicide. *American Journal of Sociology, 115*(1), 74–128; Kirk, D. S., & Papachristos, A. V. (2011). Cultural mechanisms and the persistence of neighborhood violence. *American Journal of Sociology, 116*(4), 1190–1233; Papachristos, A. V., Hureau, D. M., & Braga, A. A. (2013). The corner and the crew: The influence of geography and social networks on gang violence. *American Sociological Review, 78*(3), 417–447; Papachristos, A. V., Braga, A. A., & Hureau, D. M. (2012). Social networks and the risk of gunshot injury.*Journal of Urban Health, 89*(6), 992–1003; Ratcliffe, J. H., & Rengert, G. F. (2008). Near-repeat patterns in Philadelphia shootings. *Security Journal, 21*(1), 58–76; Papachristos, A. V., & Wildeman, C. (2014). Network exposure and homicide victimization in an African American community. *American Journal of Public Health, 104*(1), 143–150.

Subcultural street codes not only produce much delinquency, crime, and violence, but also these violent acts have serious impacts on the social and cognitive development of youth residing in neighborhoods characterized by the street code. For instance, Sharkey (2010) analyzed 6,041 homicides occurring in Chicago between 1994 and 2002. Chicago has a heavy gang presence, and many of its homicides reflect the impulsive, reactive behaviors described in the code of the street. Sharkey found that among homicide exposure reduces vocabulary and reading assessment scores by 0.5 and 0.66 standard deviations, respectively among African American youth. Those living in the most violent neighborhoods spend at least one quarter of the year, or approximately one week out of every month functioning at a lower cognitive level due to the effects of homicide.

Not all research on the code of the street is negative, and not all of it focuses on street people. Another important concept in this area of research is street efficacy. **Street efficacy** is the perceived ability to avoid violent confrontations and be safe even in negative, violent environments. In other words, it describes a person who behaves in prosocial ways even in the face of street environments. In a study using data from the Project on Human Development in Chicago Neighborhoods, Sharkey (2006) examined the association between street efficacy and violent criminal behavior, including behaviors that were potentially associated with homicide, such as shooting someone or shooting at someone. In several models, street efficacy was negatively associated with violence even while controlling for verbal ability, impulsivity, parental supervision, domestic violence, family criminality, marijuana use, alcohol use, school violence, and prior violence. He also controlled for neighborhood factors including concentrated disadvantage, collective efficacy, and neighborhood violence. Youth with greater street efficacy were also less likely to use violence and less likely to associate with delinquent peers.

Sharkey also found that youth in severely disadvantaged neighborhoods had less confidence in their ability to avoid violence in large part due to the sheer presence of street code youth and situations that were laden with street code-violence. This comports with Anderson's assessment that even decent people had to be fluent in the street code for self-protection and use violence—or at least give the impression that they would use violence—to resolve social situations.

Of all the theories in this book the one that perhaps most obviously relates to homicides as they appear on the evening news is Anderson's the code of the street. Given the disproportion black involvement in homicide, and given how many of these homicides are caused by minor slights and trivial signs of disrespect, it seems to have considerable salience. Nevertheless, there are some caveats that should be considered.

First, even in very disadvantaged neighborhoods in Chicago, the use of serious interpersonal violence is nevertheless relatively low. For example, the violent item with the highest prevalence in Sharkey's (2006) study using the Project on Human Development in Chicago Neighborhoods data is hitting someone with whom you do not live (17.3 percent). The prevalence of other forms of violence are also low including throwing objects/bottles at someone (6.6 percent), threatening to hurt someone physically (5.2 percent), gang fighting (3.2 percent), and attacking someone with a weapon (2.1 percent). For potentially homicidal forms of violence, the prevalence is even lower. Less than 1 percent of youth in the sample shot at someone and just 0.4 percent actually shot someone. Thus even in the worst, most street code saturated environments, serious violence is rare and homicide rarer still.

A reason for this is that Anderson's theory likely underemphasizes the importance of antisocial traits in favor of a sociological and social psychological explanation. The mechanisms that are described in the code of the street are essentially indicators of other highly antisocial traits, such as hostile attribution bias, impulsivity, or even psychopathy (DeLisi, 2014a). In this way, what appears to be street code murders might simply be the outcome of highly antisocial, poorly tempered, poorly self-regulated criminals coming together, with guns.

Finally, it could also be that the negative environments that Anderson's theorizes are the causes of the street code might actually be the products of their underlying antisocial traits and other deficits. For example, Massey (1995) suggests that high rates of black poverty and high rates of black segregation engender high crime rates and antisocial adaptations such as the street code. In this way, poverty and segregation "forces" blacks into crime and even homicide as a behavioral response to these negative conditions. But if crime rates are significantly higher in the poorest, most isolated contexts, it could also be the case that all of these "environmental" factors are the net result of a collectivity of highly antisocial individuals. The assorted deficits of street criminals results in unemployment, poverty, public assistance, physical disorder, a street code, crime, and violence. It is a chicken and egg argument, but the wide range of negative life circumstances of street offenders likely stems from their deficits and refusal to engage in the standard behaviors of conventional status. Some examples of these negative conventions are seen in the next chapter on lifestyles and their association with homicide.

CHAPTER 5

Homicide and the Lifestyle Perspective

Involvement in risky activities and criminal behavior are lifestyles that disproportionately contribute to involvement in homicide—as offender and victim.

Conceptual Background

On September 6, 1949, Howard Unruh methodically walked through his neighborhood in East Camden, New Jersey, and shot several neighbors, shopkeepers, and patrons. Over a 12-minute period that eventually became known as the "walk of death" Unruh murdered 13 victims and attempted to murder an additional three persons. At the time, Unruh was an unemployed World War II veteran who lived with his mother in her apartment. A closeted homosexual, Unruh would travel to Philadelphia to have anonymous sexual encounters with men then return to his isolated existence. Also a paranoid schizophrenic, Unruh kept a diary of his neighbors whom Unruh was convinced were talking behind his back. These diary entries contained codes such as DNDR (Do Not Delay Retaliation) indicating that Unruh planned to commit violence against them (Schechter, 2003). Found incompetent to stand trial, Unruh would be placed in psychiatric facilities for the next 60 years until his death at age 88 in 2009 (Goldstein, 2009).

In summer 2012, Rodney Alcala pled not guilty to the murder of Cornelia Crilley in 1971 and Ellen Hover in 1977. A former contestant on the 1970s game show *The Dating Game*, Alcala was sentenced to death in California for five homicides that he committed in that state between 1977 and 1979. Alcala was found with hundreds of photographs of women and children with many in suggestive, often sexual poses. He would lure his victims using his employment as a photographer (Peltz, 2012). In late 2012, Alcala changed his mind and plead guilty to these murders for which he was sentenced to 25 years to life in January 2013 (Rudegeair, 2013). It is believed that Alcala killed potentially hundreds of victims.

More recently, rap mogul Marion "Suge" Knight was charged with murder in January 2015. The cofounder of Death Row Records, Knight has not only been successful in the music business, but also has been in consistent trouble with the law with multiple arrests and imprisonments for a variety of violent crimes. According to the most recent allegations, Knight got into an argument with two men at a restaurant then followed them to a parking lot about 20 minutes later. There, Knight hit the men with his pickup truck, backed over them, and fled the scene. One died and the other is in the hospital (Associated Press, 2015).

Aside from the homicidal and (currently) allegedly homicidal conduct, what do these cases have in common? All of the offenders engaged in violence as an outgrowth of their day-to-day lives, and more generally, their lifestyle. For Unruh, the lifestyle was an isolated, lonely existence other than closeted excursions to another city for sexual encounters. Suffering from increasing mental deterioration, Unruh traveled little outside his immediate orbit and those connections produced feelings of paranoia and resentment. For Alcala, life was more extravagant and involved frequent access and opportunity to young women in the course of his work life. In fact, his work life was a guise to lure these women to remote locations and other private settings where he could commit sexual violence. For Knight, life was even more extravagant and involved parties, working, and multiple opportunities for skirmishes with others as a consequence of his gang-oriented, criminal lifestyle. This lifestyle often led to trouble with others, and that trouble could smolder to homicidal violence.

Although concern about crime is nearly universal, it is important to realize that not all individuals in a society are equally likely to commit crime or be victimized by crime. This includes being a homicide offender, homicide victim, or both. A variety of features of an individual's daily habits, associations, travel patterns, place of education and/or employment, and the amount of time he or she spends in various activities influences whether and how frequently crime is likely to occur. Whereas most people are generally safe in their daily environments, others are at tremendous risk of being victimized even fatally victimized.

Criminal involvement is largely stratified by the roles, behaviors, and customs of various social statuses including age, gender, race, and social class. According to **lifestyle theory** (Hindelang, Gottfredson, & Garofalo, 1978), criminal offenders and victims tend to "match" demographically because crime represents social interaction and social access among similarly situated people. For instance, Hindelang and colleagues (1978) noted that people tend to associate with others who are most like themselves, a process they referred to as **homogamous interaction**.

This means that adolescents and young adults are most inclined to associate with and spend most of their time with adolescents and young adults. Older adults associate with older adults with whom they have much in common and shared life experiences. Racial and ethnic groups tend to group together again because of proximity and shared cultural and life experiences. Males often have males as their best friends, and women tend to have other women as their social network. Different lifestyles unfold from these interaction patterns, and lifestyles place one differential at odds for crime and violence. For evidence of these differences, see Figure 5.1.

Thus, adolescents are more likely than much older adults to engage in delinquency and be victimized. The same logic applies for sex (males are overrepresented compared to females), race (blacks are overrepresented compared to whites), and social class (severely disadvantaged persons are overrepresented compared to affluent persons). Various lifestyle characteristics, such as going to bars or dance clubs which are crowded with alcohol-using persons at night are intrinsically more potentiated for crime than going to sleep at 9 PM. In other words, it is not necessarily the status of a person that makes them more likely to commit crime and be victimized, but it is the way that they live, and the things that they do.

Drawing on his nearly three decades of experience working in the federal Bureau of Prisons, Walters (1990, 1994, 2012; White & Walters, 1989) developed a theory of lifestyle criminality. **Lifestyle criminality** is a life

	Percent of —			Rate per 100,000	
	Victims	Offenders	Population	Victims	Offenders
Total	100%	100%	100%	7.4	8.3
Age					
Under 14	4.8%	0.5%	20.0%	1.8	0.2
14–17	5.2	10.6	5.8	6.6	15.0
18–24	24.4	37.5	10.6	17.1	29.3
25–34	28.7	28.0	15.6	13.7	14.9
35–49	22.8	17.1	21.1	8.0	6.7
50–64	8.9	4.9	14.7	4.5	2.7
65 or older	5.1	1.6	12.3	3.1	1.1
Sex					
Male	76.8%	89.5%	48.9%	11.6	15.1
Female	23.2	10.5	51.1	3.4	1.7
Race					
White	50.3%	45.3%	82.9%	4.5	4.5
Black	47.4	52.5	12.6	27.8	34.4

Figure 5.1   Age, sex, race and homicide.

Source: Modified from Cooper, A., & Smith, E. L. (2011). *Homicide trends in the United States, 1980–2008. Annual rates for 2009–2010.* Washington, DC: U.S. Department of Justice, Office of Justice Programs, Bureau of Justice Statistics.

pattern of irresponsible, self-indulgent, interpersonally intrusive, and social rule-breaking behavior. According to lifestyle theory, these components are distinct yet interrelated. The irresponsibility component reflects a generalized unwillingness to be accountable for one's behavior. It involves a neglect of the social and moral obligations to others. Examples of this include frequent absenteeism from school and work, poor financial management (e.g., personal bankruptcy, not having a savings or checking out, etc.), and failure to support one's family and children. The self-indulgent component is comprised of a lack of self-restraint and repeated desire to search for personal pleasure. Examples of this tendency are being unfaithful in marital or romantic relationships, substance abuse, and a lack of attachment or commitment to others.

Interpersonal intrusiveness is theorized to be the most destructive aspect of the criminal lifestyle because it involves aggressive or violent acts, expressions of interpersonal hostility, abuse of others, and a desire to control others. Examples of this are the repeated acts of harm and violation of other's rights that lifestyle criminals impose. Social rule breaking is a blatant disregard for societal norms and problem with authority. Examples of this are consistently getting into trouble at school and work, suspensions, expulsions, terminations, and repeated arrests for crime and noncompliance with the juvenile and criminal justice systems.

Perhaps because of the author's practitioner orientation, Walter's lifestyle theory is very critical of mainstream sociological theories of crime because they do not offer a believable explanation for the realty of offending. White and Walters commented (1989, p. 259):

> "Most contemporary theories of crime are, in fact, myths based more on sociological philosophy than empirical fact. We have suggested that if society is to come to grips with crime, we must begin by rejecting these myths and begin focusing our efforts on developing a more realistic, pragmatic approach to understanding persons who commit crime as a part of a general lifestyle. These criminals, although relatively small in number, represent a growing subclass of society responsible for a disproportionate share of the criminal activity in this country."

A final part of lifestyle theory is disresponsibility. **Disresponsibility** is an intellectual effort or rationalization in which a person attributes his or her actions to other causes and other people. Also known as blame externalization, disresponsibility is commonly seen when serious offenders blame others, such as the police or even their victims, for their arrest record and the legal consequences of their conduct. Disresponsibility is also commonly seen in drug offenders who refuse to acknowledge their responsibility for their addiction.

Another lifestyle criminological theory is routine activities theory that is also examined in Chapter 2. Advanced by Cohen and Felson (1979), routine activities theory simply indicates that crime occurs when three situations converge in time and space. There is the presence of a motivated offender, the presence of a suitable target, and the absence of capable guardians. Cohen and Felson also directly addressed the importance of lifestyle factors toward understanding crime. They defined lifestyles as "recurrent and prevalent activities (especially formalized work, provision of food and shelter, and leisure activities) which provide for basic population and individual needs" (1979, p. 593). One's lifestyle differentially places one at risk for victimization based on their differential contact with motivated offenders, potential victims, and sanctioning agents, such as police officers.

Unlike most criminological theories that tend to focus on delinquency and generally nonhomicide forms of crime, Cohen and Felson directly addressed the concept of predatory violence because they asserted that routine activities and lifestyles directly explained trends in "direct-contact predatory violations." In their theory, the authors also analyzed crime trends and found a significant increase in murder in post-World War II America. Specifically, they found there was a 47 percent increase in the rate of family or relative killings, but a 294 percent increase in the murder rate among known felons. These trends were linked to lifestyle patterns that changed the ways that offenders, victims, and (lack of) police interacted in public life.

With the lifestyle perspective in mind, it is also important to note the relationship between homicide offender and victim. According to a recent report from the United States Department of Justice, more than 78 percent of homicides occurring between 1980 and 2008 involved nonstrangers. Of these more than 49 percent were acquaintances or friends, 12.4 percent were family members, 10 percent were spouses, and 6.3 percent were dating. In other words, nearly 80 percent of homicides over a nearly three decade span involved persons who daily, routinely associated with one another often in intimate or family relations (Cooper & Smith, 2011). Often, people who are very familiar with one another have similar lifestyles and occupy similar social, educational, and work niches. And for the 22 percent of homicides that involved strangers, it was often the case that offender and victim were similarly engaged in matching lifestyles and day-to-day activities.

In short, lifestyle theories argue that persons who are around serious offenders, who are around dangerous offenders, who place themselves in situations that are unstable and involve the presence of weapons (e.g., guns), drugs, and alcohol, who are not often in well-regulated, structured activities, and who are not surrounded by persons who can supervise, control, or police the situation are prone for violence. The empirical linkages of lifestyle theory to various forms of homicide are examined next.

Empirical Linkages to Homicide

Although it was developed mostly to pertain to delinquency and crime generally, the lifestyle perspective is certainly also seen in homicide. Several studies using a variety of research methods and data sources have provided support for the lifestyle perspective as it relates to fatal criminal violence. In his study of homicide in Northern Sweden from 1970 to 1981, Lindqvist (1986) found that homicide offenders and victims very strongly matched on a variety of demographic, lifestyle, and behavioral characteristics. One of the strongest correlates of homicide offenders and victims was alcohol use and frequenting bars and establishments were alcohol was served, and which often served as the breeding ground for disputes that became homicides.

Certainly the criminal lifestyle lends itself to experiencing a homicide either as offender, victim, or both. For example, Barker and Human (2009) examined the criminal activities of four outlaw motorcycle clubs: Hells Angels, Outlaws, Bandidos, and Pagans. They found that homicides were relatively common features of these gangs' overall criminal repertoire. In some cases, murders were spontaneous expressive acts. In other cases, the murder of rivals were committed as part of ongoing instrumental enterprises of the gang. Other times, murders were planned aggressive acts or short-term instrumental acts, such as the murder of prison guards. Since so much of these gang members' daily activity was linked to serious and often hardcore criminal activity, it is no wonder that homicides were a small yet significant part of their life.

A striking example of the salience of lifestyle to homicide is to compare the behavioral outcomes of serious offenders when they are in highly structured, controlled environments, such as jail or prison confinement and their usual life on the street. Compelling evidence is seen at in both the transition from jail to street and from prison to community. Using data on more than 150,000 persons released from New York City jails between 2001 and 2005, Lim and colleagues (2012) matched the released offenders to controls based on age, sex, race, and neighborhood. They found that the risk of homicide among released prisoners was twofold higher than those in the control group. In the first 2 weeks after release from jail, former jail inmates were greater than five times more likely to be murdered and greater than eight times more likely to die from drug overdose (Lim, Seligson, Parvez, Luther, Mavinkurve, et al., 2012).

Similarly, Scheyett and her colleagues (2013) recently examined mortality patterns of felons recently released from prison. Using data from the North Carolina Department of Corrections and North Carolina Violent Death Reporting System, they found that 64 percent of the violent deaths of prison releases were homicides. The homicides occurred as the result of an argument or part of ongoing criminal activity. Six percent of the violent deaths were homicides as the result of legal intervention, or justified police killings. Thirty percent of the violent deaths were suicides. These were triggered by depression, relationship problems, and other problems relating to continued involvement in the legal system. Furthermore, a large study of more than 30,000 inmates released from prisons in Washington found that homicide played an important role in the early mortality of former prisoners. Compared to those in the general population, the risk of death for former prisoners was 13 times higher in the first 2 weeks of their release (Binswanger, Stern, Deyo, Heagerty, Cheadle, et al., 2007). In addition to homicide, other causes of mortality were also lifestyle related including drug toxicity and cardiovascular disease which is heavily dependent on lifestyle.

Sometimes the lifestyles of homicide offenders and victims are considered so deviant that homicidal behavior is partially extended because of a lack of police involvement. An interesting case is Ronald Dominique. Dominique raped and murdered at least 23 men in Louisiana between

1997 and 2006. A criminal offender with prior arrests for rape, assault, disturbing the peace, harassment, drunk driving, and other who led an impoverished existence, Dominique met other gay men or male hustlers who would have sex with men in exchange for money or drugs. Under the guise of going to his house to buy and use drugs, Dominique would bind or handcuff them, rape them, and then murder them. Early police contacts were not aggressively pursued because it was unclear whether these were abductions or whether they were simply low-level criminals engaged in a sex and drug lifestyle (Forsyth, 2015). Ultimately, Dominique was arrested in December 2006 and confessed to the rape and murder of 23 men to avoid the death penalty. He is serving eight life sentences at the Louisiana State Penitentiary.

Drawing on criminal justice, health care, and U.S. Census data, Broidy and her colleagues (2006) examined the overlap in social contexts and lifestyles among all known homicide offenders and victims in Bernalillo County, New Mexico between 1996 and 2001. Among the 332 homicide incidents, they found that 86 percent of offenders and 85 percent of victims were seen in the emergency department on at least one occasion for traumatic injuries relating to being assaulted or being shot. Emergency visits were also disproportionately related to drug overdoses, alcohol poisoning, and accidents relating to drug usage. Moreover, the majority of offender and victim healthcare usage was via the emergency department and during nontraditional business hours between 10 PM and 4 AM.

They also found that homicide offenders and victims lived in environments where violence and victimization were facilitated by low guardianship, opportunity, and exposure to motivated offenders. Their neighborhoods had many vacant houses, high proportion of renter-occupied units, and few intact families. The residents of these neighborhoods tended to be young, single males with lower education and wealth (Broidy, Daday, Crandall, Sklar, & Jost, 2006).

Both offenders and victims also had extensive criminal histories that portray a lifestyle of crime, violence, and victimization. Nearly half of homicide victims had an arrest history and 57 percent of offenders did. Nearly 40 percent of victims and nearly 50 percent of offenders had an arrest history for violent crimes, such as rape, armed robbery, domestic violence, and other assaults. Five percent of homicide victims and nearly 11 percent of homicide offenders had previously been arrested for homicide!

Using data on three cohorts of releases from the California Youth Authority, Ezell and Tanner-Smith (2009) examined lifestyle and other behavioral factors as predictors of homicide victimization. They found that although drug and alcohol problems were not predictive of being murdered, broader antisocial lifestyle factors were. Youth who had more extensive arrest histories for violent crime, who had multiple family members who were engaged in criminal behavior, and who were involved in gangs were significantly likely to be murdered.

Indeed, as the latter finding indicates a clear example of lifestyle theory is seen in gang homicides. According to Decker (1995, 1996), the quick rise and fall of gang homicides is consistent with the loose organization of gangs, its generally weak leadership, and a lifestyle of hanging around and committing crime. Most gangs are loosely organized and seemingly waiting for something to unite them, and that something is often an attempted or completed homicide. The uniting element is real or perceived threats from some other "outgroup" usually a similarly disorganized set of youths from another neighborhood. Very quickly, the threat is framed as an enemy to the gang. This shared perspective serves to increase the cohesion of the gang and justify the use of violence to "respond" to the real or perceived threat posed by the gang's enemy. Some short-lived act of violence—such as a drive-by shooting—occurs and rapidly de-escalates until the process begins again.

Decker described this process as proceeding through seven steps. First, young offenders have loose bonds to the gang. Gang members often also have lots of idle time on their hands since they are likely to drop out of school, disengage from the labor market, and generally withdrawal from conventional societal activities. Second, there is collective identification of a threat from a rival gang that reinforces the use of violence, expands the number of gang members, and increases cohesion. Third, there is a mobilizing event—possibly, but not necessarily, violence that contributes to escalation of activity, which is the fourth step. Fifth, there is a homicide followed by rapid de-escalation (the sixth step), and finally, retaliation.

It would be much more difficult for this unfolding of gang homicide to occur if gang members were working 8–12 hours per day, or were fully enrolled at school, or were conducting their activities in broad daylight during normal business hours. But late at night and in the early hours of the morning, when most conventional people are asleep to prepare themselves for the next day of work or school, the gang lifestyle enables murder.

A variety of other studies have linked lifestyle factors and the routine daily activities of individuals to variations in homicide. In his study of 1,748 homicides selected from Chicago, Dallas, Memphis, Newark, Philadelphia, Oakland, San Jose, Saint Louis, and an anonymous city in the western United States, Clark (1995) examined homicides that were perpetrated by lone versus multiple offenders. He found that multiple offender homicides were significantly more likely to occur at a place of employment. This was largely because many armed robberies of businesses involved multiple assailants. Conversely, lone offender homicides were more likely to involve victim precipitation and involve situations where the victim had been drinking alcohol.

In a study of 54 offenders who had murdered at least ten victims, Godwin and Canter (1997) the lifestyle distances in terms of the locations where killers initially encountered their victims and the location where they ultimately dumped the victim's body. The overall average distance from the serial killer's residence to where they first encountered their victim was a mere 1.46 miles as part of the offender's daily routines. This suggests that daily activities can serve as the opportunity structure for a serial killer to observe a desired victim. In terms of body disposal after the killing, the average distance was just over 14 miles from their residence. In other words, trolling for victims and dumping their bodies fit into the mundane circumstances of the offender's lifestyle.

Pizarro, Zboga, and Jennings (2011) examined more than 500 homicides occurring in Newark, New Jersey, from 1997 through 2007. They discovered considerable overlap between homicide offenders and their victims. They were overwhelmingly male, black young adults with considerable gang involvement and drug history. The majority of offenders and victims had arrest histories for violence, weapons, drugs, and property crimes. More than 73 percent of the killings were motivated by an escalating dispute, gang or drug related, or robbery related. Overall, 87 percent of homicide offenders and 75 percent of their victims were engaged in some type of criminal lifestyle.

Other research on homicide in Newark likened it to an infectious disease whereby homicide offenders and their criminally involved victims essentially operated as infectious agents (Zeoli, Pizarro, Grady, & Melde, 2012) based on their deviant lifestyles. Rydberg and Pizarro (2014) produced similar findings. They found that 76 percent of homicides were cleared when the victim did not have any indicators of deviant lifestyle that would reflect low or weaken social bonds to society. Conversely, victims who had three or more indicators of deviant lifestyle resulted in cases that were solved just 40 percent of the time. Thus, the haphazard lifestyle of homicide victims made it more difficult for investigators to close their cases.

The lifestyle of serious offenders is so dangerous, that at times, being in state custody is safer than being on the street. In an assessment of all public and private juvenile justice facilities in the United States, Gallagher and Dobrin (2006) found that detained delinquents were significantly less likely to die from homicide and accidents while under correctional supervision. However, they were 200 percent more likely to die from suicide and about 50 percent more likely to die from illness.

Box 5.1   Prostitutes as Victims of Serial Homicide

Lifestyle theory enjoys a particular amount of intuitive appeal because of empirical differences between various persons and their likelihood of being affected by crime. Individuals who place themselves in "riskier" situations and contexts, such as crowded bars, parties with intoxicated individuals, and neighborhoods and residences known for drug activity are significantly more likely to be victimized than persons who do not place themselves in these situations. And in the most dangerous and risky environments, the likelihood of harm is even higher.

Nowhere is this more evident than among prostitutes. Prostitution is an extraordinarily dangerous occupation characterized by little social support (prostitutes commonly flee abusive households and are often transient), substance abuse, and exposure to potentially violent customers. For example, a study of 1,969 women who worked as prostitutes in Colorado Springs, Colorado between 1967 and 1999 found a workplace homicide rate of 204 homicides per 100,000 persons. To put this rate into perspective, the most dangerous workplace homicide rate for women is 4 homicides per 100,000 for liquor store workers and for men is 29 homicides per 100,000 for taxicab drivers (Potterat et al., 2004). In other words, the workplace homicide rate for women working as prostitutes is 51 times greater than the next most dangerous job among women. Prostitution violence is also not limited to prostitutes as victims. Although prostitutes are most likely to be murdered by clients or customers, prostitutes are also most likely to murder their clients or customers. In addition, pimps are most likely to be murdered by other pimps (Brewer et al., 2006).

The lifestyle of prostitutes also makes them particularly susceptible to be victims of serial homicide offenders. The notorious Green River Killer, Gary Ridgway, murdered 49 women prostitutes. As Levi-Minzi and Shields (2007, p. 77) noted, "It was here that one man was responsible for the horrific fusion of his world of serial sexual murder and the underground world of prostitution. This man was Gary Leon Ridgway, the Green River killer." His personal rationale points to the inherent lifestyle dangers of prostitution:

> I picked prostitutes as my victims because I hate most prostitutes and did not want to pay them for sex. I also picked prostitutes as victims because they were easy to pick up without being noticed. I knew they would not be reported missing. I picked prostitutes because I thought I could kill as many of them as I wanted without getting caught. (cited in Quinet, 2011, p. 81)

Diverse researchers have produced similar estimates of how many serial murder victims are prostitutes. Brewer and his colleagues (2006) estimated that prostitutes accounted for 35 percent of serial murder victims.

Drawing on homicide data from 1970 to 2009, Quinet (2011) reported the prostitutes accounted for 32 percent of all U.S. serial murder cases.

Finally, these cases are much more unlikely to be solved than cases involving nonprostitute victims in large part because of the sheer lifestyle differences between the victims. As Bell, Busch, Hotaling, and Monte (2002, p. 1094) suggested, "Prostituted women are extremely vulnerable to violence because of the secrecy and illegal nature of their work. They are among the few women in society who voluntarily get into cars with unfamiliar men, and as a result, they are prime targets of serial killers." Indeed, for these reasons, once prostitutes get into that car, they are seriously at risk for homicide victimization, and moreover, at risk of never being found again.

Sources: Potterat, J. J., Brewer, D. D., Muth, S. Q., Rothenberg, R. B., Woodhouse, D. E., Muth, J. B., ... & Brody, S. (2004). Mortality in a long-term open cohort of prostitute women. *American Journal of Epidemiology, 159*(8), 778–785; Brewer, D. D., Dudek, J. A., Potterat, J. J., Muth, S. Q., Roberts, J. M., & Woodhouse, D. E. (2006). Extent, trends, and perpetrators of prostitution-related homicide in the United States. *Journal of Forensic Sciences, 51*(5), 1101–1108; Quinet, K. (2011). Prostitutes as victims of serial homicide: Trends and case characteristics, 1970–2009. *Homicide Studies, 15*(1), 74–100; Levi-Minzi, M., & Shields, M. (2007). Serial sexual murderers and prostitutes as their victims: Difficulty profiling perpetrators and victim vulnerability as illustrated by the Green River case. *Brief Treatment and Crisis Intervention, 7*(1), 77–89; Busch, N. B., Bell, H., Hotaling, N., & Monto, M. A. (2002). Male customers of prostituted women exploring perceptions of entitlement to power and control and implications for violent behavior toward women. *Violence Against Women, 8*(9), 1093–1112.

© Dm_Cherry/Shutterstock, Inc.

Due to the dangers of their lifestyle and occupation, prostitutes account for more than 30 percent of the victims of serial murderers in the United States.

Lifestyle theory is important for understanding lethal violence among subgroups in American society. For example, Bailey and colleagues (1997) studied lifestyle and household risk factors for lethal violence among women, and produced several important findings. Their data included 143 homicides and 123 suicides over a 5-year span of female victims in Shelby County, Tennessee, King County, Washington, and Cuyahoga County, Ohio. These victims were matched to controls that were similar demographically. Living alone significantly increased the likelihood of being both a homicide and suicide victim. Many women obtain firearms for self-protection, but ironically, having a firearm in the home increased the risk of suicide nearly fivefold, and increased the risk of homicide victimization more than threefold. In addition, illicit drug use by a member of the household, prior domestic violence, and prior arrest of any member of the household significantly elevated the risk of homicide victimization for women. In other words, involvement in an antisocial lifestyle with intimates who use drugs and are frequently contacted by the criminal justice system increases the likelihood of violent death.

Roberts and Willits (2011) examined lifestyle factors and routine activities as potential predictors of eldercide in 195 American cities. They hypothesized that elderly persons are at risk for certain types of homicide (e.g., accompanying a burglary, robbery, or sexual assault) given their failing health, inactivity, and social isolation. They found that cities with greater numbers of older adults living alone, greater numbers of older adults with a disability, and more robberies had more felony-related eldercides. Other factors such as older adults who were not working were associated with argument-based eldercides.

Lifestyle factors also figure into the increased risk of homicide among persons with certain types of mental illness. A study of 281 released male forensic patients in Finland is revealing. Tiihonen, Hakola, Eronen, Vartiainen, and Ryynänen (1996) found that these patients were 300 times more likely than those in the general population to commit a homicide in the year following their release. These patients also had stopped taking their medication and stopped attending therapy or treatment sessions for their schizophrenia. The result was a transient, unstructured lifestyle that dramatically increased the risk for murder.

Public health research demonstrates the antisocial lifestyles of homicide offenders, and also homicide victims. A study of emergency department (or emergency room) use among persons who were ultimately involved in a homicide event is illustrative. Most individuals who ultimately commit homicide or are victims of homicide lack health care, do not regularly use health care services, and do not even have a primary care physician. About 75 percent of homicide offenders and 70 percent of homicide victims do not have a regular doctor (Crandall, Jost, Broidy, Daday, & Sklar, 2004). In addition, some of the most common causes of emergency department use among homicide-involved persons are for assaults, drug overdoses, and firearm injuries. Homicide offenders were specifically more likely to resort to emergency department use for drug overdoses and firearm injuries.

In a case-control study of 105 homicide victims and 105 nonvictims, Dobrin and Brusk (2003) indicated that homicide victims are substantially more antisocial than nonvictims. Ever having been arrested increased the likelihood of being murdered by a factor of 10. This produces an attributable risk of 90 percent which means that 9 out of 10 homicides among those who had been arrested was the result of the exposure of having been arrested. Any property arrest increased the likelihood of homicide victimization by a factor of 11.2. This equates to an attributable risk of 91 percent. Any drug arrest increased the likelihood of homicide victimization by 12.1, or an attributable risk of 92 percent. Any violent arrest increased the likelihood of homicide victimization nearly sixfold which produced an attributable risk of 83 percent. When age, race, and sex are controlled, homicide victims are 5.3 times more likely to have ever been arrested than nonvictims. Moreover, they are 5.9 times more likely to have a property arrest, 2.5 times more likely to have a violent arrest, and four times more likely to have a drug arrest.

Indeed, risky lifestyles exponentially increase the likelihood of death for homicide offenders. Putkonen and her colleagues (2001) examined 10 years of homicide data from Finland and found that women who had committed homicide were much more likely to die from unnatural causes, such as a drug overdose. Specifically, homicidal women were more than *200 times more likely* than nonhomicidal women to die from unnatural causes! Moreover, homicidal women had a more than *400-fold greater risk* for suicide than women who had not murdered (Putkonen, Komulainen, Virkkunen, & Lönnqvist, 2001).

Lifestyle theory illuminates the ways that relatively routine activities manifest in lethal violence, and that most forms of homicide unfold from the lifestyles of potential homicide offenders and victims. An exception to this is seen in serial sexual homicide where the homicide offender behaves like a predator who stalks prey. Chan, Beauregard, and Myers (2014) recently compared 73 single-victim sexual homicide offenders to 13 serial sexual homicide offenders among a cohort of inmates in high-security Canadian prisons. They found that serial murderers were more likely to premeditate their crimes, indeed 85 percent of them engaged in structured premeditation of their killings. They were less likely to know the victim, but more likely to target the victim because of distinctive physical or personality characteristics. About 85 percent of serial sexual murderers engaged in deviant sexual fantasies within 2 days of their murders. These characteristics reflect the hunting behavior of serial murderers and also shatter the typical circumstances that accompany normal homicides as anticipated by lifestyle theory.

Lifestyle theory focuses on how individuals choose to live, but generally leave unexplained what force could be prompting persons to live such a hectic and disorganized life. A theory that articulates a driving force for negative lifestyles and all sorts of negative behaviors is explored in the next chapter.

CHAPTER 6

Homicide and the
Self-Control Perspective

Many homicides result from relatively normal interpersonal disputes where
one individual loses their temper—or loses control—and kills a family
member or friend.

Conceptual Background

In 1996, neuroscientists published a case study of a 65-year-old man with
no criminal history and no previous use of violence who strangled his wife
after she scratched his face during an argument (Relkin, Plum, Mattis,

81

Eidelberg, & Tranel, 1996). He was unaware of his rationale or motivation for abruptly murdering his wife. A magnetic resonance image (MRI) indicated that he had a large cyst in the left frontal region of is brain that had displaced his left middle cerebral artery. Subsequent testing indicated reduced EEG amplitude in the left frontotemporal region and a positron emission tomography (PET) scan indicated significantly reduced glucose metabolism in the affected left frontal region. They concluded that these neurological problems contributed to his sudden, impulsive, spur-of-the-moment decision to commit murder, a behavior heretofore that would have been impossible to predict based on prior behavior. It was a one-time only display of impulsive low self-control that resulted in homicide.

To the lay person, the basic ability to control one's thoughts and behaviors goes a long way toward explaining many and perhaps most outcomes in life. When asked to consider those who consistently get into trouble, a common observation is that the person lacks self-control. Conversely, when asked to explain why a person it physically fit, or financially secure, or enjoying a successful career, a common observation is that the person has good or even great self-control. Indeed, "The human capacity for self-control has been an enduring theme in philosophy, poetry, politics, and theology throughout history" (Heatherton & Baumeister, 1996, p. 90).

Self-control is the basic ability to regulate one's emotions and behaviors especially toward long-term consequences versus short-term benefits. Self-control has been cited as an important reason for behavioral differences between criminals and noncriminals and for differences between those who commit violent acts, such as murder and those who do not. As Toby (1957, p. 16) advised, "Clinical study reveals that the impulses to steal and murder and rape are universal. Apparently, the difference between the law-abiding adolescent and the hoodlum is not that one has impulses to violate the rules of society while the other has not." Instead, the difference is self-control.

Although it is a simple explanation, the notion that self-control or the lack thereof explains most behavioral outcomes is difficult to retort. Indeed, the concepts of willpower and temper relate to the ability that an individual has to regulate their conduct and emotions. This is important given the normative processes that immediately precede many homicides. From a self-control perspective, these offenders lacked willpower or were too poorly tempered to turn away from the homicide incident.

Self-control is also central to how the criminal courts define homicidal behavior. For example, the decision to distinguish murder from manslaughter rests on self-control. Weihofen and Overholser (1947, cited in Brenner, 1953, p. 283) observed, "The provocation which at common law reduces a homicide to manslaughter must be such as is calculated to produce hot blood or passion in a reasonable man, an average man of ordinary self-control." Unlike other criminological theories, self-control is related to homicide even in matters of jurisprudence.

Several scholars across the social sciences and humanities have utilized self-control as a key concept to explain behavior, and particularly maladaptive behaviors like crime and violence. In Dante's *The Divine Comedy*, various violations of self-control resulted in differential placement in the various circles of Hell. The lustful were sent to Circle 2 of Hell. Gluttons were sent to Circle 3 and the wrathful sent to Circle 5. Murderers were sent to Circle 7 of Hell only two stages removed from Circle 9 which was the final circle of Hell (Barry, 2013). The implication is that violations of self-control or self-regulation were sinful and compatible with criminal behaviors including homicide.

In psychiatry, the disorder Intermittent Explosive Disorder expressly links self-control and violence. **Intermittent Explosive Disorder** is characterized by recurrent episodes of aggression involving violence or destruction of property that are out of proportion to provocation or precipitating stressors. It is the only disorder in the Diagnostic Statistical Manual for Mental Disorders that has impulsive aggression as its core feature. Some adolescents with the disorder engage in hundreds of violent rage attacks per year (McLaughlin, Green, Hwang, Sampson, Zaslavsky, & Kessler, 2012) thus it has great potential to manifest in homicidal behavior.

In psychology, additional models have been developed that link self-control to crime, violence, and even homicide. Several scholars (e.g., Joireman, Anderson, & Strathman, 2003; Zuckerman, 2007) point to **sensation seeking** which is a tendency to seek novel experiences and excitement often in an impulsive way. In their models, sensation seeking and impulsivity contribute to a general behavioral tendency that discounts future costs of behavior. When combined with high trait anger and trait hostility, there is increased likelihood to use aggression in interpersonal disputes and an increased desire to retaliate against persons who are viewed as threats. Thus, persons with this mixture of personality traits "run hot" emotionally, and can rather easily be led into aggressive disputes such as assaults which can serve as the starting point for an exchange that can result in a homicide.

Finkel and colleagues have developed **I³ theory** (DeWall, Finkel, & Denson, 2011). I³ (pronounced I cubed) presents three Is that relate to aggression. The first I is for *instigation* which relates to normative social dynamics that can produce aggressive reactions, such as being insulted or rejected. The second I is *impellance* is dispositional or situational factors that cause the person to experience a strong urge to use aggression. These can be dispositional anger, extreme pain, or extreme frustration. The third I is *inhibition*. Persons who are disinhibited are less likely to override psychological and physiological reactions to anger and provocation, and instead respond to these stimuli with violence. Conceptually, the three Is are an easy and intuitive template for an individual who will experience considerable opportunities to use aggression in everyday disputes, and this aggression could theoretically include homicide.

Without question, the most visible self-control theory in criminology and criminal justice is the Gottfredson and Hirschi's (1990) **self-control theory** advanced in their book *A General Theory of Crime*. In their landmark book, Gottfredson and Hirschi (1990) boldly theorized that a single construct—namely self-control—is the indispensable thing that explains behaviors in life. In terms of criminal behavior, it is low self-control that causes crime and other forms of negative or maladaptive behaviors. From this theoretical perspective, the reason that serious criminal offenders also often smoke, drink alcohol, abuse drugs, cheat on their spouse or significant other, abandon their family responsibilities, cut class, refuse to do their homework, quit school, quit jobs, are often fired from jobs, and the like is that they do not have the wherewithal to handle these responsibilities.

Their self-control construct had six distinctive elements of subcomponents:

- *Low gratification delay*: persons with this tendency crave immediate gratification of their desires and have considerable difficulty waiting for longer term rewards. Gratification delay is required for most responsibilities in life especially educational and work demands, thus persons who are unwilling to invest the time to earn a delayed reward (e.g., diploma, degree, tenure, and higher salary) will face hardships in school and work.
- *Low persistence*: persons with this tendency similarly have little persistence or perseverance in completing challenges or basic responsibilities that are not immediately resolved. The lack of wherewithal also impacts interpersonal relationships thus those with low persistence would be less likely to maintain long-term relationships including marriage.
- *High activity-level/physicality*: persons with this tendency prefer action-oriented activities, have a high activity level, and can be hyperactive. They find it difficult to be calm and relaxed and instead seem to crave action and be sensation seeking.
- *Temper*: Those with a quick, hot, or bad temper (several characterizations exist) have difficult subordinating emotional reactions and instead respond very quickly and impulsively when threatened, disrespected, or annoyed. Having a bad temper significantly increases

opportunities for negative social exchanges, arguments, and fights—conditions that often are the raw material for violence.

- *Low cognitive or verbal skills*: Those with lower verbal intelligence are less able to resolve problems or disputes verbally or intellectually, and instead use force to settle disputes. Cognitive deficits also create problems for educational and work functioning.
- *High self-centeredness or narcissism*: Persons with this tendency always put their own wants and needs first ahead of the wants and needs of others, including family members and friends. It reflects self-absorption across contexts and also encompasses criminal behavior as a personal want.

In Gottfredson and Hirschi's (1990, p. 157) view:

"People who lack self-control tend to dislike settings that require discipline, supervision, or other constraints on their behavior; such settings include school, work, and, for that matter, home. These people therefore tend to gravitate to "the street" or, at least in adolescence, to the same-sex peer group. Yet individuals with low self-control do not tend to make good friends. They are unreliable, untrustworthy, selfish, and thoughtless. They may, however, be fun to be with; they are certainly more risk-taking, adventuresome, and reckless than their counterparts."

Their book has generated an incredible amount of tests and research activity, and at this writing has been cited more than 7,000 times making it one of the most cited criminology books in history. Moreover, low self-control has been empirically linked to a vast number of conduct problems, delinquency, crime, and violence (Buker, 2011; DeLisi, 2011; de Ridder, Lensvelt-Mulders, Finkenauer, Stok, & Baumeister, 2012).

Unlike most theories of crime and delinquency, Gottfredson and Hirschi (1990) explicitly wrote about how their central theoretical construct was associated with homicide. According to them, homicide is the most mundane and easily explainable crimes because most homicides occur under rather predictable situations involving people who know one another. That most homicides are perpetrated with a firearm also comports with the theory, because it requires very little skill or long-term investment process to squeeze a trigger. Instead, most homicides involving guns are quarrels or arguments occurring when one or both parties are intoxicated. The way to "resolve" these quarrels or arguments is to make the person stop by shooting him or her (usually him). In other words, homicide offers those who commit it a short-term immediate benefit without consideration of the long-term and rather serious legal consequences. As Gottfredson and Hirschi (1990, p. 33) suggested, "[t]he benefits of homicide are not large, profound, or serious. They are, on the contrary, benefits of the moment, and the effect of alcohol or drugs may be found precisely in their tendency to reduce the time-horizon of the offender to the here and now."

Moffitt and her colleagues (2011; Israel et al., 2014) evaluated the predictive validity of childhood self-control on a range of life outcomes during adulthood. The findings were startling. Persons who displayed low self-control during childhood reported a range of difficulties at age 32 years. These included worse physical health, greater depression, higher likelihood of drug dependence, lower socioeconomic status, lower income, greater likelihood of single-parenthood, worse financial planning, more financial struggles, and most importantly for a criminological audience, more criminal convictions. Indeed, 45 percent of participants with low self-control during childhood had criminal convictions at age 32, a level that is nearly fourfold higher than the prevalence of criminal convictions for persons who had higher childhood self-control.

In addition, self-control is relatively and in some cases absolutely stable across the life-course which is consistent with theoretical expectations. For instance, a large-scale study of approximately 20,000 children in the United States found little evidence of changes in self-regulation capacity over a 5 year span from kindergarten through fifth grade (Coyne, Vaske, Boisvert, & Wright, 2015). In addition, self-regulation was most stable among children with the greatest deficits in it suggesting that those who are unable to control their behavior are likely to suffer from this fundamental deficit throughout life.

Despite the popularity of self-control theory in criminology it has not been widely linked to homicide offending in large part because criminology generally uses general population samples that contain few if any homicide offenders. Nevertheless, diverse works in the social sciences have explored empirical linkages between self-control theories and homicide, and these are examined next.

Empirical Linkages to Homicide

In the big picture of things, there has been a staggering reduction in the role of violence and lethal violence over the last several centuries of human history. In his bestselling treatise *The Better Angels of Our Nature: Why Violence Has Declined*, Pinker (2011) suggested that several social forces have not only reduced the incidence of violence including homicide, but also these social forces have increased public revulsion to these forms of violence. According to Pinker, a general civilizing process has occurred since the Middle Ages via the expansion of the state, the expansion of commerce and the general prosperity that flows from it, and expansion of cultural cosmopolitanism that increasingly viewed violence and murder as brutish and "beneath them."

Thus, from a general historical perspective, as nations become more modernized and social life is defined by self-control, they experience fewer homicides (Eisner, 2001). More recently, Eisner (2014) offered a historical account which suggests that the civilizing process that typifies societies as they develop result in increase in self-control because they promote civility, self-discipline, and long-sightedness. Using historical sources, Eisner advanced that the eleventh to twenty-first centuries can be understood as five epochs of civilizing processes and greater focus on self-control. A major result of these advances is a reduction in homicide.

The *courtization of warriors* era spanned the eleventh to thirteenth centuries and included several societal advances that increased self-control and decreased homicide. These included courtliness as a new ethic, which was characterized by modesty, patience, restraint, and elegance, the limitation of retaliation rights, the beginning of state monopolization over legitimate use of force, and the beginning of state-run criminal justice based on written procedure, or simply, law.

The *early absolutist state* spanned the fifteenth to seventh centuries and was characterized by increasing power and centralization of the state that limited the ability of citizens to exercise violence.

The *social disciplining revolution* spanned the sixteenth to eighteenth centuries and included police control over daily behaviors, cultural emphasis on frugality, duty, deference, and orderliness, the promotion of an ethic of inner control by the church, and public fight against disorderly pastimes and behaviors.

The *bourgeois civilizing offensive* spanned 1830 to 1900 and included universal schooling, temperance movements that emphasized self-control, and the ideal of domesticity and respectability to promote inner-directed family harmony.

The *securitization and new culture of control* spans approximately 1980 to the present includes intensive control of antisocial behaviors, enforcement of discipline and propriety, and expanding infrastructure of crime prevention and community, and initiatives against welfare dependency (Eisner, 2014).

Other studies at the microlevel have also shown the importance of self-control to homicidal behavior. In an archival study of 231 incidents of parricide or mass murder covered in the *Chicago Tribune* and the *New York Times* between 1851 and 1899, Shon and Roberts (2010) found that most of these homicidal acts originated as spontaneous acts usually during the course of an argument that ultimately led to murder and in some cases, multiple murder.

Drawing on data from an epidemiological sample of more than 43,000 participants, Larson, Vaughn, Salas-Wright, and DeLisi (2015) examined the linkages between self-control and various forms of criminal violence. Although their study did not focus on homicide, it contained other violent acts that often serve as the precipitants of homicide. They found evidence of a small group of about 6 percent of persons who display very low self-control and Narcissistic Personality Disorder. A tendency toward narcissism is included in Gottfredson and Hirschi's theory. For example, persons in this group were much more likely to bully others, commit rape, commit robbery, start fights with strangers, and engage in a variety of forms of domestic violence. Indeed, they were nearly eight times more likely to rape and about five times more likely to commit intimate partner violence. They also were nearly four times more likely to threaten someone with a gun or knife. Thus, it appears the particular combination of self-love or narcissism and low self-regulation is a potent cocktail that can result in varied forms of violence up to and likely including homicide.

Self-control theory also is helpful for understanding why there is so much overlap between homicide offenders and homicide victims in terms of social and demographic characteristics. According to Gottfredson and Hirschi (1990, p. 17), "It turns out that victims and offenders tend to share all or nearly all social and personal characteristics. Indeed the correlation between self-reported offending and self-reported victimization is, by social science standards, very high." In a study of 60 parolees from the California Youth Authority who were murdered within 5 years of their release, Piquero, MacDonald, Dobrin, Daigle, and Cullen (2005) found that parolees with lower self-control were more likely to be homicide victims. Among the offenders, an increase in low self-control from its minimum to its maximum value increased the odds of being murdered by nearly 170 percent! They also found that low self-control was not associated with any type of death, but was instead limited specifically to homicide victimization.

Interviews with active violent offenders also show how impulsive decisions reflecting poor self-control can result in homicide. In their qualitative study of carjackers, Hochstetler, Copes, and Williams (2010, p. 503) published this offender commentary about the use of violence, and how quickly it can unfold:

> Definitely I'm violent, don't get me wrong. I'll fight. Here in the prison, here I'm on the boxing team. But fighting's not everything.... But [a co-offender], you know, he's not like me. We get along good

as a team, you know in situations,but as far as being a lot alike, we're nothing alike. He'll kill somebody! I mean I'll do whatever, but when it comes to killing somebody out of cold blood for no reason—that's not me. Carjacking the whole time you're doing it you'rethinking, "Yeah, if he don't give it up, I'll kill him." Once you get there, it's not so easy. Aiming the gun flashing it around—that's easy. Pulling the trigger it's a lot harder than people think.

In their study of 2,160 jail inmates, Ward, Fox, Tillyer, and Lane (2015) reported that offenders with low self-control were most likely to be violent victimized including potentially homicidal victimization such as being shot or stabbed during a robbery, carjacking, or home invasion. Similarly, others (Franklin, 2011; Franklin, Franklin, Nobles, & Kercher, 2012; Turanovic & Pratt, 2014) found that persons with low self-control were more likely to be violently victimized in a variety of ways, including some that potentially could result in homicide, such as aggravated assault with a weapon and sexual assault.

Other conceptual models are similar to self-control theory and advance the basic idea that poor self-regulation is a key ingredient for antisocial behavior and violence. For example, Megargee (1966) advanced that homicide offenders can be understood by a two-part typology of overcontrolled and undercontrolled persons. Overcontrolled individuals are those who display rigid inhibition of the expression of aggression whereas undercontrolled individuals generally lack inhibition at controlling aggression. Although both types are involved in homicide, there are likely behavioral differences with undercontrolled individuals faring worse in terms of their criminal careers.

Blackburn (1971) reported evidence of four personality types of murderers that generally centered on the role of impulsivity and self-control. Only one group was able to regulate its impulses, these were offenders who were overcontrolled and had higher levels of internalizing symptoms. The other groups were characterized as paranoid-aggressive, depressed-inhibited, and psychopathic. All of them presented with problems with impulse control and self-regulation deficits that was mixed with diverse forms of other psychopathology.

In their study of 164 male murderers imprisoned in Georgia and their subsequent parole risk, A. Heilbrun, L. Heilbrun, and K. Heilbrun (1978) found that those who committed impulsive murders also were most likely to fail on parole because of their low self-control. Moreover, blacks were more likely than whites to commit impulsive homicides, and their greater parole failure reflected a basic deficit in complying with the conditions of parole. In other words, low self-control was predictive of both the original homicide and the subsequent parole violation.

McGurk (1981) compared overcontrolled and undercontrolled homicide offenders and found that undercontrolled murderers have more extensive criminal careers, have greater psychiatric problems, display more suicidal ideation, and engage in more institutional misconduct while in prison. In their study of criminal offenders including a sample of 80 premeditated murderers, Holcomb, Adams, and Ponder (1985) found evidence of five latent groupings of personality styles among these offenders. Overall, their personality functioning coalesced around low self-control and reflected little planned direction and control in their lives and their behavior. Overwhelmingly, the homicide offenders were characterized as undercontrolled.

Box 6.1   Homicide Reflecting *High* Self-Control

Details left at the scene of a sexual homicide reveal much about the psychopathology and self-control of the murderer.

There is no denying the association between low self-control and various forms of antisocial behavior; however, an interest paradox also exists between self-control and certain types of homicide offenders. In an important work that sought to differentiate the murder scenes of sexual homicides and potentially draw inferences from the crime scenes to profile the offender, Ressler, Burgess, and Douglas (1988) advanced a typology of sexual homicide offending. On one hand was a **disorganized**

sexual murderer whose offense was spontaneous, whose victim was known but depersonalized, and who engaged in minimal conservation during the attack. The disorganized killer's murder scene was random and sloppy, characterized by sudden violence with minimal use of restraints, and sexual acts after death. The victim's body was left in view at the death scene and importantly, weapons and other forensic evidence were often present at the scene. This killer is sloppy.

In contrast, the **organized sexual murderer** committed a planned killing of a targeted stranger who was personalized. There was controlled conservation during the killing, use of restraints, aggressive acts before death, and demand for submission. The entire crime scene of the organized killer reflected control. The victim's body was hidden, often transported, and there was an absence of weapons or other forensic physical evidence. Taken together, the Ressler et al. (1988) typology painted a picture of two very different perpetrators in terms of their functioning, their competence, their mastery over their murder victim, and their *control* over their murder scene.

Although the typology has some limitations (Sewall, Krupp, & Lalumière, 2012), it is a useful way to conceptualize sexual murder. In a comparative study of murderers, rapists, and general felons, Kozma and Zuckerman (1983) found that murderers had better self-control than general felons in terms of their ability to regulate their conduct during prison confinement. Beauregard and Martineau (2014) recently the crime scene behaviors of 350 sexual homicide offenders and found that organized killers, who displayed high self-control during and after their killings were able to delay the number of days until the body was discovered and avoid having the police solve the case. Thus some of the most extreme offenders, those who commit sexual homicide, embody high self-control and use this asset to further their violence and forestall criminal justice system interventions.

Despite the self-control differences between organized and disorganized sexual murderers, it is also important to note that the immediate decision to commit the murder is itself usually a spur-of-the-moment decision based on an apparent opportunity (Hazelwood & Douglas, 1980). Thus even among homicide offenders whose killing repertoire suggests control there is fundamentally the element of low self-control.

Sources: Ressler, R., Burgess, A., & Douglas, J. E. (1988). *Sexual homicide: Patterns and motives.* Lexington, MA: D. C. Heath; Kozma, C., & Zuckerman, M. (1983). An investigation of some hypotheses concerning rape and murder. *Personality and Individual Differences, 4*(1), 23–29; Beauregard, E., & Martineau, M. (2014). Does the organized sexual murderer better delay and avoid detection? *Journal of Interpersonal Violence,* doi: 0886260514555129; Sewall, L. A., Krupp, D. B., & Lalumière, M. L. (2013). A test of two typologies of sexual homicide. *Sexual Abuse: A Journal of Research and Treatment, 25*(1), 82–100; Hazelwood, R. R., & Douglas, J. E. (1980). The lust murderer. *FBI Law Enforcement Bulletin, 49*(4), 18–22.

Still others connect low self-control to more fundamental differences in temperament and personality. In their general theory, DeLisi and Vaughn (2014) theorize that low effortful control and high negative emotionality are the cornerstone temperamental constructs that predict problem behaviors from infancy through adulthood. According to their theory, those with self-regulation deficits are generally unable to control their impulses and frequently get into trouble. Moreover, they tend to experience the world in a negative way and experience negative emotions like anger, hostility, and irritability. These traits, combined with the low self-regulation, tend to annoy others and lead to frequent aversive interactions. Over time, this contributes to ever more problem behaviors.

Although the theory has not been empirically linked to homicide, it is not difficult to imagine how an impulsive, poorly controlled person with lots of negative emotions could perpetrate and be victimized in a violent way. For instance, Perdue and Lester (1974) studied 50 convicted murderers and measured their temperamental profiles. The most common features were aggressiveness, negativity, lack of cordiality to others, unsympathetic to others, and low on self-mastery and self-regulation. In a study of 105 Canadian juvenile homicide offenders, Woodworth, Agar, and Coupland (2013) found that most juvenile homicides reflected considerable reactivity suggesting that basic deficits in self-regulation and emotional control contributed to their lethal offenses.

Impulsive homicide offenders present with a range of relatively specific behavioral features. They experience intense autonomic arousal during the murder with heightened emotional experience. The murder is reactive and immediate, instinctual, and intended to remove or neutralize a threat in order to produce homeostasis. These features are very different from premeditated murders. For instance, Hanlon and colleagues (2013) compared homicide offenders whose murders were impulsive versus premeditated and produced several findings that relate to self-control and neurocognitive processes relating to self-regulation. Impulsive murderers also had severe background characteristics that negatively affected their behavioral control. About 93 percent had histories of substance use, 34 percent had history of mood disorders, and nearly 60 percent had developmental or learning disorders. Ninety percent had prior head trauma and neurological complaints. About 30 percent were significantly abused during childhood and 46 percent had a history of violent crime. Impulsive murderers also displayed multiple executive dysfunction including lower IQ, lower verbal IQ, lower verbal comprehension, lower perceptional organization, lower processing speed, and more impaired memory (Hanlon, Brook, Stratton, Jensen, & Rubin, 2013).

More recently, de Padua Serafim, de Barros, Castellana, and Gorenstein (2014) compared the personality and temperamental traits of 40 murderers with psychopathy, 40 murderers without psychopathy, and 38 controls who were both noncriminal and nonpsychopathic. They found that psychopathic murderers scored higher on novelty seeking, lower on harm avoidance, lower on reward dependence, lower on persistence, lower on self-directness, lower on cooperativeness, and lower on self-transcendence than controls. These effects were very large suggesting that psychopathic murderers are extremely lacking in self-regulation. Moreover, they also displayed significantly worse personality and temperamental profiles to other murderers albeit ones who are not psychopathic.

Self-control broadly centers in person-specific deficits that engender a host of negative behavioral outcomes including violence and even homicide. An allied perspective—social control theory—is examined next which shows how those individual deficits produce status and role problems that similarly are associated with deviance.

CHAPTER 7

Homicide and the Social Control Perspective

Social control theory asserts that social bonds connect us to others in society and prevent criminal behavior. Those without social attachments are at greater risk for homicide offending and victimization.

Conceptual Background

In contemplating homicide, humans have consistently evoked moralistic explanations that attribute evil to persons who commit bad acts, especially homicide. In Christianity, the doctrine of **Original Sin** characterizes

95

the notion of sin that typifies humanity because of Adam's succumbing to temptation in the Garden of Eden. From this perspective, humans are by definition flawed and prone to sinful behavior. In philosophical terms, this suggests that humans are more bad than good and when the behavior in question is homicide, it is easy to attribute tremendous badness to the homicide offender. As Aristotle indicated in the *Nicomachean Ethics*, "A bad man can do a million times more harm than a bear."

In criminology, the theoretical perspective that is rooted in an original sin viewpoint of humanity and human behavior is social control theory. **Social control theory** takes a more negative view of human nature and points to the factors, processes, roles, and relationships that prevent individuals from committing crime. Unlike other criminological theories which try to answer the question, "Why do people commit crime?" control theorists pose the question "Why don't people commit crime?"

A variety of social control explanations for delinquency and other problem behaviors have been advanced by sociological criminologists. For example, Reiss (1951) suggested that delinquency was the result of the failure of both personal controls—which are internalized—and social controls—which exist externally to adequately restrain the antisocial tendencies of adolescents. Specifically, youth who had weak ego development or weak superego development were theorized to be more delinquent than those who had strong and intact egos and superegos. Empirically, Reiss discovered that juvenile delinquents with healthy egos and superegos were nearly three times less likely to fail on probation as those with weak egos or superegos.

The idea that self-concepts are important as both insulator from and risk factor for delinquency was also espoused among other criminologists. Reckless, Dinitz, and Murray (1956) queried sixth grade teachers in the highest delinquency areas of Columbus, Ohio, to nominate boys who they thought would never engage in antisocial conduct. The characteristics of boys who appeared "insulated" from delinquency including a heightened sense of social responsibility, strictness about right and wrong forms of conduct, and close bonds with their parents. In other words, an intact and strong superego was viewed by teachers as a significant buffer against engaging in maladaptive behaviors.

In a subsequent study by Reckless, Dinitz, and Kay (1957), teachers were asked to nominate boys who they thought were definitely heading for juvenile court involvement due to their delinquent conduct. They hypothesized that "adverse concepts of self and others might set the trend toward delinquency, in the sense that the young person has no internalized resistance to the confrontation of a bad neighborhood, bad home life, and bad companions" (1957, p. 566). In addition to coming from larger and often "broken" homes, delinquent-nominated youths had a significantly lower sense of social responsibility.

In a 4-year follow-up study of the "good" boys in high delinquency areas, stability was found in that good boys continued to display healthy superego development in terms of their responsible, moral behavior (Scarpitti, Murray, Dinitz, & Reckless, 1960). Similar stability was found at a follow-up study of "bad" boys with poorer self-concepts (Dinitz, Scarpitti, & Reckless, 1962). Once established healthy superego developmental facilitated prosocial behavior and similarly, once established unhealthy superego development facilitated antisocial behavior. In total, Reckless and his colleagues indicated that healthy self-concept is critical in the "containment" of delinquency. This would later be known as **containment theory**.

Containment theory suggests that inner (internal) and outer (external) forces serve as "pushes" and "pulls" that act on young people and differentially insulate them or expose them to delinquent behavior (Reckless, 1967; Reckless & Dinitz, 1967). In Reckless' work, the component that was most clearly consistent with Freudian psychoanalytic theory is inner containment. Inner containment is comprised of four subcomponents. The most important is self-concept, which reflects quality socialization and the internalization of conventional modes of conduct. In other words, youth with a strong self-concept have an intact superego. This is important on two fronts. First, boys with a strong self-concept display an overall understanding of the appropriate ways to behave, and second, their good behavior reflects well on their parents who have appropriately socialized them.

Norm retention is the second part of inner containment and relates to the degree that the youth is committed and adheres to rules and laws. It speaks to the recognition of fundamental right and wrong inherent in conduct. Adherence to rules and laws occurs at home, in school, and in the community. Frustration tolerance is the capacity of the person to handle the frustrations of daily life and remain controlled in one's behavior. Doing the right things in life and behaving in a prosocial manner requires considerable effort. In addition, day-to-day events do not always go in the youth's favor, thus there is ample frustration in life. According to containment theory, good boys are able to handle this frustration, bad boys struggle with it. The fourth component, goal orientation, relates to the sense of direction in life. Those with strong self-concepts have a long-term vision of life that involves school completion, work, and family responsibilities. Those with weak self-concepts are less invested in goals, and lead an aimless, less driven life.

Other criminologists of this era wrote similar statements about how social control affected delinquent and criminal behavior. For example,

Short and Strodtbeck (1965, p. 230) indicated, "The failure of individuals to make satisfactory adjustments in any institutional sphere inevitably handicaps their ability to achieve future goals. Our gang boys fail often in school, on the job, in conventional youth-serving agencies, and in the eyes of law enforcement officials (and therefore in the public eye). They fail more often in each of these respects than do the non-gang boys we have studied, both middle and lower class."

Nye (1958) expanded on the ideas of Reiss, Reckless, and others by suggesting three forms of social control. Direct controls are those in which punishment is threatened for antisocial behavior and compliance is rewarded by parents. Indirect controls are those whereby an individual abstains from antisocial behavior because such acts would cause pain, suffering, and disappointing to his or her parents, siblings, or peers. Internal controls are those in which an individual's conscience prevents involvement in antisocial conduct.

Box 7.1   Social Control Theory in the Murder in Britain Study

The Murder in Britain Study is a large-scale effort to study various types of homicide in the United Kingdom. It contains three sources of data including national homicide indices for England, Wales, and Scotland, case files of a sample of 866 men and women (there were 80 total female murderers) who were convicted of murder and in-depth interviews with 200 men and women currently in prison for murder.

Using a subset of cases files, Dobash, Dobash, Cavanaugh, and Lewis (2004) compared 424 men who murdered other men to 106 men who murdered an intimate partner. They found many significant differences between these types of murderers, and they broadly related to social bonds and involvement in conventional society from childhood through adulthood. Both types of killers had parents with multiple problems involving alcohol abuse, crime, and violence. More than 41 percent of men who murdered men came from parents with a broken relationship compared to 29 percent for men who murdered an intimate partner.

During childhood, both types of murderers had problems in school, displayed disruptive behaviors, evidenced mental health problems, and used drugs and alcohol by age 16. Aside from mental health problems, men who murdered men were significantly more severe in their school problems and behavior problems than men who murdered intimate partners. Their behavior problems created an assortment of problems including repeating a grade, school suspension, and ultimately school dropout. More than half of both types of murderers left school by age

16. In turn, these disengagements from conventional school bonds facilitated involvement in diverse forms of criminal behavior and justice system involvement.

During adulthood, the murderers were generally characterized by low attachment, low involvement, low commitment, and apparently low belief in conventional behavior. Nearly three-fourths of men who murdered men and half of men who murdered their partners were unemployed. A substantial minority or majority of them abused alcohol, abused drugs, had mental health problems, engaged in persistent criminal behavior, and perpetrated violence in general. Most of them, between 72 and 82 percent, had convictions as adults. Like their parents, the homicide offenders in the Murder in Britain Study had dysfunctional and broken intimate relationships that were often characterized by abuse, discord, and violence.

To summarize, while men who murdered men were consistently worse in their behaviors than men who murdered intimate partners, both groups illustrated the logic of social control theory. Those who engage in antisocial behavior often do it at the complete expense of conventional behaviors that serve to bond prosocial people to society, and to one another.

Source: Dobash, R. E., Dobash, R. P., Cavanagh, K., & Lewis, R. (2004). Not an ordinary killer— Just an ordinary guy: When men murder an intimate woman partner. *Violence against Women, 10*(6), 577–605.

Without question, though, the most influential, famous, and highly cited work in social control theory is Hirschi's *Causes of Delinquency* (1969) and his social bond theory. **Social bond theory** asserts that persons with weak or nonexistent bonds to others and society are more likely to engage in antisocial behavior. Conversely, persons with strong, intact bonds to others and society are less likely to engage in antisocial behavior. Because it advocates the more pessimistic conceptualization of human behavior, social bond theory essentially argues that individuals must be kept busy, occupied, and involved in order to stay out of trouble. When bonds are absent, individuals are likely to resort to their natural tendency, which is antisocial conduct.

The social bond is comprised of four interrelated parts. These are:

- **Attachment**: the affectional ties to family and friends that reflects the internalization of social and behavioral norms. Attachment is essentially the conscience because strong affectional ties mean that an individual will adjust their behavior to avoid hurting or disappointing another person to whom they are close. Persons who are strongly attached to their parents thus are more likely to be prosocial instead of antisocial because prosocial conduct makes others happy whereas antisocial behavior makes others sad, angry, or disappointed.

- **Commitment**: the extent to which individuals invest in conventional, prosocial behavior. It is the same concept as Toby's stake in conformity. Commitment to family, educational, and work responsibilities indicates an investment in these relationships, and investments are not likely to be broken by negative or antisocial conduct. Conversely, individuals with low commitment are not as affected by damaging family, school, and work relationships and status, thus antisocial conduct is less costly.
- **Involvement**: the engagement or participation in conventional activities. Prosocial people are kept rather busy because they are involved in going to school, studying, playing sports, participating in extracurricular activities, working, being part of a family, helping around their house, going to church, participating in social events, and many others. These activities leave little time to engage in antisocial behavior, crime, and violence.
- **Belief**: the endorsement of social and legal mores such that norms and laws should be obeyed. Those who believe in the legitimacy of rules and regulations are more likely to follow them and be compliant in their behavior accordingly. Conversely, those who view rules as illegitimate or simply choose not to believe them will be deviant.

Social control theories have a very intuitive appeal because the social situations of criminal offenders often reflect weak or non-existent social bonds and are supported by scores of data. Whereas prosocial people are usually employed, antisocial individuals are chronically unemployed. Whereas prosocial people strive for the highest educational attainment possible including university degrees, antisocial individuals commonly drop out of school during high school or even middle school. Whereas prosocial people are deeply committed to their spouse, children, parents, siblings, and other family, antisocial individuals commonly abandon their family and reject supporting them. The application of social control theories to homicide offending and victimization is examined next.

Empirical Linkages to Homicide

Earle Leonard Nelson's life and criminal career shows the relevance of social control theory to homicide. Born in the late nineteenth century, Nelson's parents died when he was a toddler and his childhood was characterized by strange and often erratic behaviors that seemed to intensify after a traumatic brain injury. During adolescence, Nelson committed an assortment of criminal offenses including burglary, child molestation, rape, and escape from prisons and state mental hospitals. Between 1926 and 1927, Nelson would murder 21 females and one male and the victims' ages ranged from 8 months to 66 years. He would also sexually assault the victims including necrophilia. Known as the Gorilla Man, Nelson was executed by hanging in 1928 (Schechter, 2004). Most of his murders involved the killing of women who were landlords as Nelson was essentially a drifter who would contact them under the pretense of needing a room for rent. He was adrift and unattached.

Research on many types of homicide offenders has shown that their family backgrounds where the social bonds are formed and solidified are often chaotic, dysfunctional, abusive, and at times, simply horrifying. It is common for many homicide offenders to be exposed to early life physical abuse, physical, medical, and emotional neglect, emotional and verbal abuse, sexual abuse and victimization, exposure to pornography, drugs, and criminal behavior (Arrigo & Griffin, 2004; Arrigo & Purcell, 2001; Burgess, Hartman, Ressler, Douglas, & McCormack, 1986; Gresswell & Hollin, 1994; Twemlow, 2003). These experiences significantly damage the developing individual's ability to form prosocial, connective bonds with others.

In developmental psychopathology, the result of these experiences and the broken social bonds is disorganized attachment. **Disorganized attachment** is the result of abuse, neglect, and poor parenting that impairs the ability of the child to form social bonds and contributes to a host of mental health and behavioral problems. The conflicting and difficult events that disorganized attachment creates are described by van IJzendoorn, Schuengel, and Bakermanns-Kranenburg (1999, pp. 226–227). "Maltreating parents, for example, are supposed to create disorganized attachment in their infants because they confront their infants with a pervasive paradox: they are potentially the only source of comfort for their children, whereas at the same time they frighten their children through their unpredictable abusive behavior. The parent is thought to be a source of fear for the child and at the same time the only attachment figure who can provide relief from distress. The incompatible behaviors of flight and proximity seeking are proposed to lead to temporary breakdown of organized attachment behavior."

Disorganized attachment is significantly linked to violence and other criminal behavior (Cyr, Euser, Bakermans-Kranenburg, & van IJzendoorn, 2010; Maniglio, 2012; Ogilvie, Newman, Todd, & Peck, 2014; Savage, 2014) and is a common background feature among homicide offenders especially those who perpetrate serial, mass, and spree homicide (Campbell & DeNevi, 2004).

Based on these findings, it is clear that many homicide offenders will have deficits in forming effective social bonds due to the litany of neglect, abuse, and deprivation in their family backgrounds. Another body of research has examined specific social bonds to family, school, work, and conventional institutions and their relation to homicide. For instance, Langevin and Handy (1987) found that homicide offenders in national and psychiatric samples in Canada were generally single, unattached, unemployed, had financial problems, and otherwise had low, weak, or nonexistence social bonds. They often had limited romantic or sexual relationships, and experienced considerable dysfunction and inadequacy in the relationships that they did have. Even if they wanted to have strong connective bonds to others, they were either unwilling or unable to consistent demonstrate attachment, commitment, involvement, and belief and thus were unfettered by the connections that bind conventional individuals to society.

Loeber and his colleagues (2005) performed a study that illustrates the salience of social bonds, and antisocial bonds, in the lives of violent offenders, delinquents, and homicide offenders. Using data from the Pittsburgh Youth Study (PYS), Loeber and his collaborators compared 33 youth who

© Lightspring/Shutterstock, Inc.

Social bonds are often destroyed in abusive, neglectful, deviant homes where disorganized attachment is created. Many homicide offenders develop disorganized attachment from these abusive backgrounds.

were convicted of homicide, 193 youth who were convicted of other serious violence, and 498 youth who self-reported various acts of serious violence.

In terms of peer and school factors, there are many deficits among the youths with homicide convictions. Their peer bonds involved other anti-social youth, unconventional peers, and peers who used drugs and alcohol. School bonding was also low with a large proportion displaying low academic achievement and more than half indicating low motivation for school, high levels of truancy, and being old for their grade which is an indicator of being held back or failing a prior year in school.

In addition, the homicidal youth displayed attitudes that were unlikely to help them believe, commit, get involved, and attach to conventional social institutions such as school and work. They were significantly likely to have positive attitudes toward problem behavior, positive attitudes toward substance use and believed that they were unlikely to be caught for committing delinquency and violence. Indeed more than 73 percent had positive attitudes toward crime. Obviously, youth who this negative of a profile face many obstacles in establishing strong school and work commitments that will contribute to being a functioning member of society.

Drawing on PYS data when 37 participants had been convicted of murder, Farrington, Loeber, and Berg (2012) found that several behavioral indicators differentiated young homicide offenders from their antisocial peers. Having a disruptive behavioral disorder, serious delinquency, peer delinquency, cruelty toward people, school suspension, truancy, having positive attitudes towards delinquency and drugs, and covert behaviors significantly increased the odds of a homicide conviction with odds ratios ranging from 1.9 to 4.9.

There were also offense-specific effects whereby involvement in robbery, aggravated assault, gang fights, weapons offenses, burglary, vehicle theft, and several forms of larceny/shoplifting were significantly associated with homicide perpetration. These effects were more robust when predicting homicide through age 14 years. Other studies of the PYS data similarly show that young homicide offenders and homicide victims have lives that are characterized by broken social bonds in multiple life areas.

For instance, Farrington, Loeber, Stallings, and Homish (2012) reported that most homicide offenders and victims came from broken homes, were poorly bonded to school and had several academic problems, had parents that were involved in crime and unemployed, and generally were not connected to conventional society. Specifically, coming from a broken family increased the odds of becoming a convicted murderer by fivefold, being suspended from school also increased the odds fivefold, and being chronically truant from school doubled the risk of homicide offending (Loeber & Ahonen, 2013; also see, Loeber & Farrington, 2011).

The importance of social control theories and especially social ties are important for understanding a variety of homicide offenders and types of homicide. For example, social ties are critical for understanding homicide-suicide. Stack (1997) examined data on 16,245 homicides in Chicago spanning 1965–1990. He found dramatic differences in the victim characteristics for homicides compared to homicide suicides. In homicide suicides, the victim was the offender's spouse in five times as many cases as in homicides. The victim was the offender's ex-lover in greater than nine times as many cases as in homicides, and the victim was female in four times as many cases. These romantic and family bonds also strongly affected the decision of the homicide offender to then take his or her own life. Controlling for other demographic variables, killing an ex-spouse or lover increased the risk for suicide nearly 13-fold. Odds of suicide are increased more than ten-fold after killing a child, eightfold after killing a spouse, sixfold after killing a boyfriend or girlfriend, and nearly twofold after killing a friend. Stack concluded (1997, p. 448), "In these cases, the bond that once held a couple together is officially broken. The loss is final; it is no longer just threatened or simply coming in the future. For persons very dependent on the old bond, this loss of their love object can be unbearable."

Similarly, drawing on data from the National Violent Death Reporting System and spanning 17 states, Logan and colleagues (2008) found that several life-event factors were the triggering events in homicide suicides. These included conflicts with one's spouse, other relationship problems, loss of employment, and financial problems. These family, work, and financial relationships are essential for maintaining a person's connectedness to the social structure. And when these relationships are severed particularly if the change is sudden, homicidal behavior can ensue (Logan, Hill, Black, Crosby, Karch, et al., 2008). Similar social ties-homicide links have also been shown among homicide offenders with schizophrenia (Fazel, Baxrud, Ruchkin, & Grann, 2010).

Other studies based on cross-sectional designs indicate that juvenile homicide offenders are relatively comparable to other violent delinquents on many social, behavioral, and developmental background factors. For instance, Dolan and Smith (2001) compared 46 juvenile homicide offenders to 106 juvenile arsonists and found that homicidal youth had higher prevalence of father psychopathology, frequent school changes, and alcohol abuse and alcohol intoxication at their homicide event. On the other hand, homicidal youth were less likely to have a psychotic disorder and less likely than arsonists to have participated in professional counseling/treatment services.

Using Canadian National Parole Board data, Cale and his colleagues (2010) compared 86 offenders who committed murder between 1975 and

2005, were confined, released, and then murdered again to 84 murderers who committed only one homicide. They found that the multiple murderers were prone to unemployment throughout their adulthood. They also lost family and community supports as a consequences of their first homicide and confinement. In other words, their adult years were comprised of weak social bonds, lengthy periods in jail and prison, and additional time with weak attachments to family, work, and community. Absent these informal social controls, many former homicide offenders engaged in multiple risky behaviors including drug addiction, alcoholism, involvement in a criminal lifestyle, and ultimately, another homicide (Cale, Plecas, Cohen, & Fortier, 2010).

In an 8-year study of 363 juvenile homicide offenders in England and Wales, Rodway and her colleagues (2011) similarly reported a history of family dysfunction, educational difficulties and attendant school problems, and discipline problems. There was also high prevalence of physical abuse, emotional abuse, sexual abuse, and domestic violence in the home lives of homicide offenders. These conditions make the development of effective prosocial bonds even more challenging (Rodway, Norrington-Moore, While, Hunt, Flynn, et al., 2011).

Homicide experiences that occur early in life can impose deficits that make the establishment of social bonds more difficult. A study of the experiences of boys who survived intraparental homicide is illustrative. Steeves, Laughon, Parker, and Weierbach (2007) noted that between 2,000 and 3,000 children each year have the horrifying experience of one parent murdering the other. Several features of this type of homicide are relevant for understanding social control theory. First, because one parent is deceased and the other is usually sentenced to a lengthy term in prison, the child loses both parents as a result of the murder. This necessitates moving in with extended family or becoming wards of the state. This can result in dramatic changes in socioeconomic status, changes in where the child lives, changes to where the child attends school, and changes to the friendship networks that the child has access to.

All of these changes are significantly disruptive and impair the attachment, commitment, and involvement bonds. Upwards of 85 percent of children who experience uxoricide has difficulty in school after the event with creates educational problems and also contributes to psychological maladjustment and stress. In other words, the homicide reduces their school bond by affecting their ability to perform academically.

The relevance of social control theory to homicide is clearly seen in cases of mass murder. Although a variety of traits and circumstances contribute to a mass murder, it is often the case that a recent disconnection serves as the spark to this form of violence. These disconnections are often the severing of a previous bond or relationship that served to socially control the offender, such as the loss of a job, spouse, or significant other. As Gresswell and Hollin (1994, p. 11) concluded in their review of multiple murder, "there is a precipitating event such as unemployment or divorce; and finally the perpetrator experiences a breakdown of 'social controls,' for example a move to a new town or the loss of an important relationship." These sudden changes shatter the calming effects of social bonds, and mixed with other precipitating factors, contribute to mass murder.

Relatedly, Auxemery (2015) described the mass murderer as a psychological crisis that is both homicidal and suicidal. He notes that mass murderers experience tremendous suffering—both real and perceived—and imagine that many individuals and groups in society are to blame for their suffering. These targets are viewed by the offender as responsible for his failures in life and lack of achievement of important milestones. To put a social control spin on this, mass murderers have generally low social bonds and often have considerable alienation and angst in the relationship realm, in the workplace, and in the case of school shooters, in the classroom.

Similarly, elements of social control theory are also seen in the biographies of sexual homicide offenders. Sewall, Krupp, and Lalumiére (2013) analyzed data from 82 serial sexual homicide offenders who were selected from the TruTV website that contains biographical, criminal history, and offense information on serial killers. Factor analyses and cluster analyses indicated three general types of perpetrators who were labeled as sadistic, competitively disadvantaged, or slashers. The competitively disadvantaged group is aptly named because it embodies offenders who are low functioning and generally have weak social bonds to society. These offenders performed poorly in school, have meager work histories, have checkered family backgrounds, and occupy the lowest socioeconomic rung of society.

Stefanska and her colleagues (2015) conducted a study of offense pathways among nonserial sexual homicide offenders using data from the United Kingdom. They discovered substantial evidence of weak social bonds among these offenders. For instance, the unemployment rate among the sample was 28 percent and the proportion that was not working full time was 60 percent. These employment data are dramatically higher than the general population. In addition, the homicide offenders displayed an assortment of emotional, cognitive, and relationship problems that influenced their criminal offending and drove the motivation for their sexual murder (Stefanska, Carter, Higgs, Bishopp, & Beech, 2015). Indeed, many of the offenders perpetrated postmortem sexual acts, postmortem mutilation, and postmortem biting—behaviors which point to the depths of their relationship dysfunction and sexual dysfunction.

Although social control perspectives have a long history in criminology, there are still innovations that link its theoretical ideas to homicide. A recent example is Lo, Howell, and Cheng's (2013, 2015) **multiple disadvantage model** which attempts to explain the large homicide victimization differences experienced by whites and African Americans. The model suggests that several negative statuses that blacks are more likely than whites to possess contributes to the former's greater likelihood of homicide victimization. Fundamentally, these disadvantages relate to nonexistent or weakened social ties, including lower educational attainment, lower socioeconomic status, lower likelihood of employment and stable employment, less likely to be married, and lower social support. In turn these weakened social controls contribute to mental health problems and lifestyle factors (e.g., heavy drinking, drug use, drug selling, gun carrying, and others) that further deteriorate attachment to conventional social institutions.

Their model is supported by data presenting the black to white homicide ratios from 1950 to 2008. In 1950, the black: white ratio was 12.4 for males, by 2008, it was 6.4 which although dramatically high is about half of its historic value. For females, the ratio has declined from 7.9 in 1950 to 2.9 in 2008. These data coincide with large advances in socioeconomic status among blacks over the latter half of the twentieth century and current era. In a recent test using data from the 1993 National Mortality Followback Survey, Lo and colleagues found that white, black, and Hispanics who were murdered were significantly likely to be unmarried, unemployed, not homeowners, and be involved in alcohol-related incidents. In other words, they displayed weak social bonds.

Social control theory is useful for understanding whether homicides are cleared by arrest and ultimately solved. In the 1960s, approximately 90 percent of U.S. homicides were cleared by arrest. This rate hovered between 60 and 70 percent since 1985 and declined to a low of 62 percent in 2006 (Quinet & Nunn, 2014). Generally, homicides involving individuals who had stronger social bonds, such as employment, stable residency, stable family relationships, and the like are more likely to be solved. Cases involving persons with weaker social bonds, such as those involved in the drug and criminal underworld, are less likely to be solved.

Rydberg and Pizarro (2014) produced similar findings. They found that 76 percent of homicides were cleared when the victim did not have any indicators of deviant lifestyle that would reflect low or weaken social bonds to society. Conversely, victims who had three or more indicators of deviant lifestyle resulted in cases that were solved just 40 percent of the time.

Of course, social control theory is not universally supported by empirical data. A major limitation of the theory centers on the many homicide offenders who have good social bonds and are connected to conventional social institutions. This is seen among some of the most infamous homicide offenders in American history. For example, John Wayne Gacy was raised in an abusive home by an abusive, alcoholic father who subjected Gacy to considerable physical, verbal, and emotional abuse including frequent belittling. At school, Gacy was an unsuccessful student who attended multiple high schools and dropped out from high school although he would complete an associate's degree prior to getting married.

Despite being married and fathering two children, Gacy engaged in diverse forms of sexual deviance and substance use including sexually assaulting two teenage boys, crimes for which he was sentenced to 10 years imprisonment. Paroled after serving just 18 months, Gacy was arrested at least twice for sexual assaults against adolescent males but the cases were dismissed.

Although employed, having been married, and being active in civic organizations, Gacy also coerced, enticed, or abducted dozens of young males for the purposes of sexual assault and murder via strangulation. Gacy was convicted of 33 counts of murder and buried the remains of many of them in the crawl space under his home. For these heinous crimes, Gacy was sentenced to death in 1980 and ultimately executed in 1994 (DeLisi, 2013).

In other words, Gacy appeared to have healthy attachment, commitment, involvement, and belief in conventional activities and was able to achieve these milestones despite a less than optimal upbringing. Many homicide offenders on the evening news are also often employed, have families, hold leadership positions, and appear to be strongly bonded to society, yet they appear to come unglued at some point and perpetrate homicidal violence. One reason why apparently high-functioning people one day decide to commit homicide relates to their position in the social structure and how well they truly are achieving the American Dream. On that note, Institutional Anomie Theory is examined in the next chapter.

CHAPTER 8

Homicide and the Institutional Anomie Perspective

© Bruce Rolff/Shutterstock, Inc.

Sociological theories like institutional anomie theory attribute the causes of homicide to American social and economic structure.

Conceptual Background

Mark Barton was a college-educated, married man with a family who lived a comfortable middle class existence. In July 1999, Barton walked into two day trading firms in Atlanta, Georgia, and murdered 12 people and attempted to murder 13 others by shooting them with a firearm. Hours after these killings, Barton committed suicide as police were about to make contact with him. Later, it was discovered that Barton had beaten his wife and two children to death with a hammer in the days before the mass murder. In other words, over a span of about 48 hours, this seemingly normal, relatively successful person caused the deaths of 16 people including his own.

After the carnage, investigators found a type-written confession on Barton's computer. In the 2 weeks prior to the shootings, Barton had lost $105,000 due to his investment in volatile stocks, and he was estranged from his wife. In his confession, Barton expressed, "Words cannot tell the agony. Why did I? I have been dying since October. Wake up at night so afraid, so terrified that I couldn't be that afraid while awake. It has taken its toll. I have come to hate this life and this system of things. I have come to have no hope."

This was not the first time homicide touched the life of Mark Barton. In 1993, his first wife and her mother were also found bludgeoned to death similar to the modus operandi he used to kill his current wife and children. Barton was the only suspect in these killings, but was not charged. He was also accused of sexually molesting his daughter when she was 3 years of age. During the investigation for that crime, Barton was deemed by a psychologist to have homicidal ideation (Sack, 1999).

Given the social and economic turmoil of his life, the statement that Barton indicated about the "system of things" is intriguing because it suggests that the social and economic structures of society played some role in his homicidal behavior. This notion is the basic idea of this chapter.

As shown in Chapter 10, there is a long history in sociological criminology that points to the role of the social structure or the stratification system and criminal behavior (e.g., Merton, 1938). **Stratification** is the informal hierarchy of a society divided into social classes that are based on educational attainment, income, and wealth. From one's socioeconomic status, power is derived. In sociology, the stratification system is viewed as a powerful cause of behavior and is largely responsible for the disproportionate involvement of the poor in antisocial and violent behavior.

Building on anomie theory, Cloward and Ohlin (1960) identified three delinquent subcultures that are contingent on social structure, opportunities in that structure, and social class. A criminal subculture emerges in stable neighborhoods that provide children with illegitimate opportunities to become successful criminals. In these environments, there are adult role models who are successful criminals inasmuch as they commit antisocial acts and disengage from conventional activities such as school, work, and family responsibilities.

A second delinquent subculture is the conflict subculture. This subculture develops in disorganized slums, where waves of migration produce social and cultural rootlessness and conflict. In these neighborhoods, children have only a few opportunities to be successful. The adult criminals who live there are failures, so there is no integration of different age levels because the adult offenders have no useful knowledge to pass on. In addition, the adult criminals have neither the ability nor the inclination to help neighborhood delinquents reduce their violent activity. The absence of legitimate and illegitimate opportunities frustrates children, and they vent their frustrations by turning to violence. Although Cloward and Ohlin were theorizing about the development of juvenile delinquency, it is easy to see how criminal and conflict subcultures characterize the impoverished, abusive, and negative environments that homicide offenders often experience.

The third delinquent subculture is the retreatist subculture where individuals do not live up to the expectations of conventional society or the criminal underworld. In this sense, they are "double failures" and retreat from society often into transiency and addiction. The retreatist subculture is what typifies the lifestyle and behavior of drifter homicide offenders who disproportionately commit serial murder.

Against this background, Messner and Rosenfeld introduced institutional anomie theory in their book *Crime and the American Dream* (1994). **Institutional anomie theory** is a structural explanation which argues that cultural focus on achievement and wealth is a source of homicide in the United States. In other words, pursuit of the American Dream is problematic because of the stratification and the extreme cultural emphasis on achievement and money in the United States serves as a causal force for homicide. To paraphrase Mark Barton's words from his confessional note, the system of things is the U.S. economic and social structure, and it can contribute to homicide.

Institutional anomie theory points to several values that typify American culture:

- **Achievement orientation:** a fundamental marker of success in American society relates to the achievement of various milestones. Failure to achieve these milestones is consistent with failure.
- **Individualism:** individual autonomy, individual rights, and self-determination are fundamental values that drive the need to accomplish goals on one's own.
- **Universalism:** this is the notion that all Americans should generally strive for achieving the same cultural goals.
- **Fetishism of money:** the accumulation of wealth is an end goal in itself and is the primary metric on which people are evaluated.

With these values in mind, institutional anomie theory asserts that social institutions largely function to facilitate these American values. Of the four major social institutions that are described: the family, educational institutions, the political system, and the economy, the latter is given priority over all the others. In other words, although achievement in the family, school, and politics are viewed as laudable goals, they pale to the achievement of great wealth, or at least the desire to achieve wealth. According to Messner and Rosenfeld, this creates an imbalance in the social institutions because the others are subordinated to economic concerns.

The institutional imbalance produces three effects. First, the family, education, and political spheres become devalued in relation to the economy. Second, other social institutions must accommodate the needs of the economy. Thus the economic strife that many homicide offenders perceive places pressure on their family responsibilities. Again, to use the Barton example from the beginning of this chapter, it was ultimately economic stressors that created a wage in his family that led to their homicides. Third, there is a general commodification of the other institutions where they are essentially valued in ways that are consistent with the economy. Everything becomes competitive and achievement based.

Over time, other social institutions, such as the family, become less capable of informally socially controlling behavior. But more generally, societal institutions that cannot keep the economy in check have reduced social control which enables violence. Messner and Rosenfeld observed that nations with stronger and more extensive social welfare policies have fewer homicides than nations like the United States where the economy is, uniquely, foremost.

Recently, Messner and Rosenfeld clarified the theory by suggesting that institutional structure, institutional regulation or legitimacy, and institutional performance are also important for understanding homicide (Messner, Rosenfeld, & Karstedt, 2013). These aspects of social institutions are seen in the relationship between institutional structure and historical variation in homicides in nations worldwide, the impact of changes in institutional legitimacy on homicide in the short-term, and changes in homicide rates. Basically, these more recent comments clarify the nature of the institutions not just whether they are devalued relative to the economy.

Although institutional anomie theory is its own independent theory, it is conceptually related to other conceptual approaches in criminology that similarly address the role of welfare and the public good in explaining crime (Beeghley, 2003). Also, whereas institutional anomie theory is like its title implies, institutional, and thus at the aggregate level, two other conceptual models address the individual-level implications of anomie and a society's inability or unwillingness to care for its citizens. As Roth

(2011, p. 547) observed, "The degree of empathy and fellow feeling among the members of a society also has a powerful effect on the homicide rate. Nothing suppresses homicide within a social group more powerfully than a sense of connectedness that extends beyond the bounds of family and neighborhood and forges a strong bond among people who share race, ethnicity, religion, or nationality."

From healthy institutions flows social support. Cullen (1994) advanced that **social support** is the relationships that meet *expressive needs* which are the emotional connections to others that serve to bolster an individual's self-worth and *instrumental needs* which are the material support, guidance and advice of an individual. Social support occurs at multiple levels including the societal level, community level, and individual level and serves as the infrastructure on which social bonds and social connections are built. Social support encompasses the nurturing, help, and assistance that family and friends provide to make life easier and help people deal with the challenges of life. Generally, healthy, more prosocial individuals enjoy considerable social support whereas antisocial individuals disproportionately suffer from limited social support.

In *Crime and Coercion: An Integrated Approach to Chronic Criminality*, Colvin (2000; also see, Colvin, Cullen, & Vander Ven, 2002) theorized that coercion in people's lives contributes to anger and other negative emotions that negatively affect their social psychological functioning. To Colvin, coercion is implicit in most theories of crime in that it embodies the negativity in causal factors (e.g., strain, peer rejection, negative parenting) that push individuals along an antisocial pathway. A related construct is the consistency with which coercion is applied ranging from consistent to erratic. Thus, Colvin's **differential coercion theory** suggests that the blend of coercion and consistency of that coercion manifest in psychological and behavioral outcomes.

Colvin advanced four ideal types in terms of their psychosocial functioning and behavioral styles. The first is a person exposed to consistent noncoercion which is the most conventional, prosocial type of social control. Such a person is characterized by high self-efficacy, high self-control, internal locus of control, low anger, and no coercive modeling. Given these protection factors, individuals exposed to consistent noncoercion have a strong disposition for prosocial behavior and are very unlikely to engage in antisocial behavior. The second type is an individual exposed to erratic noncoercion. An example of erratic noncoercion is permissive parenting where a parent is lax and does not fully invest in their children and perhaps uses financial overtures to "buy" good behavior. Children exposed to this form of control also have high self-efficacy and low anger, but their social bond to parents is less strong and their self-control is lower. As a result, youth are theorized to be susceptible to experimenting with deviant activities, such as drug use and engage in minor forms of delinquency.

The other two ideal types include individuals who are exposed to coercive interactions. Individuals exposed to consistent coercion are characterized as having low self-efficacy, high self-directed anger, weak social bonds, rigid self-control, and an external locus of control. They are theorized to be susceptible to serious mental illness especially depression and overall have low probability of prosocial behavior. Given their psychosocial profile, individuals who have been consistently exposed to coercion are also at risk to commit severe forms of explosive crime, such as homicide. Despite this, there is also low probability of general delinquency, instead the psychopathology of this type relates more to mental illness.

The final type in Colvin's (2000) typology—those exposed to erratic coercion—is the most severe. Their psychosocial profile is characterized by low self-efficacy, high other-directed anger, weak social bonding, coercive modeling, low self-control, and external locus of control. Persons exposed to erratic coercion are theorized to be most at risk for lifelong conduct problems and have a predisposition for serious and predatory forms of criminal behavior.

© SinishaKarich/Shutterstock, Inc.

Excessive cultural focus on money at the expense of other institutional relationships produces alienation, conflict, and desperate motivations that can manifest in homicidal behavior.

Institutional anomie theory is interested in the balance between social institutions, especially the economy, work, and the family, and the complex and at times competing role expectations they create. In the event that certain social institutions impose more responsibilities on an individual, the person could experience strain because of less involvement in other social institutions. The common dilemma of work-life balance is an example. Many people find it challenging to handle their spousal and parent roles in the face of economic and work pressures. As work obligations require more time, less is available for the family. Over time, these strains contribute to negative outcomes and potentially even violence because more emphasis, priority, and status is provided to economic goals compared to noneconomic ones.

Empirical Linkages to Homicide

A modest literature has examined institutional anomie theory and related theories for their association to homicide. Because the theory is relevantly new, it does not have the extensive track record of older criminological perspectives. Unlike most perspectives in this book, these tests focus on the macro or aggregate level and compare homicides between nations, counties, or other aggregate areas.

To date, criminologists have examined institutional anomie theory as a potentially useful explanation for homicide. Using data from 45 nations, Messner and Rosenfeld (1997) found that nations that provide social welfare that protects individuals from pure market economic forces have fewer homicides. Similarly, Savolainen (2000) found that the effects of economic inequality on homicide were more pronounced in nations that had few social safety nets in place. In a study of the theory using data from Russia, Kim and Pridemore (2005) found that economic change and poverty were associated with homicide whereas family strength and polity were negatively associated with regional homicide rates. However, they also found that strong social institutions did not reduce the effects of poverty on homicide which was contrary to expectations.

In an investigation using data from the Supplementary Homicide Reports for 454 U.S. urban counties, Maume and Lee (2003) found that family income inequality was a predictor of total, instrumental, and expressive homicides. This is important because it suggests family-economic institutional problems result in both predatory, cold-blooded murders as well as reactive, hot-blooded murders. They also found that noneconomic institutional forces can buffer the effects of economic motivation on instrumental homicide. In other words, the family, political realm, or education can shield individuals from economic-based instrumental murders, such as robbery-homicides or murders that are motivated by desire for insurance money.

Using data from 45 nations, Levchak (2014) examined whether globalization in the worldwide economy contributed to rapid social change, anomie, and homicide. He found that net investment in a country which is associated with economic dominance was positively associated with homicide. Nations like the United States have high foreign investment and high homicide rates whereas nations like Japan have low foreign investment and commensurately a low homicide rate.

Nivette and Eisner (2013) examined whether institutional legitimacy plays a role in homicide as more recently theorized by Messner and Rosenfeld. Using data from 65 nations, Nivette and Eisner evaluated the legality of a society's institutions which is the state's capacity to obey its own laws, the justification of a society's institutions which is the degree to which civil and political values coincide, and the consent of a society's institutions which is the level of behavioral consent of the residents of the nation. Of these institutional dimensions, they found that the more legitimate a nation, the fewer homicides it has.

Others have found limited support for institutional anomie theory as a predictor of homicide. Using data from the United Nations, World Bank, World Values Survey, and the Heritage Foundation, Hughes, Schaible, and Gibbs (2014) examined the theoretical relevance of institutional anomie theory and homicide in 50 nations. They found generally limited support for the theory. Homicides were not more common in market economies where other social institutions were weakened. A meta-analysis of crossnational predictors of homicide similarly found that region was among the most important causes, particularly Latin America location. In addition, measures of democracy and economic development had weaker effects on homicide, which generally runs counter to institutional anomie theory (Nivette, 2011).

There have also been a handful of studies to explore the association between social support and homicide. Drawing on data from 46 nations spanning the time period of 1989 to 1995, Pratt and Godsey (2002) examined the relation between social support and homicide. They found that nations with lower social support had more homicides net the effects of economic inequality, proportion urban population, sex composition, and a human development index.

In a related study, Pratt and Godsey (2003) found that nations with greater social supports in place had lower homicide rates. Nations with greater economic inequality which touches on the issue advanced in institutional anomie and other theories had higher homicide rates. Social support also was found to interact with economic inequality to produce higher homicide rates among these 46 nations. These effects persisted with the United States in the models, and without. This is important because Messner and Rosenfeld speculate there is an exceptional quality to the United States regarding its very high homicide rate, but the same institutional trends were also seen in other nations.

In her investigation of social support and homicide utilizing data from 51 nations, Altheimer (2008) employed five measures of social support. These included general social support which was the percentage of a nation's economy spent on benefits and services to workers, education expenditures, health expenditures, decommodification index which is the ease of access to welfare benefits, and a human development index. She found that nations with more social support generally have lower homicide rates, and that social support buffered the effects of ethnic heterogeneity on homicide.

Furthermore, Eisner and Nivette (2012) observed that nations with the highest homicide rates, such as Colombia and El Salvador in Latin America, Congo and South Africa in Africa, and Russia in Europe are characterized by state corruption, low investments in public health, and education, low state stability, high inequality, and ethnic cleavages. In contrast, low homicide nations have a stable, functioning government, effective health care, viable social institutions, and lower social inequality. These general snapshots are consistent with the institutional anomie perspective.

Lee and Pridemore (2014) examined population well-being and homicide rates in 102 nations. They examined the Human Development Index which is a composite measure of quality of life that is consistent with social support. In includes life expectancy, literacy, school enrollments, and standard of living. Nations with lower Human Development Index scores had significantly higher homicide rates. Conversely, nations that furnished educational opportunities and material resources and offered a better overall sense of communal well-being had lower homicide rates.

Social support theory also has implications for homicide offenders who repeat their homicidal behavior after release from confinement. Using Canadian National Parole Board data, Cale, Plecas, Cohen, and Fortier (2010) compared 86 offenders who committed murder between 1975 and 2005, were confined, released, and then murdered again to 84 murderers who committed only one homicide. They found that the multiple murderers were prone to unemployment throughout their adulthood and lost family and community supports as a consequence of their first homicide and confinement. This lack of social support left them feeling isolated and usually enmeshed in a drug and crime lifestyle that culminated in another murder.

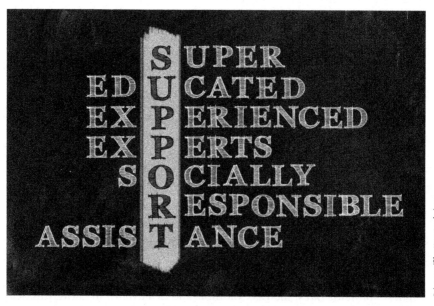

© ivosar/Shutterstock, Inc.

Social support theory indicates that offenders with fewer connections and supports from others are more likely to commit crime, and even perpetrate homicide.

Box 8.1   The American Dream, Money Obsession, and Murder

Although institutional anomie theory is a structural approach that explains homicide among nations, counties, and regions, the logic of the theory is also relevant to individual offenders. One case that seems to exemplify the theory is Andrew Cunanan. Cunanan was raised and schooled in affluence in La Jolla San Diego, California; however, there was evidence that his wealthy upbringing was a façade. His father was suspected of embezzlement and the family's financial situation was tenuous.

Cunanan nevertheless enjoyed the finer things in life, and socialized in affluent areas where he prostituted himself to older men who were financially successful. He engaged in sadomasochistic behaviors, was a drug user, and made pornographic films as part of the gay underworld of San Francisco. Cunanan also engaged in a variety of criminal behaviors and illustrated several features of psychopathic personality including superficial charm, grandiosity, sexual promiscuity, exploitative interpersonal style, low empathy, and versatile criminal endeavors.

In the spring and summer of 1997, Cunanan perpetrated a nationwide crime spree that included five homicides in Minnesota, New Jersey, and Florida. His final murder victim was fashion and business mogul Gianni

Versace. Cunanan murdered his victims in a variety of ways that included bludgeoning, stabbing, torturing, and shooting. He committed suicide approximately 1 week after the Versace killing, and at the time was one of the most wanted criminals in the United States.

Cunanan did not leave a suicide note, thus his motivation for the murders is not known. Nevertheless, a recurrent theme in his life centered on the prominence of money and the desire to live an affluent life at the expense of involvement in other social institutions including family, school, and work. To Cunanan, money and the appearance of money were paramount, and he murdered to try and achieve it.

Source: Esposito, D. (2006). Case study: Andrew Cunanan. In J. E. Douglas, A. W. Burgess, A. G. Burgess, & R. K. Ressler (Eds.), *Crime classification manual: A standard system for investigating and classifying violent crimes* (pp. 448–452). San Francisco, CA: Jossey Bass.

Not all examinations of institutional anomie theory are positive. Other studies have provided more equivocal evidence for the social support perspective on homicide. Kim and Pridemore (2005) utilized data from 78 Russian regions to examine whether social support influenced homicides rates. They found that regions with more negative socioeconomic change had more homicides, but also found that direct social support expenditures did not influence the homicide rate. In other words, although periods of rapid socioeconomic change can produce more homicides, it is expected that direct state support to residents would reduce homicide. In the Russian context, this did not occur.

Although institutional anomie theory is a macro theory, its principles trickle down to individuals and make intuitive sense in understanding specific forms of homicide, such as the financially obsessed and stressed case of Mark Barton. Beyond criminology, other social scientists and social commentators have pointed to the transformation of American social institutions and how traditionally strong institutions most notably the family and education seem to have been subordinated to the economy. This great disruption (Fukuyama, 1999) produces an unsettled, insecure feeling among many and can contribute to antisocial behavior. Social support, an idea that flows well from concern about how America's social institutions interact and mutually influence the other, also seems important for understanding the life context of many homicide offenders. Across disciplinary and theoretical perspectives in this book, there is a sense that many homicide offenders are isolated, alone, and adrift in a society that does not provide adequate services or oversight to help them.

The next chapter points to more specific mechanisms and learning processes that show how individuals become equipped with the values, attitudes, and behaviors to perpetrate homicide.

CHAPTER 9

Homicide and the Social Learning Perspective

Social learning theories attribute homicide to exposure to violent peers and the internalization of attitudes that are favorable to the use of violence.

Conceptual Background

Lawrence Bittaker and Roy Norris are among the most infamous criminals in California history. Both Bittaker and Norris had troubled childhoods and exhibited chronic antisocial behavior during their adolescence and adulthood that included many arrests and periods of confinement.

121

They happened to meet while in prison during the mid-1970s and developed a plan to abduct and rape teenage girls. Although Norris was a repeat rapist and sexual offender, Bittaker was more sadistic and psychopathic and indicated that in addition to sexual violence, they should murder their victims. Homicide was the motivator. In 1979, Bittaker and Norris put their plan into action by luring teenage girls into their van and then perpetrating unfathomable torture, rape, and murder on at least five victims. After their arrest, Norris pled guilty to these crimes in exchange for life imprisonment and agreeing to testify against Bittaker, who was older and considered the leader of the two. For his crimes, Bittaker was sentenced to death. Both still reside in prison in California. Even seasoned investigators indicated that Bittaker and Norris were among the most violent and disturbed offenders evidenced by their audio recordings and photographs of the rapes and murders (Schechter, 2003).

In their own right, Bittaker and Norris were extremely violent offenders, but it was after their relationship that a new level of barbarity was produced. These offenders point to the role of learning and exposure to peers as a powerful influence on antisocial behavior. This is the essence of **social learning theory**, the idea that humans learn values, beliefs, and behaviors from others and these learning processes manifest in behavior.

One of the most influential learning theories is Sutherland's (1947) **theory of differential association**. The theory is guided by nine principles that are sociological and social psychological in their approach and summarized and condensed here. Sutherland asserted that antisocial behavior is learned and not inherited. Biological and hereditary factors are rejected as explanations for the cause of delinquency, and Sutherland believed that only sociological factors explain why youth commit crime (of course, Chapter 16 illustrates that such a view is incorrect).

Sutherland theorized that antisocial behavior is learned through interaction with others by way of verbal and nonverbal communication. Third, the learning occurs in intimate groups, and it is in these intimate groups that children learn techniques for committing crime as well as the appropriate motives, attitudes, and rationalizations for doing so. The learning process involves exposure not only to the techniques of committing offenses, but also to the attitudes or rationalizations that justify those acts.

Unfortunately, there is no shortage of appalling incidents where parents, family members, and caregivers expose children to unconscionable depravity and antisocial conduct. These serve as the rearing environments that can result in homicide victimization and offending. For instance, a 26-year old mother was sentenced to 25 years in prison for felony murder and felony abuse of a child in which she encouraged her boyfriend to sexually abuse the child beginning when the child was just 1-month old.

In graphic text messages, the mother invited her boyfriend to rape her daughter. Ultimately, the boyfriend raped, beat, and strangled the child when she was four months old (Associated Press, 2015).

Sutherland theorized that the specific direction of motives and drives is learned from definitions of the legal code as being favorable or unfavorable. The term "definitions" refers to attitudes. Attitudes favoring law breaking are common, for instance, among youths who engage in vandalism against schools. An individual becomes delinquent or antisocial when exposure to definitions favorable to the violation exceeds the exposure to definitions unfavorable to the violation of law. This is the core of the theory of differential association. Importantly, definitions favorable to the violation of law can be learned from both criminal and noncriminal people.

The tendency for antisocial behavior is affected by the frequency, duration, priority, and intensity of learning experiences. The longer, earlier, more intensely, and more frequently youths are exposed to attitudes about delinquency (both pro and con), the more likely they will be influenced. Sutherland used the term intensity to refer to the degree of respect a person gives to a role model or associate. This attests to the importance of parents and other early role models. Learning delinquent behavior involves the same mechanisms involved in any other learning. While the content of what is learned is different, the process for learning any behavior is the same. Finally, all forms of behavior (antisocial and prosocial) are expressions of the same needs and values.

Burgess and Akers (1966) overhauled Sutherland's differential association theory by refining its focus and making the learning mechanisms more explicit. For instance, they omitted the ninth principle of differential association for their modified theory, and also made the language of social learning—particularly the influences of B. F. Skinner's work—more explicit. The result is **differential association-reinforcement theory** which suggests that crime is produced by learned and reinforced according to operant conditioning principles. Differential association-reinforcement theory is organized along seven propositions. First, Burgess and Akers posited that crime is learned according to the logic of operant conditioning (e.g., positive and negative reinforcement and positive and negative punishment). Second, Burgess and Akers suggested that crime is learned in nonsocial situations that are reinforcing or discriminative and in social interactions where the behavior of other persons is reinforcing or discriminative. Third, Burgess and Akers advanced that the primary part of learning criminal behavior occurs in groups that are the main source of reinforcement for the individual. Fourth, Burgess and Akers suggested that learning attitudes, techniques, and avoidance procedures that relate to committing crime depend on the individual's existing reinforcement contingencies. This means that learning is facilitated by the persons and things that already serve as reinforcers for the individual.

Fifth, Burgess and Akers indicate that behaviors that are learned and the frequency of their occurrence depend on the individual's existing reinforcers, and the rules by which these reinforcers are applied. Sixth, Burgess and Akers theorize that crime is a function of norms that are discriminative for criminal behavior, and the learning of crime occurs when it is more reinforcing than the learning of noncriminal behavior. This proposition is a reformulation of Sutherland's sixth principle. Seventh, Burgess and Akers suggest that the strength of criminal behavior is a direct function of the amount, frequency, and probability of reinforcement.

By expanding differential association to include reinforcement, Burgess and Akers' work is a broader theory that encompasses the more specific differential association and the generality of social learning. For all intents and purposes, criminologists generally use the terms "differential association," "differential reinforcement," and "social learning" interchangeably.

Akers has also advanced a social structural theory called the *Social Structure and Social Learning (SSSL) model*. The SSSL model suggests that four major components of social structure that work as the infrastructure for social learning processes to manifest. Differential social organization refers to community-level factors such as size, population, density, and ethnic composition. Differential location in the social structure refers to demographic characteristics. Differential social location refers to primary and secondary relationships and the social contexts in which they occur. Theoretically defined structural variables, such as social disorganization is borrowed from classic Chicago-school sociology and relates to negative features of neighborhoods (e.g., poverty, renters compared to homeowners, high residential mobility, low social trust, low collective efficacy). Disadvantaged social settings and social location creates greater opportunities for delinquent peer association and thus crime compared to more advantaged locations.

Box 9.1   The Hillside Stranglers

The Hillside Strangler case terrorized Los Angeles during 1977 and 1978 when at least 10 women were kidnapped, raped, tortured, and murdered over a 4-month period. The defendants in the case were cousins Angelo Buono and Kenneth Bianchi. Although both were psychopathic and sexually sadistic, there was also an interesting family dynamic to their relationship. Buono was nearly 20 years older than his cousin, was more socially adept, and was the dominant figure in their relationship. Buono had an extensive criminal history and kept women involved in prostitution and sexual slavery. He exposed his younger cousin to these behaviors, and soon their pimping and sexual appetites escalated to the murders. The two quarreled after the initial police investigation, and Bianchi fled California shortly after the Los Angeles murders and committed an additional two murders in Washington State (for these crimes, Bianchi is still serving life imprisonment). Buono died of natural causes in prison in California.

There are several applications of social learning theory to the Hillside Strangler case:

- The life histories of Buono and Bianchi are consistent with the modal habitual offender who experiences considerable failure in family, school, and work responsibilities while also committing an array of crimes. Moreover, the cousins likely met diagnostic criteria for psychopathy and sexual sadism, and their tortuous violence is evidence. Based on these descriptions, it is clear that Buono and Bianchi had definitions favorable not only to crime, but to abduction, rape, and murder.
- Given Buono's advanced age and status over Bianchi, it is likely that Buono's sexually deviant behavior served as a role model for his younger cousin. In turn, Bianchi imitated these behaviors during the course of the 10 abduction, rape, murders that were committed in Los Angeles. It is clear that the imitation was internalized for Bianchi as he committed two additional homicides in Washington State without the guidance of Buono.
- Buono and Bianchi engaged in sexual homicidal behavior and found that behavior to be highly reinforcing. Given their prior engagement in sex crimes, prostitution, pimping, and sexual deviancy, the cousins displayed pathologically disturbed sexual interests or paraphilias. Over time, the addition of murder complemented the reinforcements that sadistic sexual behavior provided.

Finally, the Hillside Strangler case demonstrates the synergistic effects that occur when antisocial individuals associate and mutually influence behavior. For this case, the extreme, pathological psychopathology of Buono and Bianchi coupled with their family relationship and learning processes resulted in extreme violence.

Source: DeLisi, M. (2013). *Criminal psychology*. San Diego, CA: Bridgepoint Education.

Another classic criminological learning theory is neutralization theory. **Neutralization theory** suggests that individuals are generally conventional but learn various forms of rationalization to morally free themselves to commit a misdeed. Sykes and Matza (1957) advanced a theory of delinquency in which adolescents adopted one of five forms of neutralization. These were the denial of responsibility, the denial of injury, the denial of the victim, condemnation of the condemners, and appealing to higher loyalties. Denial of responsibility is refusal to acknowledge or accept that one has committed a crime. Denial of injury and denial of victim are similar in that they are neutralizations that minimize the pain, suffering, or harm that the criminal behavior caused. Condemnation of the condemners is to turn the tables and impugn the legitimacy of those who respond to the criminal act. Criminal behavior that is said to be committed in protest of the police is an example. Appeal to higher loyalties is a way to suggest that criminal behavior is excused because it was done for a higher reason, such as loyalty to family or a gang.

Although Sutherland believed that the learning process occurs equally across environments, other learning theorists point to structural differences that affect how intensely deviance is learned. Simple exposure to violence in the most socially disorganized of neighborhoods creates multiple negative consequences. Cicchetti and Lynch (1993) developed an **ecological-transactional model of community violence**, which suggests that broad exposure to violence in the community stresses the ability of parents to protect their children from the pernicious effects of violence. Because of the toxic influences of gang activity and community violence, it becomes increasingly difficult for such parents to effectively monitor the activities of their children and adolescents. Over time, exposure to violence sets youth on a trajectory of increasingly declining parental monitoring. Cicchetti and Lynch's theory partially accounts for the entrenched nature of family dysfunction, gangs, and youth violence that characterize disorganized neighborhoods. For example, based on data from the National Longitudinal Study of Adolescent Health, Kort-Butler (2010) described this behavioral underworld as characterized by high levels of general delinquency, violent delinquency, experienced victimization, witnessed victimization, negative emotions, group fights with peers, and low socioeconomic status. About 14 percent of youth in her sample indicated that they expected to be murdered by age 21.

Spano, Rivera, Vazsonyi, and Bolland (2008) tested the ecological-transactional model of community violence using data from the Mobile Youth Survey—a sample of 360 youths living in 12 high-poverty neighborhoods in Mobile, Alabama. They found evidence of mutually reinforcing effects between exposure to community violence and parenting. Put simply, more violence exposure led to decreased parental monitoring; when dramatic exposure to violence occurred, this negative impact on parenting accelerated. Thus, community violence not only fuels the likelihood that youths will become juvenile delinquents and victims but also undermines the ability of parents to protect their children from these effects. In later work, Spano, Rivera, and Bolland (2010) examined longitudinal data from the Mobile Youth Survey to assess developmental patterns in chronic violence. They found that youths who were gang members at the first wave of data collection were between 600 percent and nearly 1,100 percent more likely to be chronically violent. By comparison, youths with chronic exposure to violence were 3,150 percent more likely than their peers to engage in chronically violent behavior at wave five.

Empirical Linkages to Homicide

Social learning processes can be seen in many forms of homicide offending. As seen in Figure 9.1, about one in five homicides in the United States involve multiple offenders, and about one in twenty involve multiple victims (Cooper & Smith, 2011). And as shown in Figure 9.2 and consistent with findings from social learning theory, group effects or multiple offenders are more commonly seen in homicide perpetrated by adolescents and young adults compared to older adults.

Although homicide offenders commonly present with a range of individual-level deficits, it is also true that many homicide offenders (and

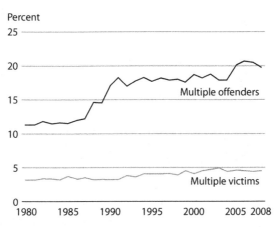

Figure 9.1   Multiple offenders and victims in homicide, 1980–2008.

Source: Modified from Cooper, A., & Smith, E. L. (2011). *Homicide trends in the United States, 1980–2008. Annual rates for 2009–2010.* Washington, DC: U.S. Department of Justice, Office of Justice Programs, Bureau of Justice Statistics.

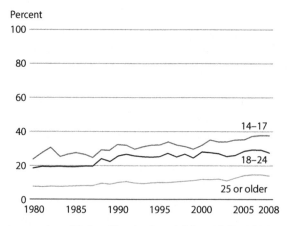

Figure 9.2 Age and multiple offender homicides, 1980–2008.

Source: Modified from Cooper, A., & Smith, E. L. (2011). *Homicide trends in the United States, 1980–2008. Annual rates for 2009–2010.* Washington, DC: U.S. Department of Justice, Office of Justice Programs, Bureau of Justice Statistics.

antisocial persons generally) were raised in appallingly abusive homes. In these homes, there was ubiquitous exposure to negative role models and belief structures that are conducive to antisocial behavior and violence. Early case study research documented parental abuse and cruelty toward their children throughout the young lives of juvenile homicide offenders (Duncan & Duncan, 1971; Duncan et al., 1958). Often, the homicides in these cases were seen as the culmination of a lifetime of horrific treatment at the hands of their parents. Many homicide offenders were also reared in explicitly antisocial homes where parents, siblings, and acquaintances not only exposed youth to antisocial behaviors but also often cultivated and promoting these negative behaviors.

Many criminological studies have shown the relevance of social learning theories to homicide offending and victimization. In a case-control study comparing 21 male juveniles convicted of homicide to 21 convicted burglars incarcerated in the United Kingdom, Hill-Smith, Hugo, Hughes, Fonagy, and Hartman (2002) identified several risk factors that differentiated murderers from their antisocial peers. Youth convicted of murder were more likely to have been reared by emotionally and physically harsh parents, to have mothers and fathers who had been arrested and to have had generally greater and more extensive educational and school problems. In other words, they had considerable exposure to antisocial role models, namely their parents, which provided myriad learning opportunities for violence and antisocial behavior.

Another illustration of social learning principles in homicide is seen in cases where children witness the killing of their mother. Not surprisingly, children who witness their mother being murdered—usually by the child's father, suffer from a range of negative experiences (Burman & Allen-Meares, 1994; Lewandowski, McFarlane, Campbell, Gary, & Barenski, 2004). These include PTSD symptoms, psychiatric disturbance, reduced school functioning, increased behavioral problems, and, most unfortunately, role modeling for serious violent behavior. Many women who are killed by their domestic partner were also previously abused, and that abuse often extends to the children. Thus, witnessing one's father murder one's mother is an extremely harrowing event that can set into motion further violence. Moreover, despite the benefits of psychological treatment, many children who have witnessed their mother's murder do not receive services (Lewandowski et al., 2004).

Many gang youth, for example, had parents and siblings who socialized them into gang life (DeLisi, Spruill, Peters, Caudill, & Trulson, 2013). And one of the main criminal outcomes of gang life is homicide offending (DeLisi, Spruill, Vaughn, & Trulson, 2014). As shown by McCuish, Bouchard, and Corrado (2014), social learning is relevant to the recruitment of homicide co-offenders among gang members. In their study, gang members who are planning to murder gang rivals or even another member within their gang tend to select similarly antisocial peers to help perpetrate the homicide. In this way, a sort of murderous homophily occurs.

Jenkins (1990) conducted a study of those who share murder, that is, those who perpetrate homicide with multiple offenders. Using archival records in the United States of multiple offender homicides in which there were 10+ victims between 1971 and 1990, Jenkins found several dynamics that linked codefendants in these cases. Many of these reflected learning processes by which a younger offender learned how to kill by following an older role model. Jenkins documented several relationships among those who share murder including a dominant male with a submissive female partner, a dominant male with a submissive male partner, a dominant female with a submissive male partner, apparently equally dominant partners or "co-killers," and others. Similarly, Juodis, Woodworth, Porter, and ten Brinke (2009) compared 84 single perpetrator homicides to 40 multiperpetrator homicides using Canadian data. They found that multi-perpetrator killings tended to involve younger offenders (among whom social learning effects are more pronounced), instrumental motives, such as robbery, and involve male victims. Group homicides also were more likely to involve alcohol use and have more gratuitous violence. Thus it appeared that the group dynamics fueled the motivation to commit murder and continue to inflict violence during the crime event. Conversely, single perpetrators killings were more likely to target female victims and involve sexual behavior and abuse.

Social learning is also seen in forensic-oriented constructs that relate to homicide. For example, Schlesinger (2002) conducted a case study of an offender who first stalked and later murdered the object of his affection. Schlesinger described this as a **catathymic process**, whereby an individual perceives that the only way to resolve an extraordinary inner conflict is to perpetrate murder. The idea was advanced by Wertham (1937). According to Schlesinger, the obsessed person undergoes an incubation period where there is increased preoccupation with the target. The incubation can last days to years in duration. This obsession creates extreme tension and stress within the individual. Underling the obsession is a deep-seated, learned personal problem, such as fear of intimacy or sexual inadequacy that similarly creates significant tension. Over time, the tension reaches a boiling point where it is no longer tolerable, and the offender murders the object of his obsession to alleviate the catathymic experience.

In a creative study, Atchison and Heide (2011) utilized multiple criminological theories including social learning theory to understand the homicidal behavior of Charles Manson and his "family" of followers. A career criminal, Manson is among the most notorious criminal offenders in American history, and he orchestrated eight homicides perpetrated

© andrey_l/Shutterstock, Inc.

In a catathymic process, an offender perceives that the only way to resolve an extraordinary inner conflict is to commit murder.

in July and August 1969 in Los Angeles. Drawing on Akers' (1985) social learning theory which contains differential association, differential reinforcement, definitions, and imitation, Atchison and Heide examined how these social learning processes influenced Manson and his followers' violent conduct. In his early life, Manson was placed in boys' homes, reform schools, and various correctional settings where he was exposed to numerous other youth who were antisocial and advocated various ways to continue to violate the law. His placement in adult jails and prisons continued throughout adulthood. In fact, Atchison and Heide (2011) calculated that Manson has spent 81 percent of his life in correctional or confinement settings. Moreover, his followers, such as Tex Watson, Susan Atkins, Patricia Krenwinkel, Lynette Fromme, Leslie Van Houten, and others were young, impressionable, troubled, vulnerable individuals who were exploited and controlled by Manson. Manson's use of sex, drugs, and various manipulations exerted tremendous control over his followers, and inspired them to do anything he requested, even murder.

Other criminologists have utilized the social learning perspective to advance explanations for specific types of homicide, such as serial murder and sexual homicide. Using case studies of Carroll Cole (who was eventually charged with 16 homicides and executed in 1985), Jeffrey Dahmer (who was eventually convicted of 15 homicides and was murdered in prison in 1994), Edmund Kemper (who eventually murdered ten people and is serving life imprisonment), Henry Lee Lucas (who was linked to more than 60 homicides and died in prison), and Arthur Shawcross (who eventually was charged with 11 homicides and died in prison) Wright and Hensley (2003) applied social learning theory to these severe serial murderers. They suggested that all humans seek affection and approval from their loved ones particularly their parents. In the event of receiving abuse, neglect, and humiliation instead—which typifies the family backgrounds of these offenders—an individual feel tremendous sadness and frustration.

Through continuously reinforced experiences, this frustration builds; however, the fledgling serial killer is unable to vent his frustration to a physically more formidable parent. Instead, less physically imposing creatures, namely small animals, become a substitute for the frustration and rage that is intended for the parent. The use of aggression, such as killing small animals, helps to alleviate the frustration. Over time, the offender will "graduate" from killing animals to killing humans and the victims often symbolically represent the initially hated parent. According to Wright and Hensley (2003, p. 83), "The torture and ultimate death of the animals made the killers feel as if they had gained some retribution for their pain and suffering. Thus, within the framework of the graduation hypothesis, children who are cruel to animals may then graduate to aggressive behaviors toward humans." Thus although serial murder is an extraordinarily rare behavior, it is nonetheless motivated by the same habituated learning principles of mundane behavior.

Similarly, Chan, Heide, and Beauregard (2010) suggest that several features of sexual murderer's lives illustrate how differential association, differential reinforcement, definitions, and imitation contribute to their ultimate murderous behavior. Most sexual murderers are reared in highly dysfunctional home environments characterized by physical, emotional, verbal, and often sexual abuse. They also tend to witness extreme violence in the way of domestic violence or ongoing criminal behavior displayed at home. In other words, they develop strong deviant behavioral learning processes via their direct and indirect associations with primary family members and peers. These relationships impose frequent and intense exposure to antisocial attitudes, values, and behaviors that ultimately form the offender's own belief system.

Chan and his colleagues (2010) theorize that sexual murderers learn attitudes and behaviors conducive to sexual violence in two ways: interaction with primary groups and emulation of primary group role models. Many were exposed to pornography and deviant sexual behavior in the home (e.g., mother engaging in prostitution in front of her children, criminals engaging in sexual violence at the home, physical and sexual abuse of the children, incest, and others). In addition, the use of pornography—and often extraordinarily violent pornography—is often extensive. This provides a vicarious exposure that supplements that direct exposure. Taken together, these learned experiences, attitudes, and values contribute to a fantasy world involving sexual violence that is continually reinforced with pornographic consumption. Over time, these sexual fantasies transition from mere fantasy to reality.

In an ingenious study, Coston (2014) examined techniques of neutralization among serial murderers by sending 75 convicted serial sexual homicide offenders a mail survey. Of these, 38 murderers responded to the questionnaire and indicated their endorsement for the five techniques of neutralization. The most common neutralization was denying the victim, such as claiming that prostitute victims are not "really" victims. More than one in four denied responsibility for their crimes despite their conviction status. And 18 percent appealed to higher loyalties albeit in antisocial ways. Nine of the convicted murderers indicated that "a lot of people think of committing multiple murders, I just did it." None of the homicide offenders denied injury or condemned the condemners. That so many of these offenders perceived that many people contemplated committing multiple homicide attests to their truly deviant cognitions.

Network analyses have shown how immersion in social networks with extensive exposure to violent offenders and gang members exponentially increases the likelihood of homicide risk. For instance, Papachristos and Wildeman (2014) recently studied a cohort of 3,718 high-risk individuals in high-crime African American neighborhoods in Chicago where 41 percent of all gun homicides occurred in just 4 percent of neighborhoods. They found that being a member of the largest, densest network of high-risk persons increased the likelihood of being murdered by 3,080 percent! In addition, each social tie removed from a homicide victim decreased one's own odds of being a homicide victim by 57 percent. In other words, having high differential association with violent, high-risk people dramatically increased the likelihood of being murdered. And commensurately, the further removed from a murder victim, the less likely one was to be murdered also. Overall, their study shows the power of network exposure and the traction that associations with violent others can have on one's own homicide risk.

Not all putatively learned content impacts homicide. Markey, French, and Markey (2014) recently examined the association between violent movies and homicide from 1960 to 2012. They found a negative and nonsignificant relationship suggesting that claims that violent films cause murder are overstated. For example, in 2012, movies were 177 percent more violent than the average film violence during this period, but homicide in 2012 was 35 percent lower than the mean homicide rate from 1960 to 2012. And PG-13 movies showed 83 percent more gun violence in 2011, a year when gun homicides were 33 percent below the mean and homicide was down 31 percent from the mean. The authors concluded that "Contrary to the notion that trends in violent films are linked to violent behavior, no evidence was found to suggest this medium was a major (or minor) contributing cause of violence in the United States" (Markey et al., 2014, p. 11).

Learning is an important part of all life processes and behaviors and has rather extensively been applied to homicide in a variety of ways and using a variety of data sources. The basic notion that exposure to those in primary relationships and the day-to-day exposures that accompany the vicissitudes of life are intuitive. In the lives of many homicide offenders, it is relatively clear that they learned to perpetrate this severe form of crime in part because of their own exposure to violent offenders, victimization, and other learning processes. Some of these negative processes, or strains, are examined in the next chapter.

CHAPTER 10

Homicide and the General Strain Perspective

© Joseph Sohm/Shutterstock, Inc.

Agnew's general strain theory points to economic, interpersonal, and emotional strains as the immediate causes of criminal violence.

Conceptual Background

The concept of strain has been central to sociological theorizing about criminal behavior. In his influential model, Merton (1938) suggested that **anomie**, a condition of normlessness where an individual is uncertain how to behave, resulted from an economic system with differential access to achieve cultural goals. Although mostly everyone in a society is exposed to similar cultural images about what it means and what it takes to achieve success, not everyone perceives they have an equal likelihood of actually achieving success. In Merton's work, people known as innovators would use illegal means to achieve success.

For several decades in criminology, the notion of anomie or strain from the social structure was economic in nature. However, it was also recognized that strains can be emotional in nature and that emotional states are likely what are most strongly associated with crime, especially the use of violence. For example, although it predated general strain theory, the basic logic of general strain theory was anticipated by other criminologists. Consider this quotation from Williams and Flewelling (1988, p. 423), "it is reasonable to assume that when people live under conditions of extreme scarcity, the struggle for survival is intensified. Such conditions are often accompanied by a host of agitating psychological manifestations, ranging from a deep sense of powerlessness and brutalization to anger, anxiety, and alienation. Such manifestations can provoke physical aggression in conflict situations."

The creator of general strain theory is Robert Agnew (1985, 1992). **General strain theory** suggests that delinquency or problem behaviors generally result from three social psychological processes. These are (1) actual or anticipated failure to achieve positively valued goals, (2) actual or anticipated removal of positively valued stimuli, and (3) actual or anticipated presentation of negatively valued stimuli. In subsequent works, Agnew (2001) indicated that these various strains are particularly likely to result in crime or violence if they are seen as unjust and undeserved, are extreme, arise from negative or criminogenic settings, or reflect pressure to engage in crime due to other offenders being present.

Agnew has also broadened his conceptualization of strains to include four types. These are:

- **Anticipated strains:** strains that are expected in the future and that can cause negative emotions currently.
- **Objective strains:** observed strains that create negative emotions and problem behaviors.
- **Subjective strains:** perceived strains that create negative emotions and problem behaviors.

- **Vicarious strains:** third-party strains where an individual observes another having strain and it negatively affects them emotionally or behaviorally.

In other words, general strain theory broadens the scope of strain or anomie theories to include the importance of relationships and other stimuli that are important to an individual. In addition, the theory articulates that what is real and what is perceived do not have to be the same but can produce the same consequences. For instance, education in the United States is freely available to everyone, yet many offenders perceive that it was not really available to them, and thus use it is a rationalization to commit crime. The theory also points to the importance of both positive and negative stimuli in the creation of problem behaviors.

General strain theory was not developed as a theory of homicide, but instead to explain general delinquency. However, the theoretical principles can also be applied to homicide offenders. Indeed, one of the most salient features of homicide offenders is the sheer number of negative or aversive stimuli that have occurred in their life ranging from childhood abuse to sexual abuse to substance abuse to imprisonment and others. It is easy to see how these negative stimuli can foster very negative, angry, and often fatalistic feelings that can serve to drive violent behavior.

Since introducing general strain theory, Agnew has continually developed and extended the theory to apply to different communities particularly those characterized by poverty, social disadvantage, and high crime rates. According to Agnew (1999):

- Communities with economic deprivation, inequality, high population density, and high nonwhite populations are more likely to select and retain strained individuals. Because these individuals are not upwardly mobile and cannot afford to live elsewhere, they must live in more stressful, strain-inducing environments.
- In these settings, individuals fail to achieve positively valued goals via the traditional ways of education and job advancement. Instead, fast money, status/respect, and the desire to be treated in a just manner become primary motivations.
- Their socioeconomic location increases feelings of relative deprivation compared to those who are achieving positively valued goals.
- Affected communities become dominated by negative stimuli and generally lack positive stimuli. These forces increase the sensitivity of residents to certain types of aversive stimuli and increase their exposure to aversive stimuli including economic deprivation, family disruption, incivility, social disorganization, and other strains.

- The aggregate effect of exposure to negative stimuli increases negative emotions like anger and frustration which can have direct effects on violent crime.
- This contributes to increased interaction with others who are similarly angry and frustrated and increases the likelihood of conflicts.
- These conflicts contribute to criminal responses to strain including assaults, shootings, and even homicide stemming from disagreements.

More recently, Agnew (2007) explored how these conditions and the role of strain in specifically producing criminal violence including homicide. He recognized that criminal offenders often have limited skills and resources for legal coping. Among other things, they have low intelligence, low constraint, low self-efficacy (i.e., the belief that they have the ability to cope with strain), and poor social- and problem-solving skills. This negative bag of tricks makes the use of violence more appealing. In addition, violent offenders have abundant skills and resources for violent coping with strain, such as personality traits that are conducive to handling strain by means of force.

Several chapters in this text refer to personality constructs that facilitate homicide (e.g., impulsive, low constraint, psychopathic traits). Beyond these person-specific deficits, violent offenders often have low levels of conventional social support, such as parents, teachers, and others who can provide assistance. For instance, criminologists have found that persons with more antisocial personality traits, such as lack of restraint are the very individuals who are more likely to respond to strain with violence (Agnew, Brezina, Wright, & Cullen, 2002). In addition, offenders often demonstrate little social control and are not closely monitored or supervised by others. They associate with other people who are violent and whose beliefs are favorable to using violence. Finally, there is often little cost or down-side attributed to committing homicide, and there is ample upside in the way of alleviating strain, increasing one's reputation, or simply settling a dispute. In these ways, Agnew's general strain theory is compatible with many other criminological theories.

Empirical Linkages to Homicide

The basic notion that persons who are exposed to more strains are more likely to become serious and violent offenders is broadly supported in the criminological and related literatures. A recent study is illustrative. Fox and colleagues (2015) examined the role of adverse childhood experiences as

Box 10.1   Strains and Motivations: Data from National and Psychiatric Samples

General strain theory points to various types of strain and how these experiences contribute to negative affective states and crime. Perhaps more than other criminological theories, general strain theory articulates what an individual was thinking, or was motivated by when he or she committed their crime. An interesting study by Langevin and Handy (1987) compared a national sample of homicides involving 1,358 murders and a psychiatric sample of homicides involving 108 murders. The homicides were then split into two types, those that had stranger victims and those that had acquaintance victims.

The groups differed in terms of their stated motivation for the murders. In the national sample, the overwhelming motive for the stranger murders was simply to commit other crimes, such as rape, robbery, or burglary. For acquaintance murders, about 60 percent were the result of arguments or anger. In the national sample, anger was the motive in nearly six times as many acquaintance than stranger murders. Jealousy was the motive in 15 times more acquaintance than stranger murders.

In the psychiatric sample, there were many more motives for the homicides. These included sexual frustration, money problems, long-term anger, sudden provoked anger, jealousy, revenge, insult, paranoia, and various other crimes. Nearly 28 percent of stranger murders and 33 percent of acquaintance murders had no obvious motive and appeared senseless. In other words, there did not seem to be a rational linkage to a strain or stressor. Conversely, only about 4 percent of murders in the national sample both stranger and acquaintance had no known motive.

The study reinforces the differences between normal and abnormal homicides, and how the victimology whether stranger or acquaintance matters in terms of motivating factors for the killer. It also specifies that many specific strains appear to be the driver of homicides in Canada, and these data are generally generalizeable to other nations including the United States.

Source: Langevin, R., & Handy, L. (1987). Stranger homicide in Canada: A national sample and a psychiatric sample. *Journal of Criminal Law and Criminology, 78*(2), 398–429.

a predictor of serious, violent juvenile offending among a very large sample of nearly 23,000 youth referred to the Florida Department of Juvenile Justice. Adverse childhood experiences included emotional abuse, physical abuse, sexual abuse, emotional neglect, physical neglect, household violence, household substance abuse, household mental illness, and having an incarcerated household member. In other words, this list of adverse child-hood experiences is a laundry list of noxious stimuli in the home environments of serious delinquents, many of whom committed homicide and/or other serious felonies.

Each adverse childhood experience increased the likelihood of becoming a serious and violent juvenile offender by 35 percent. This means youth with all nine forms of adverse experiences were 315 percent more likely to become a serious, violent delinquent (Fox, Perez, Cass, Baglivio, & Epps, 2015). In addition, the most violent youth were more likely to have three of more of these strains and the prevalence of having 4–9 strains was significantly higher among the most violent youth. Conversely, whereas 31 percent of one-time only juvenile offenders had zero adverse childhood experiences, just 7 percent of the violent offenders had zero.

The basic personality functioning of murderers is conducive to the tenets of general strain theory. In their personality study of 112 imprisoned murderers, Biro, Vuckovic, and Djuric (1992) found that nearly half of the murderers were characterized with a hyper-sensitive-aggressive profile. This presents as "a persons who is easily offended, intolerant of frustration, prone to impulsive-aggressive outbursts, possibly introverted and dysphoric. Such a person will be always dissatisfied and disappointed with people, and is very likely to show paranoid interpretations of social situations" (Biro et al., 1992, p. 364).

As examined in Chapter 9, Atchison and Heide (2011) utilized multiple criminological theories including general strain theory to understand the homicidal behavior of Charles Manson and his "family" of followers. Manson is among the most infamous criminal offenders in American history, and he orchestrated eight homicides perpetrated in July and August 1969 in Los Angeles. Many of the events of Charles Manson's life and criminal career stemmed from his failure to achieve financial goals, the presentation of noxious or negative stimuli, and the removal of positive stimuli.

More than 80 percent of Manson's life has been spent in prison, jail, or various institutional settings for at-risk and delinquent children. A life behind bars provides many examples of chronic stressors that could result in crime and violence, and many of these happened to Manson. He was beaten by correctional staff, gang raped by other youth at the Indianapolis School for Boys, and involved in multiple other violent acts—as victim and as perpetrator—during his various confinements.

Decades in confinement surrounded by other highly antisocial men also presented a cascade of noxious stimuli that Manson would have to process later in life. In addition, Manson was largely neglected and abandoned by his mother early in life, and his wife and newborn child left him after one of his many stints in prison. These family relationships were intensely meaningful to Manson and represent the removal of positive stimuli including in general strain theory. Finally, it is important to note that Manson failed, and failed miserably, according to conventional indicators of success in society. He was often unemployed and homeless, did not succeed in any skill or vocation, and instead survived by pimping, theft, robbery, and drug selling, and produced nothing of particular value.

Recently, Eriksson and Mazerolle (2013) advanced perhaps the most comprehensive model of homicide that is explicitly rooted in general strain theory. According to Eriksson and Mazerolle, the various sources of strain affect men and women in similar and different ways, and these differences manifest in distinct forms of domestic or intimate partner homicide. For men, prevention from achieving goals is illustrated by them being unable to achieve control over their wife or family. The removal of positively valued stimuli can encompass a loss of control, relationship separation, the loss of children via child custody disputes, and others. The presentation of negatively valued stimuli can include a protection order, arrest, or suspected partner infidelity.

Together, these strains produce negative emotions such as anger, rage, and jealousy. Eriksson and Mazerolle also asserted that the negative emotions in general strain theory are conditioned by other characteristics including negative emotionality, low constraint, attitudes toward violence, peers condoning violence, attitudes of entitlement or proprietariness, and insecure attachment. Men who have some or all of these risk factors are more likely to perpetrate spousal homicide when faced with intense negative emotions and loss.

For women, prevention from achieving goals is illustrated by the disrupted maintenance of a close relationship. The removal of positively valued stimuli can include restricted freedom or the loss of identity as a happily married woman. The presentation of negatively valued stimuli can take the form of exposure to intimate partner violence (or escalated violence), abuse of children, and anticipated abuse. These sources of strain produce fear, desperation, and terror. When conditioned by other risk factors, such as low perceived social support and limited access to resources, women are potentially likely to murder their husband.

Although not a direct test of Eriksson and Mazerolle's model, intimate partner homicide data from multiple European nations including Finland, France, Germany, Italy, Netherlands, Portugal, Slovenia, Spain, Sweden, and the United Kingdom illustrate that a general strain theory approach is a useful explanatory mechanism for intimate partner homicide (Corradi & Stöckl, 2014) and understanding the various stressors or strains that cause men and women to perpetrate homicide.

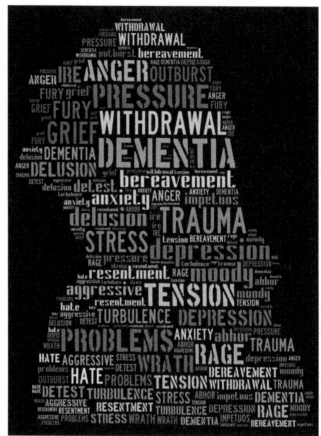

© Amir Ridhwan/Shutterstock, Inc.

Mass murders committed at schools are consistent with Levin and Madfis' (2009) application of general strain theory.

Even multiple homicides can be understood from a general strain perspective. Levin and Madfis (2009) developed a five-stage sequential model that articulates the various strains that potentially lead to a mass murder. These are chronic strain, uncontrolled strain, acute strain, and planning stage, and the massacre. Chronic strains are comprised of early-life and adolescent frustrations that contribute to an individual's social isolation. These experiences result in a lack of prosocial social supports, such as friendship networks, family, and other social contact which collectively are uncontrolled strain. An acute strain is a real, perceived, or imagined negative event that the perpetrator finds to be devastating. The acute strain initiates a planning stage whereby a multiple murder is fantasized as being a masculine solution to the powerlessness that the acute strain caused. The final stage is the mass murder itself which is usually facilitated by firearms.

On an even larger scale, Maier-Katkin, Mears, and Bernard (2009) developed a general strain theory-oriented conceptual model of crimes against humanity, such as genocide. Their main proposition is that intense, prevalent societal-level strain is caused by insecurity, danger, scarcity, deprivation, political and economic oppression, and other factors. The more strains that are felt collectively and individually, the more likely crimes against humanity will occur.

Next, strain undermines intergroup solidarity and drives individuals to rely more heavily on narrowly defined "us versus them" primary groups. These groups contribute to greater individual submission to authority and acceptance of social roles that are governed by their small primary group. Within these groups, ideology and self-interest are engendered and often exacerbate the original strains and grievances. Once these conditions are in place, the use of angry aggression becomes likely.

Although strain is a common phenomenon, it is also a powerful one in the lives of homicide offenders. Among normal homicide offenders, such as those who murder an intimate or acquaintance as a result of a mundane occurrence, such as an argument, strain can be understood as the spark that ignites a homicide. Among abnormal homicide offenders, such as those who commit sexual homicide or serial murder, a long history of strains and noxious stimuli are often present in the childhood and adolescent years, and these experiences have integral value to the offender. Indeed, these strains, including sexual abuse victimization, incest victimization, physical abuse, neglect, precocious exposure to pornography, alcohol, and drugs, and many others are often cited as the reason why the person ultimately perpetrated their homicide(s).

Although general strain theory moved away from economic factors as the primary source of strain, it also noted that anger, strain, and frustration were more likely to occur among the disadvantaged and poor. The structural perspective, which entirely takes this approach, is examined in the next chapter.

CHAPTER 11

Homicide and the Structural Perspective

The structural perspective suggests that aggregate characteristics influence the criminal behavior of individuals.

Conceptual Background

A common and interesting classroom exercise in universities across the country is to ask students to visualize the places, settings, or neighborhoods in their town or city that seem to be the most dangerous and have the highest probability of crime. These are often places that are featured on the evening news for the latest violent crime or homicide. Often, these places have few single-family homes, have few residences that are owned, but are instead rented, and have many apartments. The businesses in these locations tend to be small, service-oriented establishments that provide basic amenities or even more commonly, vices. Examples include gas stations, liquor stores, cigarette stores, check cashing stores, furniture rental stores, adult book stores, strip clubs, and the like. These settings often have empty buildings that formerly housed more substantive businesses that employed people in full-time jobs with benefits. Over time, the vacant buildings fall into disrepair and seem to invite vandalism, graffiti, and shelter for people to engage in drug use, drug selling, prostitution, and transiency.

In large urban centers, some of these places have been blighted, negative areas for generations and seemed to invite a range of social problems. Students can well visualize these places and imagine how the sheer structural characteristics of these settings seem to mold behaviors. The basic logic that place can affect human behavior is central to the structural perspective.

The founder of sociology—Émile Durkheim—was the first to describe how social change that occurred quickly as a result of economic changes had the effect of producing behavioral uncertainty among individuals. This uncertainty, or anomie contributed to weakened social integration, social turmoil, and increased the likelihood of violence behaviors including suicide and homicide. According to Durkheim (1897 [1951], p. 356), "Now, whenever society is integrated in such a way that the individuation of its parts is weakly emphasized, the intensity of collective states of conscience raises the general level of the life of the passions; it is even true that no soil is so favorable to the development of the specifically homicidal passions." The basic logic is that social structure, social change, and simply, structure, affect homicide.

Sociologists in the early and middle twentieth century described how the increasing industrialization of the United States and the frequent population growth that accompanied it led to large-scale changes in the physical and social structure of society, and in turn, had important consequences for human behavior. In a classic statement, Wirth (1938, p. 1) advised:

"[A] city is a relatively large, dense, and permanent settlement of heterogeneous individuals. Large numbers account for individual variability, the relative absence of intimate personal acquaintanceship, the segmentalization of human relations which are largely anonymous, superficial, and transitory, and associated characteristics. Density involves diversification and specialization, the coincidence of close physical contact and distant social relations, glaring contrasts, a complex pattern of segregation, the predominance of formal social control, and accentuated friction, among other phenomena. Heterogeneity tends to break down rigid social structures and to produce increased mobility, instability, and insecurity..."

In other words, the changes to the economic and population structure of society significantly affect the behavioral responses that people make, even responses to negative conditions. Thus to return to the classroom example, the reason that blighted areas tend to stay blighted over long periods of time is that the ecology has made the relations between people into such a way that they do not effectively control one another's conduct. In these types of negative environments, negativity and violence are fostered. Trend data on homicide victimization and homicide offending rates by city population seem to support the notion that more urban settings are associated with more murders than cities with lower population and hence better connections among residents (see Figures 11.1 and 11.2).

The **structural perspective** asserts that aggregate characteristics of neighborhoods, cities, states, or nations are associated with homicide rates occurring in those settings. Structural features include demographics characteristics, such as age, sex, and racial composition, family characteristics, such as percent married, single-parent households, population characteristics, such as size and density, and economic characteristics, such as poverty rate, unemployment rate, income inequality, and others. Generally, larger, more densely populated places, cities with more divorced males, and places with greater poverty or resource deprivation have more homicides

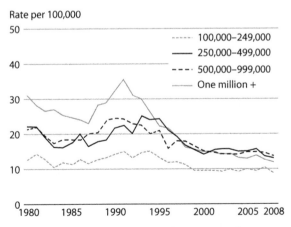

Figure 11.1   Homicide victimization rates by city population size, 1980–2008.

Source: Modified from Cooper, A., & Smith, E. L. (2011). *Homicide trends in the United States, 1980–2008. Annual rates for 2009–2010.* Washington, DC: U.S. Department of Justice, Office of Justice Programs, Bureau of Justice Statistics.

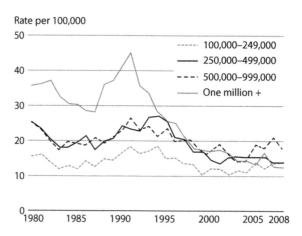

Rate per 100,000

100,000–249,000
250,000–499,000
500,000–999,000
One million +

Figure 11.2 Homicide offending rates by city population size, 1980–2008.

Source: Modified from Cooper, A., & Smith, E. L. (2011). *Homicide trends in the United States, 1980–2008. Annual rates for 2009–2010.* Washington, DC: U.S. Department of Justice, Office of Justice Programs, Bureau of Justice Statistics.

(cf., Land, McCall, & Cohen, 1990; McCall, Land, & Parker, 2010; Messner & Rosenfeld, 1999; Williams, 1984; Williams & Flewelling, 1988).

A host of structural variables are important to homicide. The reasons why these conditions facilitate homicide are diverse and include the following:

- **Poverty:** although research findings are mixed, there is generally a relationship where greater material disadvantage engenders greater involvement in antisocial behavior which increases the likelihood of conflict, and potentially homicide. A clear example of a poverty-inducing effect is seen in drug selling. For individuals who perceive they cannot pay their bills by conventional employment, there is an attraction to drug selling because it is relatively easy and can yield considerable income. However, drug selling also exposes one to criminal offenders and increases the likelihood of victimization from other offenders seeking drugs, money, or both. Many homicides stem from involvement in drug selling and other underground forms of economic activity, such as illegal gambling and prostitution.
- **Inequality or relative deprivation:** although poverty can produce homicide in absolute terms, there is also the notion that one's economic position relative to another is also a motivating force for violence. If inequality is considered to be ascribed based on one's race, ethnicity, or neighborhood, it is seen as less legitimate than inequality that is based on merit. Structural theorists suggest that this

creates resignation against the conventional society and fuels anger that often motivates violent crime including homicide. A landmark study of homicide in 125 U.S. cities or SMSAs (standard metropolitan statistical areas), for instance, found that racial and economic inequality was associated with homicide but that poverty itself was not (Blau & Blau, 1982).

- **Family structure:** several variables included percent married, percent divorced males, and percent female-headed households are associated with crime and homicide. The reason is that nonintact families are less able to adequately supervise and monitor children's behavior because of the absence of one or both parents, the unsupervised time when the present parent is working, or the refusal or inability of parents to watch their children. As a result, these youth are more likely to associate with peers who usually share their family background which exponentially increases opportunities for conflict and violence.

- **Population characteristics:** as examined in Chapter 1, there are sharp sociodemographic differences in homicide offending and victimization. Thus, geographic areas or cities with populations that are disproportionately young, male, poor, and nonwhite are likely to experience more homicide than populations that are disproportionately older, female, more affluent, and white.

In structural research, another important concept is concentrated disadvantage. **Concentrated disadvantage** typifies impoverished places where a high percentage of residents receive welfare, are unemployed, are disproportionately African American, are younger, and tend to live in female-headed households. These characteristics are believed to structure social interaction, family functioning, school performance, and value structures in negative ways that facilitate involvement in antisocial conduct. Areas of concentrated disadvantage are also characterized not only by material poverty, but also by behavioral poverty as well and usually include frequent exposure to antisocial behavior, vice, disorder, and violence.

Empirical Linkages to Homicide

Several studies have examined structural conditions to assess their association with homicide at the aggregate level. Drawing on data from 125 SMSAs in the United States, Williams (1984) conducted a structural study that included models that examined the importance of cultural factors such as anger about racial inequality and various economic factors on homicide. Whereas prior studies had questioned the role of poverty (measured by the percent of the population that lived below the poverty line), Williams found that percent poor was a strong and significant predictor of homicide. This study included controls for economic inequality, racial inequality, divorce, population size, percent African American, and percent black squared (which would be a proxy for African American segregation). Interestingly, Williams also found that the poverty-homicide linkage was generally limited to SMSAs that were not in the southern United States. In the south, the significant effect of poverty on homicide was tempered perhaps because it was driven by other regional forces such as those discussed in Chapter 3.

In a study of 168 U.S. cities with populations that exceeded 100,000 residents, Williams and Flewelling (1988) examined several structural factors including percentage poor, percentage black, justifiable homicide ratio, southern location, divorce rate, and population density for their association to seven types of homicide including family conflict, family other (referring to other circumstance or motivation), acquaintance conflict, acquaintance other, stranger conflict, stranger other, and total homicides. They found that percentage poor was significantly associated with all seven types of homicide, indeed it was the only structural measure that was so consistently significant. Divorce rate was significant for all homicides except stranger conflict and percentage black was significant for all with the exceptions of family other and stranger conflict. The other structural factors were intermittently associated with various types of homicide.

Structural risk factors are also importantly related to juvenile homicide offending and victimization, thus youth reared in places with greater concentrated disadvantage are more likely to commit homicide (MacDonald & Gover, 2005). In their study of homicide in Dade County, Florida, Massey and McKean (1985) found that places with more males, more young males, more single males, and a greater proportion of people living alone had more homicides. In addition, neighborhoods that were overcrowded, had more vacant buildings, and had buildings with multiple families residing in them also had more homicides.

In a study of 26 neighborhoods in the Manhattan borough of New York City, Messner and Tardiff (1986) found that the size of the poor population and the percent divorce or separated were the only significant predictors of homicide, while socioeconomic and racial factors were not significant. Sorensen, Marquart, and Brock (1993) examined multiple theoretical perspectives in their study of killings of felons by police officers in the line of duty. Using national data from the Supplemental Homicide Reports, they found that cities with more inequality had not only more violent crime, but also more police killings of felons. These effects persisted in models that included 169 cities with a population of 100,000 or greater and in 56 cities with population of 250,000 or greater. Cities with a higher African American population also were more likely to have police killings of felons.

A structural approach has also been utilized to theorize other specific forms of lethal violence, such as homicide-suicide. Manning (2014) suggests that homicide-suicide can be understood as a function of socioeconomic and sociocultural relations between the two individuals who are killed in the homicide-suicide event. In cases of suicide, there is relational closeness, cultural closeness, functional interdependence, superior adversary, and no third party support in characterizing the relationship between the homicide and suicide victims. In cases of homicide, there is relational distance, cultural distance, functional independence, inferior adversary, and strong third party support. To Manning, cases of homicide-suicide fall between these dimensions. For a national look at types of homicide by city size, see Figure 11.3.

		Percent of all homicides			
	Total	Large city	Small city	Suburban area	Rural area
All homicides	100%	57.7%	13.6%	21.3%	7.5%
Victim/offender relationship					
Intimate	100%	46.7%	16.0%	27.1%	10.2%
Family	100%	44.8	14.9	28.5	11.8
Infants	100%	47.3	18.5	26.2	8.0
Elders	100%	45.8	17.0	25.4	11.8
Circumstance					
Felony murder	100%	60.8%	12.6%	20.8%	5.8%
Sex related	100%	48.4	14.9	27.3	9.4
Drug related	100%	67.4	10.8	18.1	3.7
Gang related	100%	69.6	13.3	16.6	0.5
Argument	100%	53.5	15.5	21.6	9.4
Workplace	100%	30.8	16.3	38.3	14.6
Weapon					
Gun homicide	100%	59.6%	12.4%	20.3%	7.7%
Arson	100%	53.0	16.1	22.7	8.2
Poison	100%	38.0	18.3	31.0	12.7
Multiple victims or offenders					
Multiple victims	100%	47.6%	14.1%	27.2%	11.1%
Multiple offenders	100%	65.5	10.8	18.0	5.7

Figure 11.3   Characteristics of homicides by city size, 1980–2008.

Source: Modified from Cooper, A., & Smith, E. L. (2011). *Homicide trends in the United States, 1980–2008. Annual rates for 2009–2010.* Washington, DC: U.S. Department of Justice, Office of Justice Programs, Bureau of Justice Statistics.

Phillips (2002) utilized 1990 data for 129 U.S. metropolitan areas to explore how structural characteristics affected racial and ethnic differences in homicide offending. She examined a host of structural variables including family structure as indicated by percent divorced or separated, socioeconomic factors such as percent with college education, percent families below poverty level, and percent males unemployed, industrial structure such as migration and percent employed in manufacturing, and cultural factors including state gun control laws, segregation, and region. Overall she found that all of the Hispanic to white differential in homicide could be reduced if the socioeconomic conditions of Hispanics were placed on par with whites. Similarly, the white homicide rate would increase by 53 percent if they faced the same structural disadvantages as those faced by Hispanics. About half of the black to white differential could be reduced if whites faced the same structural conditions as African Americans. The homicide would be reduced by 69 percent if African Americans had the same structural features as whites.

McCall, Parker, and MacDonald (2008) examined structural features and their association with homicide rates in 83 U.S. cities with populations greater than 100,000 residents at four time periods, 1970, 1980, 1990, and 2000. They found considerable variability in the effects of structural factors on homicide. In some periods, factors were strongly and positively linked to homicide whereas at other periods there were significant negative effects. For example, resource deprivation, the size of the black population, percent of families living below the poverty line, income inequality, percent of children living with both parents, the divorce rate of males, percent unemployed, and percent of the population between ages 15 to 29 were robustly associated with homicide from 1970 to 1980, but much less associated—and often negatively associated—with homicide rates from 1990 to 2000.

In a 40-year study of American cities, Beaulieu and Messner (2010) found that the number of divorced persons, especially males, was consistently related to homicide rates from 1960 to 2000. In addition, they found that the percentage of children who do not live with two parents—a proxy for divorce—was also significantly associated with homicide. Pyrooz (2012) examined gang and nongang homicides in 88 U.S. cities drawing on data from the National Gang Center, U. S. Census Bureau, FBI Uniform Crime Report, and Law Enforcement Management and Administrative Statistics. He found that cities with greater socioeconomic deprivation, less population heterogeneity, less residential stability, and older populations experienced more gang homicides. Structural factors were differentially associated with gang compared to nongang homicides.

Box 11.1   Structural Conditions, Race, and Serial Killers

A general tenor of structural theories of homicide is that socioeconomic conditions strongly influence individual behavior and that the sheer structural differences that whites and blacks face in the United States largely explains racial differences in crime. From the structural position, it is mostly class differences that structure race differences in violence generally and homicide specifically. To what degree do structural conditions influence serial homicide, however? In an interesting study, Lester and White (2014) compared 57 African American and 205 white serial killers on 83 variables, many of which are relevant to structural explanations of crime. The results were mixed.

There was greater disadvantage relating to family problems and poverty among black serial killers. They were more likely to have family histories of imprisonment, especially among mother and father, and to have less education. White serial killers had more social deprivation relating to abuse history, being placed for adoption, and being alone and isolated during childhood.

On 50 variables, there were not significant race differences in the backgrounds of black and white serial killers. These variables related to family relationships and dynamics, family psychiatric history, the offender's criminal history, the offender's psychiatric history and psychopathology, suicidal behavior, paraphilias, personality disorders, and sexual behaviors that were committed before, during, and after their homicides. Even the motives that offender's had, such as a mission orientation, having visions, power and control, or hedonism were comparable.

Taken together, the study reveals that an aggregate perspective like the structural approach cannot be ecologically broken down to the individual level. Moreover, the structural position was not really developed to explain more aberrant forms of homicide like serial murder. On the other hand, the study could also point to the limitations of the structural approach in that allegations of extensive difference by race are perhaps overstated. Indeed, the current study shows that white and black serial killers are much more alike than different.

Source: Lester, D., & White, J. (2014). A study of African American serial killers. *Journal of Ethnicity in Criminal Justice, 12*(4), 308–316.

In another examination of structural conditions, homicide, and gangs, Costanza and Helms (2012) examined homicides occurring in 154 U.S. cities. They found that greater population, concentrated disadvantage, percent of population that is divorced, and rate of gang activity were associated with higher city homicide rates. They also found that cities with more divorced males and more crime had worse gang problems. In other words, a variety of structural conditions are responsible for worsening crime in American cities, and in turn, these structural risk factors and crime contribute to the gang problem.

Although structural theories assert that structural factors are invariant, that is, they explain homicide regardless of who lives in cities, research has shown this is not necessarily the case. In a study of 125 U.S. cities, Ousey (1999) found that structural features, such as poverty, unemployment, income inequality, female-headed households, and deprivation are more strongly linked to homicide among whites than blacks. Similarly, Ousey and Augustine (2001) examined the relationship between concentrated disadvantage, racial inequality, and juvenile illegal drug market activity among white and black juveniles. They found that concentrated disadvantage and juvenile drug markets were related to juvenile homicide but only for whites. Other researchers have similarly found that structural conditions differential affect homicide offending across racial and ethnic group (Parker & Pruitt, 2000b). However, there is evidence these features are limited to an American context. In cross-national research, the effects for population size and density and divorce were inconsistent (Pridemore & Trent, 2010).

Stansfield and Parker (2013) examined structural predictors of homicides in 168 U.S. cities in 1980, 1990, and 2000 and disaggregated the analyses for whites and blacks. Like several other studies, they reported that different structural factors were associated for homicide among whites and blacks, and these effects varied across decade. Poverty, racial residential segregation, joblessness, and family inequality were at times significant and at other times, not significantly associated with homicide. Across all of these eras, however, percent divorced males was significantly linked to homicide.

McCall, Nieuwbeerta, Engen, and Thames (2012) examined structural explanations for homicide in 117 Eastern and Western European cities. They included several measures such as the deprivation index, unemployed males, percent foreign nationals, age composition as indicated by percent who are aged 15–24 years, population structure, and region. Overall, they found that population structure was significantly related to homicide across these cities. The greater the population size and density, the greater number of homicides, and these effects were found in cities in Austria, Czech Republic, Estonia, Finland, France, Germany, Hungary, Lithuania, Luxembourg, Latvia, Netherlands, Slovakia, and the United Kingdom.

Structural research identifies the tangible components, or nuts and bolts of a region, but there are also less tangible, human products of

© Andreas Meyer/Shutterstock, Inc.

Social capital is difficult to produce and sustain in impoverished cities with few social and economic opportunities. Instead, disorder, crime, and homicide tend to flourish.

these structures. An important example is social capital. **Social capital** broadly refers to relationships with people and organizations that foster collective action and produce personal, social, and economic benefits for individuals. Social capital encompasses civic engagement, social trust, volunteerism, political engagement and activism, workplace connections, altruism, volunteering and charity, and involvement with community organizations.

Several studies have examined the role of social capital in explaining homicide in the United States. Based on data from 99 geographic areas in the United States, Rosenfeld, Messner, and Baumer (2001) found that lower social capital was associated with more homicides even while controlling for population structure, resource deprivation, age composition, male divorce, unemployment, and southern region. Also, although homicide reduced social capital in these jurisdictions, the relationship was not significant. This means that low social capital drives homicide, and not vice versa.

There are also linkages between social capital and homicide from a global perspective. In a study of social capital and homicide in 39 nations, Lederman, Loayza, and Mendendez (2002) found that nations with less public trust have more homicides. Using data from the World Values Survey, Robbins and Pettinicchio (2012) found that social activism—the total number of collective activities in which a person participated—was negatively associated with homicide rates in 56 nations. The relationship between social capital and homicide is not always in the expected direction. For instance, Messner, Baumer, and Rosenfeld (2004) analyzed data from the Social Capital Benchmark Survey for 40 geographic areas in 29 U.S. states. They found that places with more social trust and more social activism had *higher* homicide rates, which was contrary to expectations. Comparatively, places with less social trust and less social activism had commensurately lower homicide rates.

A historical study of homicide in Finland from 1759 to 2000 also cast considerable doubt on the structural approach. Savolainen, Lehti, and Kivivuori (2008) observed that although Finland is a nation with a strong welfare state and considerable structural assets, it nevertheless has a high homicide rate. Social and structurally, it is similar to comparable nations including Denmark, Norway, Sweden, and The Netherlands. Finland's homicide rate began to diverge from these peer nations in the nineteenth century. They found that the Finnish welfare state did too good a job of providing for the needs of its citizens, but was unable to control the drinking behavior that associated many Finnish homicides. According to the authors, "the Finnish homicide problem is influenced by a drinking culture featuring multiple situational correlates of lethal violence. For the most part, this cultural current is regulated by a socially supportive welfare state" (Savolainen et al., 2008, p. 85).

Although a variety of structural conditions appear to be associated with homicide, it is important to note that macro causes of homicide are variable and complex (Blumstein & Rosenfeld, 1998). Thus perhaps more than other theoretical areas in criminology, there is conflicting evidence about the various roles of structural factors when understanding homicide. A final reason—and a sharp critique of the structural position generally—is that homicide does not occur at aggregate levels but is instead an individual-level phenomenon. As such, aggregating the characteristics of individuals to larger units of analysis likely distorts the data on who commits homicide and who is killed. Indeed, the structural perspective fares much better in research that uses the neighborhood level as the unit of analysis (Krivo

& Peterson, 2000; Peterson & Krivo, 1993, 2005). Such research consistently shows that neighborhoods with structural disadvantage, social isolation, many vacant homes, high unemployment, many renters, and young populations have much higher violence and homicide than neighborhoods without these structural deficits. In addition, the structural effects at the neighborhood level are invariant by race meaning the effects are similar for African Americans, whites, and Hispanics.

The next chapter offers another structural approach—social disorganization theory—one that has figured prominently in sociology and criminology for nearly a century.

CHAPTER 12

Homicide and the Social Disorganization Perspective

Social disorganization theory explains why homicide has remained consistent in specific neighborhoods in Chicago despite complete changes in the population of those neighborhoods.

Conceptual Background

In October 2014, Darren Vann was arrested for the murder of a young woman in the gritty, crime-ridden city Gary, Indiana. Once contacted by police, Vann admitted to killing the woman then promptly told authorities where six other murdered women could be found in various vacant homes in Gary. He intimated that he has been committing murder for two decades. After his arrest, records indicated that Vann was convicted of rape in Texas and served a 5-year prison term for that crime. Several jurisdictions in Indiana, Illinois, and other states are investigating Vann to see if he was potentially responsible for unsolved homicides in their locale. To date, the alleged victims in the case (Vann is scheduled for trial in summer 2015) appeared to be prostitutes who lived and worked in the blighted areas of Gary. In these places where crime and disorder reigned, there was an increased likelihood that Vann's crimes would be successfully committed because no one was around to report the crimes to the police. It was as if no one cared.

In recounting their childhood and the neighborhood(s) in which they grew up, serious violent offenders who commit homicide often tell a very similar story. Although there are of course some exceptions, the overwhelming majority of them were raised in troubled areas that are known for high levels of crime, how levels of disorder and blight, and high levels of street offenders who carry and use knives and guns. Offenders frequently perceive that the ecology of their neighborhood importantly shaped how they grew up, who they associated with, the types of activities that preferred and participated in, the types of activities they disliked and did not participate in, and where they thought they would end up in life. In other words, the neighborhood context is perceived to influence behavior especially criminal behavior. This is the basis logic of social disorganization theory.

According to **social disorganization theory**, neighborhoods characterized by high residential mobility, ethnic heterogeneity, and high poverty levels exhibit higher crime and delinquency rates. Analyzing delinquency data from Cook County, Illinois, over several decades (spanning the years 1900–1906, 1917–1923, and 1927–1933), Shaw and McKay (1942) discovered that socially disorganized areas contain higher proportions of families on public assistance, higher proportions of families who live in poverty, less expensive rents, fewer residents owning homes and therefore living on a more unstable, rent basis, high infant mortality, and large immigrant populations. They also noted that delinquency rates in disorganized neighborhoods were generally static even though their racial and ethnic composition was quite dynamic.

Their research laboratory of sorts was the city of Chicago which was and still is a destination city for immigrants. Immigrants and racial and ethnic groups would arrive at the bottom levels of the socioeconomic structure, assimilate to the culture and increase their social mobility, and then move out of the disorganized areas. This meant that crime, violence, and disorder appeared to be ecologically fixed while the population itself experienced considerable turnover.

According to Shaw and McKay (1971, p. 418), "It may be said, therefore, that the existence of a powerful system of criminal values and relationships in low-income urban areas is the product of a cumulative process extending back into the history of the community and of the city. It is related both to the general character of the urban world and to the fact that the population in these communities has long occupied a disadvantageous position."

Sociologists at the University of Chicago like Shaw and McKay, Robert Park, and Ernest Burgess utilized Burgess' (1925) a **concentric zone model** to divide the city into zones based upon real estate values, level of disorganization, crime and violence, and others. In the concentric zone model each zone of the city has a different function and relation to crime. In Zone I was the Loop or the central business district with the highest commercial real estate values and few residences. Zone II was the zone of transition that contained more industrial factories and an outer ring of tenement and rooming board houses. The **zone of transition** contained the worst neighborhoods in terms of vice, delinquency, violence, and disorder and personified social disorganization theory. It was in these neighborhoods that the transitory nature of the neighborhoods precluded the development and maintenance of the informal social control networks that thrive and facilitate prosocial behavior in better areas.

Zone III was the working class area where the skilled workers who worked in Zone II lived. Zone IV is the residential zone, and Zone V is the commuter zone; these reflect increasingly more affluent, white-collar residents and neighborhoods that are well organized and highly functioning.

Informal social control is the ability of family, friends, neighbors, and other acquaintances to monitor and regulate other's conduct through shared values and belief systems. It is separate from formal social control, which is law enforcement. In the concentric zone model, Zones III–V moved outward from the city center in progressively more affluent suburbs. Over time, generations would flee the zone of transition toward better neighborhoods in the suburbs. But they would also flee the high levels of violence and crime in the disorganized areas.

In somewhat more colorful language, Toby (1957, p. 13) has described the crime-inducing mechanisms that occur in socially disorganized neighborhoods, or what they were colloquially once referred to as—slums:

"A slum is a neighborhood where houses are old, overcrowded, and in need of major repairs. But it is also a place where people with incapacitating problems are concentrated. Preoccupied with their difficulties, the residents of a slum are simultaneously ineffective parents and apathetic citizens. The larger the concentration of distracted persons in a community, the less capable the community becomes for united resistance to anything-including crime. 'Horse rooms' and 'cat houses' are able to locate in slums for the same reason that youngsters are permitted to 'hang-out' on street corners: troubled people don't care. Thus, it is no accident when reformatory inmates come from backgrounds where neither family nor neighborhood influences posed a strong obstacle to taking other people's property."

Indeed, criminologists from the 1920s to the 1960s noticed that crime and violence seemed to concentrate in specific geographic areas, and wondered about the ecological effects of these neighborhoods. As Bullock (1955, p. 565) noted, "Crime lives best in the disorganized areas of cities." Across several decades of data in Chicago neighborhoods where the racial and ethnic composition changed yet crime and social problems remained stable to specific places, social disorganization theorists showcase the importance of the neighborhood. The essence of social disorganization theory is that the characteristics of neighborhoods are important determinants of human behavior, including antisocial forms of behavior such as homicide. What separates organized from disorganized neighborhoods is the strength and extent of various social controls. These include private social control such as family and friend relationships, parochial social control such as community organizations and the loose ties and mutual interests that stem from individuals involvement in organizations, and public social control which includes local government and local organizations (Bursik & Grasmick, 1993).

© katz/Shutterstock, Inc.

Broken windows theory powerfully shows how the enforcement of seemingly minor crimes can result in dramatic reductions in more serious crimes including homicide.

Decades later, another ecological theory that is somewhat related to social disorganization appeared on the criminological scene. In an article in *The Atlantic Monthly*, Wilson and Kelling (1982) advanced broken windows theory. **Broken windows theory** is an ecological theory which asserts that physical disorder contributes to a breakdown in formal and informal social controls that give rise to social disorder, including crime. Metaphorically, the title means that a broken window in an abandoned building has no one to repair it because there are no tenants or the business is no longer in operation. Over time, unrepaired buildings accumulate additional broken windows and other blights and these send an ecological message that no one is able or willing to repair them. In these types of environments, it appears no one is in charge and this engenders a sense of nihilism that produces similarly disordered behavior, such as nuisance offending, drug use, drug selling, prostitution, and related behaviors.

As crime, violence, and homicide increased across the late twentieth century, urban police departments increasingly shifted their focus from order maintenance, which formerly was a tenet of law enforcement, to attempting to solve serious crimes including homicide. The lack of attention to order maintenance partially facilitated the blight of American cities in the 1970s and 1980s. As Wilson (1983, p. 280) later observed, "dealing seriously with these 'small-time' offenders seems unimportant to busy, harassed officials [police]; yet the failure to attach unpleasant consequences to minor transgressions is a sure way of reinforcing the belief that such transgressions are costless and worth repeating." Consequently, Wilson and Kelling argued that police should enforce all of the laws, including the seemingly minor ones that pertain to maintaining order.

The application of broken windows theory is credited with the remarkable reductions in crime generally and homicide specifically across the nation. In New York with William Bratton as Police Commissioner and former federal prosecutor Rudolph Giuliani as Mayor, the police practiced such frequent social control that they helped to change community norms. Zero-tolerance policies for social disorder, however minor it seemed, resulted in a dramatically safer, cleaner, and more humane city.

Although social disorganization is an older theory in criminology, it has been conceptually updated with insights from biosocial criminology. Recently, Rocque, Posick, and Felix (2015) provided an overview of the effect of living in disadvantaged, social disorganized neighborhoods on the brain. The negative features of social disorganized neighborhoods create allostatic load, which is the physiological wear and tear that results from repeated exposure to stress. In times of stress or threat, the brain initiates a range of neuroendocrine responses to handle the threat. Over time, these disrupt the person's ability to appropriately respond to stress.

Over time, this produces a range of negative behavioral and attitudinal responses including altered sensitivity to threats, stressful hypervigiliance (the tendency to perceive that every situation is dangerous or threatening), impulsivity, and a low threshold for using violence. These responses are modified by the subcultural norms in disorganized neighborhoods and culminate in the advocacy of violence, and the use of violence. In other words, social disorganization theory gets "under the skin" of the residents of disadvantaged areas and likely produces physiological processes that enable violent conduct.

Empirical Linkages to Homicide

Many investigators have studied the effect of neighborhood structure on homicide and social disorganization theory has a long tradition of in studies of homicide. In a seminal study, Bullock (1955) found that census tracts in Houston, Texas, that were mostly black or Hispanic, had low median educational levels, had high unemployment, had workforces of mostly laborers, and where buildings were in need of major repairs also had more homicides.

Bullock (1955, p. 575), noted that "The basic ecological process of urban segregation centralizes people of like kind, throws them together at common institutions, occasions their association on levels of intimacy, and thereby paves the way for conflicts out of which homicides occur." In Chicago neighborhoods, indicators of social disorganization are among the most robust predictors of homicide, especially gang-related homicide and this conclusion is based on both quantitative (Curry & Spergel, 1988) and qualitative analyses (Mares, 2010).

Social organization theory is useful for understanding violence across the United States in cities other than Chicago. Kubrin (2003) linked neighborhood disadvantage to various forms of homicide based on data from St. Louis. Indeed, in some severely disadvantaged communities, homicide is viewed as a form of self-defense whereby retaliatory homicides are viewed as appropriate responses to conflicts due to perceptions that the police are ineffective to solve problems (Kubrin & Weitzer, 2003). Also in St. Louis, various forms of social disorganization have been linked to diverse types of homicide, including murder relating to domestic violence, other felony offending, and general altercations (Kubrin & Herting, 2003).

Based on homicide data from Miami and San Diego, Nielsen, Lee, and Martinez (2005) found that neighborhoods with greater residential instability had more expressive and instrumental homicides in both cities. In addition, social disorganization factors were more strongly correlated with homicide among African Americans than Hispanics. Indeed, socially disorganized neighborhoods tend to have higher numbers of gang members, and gang members often perpetrate violent crimes with firearms. For instance, a recent study found that neighborhoods in St. Louis, Missouri, with the most gang members also have the most gun assaults, which often result attempted or completed homicides (Huebner, Martin, Moule, Pyrooz, & Decker, 2014).

In their study of homicide victims compared to nonhomicide victims in Maryland neighborhoods, Dobrin, Lee, and Price (2005) found that neighborhoods characterized by poverty, low education, unemployment, and mostly female-headed households were more likely to have murder victims. In an eight-year study of homicide in Los Angeles County, investigators found that social disorganization features of neighborhoods, including population density, racial and ethnic concentration, high school dropout rates, and unemployment explained 90 percent of the homicide rate (Robinson, Boscardin, George, Senait, Heslin, & Blumenthal, 2009). Griffiths and Tita's (2009) study of homicide in public housing developments in Los Angeles is illustrative of the geographic clustering of individuals characterized by various personal and social deficits. The five public housing developments in Southeast Los Angeles in their study were characterized by active gangs within the housing development, high homicide rates, high levels of female-headed households, and between 55 and 70 percent of households living in poverty, and overall residential instability.

The theory is also applicable to international cities. For example, Vilalta and Muggah (2014) recently found that population born in another state, residential instability, vacant housing, homes with no internal plumbing, and young population were predictive of homicides in Ciudad Juarez, Mexico, which is ground zero of the drug cartel violence that has plagued Mexico over the past several decades.

Drawing on 10 years of homicide data from the El Paso Police Department, Emerick, Curry, Collins, and Rodriguez (2014) examined the role of social disorganization factors in explaining homicide. They found that various neighborhood characteristics were associated with homicide, but the relationships depending on the type of homicide. For expressive homicides, such as domestic disputes or other arguments, concentrated disadvantage and residential instability were significant. For instrumental homicides, where there was a clear motive for the killing, residential instability was significant. For gang-related homicides, concentrated disadvantage and neighborhoods with a large Hispanic population were significant.

Homicide types are not the only data that can be disaggregated. Neighborhood factors can also be used to examine racial and ethnic differences in homicide. Chauhan and colleagues (2011) examined gun homicide in New York City from 1990 to 1999. They found dramatic racial and ethnic differences across the study period. In 1990, the black gun-homicide rate was 35 per 100,000. The rate for Hispanics was 30 per 100,000 and the rate for whites was 3 per 100,000. As the great crime decline began in 1993, the differences began to reduce. By 1999, the black gun-homicide rate was 10 per 100,000, the Hispanic rate was nearly 5 per 100,000 and the white race was about 1 per 100,000. In addition, they found that neighborhoods with higher cocaine consumption were associated with more black homicides whereas greater firearm availability was associated with Hispanic homicides. No neighborhood factors were significantly predictive of white homicides (Chauhan, Cerdá, Messner, Tracy, Tardiff, & Galea, 2011).

In his review of structural theories of homicide, Pridemore (2002) noted that social disorganization constructs were among the most consistent predictors of lethal violence. Indeed, significant effects between social disorganization variables and homicide have also been found in locations outside the United States. A study using data from the Dutch Homicide Monitor from 1966 to 2003 found that neighborhoods with greater social cohesion and less socioeconomic disadvantage had fewer homicides (Nieuwbeerta, McCall, Elffers, & Wittebrood, 2008).

Although immigration was a central concern of early social disorganization theorists, subsequent research has consistently shown that immigrants and related measures are negatively associated with homicide. For example, Graif and Sampson (2009) analyzed data from the U.S. Census and the Neighborhood Change Data Base to examine the effects of immigration on homicide in Chicago neighborhoods. They found that immigration has either no effect on homicide, or serves as a protective factor against homicide. In neighborhoods with more immigrants and fewer homicides, there were nevertheless other correlates of violence including high concentrated disadvantage, high poverty, and high African American population yet the immigrant population seemed to buffer these risk factors. In addition, neighborhoods with greater language diversity—essentially another proxy for immigrant presence—was consistently linked to lower homicide. In another study of Chicago neighborhoods, Vélez (2009) hypothesized and found that new immigrants arrive in very disadvantaged and dangerous neighborhoods. After arriving, they reinvigorate local economic opportunity structures and social networks which contribute to revitalizes neighborhood organizations, and thus, fewer homicides.

Neighborhood factors implicated by social disorganization theory have also been found to discriminate who among serious juvenile delinquents becomes a homicide offender. To illustrate, DeLisi, Piquero, and Cardwell (2014) used data from the Pathways to Desistance study, a longitudinal study of 1,354 serious youthful offenders. Even though this cohort displayed an array of risk factors, just 1.3 percent of the sample, or eighteen youth, was charged with a homicide offense. Moreover, only five out of 43 risk factors significantly predicted homicide status: age, intelligence, exposure to violence, perceptions of community disorder, and gun carrying. The latter three variables are characteristic of socially disorganized communities with high levels of concentrated disadvantage and violent crime.

The theory has also proven useful for understanding the outcomes of homicide cases. Drawing on homicide case files of 414 victims killed by 534 homicide offenders in Cleveland, Ohio, Regoeczi, and Jarvis (2013) found that socially disorganized neighborhoods characterized by concentrated disadvantage and residential instability hindered the effective prosecution of homicide cases. Basically, social disorganization reduced collective efficacy.

Collective efficacy is the informal social control mechanisms in a neighborhood characterized by mutual trust and a neighborly willingness to intervene for the common good. Examples of collective efficacy include neighbors watching children play in the neighborhood to ensure their safety and wellbeing, watching a neighbor's house while they are out of town, and dissuading youth from congregating at night. Neighborhoods with low collective efficacy produce a fear of retaliation for cooperating with the police and increase the use of self-help, street justice to resolve disputes. They found that these factors resulting in fewer arrests in open homicide cases and fewer successful prosecutions. The following case narrative illustrates the relationship between these variables:

"The 19-year old male was shot with a handgun outdoors in the early morning hours. A small bag of marijuana was found in his pocket. The victim was known to sell drugs and have a temper. The victim also had a reputation for violence and was believed to have been involved in a homicide. He was described as having a number of enemies, leading to a substantial number of suspects in this case. The police were unable to develop any solid leads in the case in spite of a number of plausible suspects and possible witnesses in the shooting" (Regoeczi & Jarvis, 2013, p. 999).

Socially disorganized neighborhoods tend to have low collective efficacy in part because high rates of crime and violence destroy the trust among residents. A study using data from the Project on Human Development in Chicago Neighborhoods found that collective efficacy was significantly and inversely related to homicide (Sampson, Raudenbush, & Earls, 1997). Locations with lower collective efficacy experienced much higher homicide rates than locations with greater collective efficacy among residents. The collective efficacy, violence, and homicide link has been documented in other American cities (Krivo & Peterson, 1996; Lee & Ousey, 2005; Regoeczi & Jarvis, 2013), cities in the United Kingdom (Odgers, Moffitt, Tach, Sampson, Taylor, Matthews, & Caspi, 2009) in addition to Chicago (Browning, 2002; Morenoff, Sampson, & Raudenbush, 2001).

Box 12.1   Broken Windows Policing and Homicide…and Politics

Wilson and Kelling's (1982) broken windows theory is the rare type of criminological theory that not only breaks through the cloistered world of academia into the mainstream, but also found its way into criminal justice practice. In the 1970s, 1980s, and 1990s, the notion that crime, violence, and disorder could be reduced was almost a daydream, but the simple, earnest policy impulse to allow the police to become more assertive in their enforcement of nuisance crimes resulted in tremendous benefits. Almost overnight, large cities began to enjoy a quality of life and sense of public safety that seemed impossible just a few years earlier (Bratton & Knobler, 2009).

Of course, success often carries with it criticism. Many in the criminology community were skeptical that police practices were producing such reductions in homicide. Although criminologists were technically correct that police practices were not the *only* reason why neighborhoods and subways were now civil, clean, and safe, zero-tolerance for disorder was a major contributor. It is likely that many in academic criminology were ideologically opposed to the policies given their disproportionate liberal leaning and the unquestionable conservative, law and order nature of the policies.

In a provocative book, Mac Donald (2003) provided comparative data that examined homicides, police shootings, and public approval of the police during the mayoral terms of Ed Koch and David Dinkins to the first term of Rudolph Giuliani, a former federal prosecutor. For example, the changes include:

- 75 percent reduction in gun homicides (2,200 to less than 683).
- 25 percent reduction in officer use of firearms.
- 67 percent reduction in shootings per officer.
- In 1993, the NYPD made 266,313 arrests and committed 23 justifiable homicides.
- In 1998, the NYPD made 403,659 arrests and committed 19 justifiable homicides.
- In 1990 compared to 1998, there was a 250 percent reduction in fatal police shootings per officer.
- From 1994 to 1996, there was a 20 percent reduction in civilian complaints per officer.
- In the spring of 1996, an Empire State Survey found that 73 percent of New Yorkers had a positive view of police, compared with 37 percent in June 1992.
- By 1998, a federal Bureau of Justice Statistics survey showed 84 percent of New Yorkers age 16 and older were satisfied with the police, including 77 percent of black New Yorkers.

- In 1998, the police performed 138,887 stop and frisks with 85percent of them on blacks and Hispanics—less than the 89percent of suspects identified as black and Hispanic by victims.
- Assuming that police stopped mostly young males, and that they stopped everybody just once, that would mean that they stopped just 11.6 percent of all minority males between ages 10 and 45.

In other words, the policing changes were well-received by the citizens of New York irrespective of the reception of criminologists. Indeed, broken windows theory is now a part of the public lexicon as an example of an ecological theory with theoretical and real associations with homicide.

Sources: Bratton, W., & Knobler, P. (2009). *The turnaround: How America's top cop reversed the crime epidemic.* New York, NY: Random House; Mac Donald, H. (2003). *Are cops racist? How the war against the police harms black Americans.* Chicago, IL: Ivan R. Dee; Wilson, J. Q., & Kelling, G. L. (1982). Broken windows. *Atlantic Monthly, 249*(3), 29–38.

Considerable research attention has also been focused on policing strategies relating to broken windows theory and their effects on reducing homicide. In a study of New York City Police precincts spanning 1988–2001, Rosenfeld, Fornango, and Rengifo (2007) found that precincts servicing neighborhoods with higher disorder, more active drug markets, and that deployed more police officers were significantly likely to practice order-maintenance policing where even small municipal and nuisance violations were heavily enforced. They found that this type of policing resulted in significant lower homicide rates. Moreover, the effects withstood the significant effects of drug market and disorder, both of which were positively associated with homicide rates.

A study of 74 New York City precincts from 1990 to 1999 produced similar results. Messner and colleagues (2007) found that increases in the misdemeanor arrest rate corresponded to fewer total homicides and these effects were significant despite controlling for other precinct characteristics including the felony arrest rate, cocaine use changes, percent male, percent under age 35 years, firearm availability, percent black, socioeconomic status, and change in police manpower. In addition, more misdemeanor arrests for quality of life types of offenses also resulted in significantly fewer gun-related homicides (Messner, Galea, Tardiff, Tracy, Bucciarelli, et al., 2007). This conforms with the logic of broken windows theory, that stopping offenders from jumping turnstiles in the subway, from loitering and causing disturbances, from drug use, drug selling, and prostitution, and from other annoying crimes also corresponds to offenders who carry guns and commit more severe offenses, including homicide.

A related and more recent study indicated more specifically how additional misdemeanor arrests can produce net declines in the homicide rate. Cerdá, Tracy, Messner, Vlahov, Tardiff, and Galea (2009) found that an increase of 5,000 misdemeanor arrests in a precinct with 100,000 people was associated with a reduction of 3.5 gun-related homicides. In addition, increased misdemeanor arrests also produced lower physical disorder which has also been linked to various crimes. What is impressive about this study is that 14 other social disorganization and structural related variables were also included in the model and controlled. These included change in percent clean sidewalks, change in percent receiving public assistance, percent male, percent young, percent black, percent Hispanic, percent foreign-born, concentrated poverty, change in felony arrest rate, change in firearm availability, and change in incarceration rate.

As is the case with any theoretical perspective, there is also occasional negative evidence or null effects. For example, Diem and Pizarro (2010) examined cities with populations greater than 100,000 residents and used the FBI Supplementary Homicide Reports to examine the effects of neighborhood characteristics and various family homicides. They found that social disorganization was significantly but negatively associated with total homicides, family homicides, intimate partner homicides, filicides, and siblicides. In a study of homicide in Newark, New Jersey, and Indianapolis, Indiana, DeJong, Pizarro, and McGarrell (2011) found no relationship between social disorganization and intimate partner homicide.

The next section of the book moves outside the traditional theories of criminology into interdisciplinary and psychiatric perspectives on homicide. The role of personality in the development of homicidal behavior is examined in the next chapter.

Section II

Interdisciplinary and Psychiatric Perspectives

CHAPTER 13

Homicide and the Personality Perspective

© kwest/Shutterstock, Inc.

Antisocial persons including homicide offenders have been shown to have specific personality traits that facilitate their problem behaviors.

Conceptual Background

A fascinating feature about personality is that everyone has one, but no two are exactly alike. **Personality** is a set of traits that generally typify the stable and relatively consistent ways that a person behaves, thinks, and feels.

Like those in the general population, criminal offenders also have unique personality features, and so do homicide offenders. This chapter highlights the scientific study of personality and the particular set of personality features that are most consistently associated with criminal behavior including homicide.

Before delving into that literature, a case study of a homicide offender with perhaps the worst personality in history is examined. Carl Panzram was a career criminal and serial murderer who was active during the first decades of the twentieth century until his execution in 1930. An incorrigible delinquent as a child, Panzram was sent to the Minnesota State Training School by his parents, a facility where he was repeatedly beaten and tortured. After his release, Panzram became a transient and chronic offender who drifted around the United States and other countries committing crime and being placed in jails and prisons.

During his childhood and in many of his incarcerations, Panzram was sodomized and at times gangraped by other inmates. These experiences instilled in him an extraordinary rage and deep misanthropic hatred of all humanity. He would get his revenge by committing a range of crimes and raping hundreds of boys and other men both during his crime sprees and during his various periods of imprisonment. Under a variety of aliases, Panzram was imprisoned in at least 10 states in the United States. Panzram estimated that he raped more than 1,000 males and murdered 21 people during his life and expressed that he did this to simply show his power and contempt for them.

His derision for humanity knew no bounds. In the 1920s, Panzram traveled to Africa where he hired eight male natives to help him hunt crocodiles. During this trip, Panzram is said to have raped and murdered all eight of them, and promptly fed their bodies to the crocodiles (Schechter, 2003). Ultimately, Panzram was sentenced to a lengthy term in federal prison in the United States, where he promised to murder at the first opportunity. He succeeded, and killed another inmate in 1929. He was subsequently sentenced to death, and hanged in 1930. Panzram exemplified the monstrous public image of a homicide offender, and was mean, antagonistic, and fueled by a limitless sense of fury about others.

One of the most influential and empirically examined structural models of personality is the **Five Factor Model of Personality**. The Five Factor Model is a structural model of personality that contains five dimensions: openness to experience, conscientiousness, extraversion, agreeableness, and neuroticism. Beginning in the 1930s with research that examined adjectives used to describe personality traits, many psychologists contributed to the development of the Five Factor Model. It became a more formal structural model in the late 1980s and early 1990s (see Digman, 2002). Although multiple instruments are used to measure the constructs in the Five Factor Model, the predominant is the NEO-PI (Costa & McCrae, 1985, 1997) and the newer NEO-PI-R (Costa & McCrae, 1992). The five dimensions of personality are:

1. **Neuroticism** refers to the chronic level of emotional adjustment and instability. It includes facet scales for anxiety, angry hostility, depression, self-consciousness, impulsiveness, and vulnerability. Persons who are high scoring on neuroticism are prone to psychological distress.

2. **Extraversion** refers to the quantity and intensity of preferred interpersonal interactions, activity level, need for stimulation, and capacity for joy. High scorers are known as extraverts whereas low scorers are known as introverts. It includes facet scales for warmth, gregariousness, assertiveness, activity, excitement seeking, and positive emotions.

3. **Openness to experience** involves the appreciation and seeking of experiences. Open individuals are characterized as curious, imaginative, willing to have novel experiences, and open to varied emotional experiences. Closed individuals are characterized as conventional, conservative, dogmatic, rigid, and behaviorally set in their ways. It includes facet scales for fantasy, aesthetics, feelings, actions, ideas, and values.

4. **Agreeableness** refers to the kinds of interactions a person has along a continuum from compassion to antagonism. High scorers on agreeableness are good natured, trusting, soft-hearted, helping, and altruistic. Low scorers tend to be cynical, rude, uncooperative, irritable, and manipulative. It includes facet scales for trust, straightforwardness, altruism, compliance, modesty, and tender-mindedness.

5. **Conscientiousness** captures the degree of organization, persistence, control, and motivation in goal-directed behavior. High scorers are organized, reliable, hardworking, self-directed, ambitious, and persevering. Low scorers are aimless, unreliable, lazy, careless, negligent, and hedonistic. It includes facet scales for competence, order, dutifulness, achievement striving, self-discipline, and deliberation.

One of the fascinating things about personality is that each person's personality is distinct and reflects a unique combination of traits. Some aspects of our personality are viewed favorably by our self and others, whereas other aspects of our personality are considered more negatively. In other words, there are things that we like about our personality, and features that we do not. At times, those negative features of one's personality rise to the level of being problematic in a clinical sense. Something that should be clear based on the many case studies of homicide offenders in this book is that many homicide offenders strongly dislike themselves and are conflicted about various components of their personality and self. These personality features are usually unresolved and can play an important role in ultimately driving the offender's homicidal conduct.

Another influential personality model is Eysenck's PEN model. Over a long career, Eysenck developed a model of personality that connected the biological and genetic foundations of personality features to personality manifestations to behaviors impacted by these personality features (Eaves, Eysenck, & Martin, 1989; Eysenck, 1967, 1977; Eysenck & Eysenck, 1985). The outcome of this work was the PEN Model. The **PEN model** indicates three primary factors of personality: psychoticism, extraversion, and neuroticism.

Psychoticism is a personality factor that is comprised of nine lower-order traits. These are aggressiveness, coldness, egocentricity, impersonality, impulsivity, antisociality, unempathic, creativity, and tough-mindedness.

Extraversion is a personality factor that is comprised of nine lower-order traits. These are sociability, liveliness, activity, assertiveness, sensation-seeking, carefree, dominant, surgent, and venturesome.

Neuroticism is a personality factor that is comprised of nine lower-order traits. These are anxiousness, depressed, guilty feelings, low self-esteem, tension, irrationality, shyness, moodiness, and emotionality.

Of the three dimensions, the psychoticism dimension is the one that most directly corresponds to the personality features of antisocial individuals. Indeed, the traits inherent to psychoticism seem to personify the image of a person who is prone to violence and who would resort to homicide given an impulsive, selfish, cold personality style.

A very different personality model is not intended to be general and capture the personality of the general population, but is instead meant to capture the very narrow universe of homicide offenders who are sadistic and psychopathic (see Chapter 19). Stone (1993, 1998) developed a personality model that measured gradations of evil. **Stone's gradations of evil model** assesses the level of inhumanity of evil of a homicide offender as a function of their behavior, sadism, and psychopathy.

The gradations of evil scale ranges from 1 to 22 with each increasing number reflecting a more evil type of homicide offender:

1. Those who kill but are not murderers, such as those who kill in self-defense.
2. Jealous lovers who commit crimes of passion and are not psychopathic.

3. Willing companions of killers who are somewhat antisocial.
4. Killed in self-defense but were provocative to victim.

And

20. Torture-murderers
21. Psychopaths preoccupied with torture in the extreme but not known to have also committed murder.
22. Psychopathic torture-murderers the majority but not all are serial murderers.

Stone's model has not been widely examined or tested in large part because it is so difficult to find homicide offenders in traditional criminological samples, and it is even more challenging to find adequate variance to encompass those who commit murder in particularly sadistic ways.

Although specific personality features are linked to problem behaviors, a personality does not clinically became a problem until it rises to the level of personality disorder. A **personality disorder** is an enduring pattern of inner experience and behavior that deviates markedly from the expectations of the individual's culture. The pattern is manifested in two or more areas including cognition, affectivity, interpersonal functioning, and impulse control.

There are five additional guidelines for diagnostic criteria for a personality disorder. First, the enduring pattern of the personality is inflexible and pervasive across a broad range of personal and social situations. This means that the basic attributes of the personality are apparently across contexts. Second, the enduring pattern leads to clinically significant distress or impairment in social, occupational, or other important areas of functioning. In other words, the personality creates problems in the family, at school, at work, among peers, and among other people in general social interaction. Third, the pattern is stable and of long duration and its onset can be traced back to earlier life stages. Fourth, the enduring pattern is not better accounted for as a manifestation of consequences of another mental disorder. Fifth, the enduring pattern is not due to the direct physiological effects of a substance, such as medication or a general medical condition, such as head trauma.

In the *Diagnostic and Statistical Manual of Mental Disorders*, three types or clusters of personality disorder have been delineated. **Cluster A Personality Disorders** are viewed as odd or eccentric personality disorders and include three kinds. Paranoid Personality Disorder is characterized by a pervasive pattern of distrust and suspiciousness of others such that their motives are interpreted as malevolent. Schizoid Personality Disorder is characterized by a pervasive pattern of detachment from social relationships and restricted range of expression of emotions in interpersonal settings. Schizotypal Personality Disorder is characterized by a pervasive pattern of social and interpersonal deficits marked by acute discomfort with and reduced capacity for close relationships, cognitive or perceptual distortions, and eccentricities in behavior.

Cluster B Personality Disorders are viewed as dramatic or emotional personality disorders and include four kinds. Antisocial personality disorder is characterized by a pervasive pattern of disregard for and violation of the rights of others. Borderline personality disorder is characterized by a pervasive pattern of instability of interpersonal relationships, self-image, affect, and marked impulsivity. Histrionic personality disorder is characterized by a pervasive pattern of excessive emotionality and attention seeking. Narcissistic personality disorder is characterized by a pervasive pattern of grandiosity in fantasy and behavior, need for admiration, and lack of empathy.

Cluster C Personality Disorders are viewed as anxious or fearful personality disorders and there are three kinds. Avoidant personality disorder is characterized by a pervasive pattern of social inhibition, feelings of inadequacy, and hypersensitivity to negative evaluation. Dependent personality disorder is characterized by a pervasive and excessive need to be taken care of that leads to submissive and clinging behavior and fears of separation. Obsessive-compulsive personality disorder is characterized by a pervasive pattern of preoccupation with orderliness, perfectionism, and mental and interpersonal control at the expense of flexibility, openness, and efficiency.

In psychiatry, Sadistic personality disorder (it was discontinued in the *DSM* after the third edition) is the most germane to homicide offenders. **Sadistic personality disorder** is a pervasive pattern of cruel, demeaning, and aggressive behavior beginning in early adulthood and indicated by four of the following criteria. These include:

- Uses physical cruelty or violence for purpose of establishing dominance in a relationship.
- Humiliates or demeans others in the presence of others.
- Has treated or disciplined someone under his or her control unusually harshly.
- Is amused by or takes pleasure in the suffering of others.
- Has lied for the purpose of harming or inflicting pain on others.
- Rules by intimidation or terror.
- Restricts the autonomy of people with whom he or she has a close relationship.
- Is fascinated by violence, weapons, martial arts, injury, or torture (Stone, Butler, & Young, 2009).

Several scholars have reviewed the criminological literature to see if specific features of the personality are more relevant to crime. For example, Miller and Lynam (2001) examined four structural models of personality including the Five Factor Model and Eysenck's PEN model among 59 studies and found the strongest evidence linking low agreeableness and low conscientiousness to crime. In their meta-analysis, Samuel and Widiger (2008) investigated the Five Factor Model and its facets among the personality disorders using data from 16 samples. Although there were many significant effects among the personality disorders, the most pertinent were for antisocial personality disorder (Chapter 24). It is characterized most strongly by low levels of agreeableness and low levels of conscientiousness.

Jones, Miller, and Lynam (2011) reviewed 53 studies to explore the association between the Five Factor Model and outcome measures for antisocial behavior and aggression. Overall, effect sizes for three of the five factors were significantly associated with antisocial behavior. There was a positive link between neuroticism and antisocial behavior indicating that people who experience greater levels of negative emotionality, such as anger and hostility are likely to commit crime. Larger effect sizes were found for agreeableness and conscientiousness, with more antagonistic and less conscientious domains associated with antisocial behavior. All five factors were significantly associated with aggression. The direction for neuroticism, agreeableness, and conscientiousness was the same for aggression. In addition, extraversion and openness to experience were negatively correlated with aggression. In sum, meta-analyses make clear that personality features are significantly related to crime, aggression, and delinquency.

The central conclusion from these works is that criminal offenders have personalities that are largely comprised of negative emotions such as anger and hostility. These negative emotions facilitate conflict and often produce opportunities for violence. With low agreeableness, offenders are also antagonistic toward other people, which is an underlying condition of most of the dynamics of homicide advanced by theories in this book. Empirical linkages between personality and homicide are examined next.

Empirical Linkages to Homicide

Some caveats are in order when considering the interrelationship between personality and homicide. First, there is a separate personality disorder—antisocial personality disorder—that has its own literature and has been

Those who are very low scoring on agreeableness and conscientiousness are significantly more likely to be aggressive, antisocial, and violent.

extensively studied for its relation to crime, violence, and homicide, indeed it constitutes Chapter 23. Second, psychopathy is also a personality disturbance with a broad relation to homicide, and it too requires its own chapter (Chapter 19). Thus with thus constructs removed, the literature on basic personality features and homicide is smaller and more fragmented.

Anecdotally, there is straightforward relation between various personality features and involvement in homicide as both offender and victim. Indeed, many of the conceptual areas in this book could be effectively reduced or characterized to personality traits. For instance, the regional explanation of homicide and the code of the street are cultural explanations of homicide, but both also reflect impulsivity, temper, anger, and hostility. Indeed, in an editorial critique of the code of the street, DeLisi (2014a) suggested that persons who are purported to advocate the street code are actually simply antisocial individuals with a set of antisocial traits that result in impulsive, reactive homicides.

Blackburn (1971) reported evidence of four personality types of murderers that generally centered on the role of impulsivity and self-control. Only one group was able to regulate its impulses, these were offenders who were overcontrolled and had higher levels of internalizing symptoms. The other groups were characterized as paranoid-aggressive, depressed-inhibited, and psychopathic. All of them presented with problems with impulse control and self-regulation deficits that was mixed with diverse forms of other psychopathology.

Homicide also reflects a deeply pathological manifestation of narcissism. Mundane homicides reflect at the most fundamental level a desire of one person to impose his wants over another. This can be as simply as ending an argument, stopping another person from talking, or retaliating against someone who looked at you the "wrong" way. In cases of sexual homicide, the act of murder (and rape) reflects what the offender wants to do to the victim. In these cases, the selfish desire to rape and kill is so strong to the offender, that the desire trumps the victim's right to live. Perhaps nothing could be more selfish, self-centered, and self-motivated.

Impulsivity is a cardinal personality feature because it is broadly linked to a multitude of problem behaviors that directly relate to antisocial behavior including homicide and indirectly to other developmental problems that are the building blocks in the lives of serious offenders. For example, the most impulsive and irritable children develop multiple negative behaviors that impair their development with peers, at school, at home, and with others and also commit the worst and most varied criminal acts (Vaughn, DeLisi, Beaver, & Wright, 2009). That research profile is fully consistent with the childhood experiences of many homicide offenders. Offenders whose behavioral style is predominated by impulsivity are much more likely to commit an assortment of criminal behaviors, engage in serious violence, and be chronic offenders (Beaver, DeLisi, Vaughn, & Wright, 2010; DeLisi & Vaughn, 2008; Vaughn, Beaver, & DeLisi, 2009). Indeed, there are greater than 400 percent more likely to be a violent career criminal.

Offenders are also low in agreeableness which is defined as antagonistic. This means that their personality features are geared to be antagonistic and ready for conflict with others. The principle of homophily suggests that humans tend to associate with others who are similar to them, thus antagonistic people seek out antagonistic others. In these cases, two mutually combative people are prone to get into conflicts, fights, and other disputes that could result in a homicide.

While personality features have been linked to homicide offending, a significantly more robust association is found for *personality disorders* and homicide (recall earlier comments about the salience of Antisocial Personality Disorder and psychopathy). Diverse studies have shown that personality disorder pervades homicide offenders,

Box 13.1   The Boston Boy Fiend

Although gruesome homicide is sometimes believed to be a modern phenomenon, it is unfortunately timeless. One reason for it is that if homicidal motivation and propensity stems from basic personality features, then homicide would be an unfortunate byproduct of particularly negative personality features.

Negative personality features certainly characterized Jesse Harding Pomeroy. In the late nineteenth century, Pomeroy had the distinction of being sentenced to death at the age of 14! Pomerory was a disturbed child who at the age of 12 and 13 abducted, molested, and physically and sexually tortured young boys. For these crimes, he was sentenced to the Lyman School for Boys. There he was also noteworthy for his sadistic and unsavory personality features. Once, a large snake found its way into a recreation area where Pomeroy and the other wards were congregating. Convinced that Pomeroy would take care of the problem, a staff worker gave Pomeroy a large stick and instructed him to kill the snake so that it would not harm anyone. Indeed, Pomeroy did bludgeon the snake to death, and did so while working himself into a violent, hypnotic, quasi-sexual frenzy. The staff worker concluded from this event that Pomeroy should never be released from custody.

But he was, in 1874, pardoned and released at age 14. Within 2 months of his release, Pomeroy murdered a 10-year-old girl and a 4-year-old boy. For these crimes, he was convicted and sentenced to death. His death sentence was commuted to life, and Pomeroy attempted to escape from prison many times. For this, he spent several decades in solitary confinement. He died in prison at age 72.

Throughout his life, Pomeroy minimized his problem behaviors, blamed others for his crimes, and was generally antagonistic, self-centered, and unconscientious. Late in life, his sentence was modified again, and Pomeroy advocated for a pardon (which was not granted). At this point, he said, "I am glad of this opportunity to show the world that I can behave myself because it may lead to further consideration and possibly a pardon. I know people think I am some sort of animal thirsting for blood. I know that they think I will pounce on the first living thing I see, human or animal, and try to kill it. I have a normal mind. I am not deranged. I will prove it to you all" (Schechter, 2000, p. 287).

Source: Schechter, H. (2000). *Fiend: The shocking true story of America's youngest serial killer.* New York, NY: Pocket True Crime/Simon and Schuster.

and the disorders are greater and more severe among more severe kill-ers, such as sexual homicide offenders (Malmquist, 2006; Myers, Chan, Vo, & Lazarou, 2010).

Drawing on a sample of 22 juvenile sexual homicide offenders, Myers and colleagues (2010) found that the prevalence of personality disorders was exceptionally high. Forty-three percent had schizotypal personality disorder, 33 percent had schizoid personality disorder, 24 percent had paranoid personality disorder, 33 percent had sadistic per-sonality disorder, 14 percent had borderline personality disorder, and 14 percent had avoidant personality disorder. An additional offender also presented with narcissistic , obsessive-compulsive, and dependent personality disorders. The juvenile sexual homicide offenders averaged three personality disorders. In addition, juvenile homicide offenders were characterized by high levels of anger and hostility, which is likely a primary emotional motivator of violent and homicidal behavior (Myers & Monaco, 2000).

Johnson and Becker (1997) presented nine clinical cases of adoles-cents who presented with intense homicidal ideation and in some cases had already attempted homicide. Two of the youth self-reported a com-pleted homicide. All of these youth endorsed fantasies of becoming serial homicide offenders. Many had psychiatric problems including depression, ADHD, conduct disorder, and substance abuse. Many of them had been sexually abused at a young age, and these experiences distorted their psy-chosexual development and their personality development.

A recurrent theme among the youth was intrusive, almost obsessive thoughts and fantasies about committing murder, and in some cases, committing suicide. They killed and tortured various animals indeed one of the youth killed more than 10 animals per day. Their personali-ties were dominated by deep antagonism and loathing of other humans, narcissistic obsessions, by a complete lack of empathy for their victims and fantasized victims, and intense and often unstable negative emo-tionality. Their fantasy lives furthered the pathology of their personality and served to distance themselves from the rights and feelings of others.

Using forensic data for 166 homicidal and 56 nonhomicidal sex offend-ers in Germany, Koch, Berner, Hill, and Briken (2011) found that 80 percent of sexual murders were diagnosed with personality disorders and nearly 40 percent were sexually sadistic. The most prevalent personality disor-ders were schizoid, antisocial, borderline, and avoidant. They averaged nearly five psychiatric disorders compared to two for the nonhomicidal sex offenders. Interestingly, the homicide offenders were not significantly more psychopathic than the sex offenders. A subsequent study of the 166 homicide offenders found that 3.3 percent of them would murder again following release from custody. In addition, 23 percent were rearrested for another sexual offense and more than 18 percent were rearrested for other violent crimes, such as assault, robbery, or kidnapping (Hill, Habermann, Klusmann, Berner, & Briken, 2008).

A study of 345 murderers with sadistic personality disorder indicated a clustering of specific traits. They displayed a gleeful delight in being cruel to others both generally and specifically during the course of their murders. The offenders exerted complete control of their victims and employed humiliation and harsh discipline (Stone et al., 2009). Sadistic sexual homicide offenders are also noteworthy for greater sexual masochism, greater likelihood of isolation during childhood, prior rape arrests and convictions, more homicides, and longer duration of the homicidal act that sexual homicide offenders who are not sadistic (Hill, Habermann, Berner, & Briken, 2006). In other words, killers with more sadistic personalities take their time during the course of the homicide, and derive great joy and satisfaction from the act of murder.

A reason why personality disorders are so strongly associated with crime, violence, and homicide is delusional thinking. Howard, Hepburn, and Khalifa (2015) reported that among offenders with severe personality disorders (approximately 30 percent were homicide offenders) and who had high levels of delusional thinking were the most violent and had the most externalizing behaviors. Their measure of delusional thinking was not indicative of psychosis, but instead reflected subclinical indicators of delusion. Items included "Do you ever feel you are being persecuted in some way?" and "Do you ever feel that you are a very special or unusual person?" The item relating to feelings of persecution is important because persecutory beliefs can be a motivating factor for a person to aggress against a victim who the offender believes is harming them.

Another concept that is comorbid with personality disorders is paraphilic behaviors. **Paraphilias** are sexual perversions or sexual deviations. Two of the most severe paraphilias that are relevant to homicide are sexual sadism and pedophilia. Paraphilias also can drive paraphilic-related disorders such as pornography addiction, extreme promiscuity, and compulsive masturbation. A study of sexual homicide offenders reported high prevalence of paraphilas and paraphilic-related disorders (Briken, Habermann, Kafka, Berner, & Hill, 2006). These conditions severely impaired the offenders' social functioning evidenced by school failure, relationship problems, social isolation, high unemployment, school problems, and abuse history.

To summarize, personality relates to homicide in two broad ways. First, normal personality traits have been shown to correlate with aggression, antisocial conduct, and even homicide among offender samples. In addition, the homicidal act itself can represent extreme, pathological manifestations of specific personality characteristics, such as impulsivity, narcissism, anger, hostility, antagonism, and others. Second, personality disorder is particularly linked to criminal offending and homicide because by definition a personality disorder causes impairment in functioning in multiple life domains. The next chapter examines where these traits came from and how they have served adaptive function throughout human history.

CHAPTER 14

Homicide and the Evolutionary Perspective

Charles Darwin.

© Nicku/Shutterstock, Inc.

Evolutionary theories conceptualize about ways that homicide has evolved as a behavioral adaptation.

Conceptual Background

The most glaring correlate of homicide is sex/gender. Although there are clear age and racial trends in homicide offending and victimization, none of these effects is as consistent and replicable as the over involvement of males in homicide. The male-homicide link is not new and has been produced in scores of data projects from diverse societies over several historical periods. That men are more likely to kill and be killed than women is natural fact. The question is: why?

If one takes an evolutionary view of male homicide, several interesting observations are noted. First, a large component of male homicide relates to their sexual partners, such as the spouse, girlfriend, or ex-romantic partners. In these cases, the homicide involves a basic emotional motivation such as jealousy, anger, or revenge. Second, another large component of male homicide involves the killing of other males, often who are seen as rivals for sexual partners. In this way, they are essentially competition for sexual resources. Third, domestic homicides involving children are differentiated by whether the children are the biological children of an offender or the stepchild of the offender. In the event of a nonbiological relation, there is more likely to be violence. All three examples reflect some of the basic logic of evolutionary psychology.

Evolutionary psychology offers answers to questions such as this and is useful for understanding the dramatic behavioral differences that pertain to men and women vis-à-vis homicide. **Evolutionary psychology** is a field of study that uses evolutionary biology principles—that humans have evolved over historical time—and their evolution reflects traits and behaviors that provided some adaptive function. More specifically, the evolutionary perspective identifies **evolved psychological mechanisms**, which are domain-specific information-processing mechanisms that relate to survival and reproduction. This means that specific sets of environmental information or inputs and their corresponding physiological and psychological mechanisms and the ways these inputs are processed are linked to specific behavioral outputs.

Evolved psychological mechanisms can show how formerly adaptive traits can result in nonadaptive or detrimental traits and behaviors today. For instance, in early human societies, males had to defend their social status by any means and that often included the use of physical violence, and at times, lethal violence. Males who were unwilling or unable to defend themselves with force were viewed as weak and as poor prospects for mate selection. This scenario is consistent with subcultural explanations of homicide such as those in Chapters 3 and 4. Today, murdering a "rival" because of some sign of disrespect serves no adaptive function other than perhaps in the most antisocial of social worlds. Instead, the most likely consequences are to be killed, to be sentenced to prison for a lengthy period, or to be sentenced to death. What worked millennia ago was no longer applicable today, but the evolved psychological mechanism is essentially the same.

Other evolutionary concepts are important for understanding their application to homicide. Intrasexual competition is also important for understanding homicide from an evolutionary vantage point. **Intrasexual competition** is the competition between same sex rivals for access to mating opportunities. Traits that enhance success in finding mates are those that will be selected for since they provide an adaptive advantage.

Another concept is parental investment theory (Trivers, 1972). **Parental investment theory** indicates that the allocation of resources to offspring at the expense of other resources is a major difference between males and females. Once males successfully complete insemination that results in pregnancy, their biological role in parenting is finished. Conversely, females sustain gestation. This is an extraordinary imbalance of personal resources allocation toward one's biological child. As such, parental investment theory indicates that the sex that has the greater investment—females—will avoid violence (and homicide) because of the sheer costs associated with engaging in such behavior. Engaging in criminal behavior during pregnancy is not advised. Females are also more discriminating at choosing their mate because of the investment.

© KaeDeezign/Shutterstock, Inc.

Parental investment theory articulates why males and females differentially engage in parenting and differentially consider the costs and benefits of homicide.

The sex that has the lower investment—males—are predisposed to engage in riskier, violent behaviors because the potential benefits are access to mates by successfully competing against a rival whereas there is no biological cost. That males are more likely to engage in riskier, more violent behaviors is seen in all mammals where females have the greater investment.

In a variety of publications, Buss and Duntley (e.g., Buss, 2005; Duntley, 2005; Duntley & Buss, 2008, 2011) advanced **homicide adaptation theory** which is a general evolutionary framework that suggests how and why homicide would have evolved as a behavioral option. The reasons that homicide could serve an adaptive purpose include the elimination of a competitor for the sexual propriety of another, the killing of a genetic relative who would not serve the offender's reproductive investment, such as the killing of a chronically ill child, preventing the attack by a rival, or self-protection, protection of one's reputation, the protection or resources, such as food, shelter, and possessions, and the elimination of nongenetic, and hence costly relatives, such as the killing of stepchildren.

The most basic motives of self-defense, defense of others, and defense of property are important because they can be easily imagined as motivations to kill in prehistoric times, and reflect the mundane circumstances that characterize homicides in the present. These basic motivations are also seen in the animal kingdom where animals kill their own kin for the theorized reasons and kill competitors for these reasons relating to competition for mates, food, and other necessities. Still another piece of evidence that supports the notion that homicide has served an adaptive function is the existence of homicidal ideation. Survey research has found that the majority of persons in community, not clinical samples, have entertained homicidal ideation and even fantasized about killing another person (for a critical look at their theory, see Durrant, 2009).

Evolutionary psychology is a field which asserts that human adaptations evolve over time via natural selection. For a trait or behavior to continue among a species, it must have some advantage over a competing trait or behavior. Ironically, this same logic pertains to homicide. According to Duntley (2012, p. 335):

> Homicide is such a unique and potentially powerful strategy with dramatic fitness consequences for both the perpetrator and the victim that it is reasonable to hypothesize that it has been subjected to evolution by natural and sexual selection. Homicide is different from other strategies for inflicting costs because it leads to the absolute end of direct competition between two individuals. The person who is killed can no longer compete with his killer. A dead

competitor can no longer directly influence the environment or social contexts that he shared with his killer. The distinct outcomes of homicide would have created equally unique selection pressures to shape human psychology specifically for contexts of homicide.

What this means is that the raw emotions that often occur prior to a homicide event, as mentioned in Chapter 1, are universal human emotions (Roth, 2011). Everyone has felt anger, resentment, or jealousy, and likely everyone has muttered "I could kill him" in everyday life. But most people of course never do commit homicide. However, the motivations for it are experienced because they have served an evolutionary purpose throughout human history.

There are many examples of how homicide has proven useful across the expanse of time. In early societies, homicide was a useful way to protect oneself and one's family against an attack, to protect food, shelter, and other possessions from a competitor, and to manage one's status in a social hierarchy. Although these examples seem archaic, they are essentially the rationale that typifies homicides occurring today.

From an evolutionary perspective, the costs of homicide also make sense. Despite the universal emotional motivations to inflict serious violence (perhaps homicidal violence) on others, the overwhelming majority of persons avoid homicidal behavior because of its steep social and legal consequences. In other words, the high costs of homicide outweigh its perceived benefits—something that regretful homicide offenders experience acutely.

© Ye Liew/Shutterstock, Inc.

Using an evolutionary framework, Daly and Wilson have demonstrated that the rate of homicide by stepparents is several hundred times higher than the rate of homicide among biological parents.

Unlike other content areas in this book, it is difficult to empirically test evolutionary psychology theory because current data cannot be used to accurately measure evolving mechanisms that occurred eons ago. However, evolutionary principles have been applied to trends and other empirical regularities about homicide, and these are examined next.

Empirical Linkages to Homicide

Evolutionary approaches have primarily been applied to understand sex differences in homicide and familial relationship and homicide. One of the leading approaches is work by Daly and Wilson. Daly and Wilson (1988a) suggest that evolutionary psychology is a useful framework for understanding family homicide. Drawing on diverse sources of data, they argue that regularities in spousal killings, infanticides, parricides, and filicides display clear evolutionary patterns. Daly and Wilson demonstrate that the closer the genetic relationship between parent and child; the lower the risk of homicide.

For example, among children aged 0–2 years, the rate of homicide among stepparents was several hundred times higher than the rate of homicide among genetic parents. In other words, parents are more likely to kill children who were biologically produced by others than their own. Similarly, **parental solicitude**, the concern about the health and welfare of their biological child evolved over time so that the child could contribute to the parent's genetic posterity by producing grandchildren. In the case of step-relationships, there is not this parental solicitude, and thus there is a greater likelihood of violence, including homicide.

The evolutionary perspective is also useful for understanding what is a prevalent form of homicide—intimate-partner homicide, or spousal homicide. Most of these are driven by male sexual proprietariness or jealousy (Daly & Wilson, 1988a, 1988b). Males are more likely than females to suspect that their partner is prone to commit infidelity than vice versa because it is advantageous to do so. Perceiving infidelity is an evolved mechanism to protect the male's investment in a partner and children, and it is better to perceive falsely (when no infidelity occurred) than to lose one's partner to a rival.

As mentioned earlier in the chapter, of all its applications, evolutionary psychology is arguably most useful for understanding sex differences in behavior, and explaining them in an adaptive context. Wilson and Daly (1992, p. 206) concluded:

Men often hunt down and kill spouses who have left them; women hardly ever behave similarly. Men kill wives as part of planned murder-suicides; analogous acts by women are almost unheard of. Men kill in response to revelations of wifely infidelity; women almost never respond similarly, although their mates are more often adulterous. Men often kill wives are subjecting them to lengthy periods of coercive abuse and assaults; the roles in such cases are seldom if ever reversed. Men perpetrate familicidal massacres, killing spouse and children together; women do not. Moreover, it seems clear that a large proportion of the spousal killings perpetrated by wives, but almost none of those perpetrated by husbands, are acts of self-defense....because they fear for their own lives.

Trend data clearly show the overrepresentation of males as perpetrators (and victims) of homicide. From 1980 to 2008, nearly 68 percent of all homicides in the United States involved a male offender and male victim. Twenty-one percent involved a male offender and female victim. Nine percent involved a female offender and male victim, and just 2.2 percent involved females as both offender and victim (Cooper & Smith, 2011).

Furthermore, the sex gap is amazingly high when considering the most pathological forms of homicide such as mass murder, spree murder, serial murder, sexual homicide, and the like. Almost always, studies of these topics use exclusively male samples because there are not viable cases of female-perpetrated violence to study. And in data sets where there are female multiple homicide offenders, there are often too few to facilitate statistical models.

In other work, Daly and Wilson (1999) describe homicide as a conflict assay. A **conflict assay** is an index of relationship-specific, demographic, and situational variations in the intensity of interpersonal conflict. From an evolutionary psychological perspective, the recurrent patterns of who is involved in homicide, and why they are often involved in homicide reflect evolved strategies. For example, the sex differences in use of firearms and intrasexual aggression is related to competition for mates.

According to Daly and Wilson (1999, p. 67), "The sex difference in intrasexual violence is one that humans share with other species with 'effectively polygynous' mating systems: species in which the variance in fitness among males exceeds that among females." This means that males will always have greater involvement in homicide than females. Another component of the conflict assay centers on the relationships between killer and killed. Daly and Wilson theorize that the intensity of conflict is strongly related to blood relation. This would explain why stepparents (usually stepfathers) and their stepchildren are involved in homicide at rates far greater than blood relatives.

Box 14.1   Filicide and Evolutionary Psychology

Given the tremendous investment that parents make in their children especially mothers if one follows the logic of parental investment theory, why would filicide ever occur? Friedman, Cavney, and Resnick (2012a, 2012b) reviewed filicide from the evolutionary perspective and summarized several observations about this form of homicide.

- Some filicides occur when children display traits that are unwanted or if the child is physically/mentally disabled because the parental cost is viewed as too high particularly in the event that the child would not be able to reproduce and thus extend the parent's genetic lineage.
- Some filicides occur because the parent does not expect that the child would live to reproductive age.
- Some children are murdered due to scarce resources available to the parent especially in the event of the child having multiple siblings to whom are greater investment has already been allocated.
- Some children are murdered because the child's paternity is uncertain and other times, children are murdered when the mother has multiple children from different fathers and the fathers display differential reproductive fitness.
- Some children are murdered to accommodate the wishes of the other parent or a stepparent.
- Neonaticides occur primarily because the mother simply did not want the child and does not want to invest any resources in the child.
- The manner of death in filicides is different depending on the familial relation of the parent. Children who are murdered by biological parents are usually either shot to facilitate an instantaneous and painless death or asphyxiated.
- Children who are murdered by stepparents are usually beaten or bludgeoned to death which reflects greater negative emotionality and less concern for suffering.

There are also striking cultural differences in the legal responses to filicide, and especially to neonaticide where the psychiatric health of the mother is given mitigative influence in some societies. Overall, the evolutionary approach is an interesting way to understand filicide especially since it intuitive is counter to the adaptive logic of the perspective.

Source: Friedman, S. H., Cavney, J., & Resnick, P. J. (2012a). Child murder by parents and evolutionary psychology. *Psychiatric Clinics of North America, 35*(4), 781–795; Friedman, S. H., Cavney, J., & Resnick, P. J. (2012b). Mothers who kill: Evolutionary underpinnings and infanticide law. *Behavioral Sciences & the Law, 30*(5), 585–597.

Although of course most stepparents do not harm their stepchildren, merely having a stepparent in the home exponentially increases the risk of child abuse and filicide. In fact, preschool-aged children are 40–100 times more likely to be murdered by their stepparent (usually stepfather) than preschool-aged children living with their biological parents (Daly & Wilson, 1988b).

From these basic evolutionary processes, other forms of homicide can develop. For instance, sexual homicide can be seen as an even more distorted form of homicide that reflects polygynous mating systems but where sexual performance and other psychological features of the male influence how the victim is sexually assaulted and killed. Consider this assessment from Ressler and Burgess (1985, p. 5):

Rape is sexually deviant behavior that exhibits absolute disregard for the worth and value of an individual. Rape fantasies range from having power and control over a victim to more violent sadistic fantasies. Those who rape before killing are seeking to dominate others, regardless of their consequences; those who sexually assault after death (necrophilia) need the absence of life to have total domination without fear of resistance and/ or rejection. In both cases, there is a high amount of sexual dysfunction, most frequently ejaculatory failure. This inadequacy is projected onto the victim and may play a part in the escalation to murder.

This rationale would explain how the pathology in sexual homicide nonetheless stems from evolved psychological mechanisms that relate to desire to acquire sexual mates.

The next chapter also takes a biological-oriented approach to homicide, but this one from the medical viewpoint. The epidemiology of homicide is examined next.

CHAPTER 15

Homicide and the Epidemiological Perspective

Epidemiologists treat homicide as a disease and have significantly advanced knowledge about the causes and correlates of homicide offending and victimization.

Conceptual Background

Epidemiology is a branch of medicine that deals with measuring how much of a particular problem, or disease, exists in a population. The measure of how much of something there is in a population is known as **incidence**. The measure of how much or what proportion of a population is affected by the disease is **prevalence**. Of course, criminal behavior is not a disease but it nevertheless can be understood and studied as a quasimedical condition in order to understand how much of it is occurring in society, who it is most affecting in society, and what its causes and correlates are. From this information, epidemiologists can develop profiles of what persons with a particular "condition" look like, and from that, how preventive efforts could reduce the incidence of the problem in society.

Epidemiology is important for understanding how much of a concept occurs in society, and unrelated research indicates how mistaken the public can often be about various topics, such as homicide. Consider this research study of student perceptions about the incidence of homicide. Vandiver and Giacopassi (1997) administered questionnaires to nearly 400 students in an introductory criminology course and to seniors majoring in criminal justice to determine how well they grasped the magnitude of the crime problem relative to other mortality conditions. They found that almost 50 percent of the introductory-level students believed that more than 250,000 murders were committed annually in the United States. There were actually about 17,000 murders and fewer than 1,000 murders committed by juveniles during the year of their study. Fifteen percent of the students estimated that more than 1 million people were murdered each year! In other words, criminal justice students overestimated the annual homicide count in the United States by nearly 60 times!

Given the uncertainty about the incidence of homicide, there are two national-level measuring systems that are designed to quantify the incidence, correlates, nature, patterns, and trends of homicide in the United States. Although they both measure homicide, they are designed for distinct purposes and collect different types of information (see Regoeczi, Banks, Planty, Langton, & Warner, 2014). One is the **Supplementary Homicide Reports** that is part of the Uniform Crime Reporting Program administered by the Federal Bureau of Investigation. The Uniform Crime Reporting Program, commonly known as UCR, was initiated in 1930 and for three decades collected aggregate data on homicide based on crimes known to law enforcement. Beginning in 1960, the Supplementary Homicide Reports program was launched to include much more detailed information. This included:

- The jurisdiction where the homicide occurred
- Temporal data including month and year
- Victim demographic information
- Offender demographic information
- Relationship between the offender and victim
- Circumstances surrounding the homicide, such as whether it was argument-based, gang-related, associated with a robbery, and others

The Supplementary Homicide Reports has two sections, one for all murders and non-negligent manslaughters including justifiable homicides and one for negligent manslaughters. The former includes all cases suspected to be murders, violence-related manslaughters, law enforcement-related killings, and homicides committed in self-defense. The latter includes cases that are determined to be unintentional killings, such as motor vehicle crashes that produce fatalities. Homicides occurring in federal prisons, on military bases, and on Indian reservations are not included in the Supplementary Homicide Reports. In this system, homicide data are voluntarily submitted by law enforcement agencies based on arrest reports. These data are submitted monthly to the FBI.

The other homicide measure is the **National Vital Statistics System, Fatal Injury Reports** which includes data based on birth and death records at the state and local level. This system began in 1933 when uniform collection and national-level reporting of birth and death records was begun. The National Vital Statistics System, Fatal Injury Reports is maintained by the National Center for Health Statistics at the Centers for Disease Control and Prevention. The National Vital Statistics System, Fatal Injury Reports mortality data include a wealth of information about the decedent including:

- Age
- Race
- Ethnicity
- Marital status
- Resident status
- Educational attainment
- Residence
- Cause of death
- Nature of the injuries sustained

The National Vital Statistics System, Fatal Injury Reports does not contain information on the suspected perpetrator of the homicide or the relationship between the offender and victim. In several ways, its protocols are more stringent or rigorous than those for the Supplementary Homicide Reports. The National Vital Statistics System, Fatal Injury Reports is mandatory, is meant to track all deaths, is based on death certificates, and the main reporting source is state vital registrars. In terms of data collection, the manner and cause of death are determined by medical examiners or coroners, and the demographic information for the decedent is recorded by funeral directors on death certificates. The National Vital Statistics System, Fatal Injury Reports captures 99 percent of deaths in the United States (Regoeczi et al., 2014).

Although they utilize different methods and have different histories, there is strong convergence between the Supplementary Homicide Reports and National Vital Statistics System, Fatal Injury Reports. As shown in Figure 15.1, the National Vital Statistics System, Fatal Injury Reports captures more homicides but the overall trends in the data over three decades are very similar. In an epidemiological sense, this is comforting to know that the overwhelming majority of homicides in the United States are being counted and recorded.

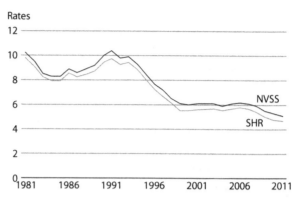

Figure 15.1 Homicide Rates in the United States, 1981–2011. Based on the Supplementary Homicide Reports and National Vital Statistics System, Fatal Injury Reports.

Source: Modified from Regoeczi, W., Banks, D., Planty, M., Langton, L., & Warner, M. (2014). *The nation's two measures of homicide.* Washington, DC: U.S. Department of Justice, Office of Justice Programs, Bureau of Justice Statistics.

Additional major contributions of epidemiological research include assessments of the overall burden of various diseases and public health issues including violence and lethal violence. Several parameters are used in this type of research.

Disability-adjusted life years (DALYs) are a measure of the state of a population's health compared to normal life expectancy or some other normalized standard. DALYs measure the gap between a specific group (e.g., homicide offenders) and the population as a whole. DALYs are the sum of due other important concepts: years of life lost due to premature mortality (YLLs) and years lived with disability (YLDs).

Years of life lost due to premature mortality (YLLs) is calculated by multiplying the number of deaths at each age by the standard life expectancy at each age.

Years lived with disability (YLDs) are a measure of the loss of health associated with a disease state compared to those who are healthy. Essentially, these measures indicate the toll that diseases exact on those who have them. In the case of homicide, they indicate the sheer human loss, disability, and burden imposed by a preventable form of lethal violence.

Epidemiological research in criminology is noteworthy for using very large samples by social science standards. Whereas most samples in criminology are in the hundreds of cases and certainly less than one thousand cases, epidemiological samples are often larger than ten thousand. From these massive samples, odds ratios are calculated to reflect the incidence of a specific disease or condition, such as an arrest for homicide, in the affected population compared to control groups or the total population. This helps to alleviate the problems of prediction in studies that did not employ an epidemiological design. Consider this quotation:

"Predicting violent behavior has been of little benefit in clinical forensic psychiatry. One reason for this is the traditional false-positive vs. false-negative approach in the case of individual subjects. Because false-positive rates have remained unacceptably high, it has been claimed that efforts to predict violence are useless for clinical decision making. When different kinds of risk are assessed in medical science, certain risk of the index subjects is usually compared with the risk of the healthy control subjects or of the total population" (Tiihonen, Hakola, Eronen, Vartiainen, & Ryynänen, 1996, p. 127).

Another important contribution of epidemiology is the case-control design. A **case-control design** or **case-control study** compares two groups. One group has a particularly characteristic, disease, or condition and serves as the cases. The other group does not have the characteristic, disease, or condition and serves as the controls. Case-control studies are commonly used to examine rare diseases in which the known effect—the presence of a rare disease—is the starting point and the case and control groups are created to find the causes. Many times, the case and control groups are matched by age, sex, race, and other factors in order for the groups to be as comparable as possible.

As mentioned in Chapter 1, homicide is an extremely rare event and even serious offenders often do not have a murder on the record. Thus, tens of thousands of persons would need to be selected to produce an adequate sample. As a result, studying homicide offenders is challenging in terms of sampling because there are often not enough homicide offenders to yield adequate power for statistical analyses. Since homicide can be likened to a rare disease, the case-control design is well-suited for homicide studies.

Empirical Linkages to Homicide

First and foremost, interpersonal violence such as homicide exacts an extraordinary toll on humanity worldwide. According to the Global Burden of Disease Study 2010, interpersonal violence caused 25,541,000 DALYs in 2010 or 371 per 100,000 in the population. Firearms assaults including firearm homicides caused 11,146,000 DALYs or 162 per 100,000 (Murray, Vos, Lozano, Naghavi, Flaxman, et al., 2013). Homicide is also responsible for scores of deaths worldwide. Based on analyses of the Global Burden of Disease Study 2010, interpersonal violence caused 4,563,000 deaths in 2010 for an age-standardized death rate of 6.7 per 100,000. Assault by firearm caused 1,962,000 deaths for an age-standardized death rate of 2.8 per 100,000. In addition, collective violence and legal interventions caused 177,000 deaths in 2010 for an age-standardized death rate of 0.3 per 100,000. Overall, interpersonal violence from homicide caused 5.2 percent of all the male deaths in the world (Lozano, Maghavi, Foreman, Lim, Shibuya, et al., 2013).

A similar burden is seen in research on mental disorders and their association with unnatural death and years of potential life lost. For example, a recent systematic review and meta-analysis indicated that overall mental disorders increase the risk of mortality by a factor of 2.2 and the median years of potential life lost was 10 years. Worldwide, about 14.3 percent of all deaths which corresponds to 8 million deaths each year are attributable to mental disorders (Reisinger Walker, McGee, & Druss, 2015). In addition, several conditions that are chapters in this book also significantly contribute to death worldwide often in the form of homicide and suicide. For example, psychotic disorders such as schizophrenia produce about 350,000 deaths. Mood disorders are responsible for 2.74 million deaths per year worldwide and anxiety disorders account for 2.41 million deaths per year worldwide. In other words, these conditions not only increase the likelihood that the affected person, or **proband**, will commit a homicide, but also increase their likelihood of dying from unnatural causes.

Epidemiological research designs permit an investigation of the long-term influence of specific variables on later outcomes among very large

© Tom Gowanlock/Shutterstock, Inc.

Worldwide, more than 5 percent of all male deaths are attributable to homicide.

samples of participants. One specific variable is firearm-related hospitalization. Using a retrospective cohort study design, Rowhani-Rahbar and colleagues (2015) examined the effect of being assaulted or shot with a firearm and subsequent risk for violent injury, violent death, and criminal offending. Compared with the general population, persons who have been hospitalized for a firearm-related injury were greater than 30 times more likely to subsequently be hospitalized for another shooting. Moreover, they were greater than seven times more likely to be murdered with a firearm. These effects were particularly pronounced among firearm victims with more extensive criminal histories (Rowhani-Rahbar, Zatzick, Wang, Mills, Simonetti, Fan, & Rivara, 2015).

Another interesting example of this research investigated the relationship between IQ in early adulthood and later risk for being the victim of homicide. Batty, Deary, Tengstrom, and Rasmussen (2008) examined a cohort of nearly 1 million men aged 18–19 who were examined for military conscription in Sweden. They found that a one standard deviation advantage in IQ conferred a 51 percent lower risk of homicide victimization. In analyses of the sample across three IQ groups (low, medium, and high), the most intelligent men were 82 percent less likely than the least intelligent men to be murdered.

An epidemiological approach is also important for understanding age, race, and sex differences in homicide offending and victimization in the United States. Chilton and Chambliss (2014) recently used Centers for Disease Control and Prevention mortality and census data along with the Supplementary Homicide Reports from the Federal Bureau of Investigation to track 30 years of homicide trends in 172 U.S. cities. These trends showed clear sex differences with male homicide rates far exceeding female homicide rates and sharp racial and ethnic differences where African Americans had the highest homicide involvement followed by Hispanics, and followed at much lower levels by whites. Their investigation demonstrated the sharp rise in homicide across the United States from 1980 to its peak in 1993 or so followed by impressive declines to the present. However, Chilton and Chambliss also demonstrated that African American homicide involvement was globally high before, during, and after the general patterning of homicide. For example, they also examined homicide trends for specific cities and found extremely high homicide victimization among black males between the ages of 15 and 29 in Atlanta, Baltimore, Chicago, Cleveland, Memphis, New Orleans, Philadelphia, and Saint Louis.

In addition to demographic characteristics, other statuses confer a much higher risk of homicide than others. Tiihonen, Hakola, Nevalainen, and Eronen (1995) examined the risk of homicide among violent offenders, some of whom had previously perpetrated homicide. Using 3 years of epidemiological data from Finland, they found that the risk of committing a homicide was 10 times higher among male homicide offenders than males in the general population. Criminal offenders with four or more prior crimes for violence were *150 times* more likely than men in the general population to perpetrate homicide!

In her program of research, Teplin has examined the longitudinal outcomes of serious delinquents who were detained in the Cook County, Illinois Juvenile Temporary Detention Center which is in Chicago, Illinois. Her project is known as the Northwestern Juvenile Project which is a cohort of 1,829 youths who were detained between 1995 and 1998. The sample is diverse by gender, race, and ethnicity but contains mostly African American and Hispanic youths. The participants in the Northwestern Juvenile Project were compared to the general population in Cook County. A recent study found that delinquents had much higher mortality than those in the general population indeed their mortality rates were 2–20 times higher than the general population depending on the characteristic of the youth (Teplin, Jakubowski, Abram, Olson, Stokes, & Welty, 2014). As shown in Figure 15.2, more than 91 percent of delinquent males died from homicide compared to 39 percent of comparison males in the general population. Although not as dramatically high, the mortality

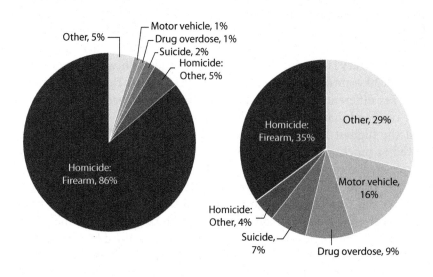

Figure 15.2 Causes of death among delinquent and general population males in Cook County, Illinois.

Source: Teplin, L. A., Jakubowski, J. A., Abram, K. M., Olson, N. D., Stokes, M. L., & Welty, L. J. (2014). Firearm homicide and other causes of death in delinquents: a 16-year prospective study. *Pediatrics, 134*(1), 63–73.

rate from homicide among delinquent girls was 41 percent with 28 percent caused by firearms. The respective rates for nondelinquent girls were 14 percent for homicide, and 7 percent for firearm homicide.

As mentioned earlier, epidemiological research is also performed with smaller samples to evaluate the characteristics that increase likelihood of homicide in a public health sense. Dobrin (2001) compared 100 homicide victims to 100 matched non-victims, and a random sample of 100 nonvictims in Prince George's County, Maryland. There were important criminological differences between the groups. Whereas just 5 percent of randomly selected non-victims and 9.5 percent of matched nonvictims had been arrested, 33 percent of the homicide victims had. Those who had been arrested were nearly five to seven times more likely to become a homicide victim. The effects varied by sample and varied by type of arrest. Drug arrests appeared to especially increase the odds of becoming a homicide victim, followed by property arrests and violent arrests. These large odds did not occur by chance which provides evidence that generalized involvement in criminal behavior increases the likelihood of being murdered one day.

One interesting study explored risk factors for homicide by using emergency room or department use. Crandall and colleagues (2004) performed a case-control design where 124 homicide victims and 138 homicide offenders were compared to randomly selected controls that were matched by age and gender. They found that homicide offenders and victims were significantly likely—more than four times more likely—to use emergency services in the three years prior to their homicide event. In fact, 85 percent of homicide-involved persons used the emergency room compared to 59 percent for controls. Several risky behaviors were predictive of future homicide involvement, including ER visit for assault (nearly fivefold increased odds), firearm injury (nearly 14-fold increased odds), and substance abuse/overdose (nearly fourfold increased odds). The prevalence of psychiatric diagnosis among homicide offenders and victims was nearly two times greater than the prevalence of psychiatric diagnosis among controls.

Drawing on data on homicides of prostitutes in Connecticut, Minnesota, Missouri, Texas, Virginia, and Washington State, Brewer and colleagues (2006) used a matched case-control design to compare those who murdered prostitutes to those who patronized prostitutes. As expected, they found that those who murdered prostitutes were more than three times as likely to have a violent criminal history of offenses, such as rape, assault, and homicide. Nearly half (46 percent) of the murderers had a violent criminal history compared to 14 percent of those who patronized prostitutes. In multivariate models, violent criminal history increased the likelihood of murdering a prostitute fivefold and a property offending history increased the risk by more than four times.

Box 15.1   The Epidemiology of Healthcare Serial Murder

Healthcare serial murder is a separate category of homicide that is characterized by five features. First, the murders and attempted murders are of patients in a healthcare setting, such as a hospital. Second, the perpetrator of the crime is a healthcare worker at the medical facility where the incident occurs. Third, two or more patients are killed or nearly killed in separate incidents than spans a period of time exceeding 30 days. Fourth, the malicious acts occur in the course or consequent to the healthcare worker's duties. Fifth, the perpetrator has the psychological capacity for committing additional malicious acts affecting patients (Kizer & Yorker, 2010). On the surface, healthcare serial murder is challenging to detect because the homicides occur in an environment where patient deaths are common, or potentially even routine, such as at a hospice location.

What is the epidemiology of healthcare serial murder? There have been more than 1,000 suspicious deaths linked to persons charged with healthcare serial murder in the past 40 years. The most common method of healthcare serial murder is the administration of a noncontrolled medication such as insulin, epinephrine, potassium chloride, or others, such as injection of an air embolus to cause a pulmonary embolism. Yorker and her colleagues (2006) found that 90 healthcare professionals have been prosecuted between 1970 and 2006. Fifty four of these were convicted, and 45 of those convicted were for serial homicide.

There have been infamous cases of healthcare serial murder as well. Charles Cullen confessed to murdering 40 patients over his homicide career and is serving multiple life sentences in prison in New Jersey. By outside appearances, Cullen was an outstanding nurse and employee, and lived a life free of crime and attached to the conventions of society. However, Cullen also was plagued by mental illness attributed to an abusive childhood, and had attempted suicide many times during his life. All of these suicide attempts were unsuccessful, and it is theorized that by killing his patients he was able to experience the death of suicide without actually having to die (Graeber, 2013). It is theorized that Cullen murdered upward of 400 victims, which, if true, would make him the most prolific serial murderer in the history of the United States.

In England, Harold Shipman was convicted of murdering 15 patients and sentenced to life imprisonment before committing suicide in prison in 2004. Shipman was convicted of unlawful killing of an additional 218 patients and is suspected in 62 other deaths for which there were not sufficient evidence to reach a verdict (Esmail, 2005). Thus, in the epidemiology of murder, healthcare serial murder contains some of the most prolific offenders.

Sources: Kizer, K. W., & Yorker, B. C. (2010). Health care serial murder: A patient safety orphan. *Joint Commission Journal on Quality and Patient Safety/Joint Commission Resources, 36*(4), 186–191; Yorker, B. C., Kizer, K. W., Lampe, P., Forrest, A. R. W., Lannan, J. M., & Russell, D. A. (2006). Serial murder by healthcare professionals. *Journal of Forensic Sciences, 51*(6), 1362–1371; Esmail, A. (2005). Physician as serial killer–the Shipman case. *New England Journal of Medicine, 352*(18), 1843–1844; Graeber, C. (2013). *The good nurse: A true story of medicine, madness, and murder.* New York, NY: Twelve.

Epidemiological research has shown that persons who commit homicide are significantly more antisocial than the general population, which is a recurrent theme in many of the conceptual approaches of this book. Cook, Ludwig, and Braga (2005) performed a case-control study of a dataset that contained all arrests and felony convictions in Illinois for 1990–2001. They also calculated the **population-attributable risk** which is the portion of homicide offenses that would be eliminated by a hypothetical intervention that reduced the offending risk of individuals with a record to the offending risk of those who lack a record. Overall, 884 persons were convicted of homicide and were compared to 7.9 million controls. Nearly 43 percent of the homicide offenders had at least one prior felony conviction whereas only 3.9 percent of controls had a felony conviction. The population-attribution risk for felony convictions was 40.3 percent. In terms of arrest, nearly 72 percent of murderers had been arrested compared to 18.2 percent of controls. The arrest population-attributable risk was 65.3 percent. Using data from 1996 to 2000, the population-attributable risk for felony convictions was 31 percent and for arrests was 58.5 percent.

In a case-control study of 105 homicide victims and 105 nonvictims, Dobrin and Brusk (2003) indicated that homicide victims are substantially more antisocial than nonvictims. Ever having been arrested increased the likelihood of being murdered by a factor of 10. This produces an attributable risk of 90 percent which means that 9 out of 10 homicides among those who had been arrested was the result of the exposure of having been arrested. Any property arrest increased the likelihood of homicide victimization by a factor of 11.2. This equates to an attributable risk of 91 percent. Any drug arrest increased the likelihood of homicide victimization by 12.1, or an attributable risk of 92 percent. Any violent arrest increased the likelihood of homicide victimization nearly sixfold which produced an attributable risk of 83 percent. When age, race, and sex are controlled, homicide victims are 5.3 times more likely to have ever been arrested than nonvictims. Moreover, they are 5.9 times more likely to have a property arrest, 2.5 times more likely to have a violent arrest, and four times more likely to have a drug arrest.

Finally, epidemiological methods have also recently been utilized in criminology to examine variation in antisocial behavior among large samples of Americans. Several findings have been produced using the National Epidemiologic Survey on Alcohol and Related Conditions also known as NESARC. The NESARC is a nationally representative sample of 43,093 non-institutionalized U.S. residents aged 18 or older and contains a wealth of items measuring substance use, psychiatric disorders, personality disorders, and various forms of externalizing behaviors. It included several externalizing behaviors that are correlated with homicide offending, including hurting other people on purpose, hitting another person so hard that they required medical attention, using weapons, physical fighting, and starting or instigating physical fights. In addition, there were several other behaviors that are essentially indicators of symptoms of antisocial personality disorder.

A study using latent class methods that found unobserved groupings of individuals within the data found that 5.3 percent of those in the NESARC were severe in their externalizing behaviors (Vaughn, DeLisi, Gunter, Fu, Beaver, et al., 2011). They committed violent behaviors at levels that were 10–20 times higher than those in the sample who were normative in their problem behaviors. Their finding was consistent with research in the criminal careers literature which indicates that about 5 percent of offenders are career criminals who are most likely to commit murder. In other words, there study shows how violence and antisocial conduct is disproportionately concentrated among a small group of severely behaved persons. Similarly, Falk and colleagues (2013) performed a large study of the Swedish population including all persons born from 1958 to 1980. This was a sample of nearly 2.4 million individuals. They found that persistently violent offenders, the type who committed homicide among other crimes, represented just 1 percent of the population yet they accounted for 63 percent of all criminal convictions. They were generally males with personality disorders, early onset problem behaviors, versatile criminal histories, and substance use.

Another useful data source for epidemiological criminology is the National Survey on Drug Use and Health which is designed to provide population estimates of substance use and health-related behaviors in the U.S. general population aged 12 years or older. Vaughn, Salas-Wright, DeLisi, and Maynard (2014) largely replicated research using the NESARC by examining latent groupings of externalizing behaviors among young Americans.

Consistent with prior research, they reported the existence of a severe subgroup that accounted for 4.7 percent of the sample. Although small in number, this small group was characterized by very high levels of involvement in all forms of externalizing and problem behaviors. For example, they sold and used drugs, carried handguns, got into physical fights, participated in group or gang fighting, and perpetrated violent attacks against other people. For some of the violent behaviors, the severe group committed crime at levels that were 50 to 70 times higher than normatively behaved youth, who accounted for nearly 73 percent of the sample. Although their study did not measure homicidal behaviors, the behavioral repertoire, propensity for violence, and recurrent involvement in fights and other confrontational situations among the severe 5 percent were consistent with the backgrounds of many homicide offenders.

Finally, epidemiological research is also helpful to demonstrate how biological and social factors interact to produce public health problems relating to homicide. For example, Freudenberg, Fahs, Galea, and Greenberg (2006) chronicled how the 1975 fiscal crisis in New York City contributed to a syndemic involving tuberculosis, HIV/AIDS, and homicide. A **syndemic** is the co-occurrence of two or more epidemics where social conditions and biological determinants interact synergistically to increase the burden of disease on the population. The fiscal crisis caused dramatic reductions in public services that in turn resulted from recessions and major downturns in the city economy. In the place of this economic malaise occurred the emergence of crack cocaine which imposed its own health and violence problems. Between 1979 and 1993, nearly 27,000 homicides occurred in the city along with nearly 50,000 cases of tuberculosis, and nearly 52,000 deaths from AIDS. The homicides produced productivity losses of $4.8 billion, quality of life losses at $12.7 billion, and overall costs of $17.7 billion.

A paradigm that takes the merging of the biological and social to the next level—the biosocial perspective—is examined in the next chapter.

CHAPTER 16

Homicide and the Biosocial Perspective

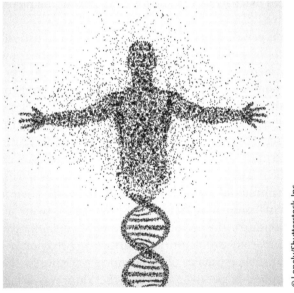

The biosocial perspective is showing how nature and nurture interact to produce complex behavioral outcomes such as homicide.

© Lonely/Shutterstock, Inc.

Conceptual Background

For most of the last century, criminology in the United States has been almost exclusively sociological in its orientation. Crime was explained by societal phenomena and the emphasis was often on units of analysis that were beyond the individual. This is why criminology has historically focuses on peer groups, neighborhoods, and counties. Indeed, the structural approaches in this book are an example.

However, there was also a ton of research on antisocial behavior conducted by scholars outside of criminology, in fields such as psychology, human development, pediatrics, social work, genetics, and the neurosciences. Gradually, some more interdisciplinary-minded criminologists began to incorporate these "outside" fields of study and use biological and social measures to understand criminology. This is known as **biosocial criminology**, which is the interdisciplinary study of crime using methods and data from multiple fields. Some of the major approaches in biosocial criminology are behavior genetics/behavioral genetics, molecular genetics/molecular genetic association studies, and brain imaging/neuroimaging (the various terms are used interchangeably). Brain imaging is explored extensively in Chapter 24 as part of the neuropsychological perspective.

Behavioral genetics research uses twin data to statistically model the relative effects of genes, similar environmental factors known as shared environment factors, and dissimilar environmental factors known as nonshared environmental factors. In recent decades, investigators have used twins as a sort of natural experiment to examine the roles of genes and environment in producing behavior. Identical or **monozygotic (MZ) twins** share 100 percent of their DNA, whereas fraternal or **dizygotic (DZ) twins** share 50 percent of their DNA. The use of twin data allows criminologists to identify the relative role of genetic factors known as **heritability**, or h^2, **shared environmental factors** or c^2, such as family environments, and **nonshared environmental factors** or e^2 that make twins different, such as peer relationships. The use of twin data allows quantitative estimates of the relative importance of nature and nurture on behavior. In other words, it permits statistical estimates of "how much" variance in crime is caused by genes, families, or peers—a question that once was debated only theoretically or philosophically, or from the sociological perspective, never debated at all.

How much variance in antisocial behavior is attributable to genetic and environmental factors? Mason and Frick (1994) performed a meta-analysis of 15 twin and adoption studies with a total sample of over 4,000 that provided 21 estimates of the heritability of antisocial behavior. The overall effect size was that 48 percent of the variance was attributable to genetic factors. Miles and Carey (1997) published a meta-analysis of 24 studies of human aggression and found that genes accounted for 50 percent of the variance. Rhee and Waldman's (2002) meta-analysis of 51 twin and adoption studies of antisocial behavior found that genes accounted for

41 percent of the variance, nonshared environmental factors accounted for 43 percent of the variance, and shared environmental factors accounted for 16 percent of the variance in antisocial behaviors. Ferguson (2010) performed a meta-analysis of 38 studies comprising 53 separate observations with a combined sample size of nearly 97,000 published from 1996 to 2006. He reported that 56 percent of the variance in antisocial personality and behavior was attributable to genes, 31 percent to the nonshared environment, and 13 percent to the shared environment. In other words, genes, family environments, and unique environments *all* contribute to the causes of antisocial behavior.

Behavior genetics research estimates the relative role of genetic factors in the etiology of crime, but it does not identify the specific genes that are implicated. Studies that use measured genes are commonly referred to as **molecular genetic association studies**. Some general information about genes is needed. In the approximately 100 trillion cells in the human body except red blood cells exists an individual's genome which is the complete genetic map of an organism. The genetic code is written in deoxyribonucleic acid (DNA). About 6 feet of DNA are packed into 46 chromosomes within each cell, 23 chromosomes are inherited from an individual's mother and 23 chromosomes are inherited from an individual's father.

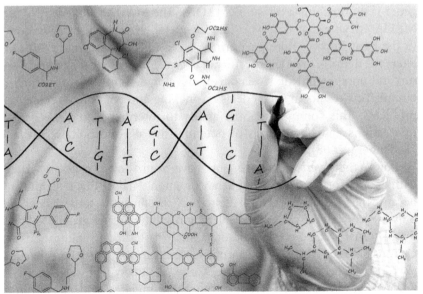

© Wichy/Shutterstock, Inc.

Biosocial criminologists are identifying genetic variants that contribute to various antisocial traits and behaviors that relate to homicide.

DNA has four major functions: it contains the blueprint or code for making proteins and enzymes, it regulates how and when proteins and enzymes are made, it carries this information when cells divide, and transmits this information from parent to child. The product of the DNA code is a **gene**, which is a distinct section of DNA in a cell's chromosome that contains the codes for producing specific proteins involved in brain and bodily functions. DNA has a unique double helix appearance similar to a ladder that is twisted continuously. The sides of the double helix are made up of sugars and phosphates. The "rungs" of the double helix are composed of two chemicals composed of atoms of carbon, hydrogen, oxygen, nitrogen, and phosphorous called nucleotides or base pairs. There are four base pairs in DNA. These are adenine which is abbreviated as A, thymine which is abbreviated as T, guanine which is abbreviated as G, and cytosine which is abbreviated as C. A always pairs with T and G always pairs with C.

The base pairs can produce subtle, and at times, obvious differences in some genes. Genes that exist in multiple forms are called **polymorphisms**, and variants of these polymorphisms, called **alleles**, confer various effects on the functionality of the gene. An important implication of polymorphisms is differential communication between neurons in the brain, a process known as **neurotransmission**. There are several neurotransmitter systems in the brain, some of which are inhibitory in nature, and others that are excitatory in nature. One of the most "famous" genes is monoamine oxidase A (MAOA). The **MAOA gene** encodes the MAOA enzyme that is responsible for metabolizing neurotransmitters in the brain such as norepinephrine, serotonin, and dopamine. MAOA alters the neurogenetic architecture of aggression because it alters serotonin and norepinephrine levels during development of the corticolimbic circuit. This results in social decision-making and emotional regulation problems. This compromises the ability to interpret ambiguous social interactions and perceptions of potential threat (Buckholtz & Meyer-Lindenberg, 2008).

Low-activity versions of the gene have been shown to be associated with various forms of antisocial behavior among males. This is significant because the MAOA gene is located on the X chromosome; thus, males have only one copy of the gene and display significantly greater genetic liability for MAOA risk alleles. Multiple meta-analyses indicate significant associations between MAOA polymorphisms and various antisocial behaviors (Byrd & Manuck, 2014; Kim-Cohen, Caspi, Taylor, Williams, Newcombe, Craig, & Moffitt, 2006). There is so much accumulated evidence for linkages between MAOA and antisocial behavior, and by implication the salience of neurotransmission to behavior, that it is commonly referred to as "the warrior gene" (Holland & DeLisi, 2015).

Empirical Linkages to Homicide

Against this biosocial backdrop, an assortment of research studies has shown the relevance of biological concepts and biosocial interactions on homicidal conduct. An intriguing study by Finnish researchers supports the notion that serious criminality and propensity for violence run in families. Putkonen, Ryynänen, Eronen, and Tiihonen (2002) examined the criminal records of 11 children of 36 homicide offenders and compared them to 220 controls that were matched by sex, age, and domicile of birth. They found that among the children of homicide offenders, there was a 24-fold increased risk for committing violent crime and 17-fold increased risk for criminality compared to those whose father was not a murderer.

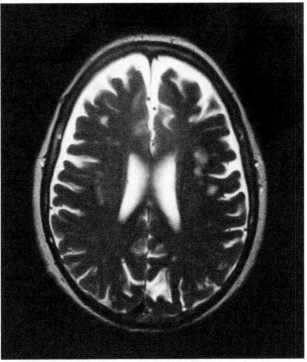

Scientists worldwide have shown how brain structure and brain functioning among homicide offenders is often different from those in the general population.

Many homicide offenders have family backgrounds—that for biological and social reasons—demonstrate intergenerational continuity in propensity to murder. For example, Harvey Robinson murdered and raped three women and committed additional attempted murders and rapes as a juvenile in Allentown, Pennsylvania. For these crimes, he was sentenced to death and was perhaps the youngest offender on condemned status in the United States (Ramsland, 2012). Of course, the juvenile death penalty was since held unconstitutional in *Roper v. Simmons* (2005), thus Robinson will never be executed, nor punished with life imprisonment without parole. Interestingly, Robinson's father committed a similar bludgeoning murder 31 years prior to his son's rampage (Garlicki, 1994).

Neuroscientists are providing significant evidence that the causes of homicide reside in brain abnormalities. In a study of 22 murderers and 22 age-matched and gender-matched controls, Raine and his colleagues (1994) examined cerebral uptake of glucose using positron emission tomography. They found that murderers had significantly lower glucose metabolisms in the lateral and medial prefrontal cortex compared to controls. However, there were not differences for posterior frontal, temporal, and parietal glucose metabolism. They also controlled for handedness, ethnicity, head injury, schizophrenia, and motivation (Raine, Buchsbaum, Stanley, Lottenberg, Abel, & Stoddard, 1994).

In a brain imaging study of 41 murders and 41 age- and sex-matched controls, Raine, Buchsbaum, and LaCasse (1997) found numerous limbic system differences. Murderers had reduced left and increased right amygdala activity, reduced left and increased right activity in the hippocampus, and greater right activity in the thalamus compared to controls. Due to concern about handedness and brain laterality, they conducted additional analyses of left and right-handed murderers and found that handedness did not account for the asymmetric limbic activity in addition to the reduced frontal activity. Recently, Yang, Raine, Han, Schug, Toga, et al. (2010) found gray matter volume reductions in the hippocampus and parahippocampal gyrus, which is involved in information processing for impulse control and emotional regulation, among homicide perpetrators who also have schizophrenia. Limbic differences also differentiate the type of murderer.

In another positron emission tomography study which measured glucose metabolism in areas of interest in the brain, Raine, Meloy, Bihrle, Stoddard, LaCasse, et al. (1998) compared cortical and limbic regions for predatory/instrumental murderers and affective/reactive murderers compared to controls. They found that affective murderers had higher right hemisphere limbic functioning and lower right hemisphere prefrontal/limbic ratios. This comports with the notion that impulsively violent offenders are unable to inhibit their emotional responses during heated confrontation. On the other hand, predatory murderers had cortical functioning that was intact and on par with controls while also having excessive right limbic activity. This is consistent with the idea that instrumentally violent people can victimize others due to impairments in the limbic system (e.g., callousness, lacking conscience).

It is important to recognize that the psychopathology demonstrated by homicide offenders it often itself suggestive of limbic dysfunction. For instance, in their study of 166 convicted sexual homicide offenders, Briken, Habermann, Berner, and Hill (2005) found that 30 percent of their sample had brain abnormalities and among these offenders half also presented with sadistic personality disorder which is characterized by the infliction of pain, humiliation, and suffering on victims for the gratification of the offender. By definition, the disorder implies the absence of empathic emotion and likely amygdala dysfunction.

An actual syndrome linking the limbic system to homicide offending has been advanced. Pontius (1997) proposed Limbic Psychotic Trigger Reaction which is characterized by motiveless, well-remembered, unplanned homicidal acts committed by an offender who was temporarily psychotic, autonomically aroused, and who displayed flat affect. Pontius documented 14 cases of Limbic Psychotic Trigger Reaction syndrome and suggested that the limbic system undergoes a seizure that is started or "kindled" by a very specific trigger that is associated with stressors in the individual's memory.

Recently, investigators conducted the first study of gray matter volume deficits in youth who have committed homicide. The authors used high resolution structural magnetic imaging and voxel-based morphometry to identify brain matter volume differences between 20 male adolescents who were convicted murderers and three control groups: 20 matched controls who were incarcerated but had not committed homicide, 21 healthy participants from the community, and 135 incarcerated controls who had not committed homicide (Cope, Ermer, Gaudet, Steele, Eckhardt, et al., 2014). Overall, homicide offenders had reduced gray matter volume compared to controls and these differences were particularly seen in the lateral temporal cortex. These brain differences were significant despite controlling for other correlates of antisocial behavior, including age, IQ, socioeconomic status, impulsivity, psychopathic personality traits, callous-unemotional traits, traumatic brain injury, current or past mental disorder diagnoses, prior criminal convictions, and substance abuse history. Moreover, they were able to correctly classify 75 percent of homicide offenders and 82 percent of non-homicide offenders based on their brain structure.

Another large research domain in biosocial criminology centers on finding genetic variants which are associated with extreme violent behaviors including homicide. As discussed earlier, one of the most frequently studied genes for a relation to serious violence, impulsive violence, and homicide is the monoamine oxidase A gene or MAOA. It is colloquially known as the "warrior gene." The MAOA gene is a functional polymorphism which means that it exists in multiple forms in the human genome and these forms, or alleles, produce a brain enzyme that is differentially efficient at degrading or regulating neurotransmitters including serotonin, norepinephrine, and dopamine. MAOA is commonly divided into two types of alleles, those that correspond to low MAOA activity and those that correspond to high MAOA activity. It is the low activity variants of MAOA that correspond to violent behavior particularly in the context of abusive or negative environments. For example, low-activity variants have been linked to gang involvement and engaging in weapons use while in a gang fight (Beaver, DeLisi, Vaughn, & Barnes, 2010).

A relatively recent innovation is to examine the rare 2-repeat allele of the MAOA gene, one that is disproportionately found in black males rather than white males. For example, Beaver and colleagues (2013) found that African American males who were 2-repeat allele carriers had significantly higher scores on a psychopathic personality measure, were nearly four times more likely to be arrested, and three times more likely to be incarcerated than African American males without the 2-repeat allele. The 2-repeat carriers also exhibited more lifetime antisocial behavior. Analyses could not be executed with white males because only 0.1 percent carried it (Beaver, Wright, Boutwell, Barnes, DeLisi, & Vaughn, 2013) compared to 5.2 percent of black males.

The 2-repeat allele of the MAOA polymorphism has also been linked to the very criminal behaviors that produce many homicides namely stabbing and shooting. Using the National Longitudinal Study of Adolescent Health similar to the prior works discussed in this chapter, Beaver, Barnes, and Boutwell (2014) found that African American males who carried the 2-repeat allele were significantly more likely than all other genotypes to shoot or stab victims and to reporting having multiple shooting and stabbing victims. In fact, they were nearly 13 times more likely to shoot or stab victims compared to those without the 2-repeat allele. It is important to note that less than 6 percent of the total sample of approximately 20,000 participants had ever shot or stabbed someone. This means that the rare variant is commensurately associated with very rare violent acts.

A recent study of Finnish prisoners, several of whom had committed homicides or attempted homicides, found associations with low-activity alleles of the MAOA gene that is involved in regulating neurotransmitters and the CDH13 gene which codes for neuronal membrane adhesion protein (Tiihonen, Rautiainen, Ollila, Repo-Tiihonen, Virkkunen, et al., 2014). Importantly, the main effect for MAOA was only seen among offenders who had committed at least two severe violent crimes. Others researchers have found significant genetic effects for the androgen receptor gene CAG short and GGN long polymorphisms (Aluja, Garcia, Blanch, & Fiba, 2011) and various antisocial traits and behaviors among murderers.

The **catechol O-methyltransferase gene**, known as COMT, is an important candidate gene for antisocial and other problem behaviors due to the major role the enzyme plays in modulating dopamine levels in the prefrontal cortex, the area of the brain that controls executive cognitive functioning. The COMT gene contains a valine/methionine polymorphism at codon 158 (Val^{158}Met) which is associated with a 40 percent reduction in prefrontal enzymatic activity (Chen et al., 2004). As a consequence, there are higher levels of dopamine in the prefrontal cortex and excess brain dopamine is associated with externalizing disorders. A study of schizophrenia patients who had committed homicide and controls who had not murdered in Israel found that those with the low-activity variant of COMT were more likely to be in the homicide group (Kotler, Barak, Cohen, Averbuch, Grinshpoon, et al., 1999).

Although much of biosocial criminology involves the use of molecular genetic association studies, other scholars have utilized a chromosomal approach to study homicide. For example, Briken, Habermann, Berner, and Hill (2006) analyzed the case histories of 166 offenders in Germany who had perpetrated a sexual homicide. They were interested in the potential role of sex chromosome abnormalities which have been shown to be rare yet substantially more prevalent in men who have murdered compared to men in the general population.

Of the 166 murderers, chromosome analysis was performed on thirteen of them, and a staggering three men displayed XYY chromosome abnormality which is the presence of a second Y chromosome. The prevalence of XYY was 1.8 percent in this sample compared to 0.7 to 0.9 percent in unselected samples of prisoners and about 0.01 percent in the general population. In other words, XYY is *180 times* more prevalent among sexual murderers than the general population.

The three murderers with XYY abnormality had severe developmental histories. Case 1 was physically abused by his father and had childhood speech problems and learning disabilities. At age 15, he was convicted of two rapes and an attempted rape and referred to a psychiatric facility. At age 17, he committed a violent offense against a girl and a year later committed a sexual homicide. He is currently incarcerated. His diagnoses include sexual sadism, pedophilia, alcohol abuse, antisocial personality disorder, and avoidant personality disorder. His PCL-R score is 28.

Case 2 was physically abused by both parents and also had learning difficulties. His first offense was a sexual assault at age 14. At age 15, he was convicted of ten additional rapes and placed in an adolescent psychiatric hospital. While there he violently victimized two other patients. At age 17, he was convicted of two additional rapes and sentenced to prison. After attempting to rape and murder two victims at age 20, he successfully perpetrated two other rape-murders and was sentenced to prison. He is sexually sadistic, has ADHD and antisocial personality disorder, and has a PCL-R score of 28.

Case 3 was physically abused by both parents, displayed gross motor and learning impairments, and had gender confusion. He committed a sexual homicide at age 17, attempted rape at age 19, sexual homicide at age 20, and attempted sexual homicide at age 21. For these crimes, he is currently imprisoned. His diagnoses include sexual sadism, transvestic fetishism, antisocial personality disorder, schizoid personality disorder, and narcissistic personality disorder. His PCL-R score is 23.

Box 16.1   Brain Scanning a Serial Killer

Randy Kraft was a relatively high functioning, high achieving person who first two decades of life seemed to be on the path to success. However, Kraft also had extremely violent impulses and desires that would make him one of the most prolific serial murderers in U.S. history.

Kraft is believed to have abducted, raped, and murdered upward of 64 or 67 males (estimates vary) between the ages of 13 and 35. All of his crimes were painstakingly premeditated and Kraft would drug his victims to subdue them then rape them. The victims were bound and often emasculated, and Kraft would insert socks into the victim's rectum. Many of the victims were also tortured and mutilated. Kraft was conflicted about his homosexuality and this conflict influenced his behaviors during the homicides. The murders occurred in multiple states, but mostly in California. Kraft was finally caught due to an innocuous traffic violation, and in 1989 was convicted of 16 homicides and numerous additional serious felonies. He was sentenced to death that year.

Renowned criminologist Adrian Raine conducted brain scans of Randy Kraft and showed the neurological functioning of a predatory, instrumental homicide offender. The functional PET brain scans showed that Kraft's brain exhibited similar prefrontal activation and functioning as a normal control and even of Raine himself (who was also scanned). However, Kraft's brain was different from impulsive, reactive murderers who display severe deficits in prefrontal activation and functioning.

This suggested that the prefrontal cortex of Randy Kraft effectively functioning normally, which is consistent with the apparently normal façade of his life....one that masked a very dark interior.

Source: Raine, A. (2013). *The anatomy of violence: The biological roots of crime.* New York, NY: Pantheon.

In the end, the biosocial paradigm has served as an important way to bridge research in the biological sciences and the social sciences to show that both fields have important contributions to homicide. The following example is illustrative. Researchers in Finland analyzed a dataset on the monthly occurrence of homicide in Finland during the years 1957–1995 that contained 4,553 homicides. They found that during winter, the homicide rate was 6 percent below the expected rate and that during the summer the homicide rate was 6 percent higher than the expected rate (Tiihonen, Räsänen, & Hakko, 1997). Trends in violent suicides such as those committed with a firearm followed the same trend. They concluded that the seasonal fluctuations in homicide and suicide corresponded to circannual rhythms of serotonin transmission.

Some of the same investigators conducted a brain imaging study of 21 impulsively violent offenders with alcoholism most of whom attempted or completed homicides, 21 age- and sex-matched control, and 10 nonviolent alcoholic controls (Tiihonen, Kuikka, Bergström, Karhu, Viinamäki, et al., 1997). They used single-photon emission tomography (SPET) with an iodine tracer to measure serotonin re-uptake in the diencephalon, striatum, and the cingulate cortex. They found that serotonin binding in the midbrain of violent offenders was significantly lower than healthy control and non-violent alcoholics. Reduced brain serotonin leads to increased amygdala reactivity to threat, which is precisely the effect seen in the impulsive homicides by intoxicated offenders. This suggests that serotonin deficit is associated with impulsive homicides among alcoholics and provides additional support for the seasonality hypothesis of homicides occurring in Finland.

Of all the areas of research, the biosocial perspective is poised to make the most exciting scientific discoveries about the causes and correlates of homicide because of its use of genetic and brain data to show how these biological constructs are affected by and influenced by various environmental contingencies. The next chapter takes a different perspective, and an important one, in that it studies homicide from the victim's perspective.

CHAPTER 17

Homicide and the Victimology Perspective

Victimology is a field of study that focuses on an often forgotten part of the homicide event—the victim.

Conceptual Background

Like most areas of criminal justice, most of the research attention is paid to offenders and this unfortunately often comes at the expense of victimization. Of course, in any homicide, there are direct victims—the person or persons who lose their life—and indirect victims who are profoundly affected by the loss as well. Any homicide is a tragedy, but as shown in Figures 17.1 and 17.2, homicide is currently at its lowest levels since about the 1950s in terms of homicide victimization rate. And the 15,000 homicide victims each year currently is significantly down from the peak of approximately 25,000 homicide victims each year in the early 1990s.

Victimology is the study of victims of crime. Criminology and criminal justice research is overwhelmingly focused on criminal offenders and criminal justice system practitioners, and while these parties are essential to understanding crime and punishment, largely overlooked or even ignored are crime victims. This is particularly the case in homicide studies where by definition there is limited ability to study the victim other than for postmortem forensic reasons. But homicide victims leave behind family, friends, and acquaintances that are significantly affected by the homicide event. In some ways, dealing with a loved one's murder is more difficult than other hardships to overcome. According to Malone (2007, p. 384), "The emotional and psychological processes following a murder do not necessarily follow the traditional 'stages of grief' model, and differ significantly in duration, intensity, and complexity—partly due to the traumatic

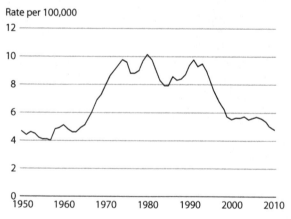

Figure 17.1 Homicide Victimization Rate, 1950–2010.

Source: Modified from Cooper, A., & Smith, E. L. (2011). *Homicide trends in the United States, 1980–2008. Annual rates for 2009–2010.* Washington, DC: U.S. Department of Justice, Office of Justice Programs, Bureau of Justice Statistics.

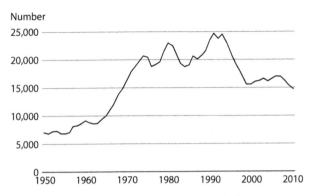

Figure 17.2   Number of homicide victims, 1950–2010.

Source: Modified from Cooper, A., & Smith, E. L. (2011). *Homicide trends in the United States, 1980–2008. Annual rates for 2009–2010.* Washington, DC: U.S. Department of Justice, Office of Justice Programs, Bureau of Justice Statistics.

nature of the death and partly due to the need to suppress grief reactions in order to deal with complex practical, legal and financial matters during the months after the death." Studies of homicidally bereaved individuals have shown there are many logistical issues that have to be addressed including funeral expenses, benefit claims and related processing, child care issues, and effectively taking over the business responsibilities of the murdered person. These logistical matters delay the ability of the person to truly begin to grieve. In addition, there are many difficulties with the criminal justice process including poor communication from investigators and prosecutors (Malone, 2007).

Depending on the relationship of the homicide offender and victim, there are unique problems that affect the survivors of homicide victims. Uxoricide, for instance, usually produces the loss of both parents, which means that their children must be raised by family, guardians, or become wards of the state. These changes necessitate major life changes in terms of the child's socioeconomic status and residency (Parker, Steeves, Anderson, & Moran, 2004). The loss of both parents often means attending a new school and having to make new friends—major changes for most children.

The media poses another potential problem. On one hand, the media can assist murder victims by providing exposure to their victimization in the event that the offender is at large or if the case is currently unsolved. Media coverage can provide the public scrutiny that facilitates the apprehension of the offender, or at the very least, applies pressure to the local criminal justice system to clear the case with an arrest. But the media can also contribute to victim trauma by being intrusive and trouncing on the private mourning. For instance, a study of the media and murder victim's families in Israel, Italy, and Switzerland found evidence of mixed but mostly negative media effects on the families of murder victims (Barak-Brandes & Shaul, 2014). Specifically, the media coverage made their suffering a public event and effectively transformed their private suffering and bereavement into a news item for public discourse.

An important construct in victimology and among crime victims is sense-making. **Sense-making** is a restorative idea whereby victims create meaning to understand their loss and assist in their postcrime event self-identity. In other words, sense-making encompasses the positive ways that an individual comes to terms with their victimization and the degree to which he or she allows the victimization process to influence one's identity.

Empirical Linkages to Homicide

Diverse methodologies have been used to examine the victimology aspects of homicide. An interesting study explored sense-making among 37 **cov-ictims of homicide**, or the family, friends, and acquaintances of murdered individuals. Based on extensive interviews with these covictims, Stretesky, O'Connor Shelley, Hogan, and Unnithan (2010) identified several criminal justice system issues that preventing healthy sense-making formation. These problems included perceptions about a lack of communication from investigators on the status of their case, perceived lower concern about the murder victim due to his or her social and demographic characteristics, lack of prosecution of the killer of their loved one, and perceptions that the police are no longer actively investigating the homicide. In effect, they found a double form of victimization whereby covictims first must face the injustice of having a loved one murdered, and then face the injustice of a criminal justice system that for a variety of reasons was not efficiently or effectively solving the case.

As shown in Chapter 1, there are sharp demographic differences in homicide offending and victimization. African Americans experience more homicides, as offender and victim, than other racial and ethnic groups in the United States. For instance, in her culturally specific model of coping with homicide, Sharpe (2014) noted that the homicide rate among blacks was 17.9 per 100,000 but just 2.92 per 100,000 based on 2010 data from the Federal Bureau of Investigation. In this regard, African Americans bear the brunt of American homicide and comprise nearly half of all homicide victims in the United States. Sharpe believes that African Americans have a culturally specific way to cope with homicide bereavement. In her model, African Americans have a legacy of cultural trauma that is defined by ancestral survivorship and anticipated hardship due to distrust of clinical and governmental entities.

After experiencing a homicide as a covictim, she suggests that African Americans experience shame, blame, stigma, and a sense of lack of justice that is uniquely related to their racial status. In terms of coping strategies, Sharpe suggests that African Americans engage in spiritual coping and meaning making, maintain a connection to their murdered loved one, collectively cope and care for others, and concealment, where the pain from the homicide is hidden from others. In the event that these coping strategies help the bereaved, there is a prosocial response to the homicide. In the event that these coping strategies are ineffective, maladaptive responses can occur.

Responding to homicidal loss is unfortunately, but perhaps predictably, associated with negative outcomes, including complicated grief. **Complicated grief** is a debilitating, chronic sense of loss where an individual is not able to overcome the bereavement process. In the event that the perpetrator of the homicide is never brought to justice, covictims of homicide can experience tremendous anger, feelings of revenge, and even PTSD symptoms. For instance, a study of 331 covictims of homicide in the Netherlands found that their dispositional and situational feelings of revenge were much lower if the homicide offender was convicted as opposed to another legal outcome (van Denderen, de Keijser, Gerlsma, Huisman, & Boelen, 2014). In addition, covictims with more feelings of revenge and PTSD symptoms were more likely to experience complicated grief and less likely to display positive social functioning.

Box 17.1   Victimology Effects after a Mass Shooting

Sadly, mass shootings are a relatively common, worldwide phenomenon. Obviously, any incident of homicide is tragic, but the sheer numbers of casualties of mass murders make them especially horrifying. The most violent mass shooting occurred on Utøya Island, Norway, on July 22, 2011, where 77 people were murdered and another 319 injured. In the United States, the most violent mass murders have become part of the national lexicon and are often referred to be the location of the atrocity, such as Virginia Tech, San Ysidro, Columbine, Luby's Cafeteria, and the University of Texas clock tower.

A particularly frightening aspect of mass murder is the seeming randomness of the violence, and the degree of unpredictability to the events. For example, Honduras has a firearm homicide rate that is 18 times greater than the United States, but Honduras has not experienced an infamous mass murder. Other nations with firearm homicide rates that are 10 times greater than the United States, such as El Salvador, Jamaica, and Venezuela have also not had a major mass murder. On the other hand, the deadliest mass murder occurred in Norway, a nation with a firearm homicide rate that is 1/90th of the United States rate (Shultz, Thoresen, Flynn, Muschert, Shaw, et al., 2014). Thus, it is difficult to predict where a mass murder will unfold next.

Persons who survive mass shootings experience a multitude of negative mental health effects. Many of them experienced extraordinary trauma, such as being shot, directly witnessing the murder of other people, some of whom were family of friends, and seeing dead bodies. These experiences often result in increased psychological distress, PTSD, depression, anxiety, and others. Other survivors of mass shootings have difficulty adjusting to life and also experience dissociation, avoidance behaviors, and problems with emotional regulation. About 30–40 percent of children who are exposed to life-threatening events like a mass murder will meet criteria for PTSD, and the severity and prevalence is even higher if the proximity to the violence is closer. And this discussion pertains to individuals who were not necessarily wounded in the mass murders. Persons who were shot and survived the mass murder can experience a range of medical problems that negatively impact their functioning, their livelihood, potentially their socioeconomic circumstances, and their mental health. In sum, mass murder initiates a cascade of negative consequences for direct, indirect, and vicarious victims of the carnage.

Source: Shultz, J. M., Thoresen, S., Flynn, B. W., Muschert, G. W., Shaw, J. A., Espinel, Z., Walter, F. G., Gaither, J. B., Garcia-Barcena, Y., O'Keefe, K., & Cohen, A. M. (2014). Multiple vantage points on the mental health effects of mass shootings. *Current Psychiatry Reports, 16*(9), 469–487.

There are important health consequences for the friends and families of homicide victims. There is considerable evidence of elevated psychopathology among homicidally bereaved persons. For example, van Denderen, Keijser, Kleen, and Boelen (2014) conducted a systematic review of the literature and found that PTSD symptoms varied from 19 to 71 percent among persons who were bereaved by homicidal loss. Moreover, between 5 and 6 percent of homicidally bereaved individuals currently displayed PTSD. In addition, homicidally bereaved persons often faced depression, complicated grief, anger, hostility, and substance abuse problems. A more recent study indicated prevalence of between

30 and 38 percent for PTSD and 80 to 83 percent for complicated grief among homicidally bereaved individuals (van Denderen, Keijser, Huisman, & Boelen, 2014).

Mastrocinque and her colleagues (2014) conducted a focus group with 28 participants from Rochester, New York, Albany, New York, and several locations in Indiana. Covictims of homicides displayed a wide range of physical and mental health changes including dramatic weight loss, dramatic weight gain, increased blood pressure, stressful hypervigilance, anxiety and depression, headaches, vague body pains, and others. These medical problems contributed to deterioration in their daily living, such as reductions in bathing and grooming and severely disrupted sleep patterns. The researchers concluded that surviving family and friends of homicide victims have an assortment of biological, psychological, social, and spiritual needs that generally are not well met by existing services, at least from the covictims' perspectives.

As a way to improve the services for covictims of homicide, some criminal justice organizations have created special liaisons (Malone, 2007). **Family liaison officers** are members of a police department who serve as a single point of contact between the police department handling

Family liaison officers can help covictims of homicide navigate and survive the bereavement process.

a homicide case and the homicide victim's family and friends. Family liaison officers are effective at providing consistent and frequent communication about the status of the investigation to family and friends. Among probation departments, a similar position also exists. **Victim liaison officers** are dedicated correctional staff who work with the family and friends of homicide victims to assist in relevant tasks, such as obtaining victims services and notification of release (if applicable) of the homicide offender.

The pain and suffering relating to a case that has not been solved is even more acute. **Cold cases homicides** are open investigations in which there has not been judicial resolution. In many cold cases, there is never even an arrest. Wellman (2014) conducted in-depth interviews with 24 cold case homicide survivors and found that they made interesting comparisons to other bereaved groups when coming to terms with their loss. They felt a sense of kinship with other persons who had also lost loved ones to homicide. These people were seen as equal to them because they had both experienced a similar loss, thus it was a lateral emotional coping. Many developed friendships with other survivors of homicide and felt that these relationships assisted them in their emotional recovery and getting on with their daily lives.

They also experienced downward comparisons to others who lost loved ones to causes other than homicide. Wellman found that covictims of cold case homicides viewed deaths from other causes as less painful and emotionally devastated than what murders produce. And the unsolved component of their cold case makes it even more emotionally heart wrenching and righteous compared to other causes of death. Unfortunately, these feelings of downward comparisons where other causes of death are viewed as "less than" a homicide produce feelings of isolation, depression, and anxiety among the bereaved.

It is important to recognize that at times another victim of homicide is ironically the homicide offender. A study of clinical data from therapy groups among 41 homicide offenders is illustrative. Adshead, Ferrito, and Bose (2014) found that homicide offenders undergo significant self-reflection as they come to terms with their homicidal conduct. First, they must accept that homicide offender is now a status that describes them. This acknowledgment brings with it tremendous guilt and anxiety and results in a changed identity. Second, they must accept how abnormal mental states both potentially influenced their homicide event and/or continues to be a part of their identity. This is especially true for homicide offenders with major mental disorders, such as schizophrenia. Although many will find it challenging or perhaps even inappropriate to consider the victimization experiences of homicide offenders, it is nevertheless important to recognize that homicide offenders often suffer considerable psychiatric distress from the reality of their criminal conduct, and the resultant punishment it denotes.

Similarly, the perpetrators of certain forms of homicide are sometimes viewed in sympathetic ways particularly if there is real or perceived evidence of mental illness in the offender. A case in point is neonaticide. Shelton, Muirhead, and Canning (2010) studied 45 U.S. cases of maternal neonaticide and found a general sense of ambivalence about these cases. According to the authors, three factors influenced feelings of ambivalence about women who kill their child within its first day of life. First, there is a perception that childbirth sets into motion emotional and physical turmoil that reduces the mother's perceived culpability for her conduct. Second, there is sentiment that neonaticide offenders are not offenders generally, in that they do not commit various forms of street crime, and thus they are more redeemable. Third, for some there is uncertainty about the personhood of a fetus or newborn. While opinions can vary on these issues, the ambivalence also seems alive in the criminal courts as 22 percent of these homicide offenders received probation for murdering their newborn child.

Finally, a powerful way to comprehend the impact of homicide is to examine a unique form of homicide: the killing of a law enforcement officer in the line of duty. The Federal Bureau of Investigation publishes a special report on **Law Enforcement Officers Killed and Assaulted (LEOKA)**. Between 2001 and 2010, 541 police officers were killed in the line of duty. Of these killings:

- 23 percent were during arrest scenarios
- 22 percent were ambush scenarios
- 18 percent were during traffic pursuits or stops
- 14 percent were during disturbance calls
- 11 percent involved suspicious individuals or circumstances
- 12 percent involved other situations

Those who murder police officers are often serious offenders. About 82 percent had prior arrests, 64 percent had prior convictions, and 43 percent had prior arrests for violent crimes (Cooper & Smith, 2011). Fortunately, the incidence of police killings has declined nearly 50 percent over the last three decades (see Figure 17.3).

That most offenders who kill police are serious offenders is fully consistent with the next chapter, which focuses on offending patterns over the

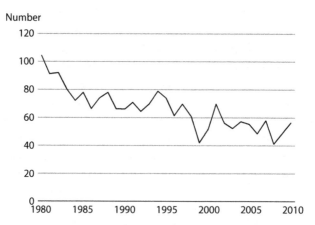

Figure 17.3 Law enforcement officers killed in the line of duty, 1980–2010.

Source: Modified from Cooper, A., & Smith, E. L. (2011). *Homicide trends in the United States, 1980–2008. Annual rates for 2009–2010.* Washington, DC: U.S. Department of Justice, Office of Justice Programs, Bureau of Justice Statistics.

life course, especially the offending patterns of those make violence and crime their life's work.

CHAPTER 18

Homicide and the Criminal Career Perspective

© Everett Historical/Shutterstock, Inc.

Many murderers, including the notorious outlaw Jesse James, have extensive criminal careers including dozens and even hundreds of arrests and convictions for a variety of crimes.

Conceptual Background

In June 2014, 34-year-old Joshua Wade confessed to murdering three men while appearing in court for a hearing to transfer his jurisdiction from state to federal prison. Wade had already been convicted of two other murders, the first occurring when he was just 14 years of age. Upset with the conditions of his prison facility in Alaska, Wade blurted out in court that he had also killed the other men in part to change jurisdiction to the federal system where he assumed the conditions of confinement would be better. Although relatively young, Wade had already been arrested for a host of crimes including carjacking, sexual assault, armed robbery, tampering with evidence, drug violations, and others. He has been in juvenile detention centers, reform schools, jails, and prisons for much of his life (Shedlock & Burke, 2014). This one offender had committed many lifetimes of violence, crime, and disorder.

As this current event attests, criminal justice practitioners have long recognized that criminal activity is not randomly distributed throughout the human population. Some people are significantly more likely than others to commit crime, and indeed, most of the theories in this book attest to the individual-level variation in criminal behavior. Most people do not commit crime, some commit a small amount of crime, and still others commit crime in bunches. These behavioral differences manifest in arrests, convictions, and involvement in the criminal justice system, such as probation, jail sentences, prison terms, parole sentences, and related correctional involvements. As such, most individuals will go their entire life without being arrested, and frankly will only be contacted by the criminal justice system for a speeding ticket. Among those who are arrested, it is often a one-off occurrence and is usually for a relatively minor offense such as traffic violations, drunk driving, or shoplifting. Others are seemingly continuously arrested throughout their life.

The sum total of this criminal activity is a criminal career. The **criminal career** is a measure of an individual's criminal activity across life. It is defined by a variety of parameters. The beginning of the criminal career is known as **onset**. Generally, onset is inversely related to the severity of the criminal career, which means that the earlier onset emerges, generally the worse the offender is. Onset is thought to reflect the emergence of a person's latent liability for problem behavior, or criminal propensity. Criminal onset can be understood like other forms of onset, such as reading ability. For example, a child who reads very early in life, such as age 2 or 3 years, likely is academically talented and has high intelligence. Conversely, a child who does not read until age 10 years likely has academic deficits and lower intelligence. In both cases, the timing of reading emergence is viewed as a proxy for the child's overall academic ability, intelligence, or "smarts."

Onset can be measured in many ways. Usually, the actual emergence of an individual's antisocial behavior predates their first arrest. Serious offenders often get into considerable trouble even during toddlerhood and throughout childhood. However, they are not usually arrested until late childhood or early adolescence. Research has shown that arrest onset is the most important indicator of onset because it is most strongly associated with criminal career severity (DeLisi, Neppl, Lohman, Vaughn, & Shook, 2013), and the age of 14 years has been shown to be a particularly strong indicator of criminal career severity and seriousness (DeLisi, 2006). Irrespective of how it is measured, onset marks the start of a criminal career.

Once a criminal career has begun, it tends to develop in unpredictable and often intermittent ways. **Intermittency** means sporadic activity where an offender is arrested multiple times in a short-period of time, then has periods of time with little to no arrests. In other words, the "pattern" is there is no clear pattern. Criminal careers do not follow a linear pattern and usually do not reflect a clear pattern of **escalation** or an increase in the severity of crimes. This means that a homicide offender, for instance, could commit murder for his first arrest or his fiftieth arrest, it is difficult to predict.

Once underway, criminal careers have a developmental course that reflects continuity, where there is continued antisocial behavior and attendant criminal justice system involvement and discontinuity, where the crime appears to decline. For example, persons who have substance dependence often commit crime at very high rates in order to obtain resources to exchange for drugs. In these cases, there is frequent arrest activity. On the other hand, persons who enter into a healthy, prosocial relationship such as a marriage often see a sharp decline in criminal activity and arrests. The frequency of criminal activity or rate of arrests in a specific period of time is known as **lambda**. In other words, criminal careers can display a flash-point or go dormant.

When a criminal career has substantively gone dormant, it goes through a period of **desistance**, or declining criminal behavior and declining criminal justice contacts until it finally ends. The end of a criminal career is known as **termination**.

Perhaps one of the most important concepts in the criminal career perspective is the asymmetry in offending whereby a small number of persons are disproportionately responsible for the bulk of serious crimes, including homicide. These are known as chronic or habitual offenders, or more simply **career criminals**. The seminal work that established the contemporary understanding of career criminals was *Delinquency in a Birth Cohort* (Wolfgang, Figlio, & Sellin, 1972). The study followed 9,945 males born in

Philadelphia in 1945 and who lived in the city at least from ages 10 to 18. The significance of this prospective, longitudinal birth cohort design was that it was not susceptible to sampling error because every male subject in the cohort was followed. They found that nearly two-thirds of the youth never experienced a police contact and that 35 percent of the population had. According to Wolfgang and his associates (1972), persons with five or more police contacts were chronic or habitual offenders. Of the nearly ten thousand boys, only 627 members, just 6 percent of the population, qualified as habitual offenders. However, the chronic 6 percent accounted for 52 percent of the delinquency in the entire cohort. Moreover, chronic offenders committed 63 percent of all Index offenses, 71 percent of the murders, 73 percent of the rapes, 82 percent of the robberies, and 69 percent of the aggravated assaults.

A second and improved study examined a cohort of persons born in Philadelphia in 1958. Conducted by Tracy, Wolfgang, and Figlio (1990), the second Philadelphia cohort contained 13,160 males and 14,000 females. Overall, the 1958 cohort committed crime at higher rates than the 1945 cohort and demonstrated greater involvement in the most serious forms of crime, such as murder, rape, robbery, and aggravated assault. However, roughly the same proportion of persons, 33 percent, experienced arrest prior to adulthood. Approximately 7 percent of the population members were habitual offenders, and they accounted for 61 percent of all delinquency, 60 percent of the murders, 75 percent of the rapes, 73 percent of the robberies, and 65 percent of the aggravated assaults.

One of the most important theoretical developments of the last 30 years is Moffitt's (1993) **developmental taxonomy**, which articulates a three part typology of individuals. Abstainers are persons who do not engage in antisocial behavior, thus they would be extremely unlikely to ever commit a homicide. Adolescence-limited offenders are persons who engage in deviance briefly during their adolescence mostly for defiance-oriented offenses that reflect the conflicts of their changing status from child to adult. This includes behaviors such as driving deviance, alcohol use, smoking, marijuana use, theft, and similarly low-level crimes. **Life-course-persistent offenders** are those that display antisocial conduct across life due to neuropsychological deficits, negative environmental contexts, and the interaction of those person- and environmental-deficits. Life-course-persistent offenders are another way to describe a career criminal, and these offenders are those who have the most serious criminal careers and who engage in the most severe types of behavior, including homicide.

In the taxonomy, abstainers and life-course-persistent offenders are pathological in statistical terms and represent only about 5 to 10 percent of a population. Conversely, adolescence-limited-offenders are normative in statistical terms and represent the remainder of a population. The tax-onomy is a heuristic device to understand highly prosocial individuals, mostly prosocial individuals who dabble in antisocial conduct in various ways, and extremely antisocial individuals who rarely dabble in prosocial conduct. Moffitt's developmental taxonomy has been extremely influential not only in criminology and criminal justice, but across the behavioral sciences (Moffitt, 2007).

Criminal career research is less of a theory per se, and more of a conceptual approach to studying the diversity of the offending population. Because homicides offenders are comparatively rare, they often do not appear in samples that criminologists are able to construct. This occurs for a few reasons. First, most people do not commit murder, thus sampling several hundred or even several thousand members of the community likely will not produce a single person who has committed homicide. And even if sampling designs do yield some homicide offenders, there usually are not sufficient numbers of homicide offenders to facilitate statistical analyses.

Second, much of criminological research is conducted for the testing of criminological theories that focus on delinquency and general criminal offending that is more common, such as theft, burglary, and drug offenses, thus the focus in not on homicide. Third, the study of homicide has historically been the province of forensic psychologists and practitioners, not mainstream criminologists who have historically been sociological in their orientation. Nevertheless, there is a sizable literature on homicide offenders from a criminal careers perspective, and that work is examined next.

Empirical Linkages to Homicide

The criminal career perspective is important for many reasons, but one of the central reasons is that it allows a lifespan perspective of criminal offenders to see how their antisocial careers develop and the course they take over time. As Ganpat and her colleagues (2014, p. 222) advised, "[a] person's criminal history is generally seen as an important manifestation of one's personal characteristics, and especially of criminal propensity, impulsivity, and self-control." This is particularly important to understand the background characteristics of homicide offenders.

In their study of more than 272,000 prisoners released from prisons in the United States in 1994, Langan and Levin (2002) reported that fewer than 2 percent of released prisoners had been convicted of homicide, but that nearly one in five committed another violent offense. And 1.2 percent of convicted murderers committed yet another homicide. It is common for homicide offenders to have extensive criminal history and considerable prison history, and to recidivate after release from confinement (Baay,

Liem, & Nieuwbeerta, 2012; DeLisi, Hochstetler, Jones-Johnson, Caudill, & Marquart, 2011).

Indeed, as shown in Figure 18.1, many homicides occur along with other circumstances that denote generalized involvement in crime, such as engaging in other felonies, sex offenses, drug crimes, gang battles, and the like. Based on the Supplementary Homicide Reports and newspaper archives, Petee, Padgett, and York (1997) examined 139 mass killers from 1965 to 1995 and found that the modal group committed felony murder, in other words their killing rampage occurred along with other criminal activity.

Firestone and colleagues (1998) compared the criminal careers and other characteristics of child molesters, some of whom had committed homicide and some who had not. Overall, they found that homicidal child molesters were much more severe in their behavioral profile than nonhomicidal ones. Homicidal child molesters more commonly

	Victims			Offenders		
Types of homicide	Total	Male	Female	Total	Male	Female
All homicides	100%	76.8%	23.2%	100%	89.5%	10.5%
Victim/offender relationship						
Intimate	100%	36.3%	63.7%	100%	70.3%	29.7%
Family	100%	54.7	45.3	100%	74.4	25.6
Infants	100%	54.7	45.3	100%	62.5	37.5
Elders	100%	57.2	42.8	100%	84.8	15.2
Circumstances						
Felony murder	100%	79.2%	20.8%	100%	93.2%	6.8%
Sex related	100%	18.3	81.7	100%	93.7	6.3
Drug related	100%	90.5	9.5	100%	95.5	4.5
Gang related	100%	94.6	5.4	100%	98.3	1.7
Argument	100%	77.2	22.8	100%	86.6	13.4
Workplace	100%	79.1	20.9	100%	91.3	8.7
Weapon						
Gun homicide	100%	82.6%	17.4%	100%	92.1%	7.9%
Arson	100%	54.7	45.3	100%	78.8	21.2
Poison	100%	56.1	43.9	100%	60.5	39.5
Multiple victims or offenders						
Multiple victims	100%	64.4%	35.6%	100%	93.6%	6.4%
Multiple offenders	100%	88.0	12.0	100	91.6	8.4

Figure 18.1   Criminal career correlates of homicide by sex, 1980–2008.

Source: Modified from Cooper, A., & Smith, E. L. (2011). *Homicide trends in the United States, 1980–2008. Annual rates for 2009–2010.* Washington, DC: U.S. Department of Justice, Office of Justice Programs, Bureau of Justice Statistics.

victimized strangers, were more psychopathic, were more likely to have antisocial personality disorder, were more likely to be sexually sadistic, and to display multiple personality disorders and other paraphilias. More than 82 percent of the homicidal group were sexually sadistic and about 53 percent were both pedophilic and sexually sadistic. The respective prevalence of those constructs for the nonhomicidal group was zero percent for both. The homicidal group also demonstrated higher levels of deviant arousal to pedophilic and adult assault stimuli. In terms of criminal careers, the homicidal group had more than 2.5 times as many arrest charges as the nonhomicidal child molesters. The homicidal child molesters also were significantly more likely to have a history of other violent arrests and convictions (Firestone, Bradford, Greenberg, Larose, & Curry, 1998).

Heide, Spencer, Thompson, and Solomon (2001) studied 59 juvenile homicide offenders of which 10 were sentenced to youthful incarceration. They found that 60 percent of the total sample was returned to prison—a conservative estimate because arrests and other nonreincarceration dispositions were not considered as recidivism. In other words, the juvenile homicide was not an aberration but instead was a signal indicator of a usually extensive criminal career. Similarly, Hagan (1997) found that more than half of youths who had been confined for murder during adolescence were subsequently returned to prison upon convictions for other serious violent crimes such as robbery, rape, kidnapping, and assault.

Based on data from 654 homicide offenders selected from eight states, DeLisi and Walters (2011) tested an interactive model where multiple-homicide offending was a function of prisonization and concurrent instrumental violent offending. They controlled for an assortment of correlates of violent offending including age, race, sex, criminal history, prior incarcerations, and contemporaneous involvement in rape, robbery, kidnapping, and burglary. The authors found that offenders with multiple prior confinements who were subsequently released and continued to commit instrumentally violent crimes were significantly likely to murder multiple victims.

Sturup and Lindqvust (2013) examined the recidivism patterns across 32 years of homicide offenders selected from Swedish population registers. They found evidence of continuity in homicide offending among individual criminal careers. About 10 percent of murderers were subsequently arrested for crimes, and 3 percent committed an additional murder. They also found that another 3 percent of offenders had committed a murder prior to their murder conviction for which they were on the register. All of these were recidivistic single-victim homicide offenders there was no evidence of serial murder.

In their study of serial murder in South Africa, Salfati, Labuschagne, Horning, Sorochinski, and De Wet (2014) found that 25 percent of the serial killers in South Africa between 1936 and 2007 had previously been arrested for homicide. In their study of inmate homicide in the Texas Department of Criminal Justice between 2000 and 2008, Cunningham, Sorensen, Vigen, and Woods (2010) found extensive evidence of juvenile and criminal history among 52 homicide offenders and their 35 homicide victims. Half of inmate killers had prior juvenile probation involvement, 44 percent of homicide offenders had been placed in detention homes or hospitals, and 18 percent of them had been committed to juvenile reformatories.

Vaughn and his colleagues (2009) conducted one of the first examinations of multiple homicide offenders that explicitly used a criminal careers perspective. Drawing on data from 160 persons who were convicted of multiple homicides, they utilized latent class analysis which allows researchers to discover unobserved groupings of persons in data. Three types of multiple homicide offenders were found. One group had surprisingly little criminal history (averaging three career arrests) and was not generally arrested until adulthood. A second group had more extensive criminal history. A third group had severe criminal records and the most prior arrests for various offenses, including prior homicides (Vaughn, DeLisi, Beaver, & Howard, 2009). Other research has similarly shown that multiple homicide offenders tend to commit an array of offenses and be mostly versatile (Wright, Pratt, & DeLisi, 2008). This means that in addition to homicide, they also commit property crimes, other nonhomicide violent crimes, drug violations, and other legal violations. For a look at the criminal careers of offenders who committed sexual homicides as adolescents, see Box 18.1.

A unique data source to examine the development of homicide is the Pittsburgh Youth Study is a longitudinal study of inner-city boys in Pittsburgh, Pennsylvania, who were in first, fourth, or seventh grades in public schools in 1987. The children are high-risk for antisocial behavior given their educational deficits (between 26 and 40 percent had been held back in school), socioeconomic situation, and family instability. Several factors have been found to predict subsequent homicide offending. These include being old for one's grade, having a young mother, mother low educational attainment, living in a bad neighborhood, having a disruptive behavior disorder, having a positive attitude to delinquency, having a positive attitude to substance use, school suspension, peer delinquency, peer substance use, and various types of delinquency including weapons carrying, gang fighting, and selling drugs (Farrington & Loeber, 2011).

Several studies have also reinforced the idea that a small number of offenders, usually around 5–10 percent, of the population not only commit

most of the crime, but are the ones primarily responsible for committing homicide. There are many examples of this empirical regularity. In
Boston during and after the crack cocaine epidemic of the late twentieth
century, Braga (2003) observed that about 1 percent of juveniles in the city
accounted for 60 percent of the juvenile homicides. Almost all of these
homicide offenders were gang-involved, chronic delinquents. The most
chronic of these offenders had 54 prior criminal arraignments, 25 prior
violent crime arraignments, 24 prior property crime arraignments, and 14
prior drug crime arraignments. The youngest of these severe offenders was
12 years of age!

As examined in Chapter 15, Cook, Ludwig, and Braga (2005) performed
a case-control study of a dataset that contained all arrests and felony convictions in Illinois for 1990–2001. Overall, 884 persons were convicted of
homicide and were compared to 7.9 million controls. Nearly 43 percent of
the homicide offenders had at least one prior felony conviction, whereas
only 3.9 percent of controls had a felony conviction. In terms of arrest,
nearly 72 percent of murderers had been arrested compared to 18.2 percent of controls. In terms of violent felony convictions, such as homicide,
rape, armed robbery, aggravated assault and related crimes of violence, 9.3
percent of homicide offenders had prior convictions compared to 0.9 percent of controls.

Box 18.1   Juvenile Sexual Homicide Offenders....30 Years Later

In terms of criminal extremity, few behaviors can match sexual homicide.
Fortunately, it is a very rare form of homicide especially among juveniles. In
fact, fewer than 10 sexual homicides by an adolescent offender are perpetrated annually in the United States. Given that it is such an extreme form of
criminal behavior, what becomes of adolescents who perpetrate it?

Khachatryan and colleagues (2014) recently studied a sample of eight
adolescent sexual homicide offenders and followed up with them 30 years
later. Not surprisingly, their behavioral outcomes were not positive and
generally reflect a life of crime. A brief profile of these eight offenders
appears below:

- Karl was 14 when he was arrested for murder and sexual battery.
  He had no prior arrests or juvenile justice system involvement. He
  was sentenced to 99 years in prison and has currently served 31
  years in confinement. He has committed no offenses during his
  imprisonment.

- Thomas was 16 when he was arrested for murder and sexual battery. He had one prior juvenile offense also occurring at age 16. He received a life sentence in which he must serve 25 years before being eligible for parole. He has escaped from prison, but was returned shortly thereafter and has been in confinement for 30 years. He has not been released.
- Gene was 14 when he was arrested for murder. Beginning at age 8, Gene had an extensive juvenile record with 12 prior police contacts including for violent offenses, such as battery. He was sentenced to 50 years in prison. He escaped once from prison and served 25 years. He has been in the community for 5.5 years and to date has not been rearrested.
- Bobby was 14 when he committed his sexual homicide. He had three juvenile arrests starting at age 12 including violent crimes, such as assault and battery. He received a 20-year prison sentence and amassed zero acts of misconduct during his confinement. He served just over 7 years in prison and was released 8.5 years ago. Since, he has been arrested twice albeit not for violent crimes and has not been recommitted to prison.
- Gus was 16 when arrested for murder, rape, and armed robbery. He had two prior arrests also at age 16 and received a 17-year prison sentence. During his jail detention, Gus committed sexual battery and ultimately served nearly seven years in prison. He has been out for over 2 years, and been arrested 12 times including four violent offenses. Gus has also been arrested for property, drug, and firearm violations and is again in prison.
- Donnell was 17 when arrested for murder, rape, and armed robbery. His juvenile career began at age 14 and included four prior arrests. He received a 22-year prison sentence. During his confinement he committed multiple violent acts including sexual battery, aggravated assault, and assault and battery. He only served 7.5 years and has been in the community for one year and three months. He has been arrested three times, including twice for violent crimes (robbery), and is back in prison.
- Andrew was 17 when arrested for murder, rape, armed robbery, and auto theft. He was first arrested at age 7 and had a staggering 14 juvenile arrests including several violent crimes, such as robbery, battery, and aggravated assault. He was sentenced to 22 years in prison. During confinement, he committed arson, and served 7.5 years. Although he has been in the community for a mere four months, Andrews has been arrested five times for multiple violent, property, drug, and weapons offenses. He has since been returned to prison.
- Jack was 18 when arrested for murder, rape, and armed robbery. His offending career began at age 9 and included 10 juvenile arrests, including multiple violent offenses such as aggravated assault and robbery. He was sentenced to 40 years in prison. During his 19 years of

time served, he committed multiple violations for battery and smug-gling contraband. He has been in the community for over 11 years, and has not been contacted by the police for new crimes.

Although none of these individuals committed another sexual homi-cide, overall their offending careers were severe (for those who have been released).

Source: Khachatryan, N., Heide, K. M., Hummel, E. V., & Chan, H. C. O. (2014). Juvenile sexual homicide offenders: Thirty-year follow-up investigation. *International Journal of Offender Therapy and Comparative Criminology*, doi: 10.1177/0306624X14552062.

© PiXXart/Shutterstock, Inc.

Michael Vaughn and Matt DeLisi have shown that the severe 5 percent of all offenders are responsible for most of the crime and violence in the United States and are the offenders most likely to perpetrate homicide.

Using large samples of data, Vaughn and colleagues found that about 5 percent of the population—who were dubbed "the severe 5 percent"—were involved in most of the externalizing behaviors in the United States. Although the sample did not contain homicide as an outcome, the severe 5 percent did commit the most severe forms of violence and other behaviors, such as frequent gun carrying, that did correlate with homicide. Consistent with Moffitt's theory, they also found evidence of an abstainer group that was psychologically the healthiest and behaviorally the highest functioning (Vaughn, Fu, Wernet, DeLisi, Beaver, et al., 2011). In terms of their profile, abstainers would be the least likely to ever commit a violent crime, and would be exceedingly unlikely to commit a homicide.

In a unique study using data from a sample of homicide offenders, nearly 200 of whom had been sentenced to death, Behnken and her colleagues (2011) examined criminal career predictors of these most serious criminal justice outcomes. They found that several measures of prior and current criminal history were associated with capital punishment including prior incarceration history, an early onset of arrest, and serious juvenile offending including homicide and child molestation. Not surprisingly, many capital defendants have led lives of serious antisocial conduct across the life course. In another study using the same data source, DeLisi (2014) found that offenders who committed rape in conjunction with homicide were significantly likely to commit multiple homicides later in their criminal career. Indeed, the most violent offender in the dataset was convicted of nine counts of homicide and 13 counts of rape.

Researchers in The Netherlands compared 2,049 homicide offenders to 3,387 violent offenders who had attempted homicide (Ganpat, Liem, van der Leun, & Nieuwbeerta, 2014) using data from the Dutch Homicide Monitor. They found that both groups had extensive criminal histories, but ironically, the attempted murderers had criminal careers that were worse than the murderers. About 68 percent of completed homicide offenders had prior criminal history that averaged 6.7 arrests and spanned 7.7 years. Thirty-eight percent had prior crimes of violence. Comparatively, 76 percent of attempted homicide offenders had prior criminal history that averaged 7.1 arrests over an 8.8-year span. Forty eight percent had prior crimes of violence. Nearly half of both samples had previously been imprisoned.

Using homicide data from Newark, New Jersey, Adams and Pizarro (2014) compared the patterns of offending specialization and escalation among gang and nongang members. Regardless of their gang status, it was clear that homicide offenders were also chronic offenders as they averaged nearly 10 arrests over their criminal career. This marker is two times higher than the usual measure of chronic or habitual criminality described earlier in this chapter. They also found that homicide offenders were heavily immersed in generalized criminal offending, and also that a large part of their daily live was comprised of involvement in the drug trade. Thus, both gang and nongang offenders were versatile and violent criminals who also happened to commit at least one homicide. Most limited their killing to one murder. Of the 348 offenders, only 20 were responsible for multiple homicides. Twenty offenders murdered two victims, three offenders murdered three victims, and one offender committed six homicides.

An ingenious way to examine the effects of habitual criminal behavior on homicide is to examine criminal deportations. Blake (2014) examined criminal deportations from the United States from 1985 to 1996 and found that 17 percent of the increase in the homicide rate of nations receiving the deportees was the result of these criminal "exports." These deportations represented 23 percent of the total increase in homicide in these developing countries.

The criminal career paradigm is also useful for understanding offenders for whom *homicide is their career.* To illustrate, Farrell, Keppel, and Titterington (2011) created an exploratory roster of 10 female serial murderers selected from their review of news archives from 1895 to 1990. These women had homicide careers that averaged about 11 years in duration, and ranged from 2 years for Aileen Wuornos to 30 years for Nannie Doss. Their homicide careers showed a contrast between the putative number of victims to the actual number of homicide charges filed against them. For instance, Genene Jones, a former pediatric nurse, is believed to have murdered between 10 and 120 infants and children but was charged with just one homicide (other charges have subsequently been added). Jane Toppan confessed to poisoning 31 victims but was charged in just three of the homicides. Tillie Klimek was believed to have poisoned eight victims but was charged with just one homicide.

Using data from Canadian offenders who have committed at least one homicide, Cale and colleagues (2010) reported extensive criminal histories especially among those who killed multiple times. On average, these offenders were first convicted for a serious crime upon adulthood, had nearly seven serious convictions by age 22, and were involved in an assortment of criminal behaviors including drug violations, other violent offenses, sexual convictions, escape, and general noncompliance with the criminal justice system.

Finally, several studies explored **recidivism**, or subsequent offending following release from criminal justice system supervision among various types of homicide offenders. Liem (2013) recently conducted a systematic review of the homicide offender recidivism literature and found that subsequent criminal careers of homicide offenders after their initial homicide are quite varied and depend on how recidivism is defined. Some studies defined recidivism as another homicide, which is the rarest likelihood of reoffending.

Between 1 and 11 percent of homicide offenders go on to commit still another homicide with the highest recidivism found among psychotic homicide offenders. Self-report studies indicate that most homicide offenders continue to commit serious crimes after their initial murder with prevalence estimates exceeding 80 percent. Various studies of homicide offenders, juvenile homicide offenders, sexual homicide offenders, and others found that recidivism for additional violent crimes, including assault, sexual assault, robbery, and others ranged between 10 and 40 percent.

There is much overlap between career criminals who commit homicide and another group of offenders who are noteworthy for their recurrent involvement in problem behaviors and their disproportionate involvement in homicide. That group—psychopaths—is examined next.

CHAPTER 19

Homicide and the Psychopathy Perspective

© xpixel/Shutterstock, Inc.

No disorder or psychological condition embodies homicide as well as psychopathy.

Conceptual Background

When most people hear the word homicide, one of the words that immediately springs to mind is psychopathy. There is good reason for this as psychopathy is the conceptual area in this book that most directly corresponds to homicide offending. Many of the most infamous criminal offenders in American history, including Charles Manson, Ted Bundy, John Wayne Gacy, Aileen Wuornos, Gary Ridgway, and, frankly, probably every serial killer ever had acutely psychopathic personalities.

Psychopathy is a personality disorder that is characterized by a suite of interpersonal, affective, lifestyle, and behavioral characteristics that manifest in wide-ranging antisocial behaviors (Cleckley, 1941; DeLisi, 2009; Hare & Neumann, 2008; Ribeiro da Silva, Rijo, & Salekin, 2012). These traits occur in various combinations and like all personality traits, are relatively stable across situational contexts and over time. This means that non-psychopathic persons do not "become" psychopathic in later stages of life. Similarly, acutely psychopathic persons do not stop being psychopathic. It is what they are.

Interpersonally, psychopaths are characterized by glib or superficial charm, narcissism or grandiose self-worth, pathological lying, and conning/manipulation. Their sense of charm is primarily intended to impose their will on others and to exploit others for their own gain. The psychopathic interpersonal style is very entitled and self-absorbed and these negative traits are expressed to an absurd degree. For instance, many sexual homicide offenders will inform law enforcement that they raped and murdered victims because these forms of violence were what was required to satisfy their sexual wants and desires.

Affectively, psychopaths are characterized by callousness and lack of empathy, failure to accept responsibility, shallow emotion, and lack of guilt or remorselessness. Here too the psychopathic personality is best seen in its interaction with law enforcement. Psychopathic murderers often refuse to acknowledge that they committed their crimes even in the face of incontrovertible evidence. And even when psychopathic murderers confess or admit their crimes, they do so in a very flat, expressionless, matter of fact style that belies the gravity of their crimes.

In terms of lifestyle, psychopaths lack realistic life goals, have a parasitic orientation, and are globally irresponsible, impulsive, and stimulation seeking. In this regard, their lifestyle is frankly similar to other criminal offenders and unsuccessful persons generally. Due to their impulsive nature and refusal or inability to comply with family, school, and work expectations, they often have severe problems achieving basic adult successes. Since they cannot compete on their own merits, psychopaths strive to live off of the contributions of others.

Behaviorally, psychopaths have poor behavioral control, evince early behavior problems, engage in juvenile delinquency, are criminally versatile, and have records of noncompliance and revocation of conditional release. The psychopathic person's behavioral problems are apparent very early and compromise their development in school and other domains. They also exhibit versatile criminal offending and often have extensive arrest histories that similarly indicate failure to comply with court sentences, probation, parole, and any supervision.

Psychopathy is apparent in childhood usually in the form of **callous and unemotional traits** which are the lack of empathy and absence of guilt and **moral disengagement** which is the tendency to engage in problem behaviors without feeling guilt, shame, or other self-conscious negative emotions. Even in the preschool period, these children can be identified for their abnormally aggressive and frequently rule-breaking behavior coupled with their refusal to admit fault or apologize. For example, Paciello, Fida, Tramontano, Lupinetti, and Caprara (2008) analyzed a large sample of adolescents and identified four developmental pathways of moral disengagement and antisociality. These included a group that was almost always moral, a group with slight moral disengagement at age 14 that declined quickly thereafter, a group that had moderately high moral disengagement until age 16 that declined quickly thereafter, and finally, a small group that had moderate to high levels of moral disengagement across adolescence and into adulthood. This small pathological group was the most psychopathic. These youths were the most delinquent, the most aggressive, and committed the most acts of violence compared to others. They were also less likely to experience guilt after committing delinquency and were rated by their peers as the most aggressive.

Although psychopathy is a single construct, there is heterogeneity within it. For instance, Karpman (1930, 1947) emphasized the role of the superego in criminal behavior and created the taxonomy of psychopathy that is today known as primary psychopathy and secondary psychopathy. **Primary psychopathy** is characterized by the absence of conscience or superego where individuals experience no neurotic feelings or inner turmoil in terms of emotional response. Behaviorally, primary psychopaths are the chilling, cold-blooded psychopathic offenders that popularize television and film.

Secondary psychopaths also display severe forms of antisocial behavior, but they also have comorbid psychiatric problems relating to what psychoanalysts called neuroses and what psychologists today call "internalizing symptoms." The main difference between primary and secondary psychopaths is the existence of conscience, which underscores the larger importance of superego development to guard against crime.

Not just a Hollywood archetype, most multiple-homicide offenders are malevolent psychopaths who recurrently inflict violence and impose a major health burden.

Millon and Davis (1998) theorized there at ten subtypes of psychopathy. The most severe type was referred to as a malevolent psychopath. The **malevolent psychopath** is the most violent, vicious, and mean-spirited type of psychopathy and the one that best characterizes multiple homicide offenders. Their description is chilling:

> "These individuals are particularly vindictive and hostile; their retributive impulses are discharged in a hateful and destructive defiance of conventional social life. Distrustful of others and anticipating betrayal and punishment, they have acquired a cold-blooded

ruthlessness, an intense desire to gain revenge for the real or imagined mistreatment to which they were subjected in childhood."
(Millon & Davis, 1998, p. 168)

Much of the psychological research on psychopathy has centered on
various measurements of the construct that have been developed. Over
the last few decades, Hare's conceptualization and measurement has been
the most widely used instrument in the forensic and legal assessment of
psychopathic offenders. That tool is the **Psychopathy Checklist-Revised
or PCL-R** (Hare, 1991, 2003). The PCL-R is a 20-item assessment checklist
with good reliability and validity. Factor analysis has revealed a four-factor
model for the PCL-R including Interpersonal (e.g., superficial charming,
pathological lying), Affective (e.g., shallow affect, lack of remorse), Lifestyle
(e.g., impulsivity, irresponsibility), and Antisocial dimensions (e.g., poor
behavioral control, criminal versatility) (Hare, 2003).

Other psychologists have translated the PCL-R into broader personality features such as those examined in Chapter 13. For example,
Lynam and Widiger (2007) suggested the following general personality
profile of a psychopathic person. They had extremely high interpersonal antagonism (or extremely low agreeableness), universal impulsivity, absence of negative self-directed affect, angry hostility, and
interpersonal assertiveness.

Recently, researchers have developed new measures to study psychopathy from the perspective of the Five Factor Model. Lynam and a host of
colleagues (2011) created the **Elemental Psychopathy Assessment** which
is a 178-item self-report measure designed to assess extreme personality
variants from the Five Factor Model that relate to psychopathy.

The Elemental Psychopathy Assessment uses four of the five factors from the Five Factor Model (Openness to Experience is not used).
Antagonism (the negative pole of agreeableness) is assessed with six scales
including distrust, manipulation, self-centeredness, oppositionality, arrogance, and callousness. Conscientiousness is assessed with three scales
including rashness, impersistence, and disobliged. Extraversion is assessed
through three scales including coldness, dominance, and thrill-seeking.
Neuroticism is assessed with six scales including unconcern, anger, self-
contentment, self-assurance, urgency, and vulnerability.

Recent research found that overall scores on the Elemental Psychopathy
Assessment were significantly correlated with reactive aggression, proac-
tive aggression, antisocial behavior, alcohol use, and substance use (Wilson,
Miller, Zeichner, Lynam, & Widiger, 2011). In addition, the Elemental
Psychopathy Assessment was significantly correlated with extant measures
of psychopathy.

There are others and increasingly more measures of psychopathy, some of which are self-reports and others are based on actuarial data based on the offender's social and criminal history. Whatever their differences, these measures attempt to capture the negativity and frighteningly generalized behavioral problems that result from psychopathy. The next section examines studies that have linked the disorder to homicide.

Empirical Linkages to Homicide

Psychopathy is such a pernicious antisocial condition that is seems almost tailor-made for serious crimes such as homicide. Indeed, a substantial body of research has found that psychopathy is significantly associated with homicide offending. For instance, Laurell and Dåderman (2007) found that 40 percent of murderers scored 27 or above on the PCL-R, the most commonly used measure of psychopathy in forensic settings and more than 31 percent scored above 30. Scores above 30 on the PCL-R are considered clinical psychopathy. In their review of the literature, Millon and Davis (1998) suggested that many murderers could be characterized as malevolent psychopaths, which is a particularly negative subtype of offender characterized as belligerent, mordant, rancorous, vicious, brutal, callous, and vengeful. In other words, there is considerable conceptual and empirical convergence between psychopathy and homicide.

Myers and Blashfield (1997) assessed 14 juveniles who had committed sexual homicide. The researchers administered the *DSM-III-R* Diagnostic Interview for Children and Adolescents (DICA-R) and the Schedule for Nonadaptive and Adaptive Personality (SNAP) which is a self-report measure that assesses personality disorder. As expected, these youths displayed extensive psychopathology, and psychopathy figured prominently. Eleven youth met criteria for Conduct Disorder and other diagnoses for ADHD, alcohol abuse, and marijuana abuse were also common. Their personality functioning reflected Antisocial Personality Disorder, Schizoid Personality Disorder, Avoidant Personality Disorder, and three of the youths were sadistic. Moreover, the youth averaged 22.4 on the Psychopathy Checklist-Revised (PCL-R) with the most sadistic sexual homicide offenders tending to have the most psychopathic personalities. Most of the youth also admitted to having violent sexual fantasies that involved abduction, rape, and murder.

Most of these highly psychopathic youth will be released from confinement in their mid-twenties, which is troubling from a recidivism perspective. Myers and Blashfield (1997, p. 507) offer a grim forecast, "Two-thirds of these youths admitted to violent sexual fantasies, and one-half admitted to feeling little or no guilt over their crimes. This is a deadly combination, particularly when one realizes that this sample will receive virtually no treatment during their incarceration, and instead will complete their adolescent development and personality maturation in a prison setting surrounded by antisocial role models."

Woodworth and Porter (2002) studied the homicides of 125 Canadian offenders, some of whom were psychopathic and others who were not. They found that more than 93 percent of the homicides by psychopaths were instrumental in nature. Comparatively, about 48 percent of homicides by non-psychopaths were instrumental. Less than 7 percent of homicides by psychopaths were reactive compared to 52 percent among nonpsychopathic offenders.

A related study (Porter, Woodworth, Earle, Drugge, & Boer, 2003) found that nearly 85 percent of sexual murderers scored in the moderate to high range on the PCL-R. The sexual homicides by psychopaths were also more violent, sadistic, and gratuitous than those committed by nonpsychopathic killers. For example, more than 82 percent of psychopathic murderers displayed some form of sadistic behavior during their killings compared to nearly 53 percent of nonpsychopathic murderers. Their concluding remarks were chilling:

"Not only are psychopathic offenders disproportionately more likely to engage in sexual homicide, but, when they do, they use significantly more gratuitous and sadistic violence…More to the point, in the absence of inhibitions relating to empathy or remorse and in the presence of a thrill-seeking motive, the psychopath may try to optimize their pleasure and the damage inflicted during the homicidal act." (2003, p. 467)

Porter and Woodworth (2007) interviewed 50 convicted homicide offenders serving time in medium or maximum security prisons in Canada to examine whether psychopathic personality affected their descriptions of their homicide events. They found that although all murderers tended to exaggerate the reactivity of their murders thus suggesting that they were less morally culpable, the psychopathic homicide offenders did so to a greater extent. Porter and Woodworth also found that psychopathic murderers almost always perpetrated instrumental murders. In fact 89 percent of their murders were premeditated. Comparatively, only 42 percent of the non-psychopathic murderers premeditated their killing. Psychopathic homicide offenders also tended to omit or change greater details of their crimes especially in ways that were self-exculpatory. This is consistent with their conning and manipulative personality.

Using data from all young male offenders in Finland who had been subjected to a forensic psychiatric examination and convicted of a homicide from 1995 to 2004, Lindberg and her colleagues (2009) explored their psychopathic traits. Of the 57 murderers in the population, one in five met criteria for clinical psychopathy. The psychopathic adolescent murderers also displayed significantly more interpersonal, affective, lifestyle, and behavioral deficits of the disorder. The psychopathic youth committed more excessive or gratuitous violence during their murder and were more likely to commit another crime in conjunction with the homicide. Their social backgrounds were much more impoverished including less likely to live with their parents, more likely to have been placed in institutions or foster care during childhood, more likely to have school and educational problems, more likely to have been in special education, more likely to have additional mental health problems, and their parents were more likely to be violent and antisocial as well (Lindberg, Laajasalo, Holi, Putkonen, Weizmann-Henelius, & Häkkänen-Nyholm, 2009).

A study using interview data from homicide offenders in the Pittsburgh Youth Study demonstrates the various other deficits of psychopathic individuals. Jolliffe, Loeber, Farrington, and Cotter (2011) compared youth who had been convicted of homicide to other violent offenders and found that homicidal youth were significantly more psychopathic than their peers. Homicide offenders scored nearly four times higher than controls on arrogance and deceitfulness, more than 26 times higher on deficient

Murders committed by psychopathic offenders have been shown to be more sadistic and gratuitous in the infliction of violence.

affective experience, more than 54 times higher on impulsive and irresponsible lifestyle, and nearly 38-fold higher on juvenile delinquency and criminal versatility as measured by the Psychopathy Checklist Screening Version (PCL-SV). Although fewer than 15 percent of delinquent controls were clinically psychopathic, nearly 67 percent of the homicide offenders were clinical psychopaths, an odds ratio of 11.5! In addition, they found that the predominant emotional reaction during the commission of their homicide was no emotional reaction, 30 percent of homicide offenders reported feeling nothing. Moreover, 42 percent felt nothing or a general sense of numbness after their offense.

Box 19.1   Psychopathy and the Only Female Serial Sexual Homicide Offender

Aileen Wuornos is believed to be the only woman in American history who independently (without a codefendant) perpetrated serial sexual homicide. Between December 1989 and November 1990, Wuornos robbed, shot, and murdered seven male victims during the context of prostitution encounters. Myers, Gooch, and Meloy (2005) published a study based on a clinical interview with Wuornos before her execution, and revealed the extent of her psychopathic personality.

Wuornos was scored at 32 on the Psychopathy Checklist-Revised (PCL-R), which exceeds the clinical threshold of 30 that is used to identify an individual as clinically psychopathic. During the forensic interview, Wuornos displayed superficial charm and displayed some of this behavior during her life. She had a cocky, braggadocios conversational style that reflected an exaggerated sense of self-worth. Her life was characterized by an excessive need for stimulation including rampant substance use, work as a prostitute, and an itinerant lifestyle. Wuornos used multiple aliases and early in life displayed proneness for deception and lying. She displayed conning and manipulation in multiple areas of life, such as having simultaneous relationships with multiple people. She revealed no remorse for killing the seven victims and indicated that she wished she had murdered more victims. Her affect was often cold and unemotional but was interrupted by bouts of extreme anger. She was callous and lacking in empathy.

Throughout her life, Wuornos lived off of others and refused to engage in conventional employment despite being able. Instead she resorted to prostitution. She had very low self-control and poor behavioral control from a young age. She was sexually promiscuous and once suggested that she had sexual relations with as many as 250,000 men. Thus she had many short-term relationships based on her work as a prostitute. In every way, Wuornos was impulsive and led a day-to-day existence that suggested no planning or consideration of long-term goals. She dropped out of school at age 15 and was globally irresponsible. She tended to not accept responsibility for her actions, including her crimes, and her criminal career including juvenile delinquency and versatile forms of adult crime.

Wuornos' life contains the extremely adverse background that is common among multiple homicide offenders. Her biological father committed suicide in prison where he was serving a life sentence for raping a 7-year-old girl. Her mother and grandparents were alcoholic and various forms of abuse were common in Wuornos' early years. In her youth, Wuornos set fires at home, at school, and in other settings and was known to have a poorly regulated and often explosive temper. She had an IQ of 81 and displayed several problems in school before dropping out at age 15 to begin a life on the streets. She attempted suicide many times and was frequently raped and brutalized in her prostitution career. She had a three-state criminal history that including a mélange of offenses, including armed robbery, burglary, auto theft, assorted drug violations, assault, obstructing police, forgery, and many others. In sum, although her gender makes Wuornos an extraordinary case, her affective, behavioral, interpersonal, and lifestyle reflect garden variety psychopathy.

Source: Myers, W. C., Gooch, E., & Meloy, J. R. (2005). The role of psychopathy and sexuality in a female serial killer. Journal of Forensic Sciences, 50(3), 1–6.

Psychopathy isat least 20 times more prevalent among prisoners than the general population, and several investigations have focused on prison inmates. In an investigation of 82 male inmates in Belgium, Declercq, Willemsen, Audenaert, and Verhaeghe (2012) found that the interpersonal component of psychopathy was significantly associated with predatory homicide offending which reflects their tendency toward narcissistic gratification (i.e., abduction, rape, and murder). Similarly, research on prisoners selected from the Netherlands similarly found that male inmates who were more psychopathic were more likely to have predatory, instrumental offenses in their criminal history including homicides (Cima & Raine, 2009). Similar findings have been demonstrated with inmates from the United States (Camp, Skeem, Barchard, Lilienfeld, & Poythress, 2013).

A study of nearly 500 adult prisoners found that when psychopathic inmates were children, they committed a range of horribly violent behaviors including forcing other children into sexual activity, assaulting and being physically cruel to others, using weapons in fights, deliberately destroying property, committing arson, and killing animals (Rogers, Salekin, Sewell, & Cruise, 2000). Many of these inmates ultimately committed homicide, some committed multiple homicides.

Speaking of when psychopathic murderers were children. A recent study examined the personality functioning of a sample of children ages 4–6 years, and found that the most callous and unemotional children had the least agreeable personalities (and thus were highly antagonistic), were the least conscientious, and had the highest scores on conduct problems (Assary, Salekin, & Barker, 2015). These findings provide support for general personality models of psychopathy and also provide insight into how early the negative traits of the disorder emerge, and how they worsen behavior.

Psychopathy is useful for understanding homicide among subsamples of the offender population. For instance, Cloninger and Guze (1970) examined the disorder (in their study referred to as sociopathy) among female prisoners 20 percent of whom had committed homicide. Female homicide offenders evinced a host of interpersonal and behavioral problems relative to other female convicts. They had poor marital and work histories, were impulsive and promiscuous, had repeated behavior problems, arrests, and involvement in the criminal justice system, and drifted about without any plan or intention. The women displayed a powerful lack of shame or guilt despite the tremendous life circumstances that their behavior had produced. Other studies of female homicide offenders found significant evidence of psychopathy that often was comorbid with other psychopathology and personality disorders (Weizmann-Henelius, Putkonen, Grönroos, Lindberg, Eronen, & Häkkänen-Nyholm, 2010).

Psychopathy is one of the primary considerations in assessments of **future dangerousness**, which is a forecast of an offender's likely future violence that is made in capital sentencing. Highly psychopathic offenders with extensive and violent criminal history are viewed as likely to continue these behaviors in the future, and this prognostication is applicable to the death penalty. A recent study found that participants who evaluated a criminal defendant as being more acutely psychopathic were also more likely to recommend a death sentence (Edens, Davis, Fernandez Smith, & Guy, 2013). This indicates how pernicious the general public believes that psychopathy is, and their assessment is largely correct.

The next chapter deals with a different risk factor for homicide offending and victimization one that is less pathological and thus much more common. The substance abuse perspective is next.

CHAPTER 20

Homicide and the Substance Abuse Perspective

Substance abusers are significantly more likely than those in the general population to be murdered and to perpetrate murder.

Conceptual Background

In 2013, Richard Ramirez, the "Night Stalker" who terrorized California in the mid-1980s with a serial murder rampage that included at least 13 victims died of B-cell lymphoma cancer. In addition, the coroner indicated that Ramirez had Hepatitis C, liver failures, and evidence of chronic poly-substance abuse. Ramirez was a noted criminal and drug abuser prior to his murder spree (Associated Press, 2013). Ramirez achieved considerable notoriety and infamy for his crimes which including an assortment of violent felonies in addition to homicide. What is often not discussed, however, is the role of substance abuse in his criminal career, in his homicides, and in his death. Ramirez is not alone, many homicide offenders and victims are also drug users.

Several of the conceptual and theoretical perspectives in this book have already made clear the important role that drug and alcohol use, drug selling, and addiction play in homicide offending and victimization. Involvement in a substance using lifestyle exponentially increases exposure to risky settings with a critically high likelihood of a homicide transpiring. Social interactions that are clouded by alcohol and drug use are more likely to become violent and escalate to a homicide. Participating in the drug trade and actively carrying narcotics, large amounts of cash, and firearms facilitates committing murder and being murdered. And several conditions in this book, from Bipolar Disorder to Schizophrenia to Antisocial Personality Disorder are significantly more likely to predict homicide in persons who also have substance abuse problems. In all of these scenarios, substance use is the elixir that makes homicide more likely.

Although there are not necessarily specific theories for the substance use-homicide relationship, there are conceptual reasons for the linkage. These include:

- *Gangs*: the predominant reason for street gang activity in the United States is drug selling and drug trafficking. Most gang members have extremely meager socioeconomic life chances, have cognitive deficits, often drop out of school, are chronically unemployed, and usually disengage entirely from the legitimate employment sector. As a result, drug selling becomes the main source of income along with public assistance/welfare receipt. Gang activity pertaining to drug selling is a major source of homicide (Cohen, Cork, Engberg, & Tita, 1998; Ousey & Augustine, 2001; Riley, 1998).
- *Guns*: a corollary of gangs is that young gang members often carry firearms to facilitate their drug selling behaviors, to discourage competitors, to protect their drugs and money, and for self-protection. Irrespective of the motivation, this substantially increases opportunities for gun assaults and homicides (Blumstein, 1995).

- *Comorbidity*: those with underlying mental health difficulties who also use drugs are at increased risk or fatal drug overdose, suicide, and homicide in part because the substances exacerbate their symptoms and contribute to violent offending and in part because of exposure to risky settings and violent peers (Hiroeh, Appleby, Mortensen, & Dunn, 2001).
- *Opportunity*: drugs and alcohol increase the likelihood of emotional, unstable interpersonal exchanges that can result in homicide. A landmark study found that alcohol and drugs in the home elevates the likelihood of being murdered in the home. Moreover, these effects also pertained to nondrinkers of alcohol who were nearly two times more likely to be murdered simply given the presence of substance use in the home (Rivara, Mueller, Somes, Mendoza, Rushforth, & Kellermann, 1997).
- *Alcohol*: beyond the home effects described above, there is also evidence of a larger cultural effect where alcohol use undermines performance in role responsibilities in social institutions that directly and indirectly relate to homicide including divorce and family conflict, unemployment, and others (Parker, 1995a, 1995b).

© Monkey Business Images/Shutterstock, Inc.

Substance use exponentially increases the likelihood of homicide offending and victimization for a variety of conceptual reasons.

Even without considering the relationship between substance abuse and homicide, it is also important to observe that substance use is a major cause of death worldwide. Based on data from the Global Burden of Disease Study 2010, alcohol use disorders caused 111,000 deaths and drug use disorders caused nearly 78,000 deaths in 2010. Alcohol death increased nearly 50 percent since 1990 and drug use deaths increased nearly 192 percent (Lozano et al., 2012). From 1990 to 2010, opioid-use disorders increased nearly 400 percent. Substance use also imposes tremendous disability.

Also from the Global Burden of Disease Study 2010, alcohol-use disorders caused 17,644,000 disability-adjusted life years and drug use disorders caused 19,994,000 disability-adjusted life years in 2010. These were increases of 34.3 percent and 52.1 percent, respectively (Murray et al., 2012).

Before examining empirical studies of substance abuse and homicide, some definitions are in order. There are differences between substance use, substance abuse, and substance dependence. **Substance use** is the ingestion of a controlled substance for the purpose of causing intoxication or to experience the physiological effects of the substance.

Substance abuse is a pattern of substance use that leads to significant impairment or distress including at least one of the following four criteria in the prior 12 months: failure to fulfill major role obligations at work, school, or home, frequent use of substances when it is physically hazardous, frequent legal problems, and continued use despite recurrent social or interpersonal problems.

Substance dependence is significant impairment or distress including at least three of the following criteria in the prior 12 months:

1. Tolerance or markedly increased amounts of the substance to achieve intoxication or desired effect or markedly diminished effect with continued use of the same amount of substance
2. Withdrawal symptoms or the use of certain substances to avoid withdrawal symptoms
3. Use of a substance in larger amounts or over a longer period than was intended
4. persistent desire or unsuccessful efforts to cut down or control substance use
5. Involvement in chronic behavior to obtain the substance, use the substance, or recover from its effects
6. Reduction or abandonment of social, occupational or recreational activities because of substance use
7. Use of substances even though there is a persistent or recurrent physical or psychological problem that is likely to have been caused or exacerbated by the substance (American Psychiatric Association, 2013).

Empirical Linkages to Homicide

Given the multitude of ways that substance use conceptually relates to homicide, investigators have analyzed diverse data to explore the drugs-homicide link. In some cases, the effects of specific drugs of abuse create physiological and psychological states that directly produce homicide. For example, a study of homicide offenders who were under the influence of amphetamines found that amphetamine-produced paranoia, emotional liability, panic, and lowered impulse control resulted in murder (Ellinwood, 1971).

Similarly, cocaine intoxication can induce cocaine psychosis where there is similar emotional liability, paranoid ideation, stressful hypervigilance, and other acute emotional states that increase the likelihood of a confrontational and violent interpersonal style. To illustrate, a study of nearly 1,000 corpses that tested positive for cocaine in New York City indicated that nearly 40 percent of the deceased were homicide victims (Tardiff, Gross, Wu, Stajic, & Millman, 1989).

There is compelling evidence that substance use and abuse plays a prominent role in homicide events, and homicide offenders (and victims) are often significantly intoxicated prior to their killing. Wieczorek, Welte, and Abel (1990) examined a sample of 1,887 convicted homicide offenders and found that half were under the influence of alcohol at the time of their murder. Moreover, homicide offenders tended to binge drink prior to their murders. The mean alcohol consumption leading up to their murder was a staggering 18 drinks.

As a general rule of thumb, approximately 50 percent of more of homicide offenders and homicide victims are intoxicated on one or more substances prior to their homicide event and their substance use far exceeds population averages. Among substance abusers, homicide perpetration and victimization is significantly more likely than nonsubstance abusers (Darke, 2010).

In a study of 1,860 homicides in three counties, 444 of which were committed in a home, Kellerman and his colleagues (1993) conducted a case-control study to examine the effects of various substance use and other factors as risks for a homicide occurring in the home. They found that assorted alcohol and drug problems dramatically increased the likelihood of homicide. In homes where drinking caused problems in the household, the odds ratio was 7.0. Those who had problems at work because of drinking or drug use or were hospitalized because of these problems were between 10 and 20 times more likely to reside in a home where a homicide occurred.

McLaughlin, Daniel, and Joost (2000) examined the substance abuse histories of 25 male juvenile homicide offenders who were serving time in correctional centers in Virginia. They found that more than half of the murders were committed by juveniles with involvement in drug selling and 28 percent of the murders were explicitly drug-related, such as a murder occurring during a drug transaction. Nearly 75 percent of the killers reported substance use and 35 percent were daily drug users. In addition, toxicology evidence showed drug use in 27 percent of the victims. In fact, 86 percent of the murders could be accurately predicted by just two variables, the victim's recent drug use and the perpetrator's substance abuse history.

In a sample of drug users selected from Sydney, Australia, Torok, Darke, and Kaye (2011) found significant interrelationships between substance use and violent delinquency whereby offenders whose violence history predated their drug use tended to have the most severe criminal careers. Based on interview data with 350 methamphetamine users who received substance abuse treatment, Brecht and Herbeck (2013) found that more than half of them perceived that their substance use made them more violent, and nearly 60 percent reported a significant history of violence that predated and co-occurred with their addiction. Those whose violence was methamphetamine related were significantly more likely to have a prior criminal history for assault with a deadly weapon, armed robbery, aggravated assault, homicide, and attempted homicide.

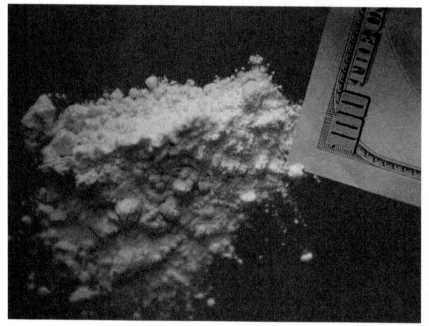

© eminkuliyev/Shutterstock, Inc.

Numerous studies have shown that drug use and drug selling significantly increase the likelihood of being murdered, committing murder, and witnessing murder.

Drawing on data from the Pittsburgh Youth Study, Farrington, Loeber, Stallings, and Homish (2012) examined early risk factors for homicide offending and homicide victimization and found that persistent drug users, marijuana sellers, and hard drug sellers were significantly more likely to commit homicide and to be killed by homicide. In addition, having an attitude that was favorable toward substance use increased the odds of homicide offending by a factor of 3.4. Based on data from more than 3,000 youth selected from the National Study on Drug Use and Health, Shook, Vaughn, and Salas-Wright (2013) found that drug selling adolescents engaged in significantly more fights, gang fights, criminal attacks, and handgun usage than non-drug sellers in the general population. These behaviors are virtually a recipe for homicide risk.

A more recent meta-analysis further supported the idea that substance use, specifically alcohol, is importantly related to homicide. Kuhns and his colleagues (2014) reviewed 23 studies that included information from 28,265 homicide offenders selected from nine nations. On average, 48 percent of homicide offenders were under the influence of alcohol at the time of their murder, and 37 percent were intoxicated. Interestingly, homicide offenders who perpetrated their killing with a firearm were less likely to be under the influence of alcohol (Kuhns, Exum, Clodfelter, & Bottia, 2014).

Hedlund, Ahlner, Kristiansson, and Sturup (2014) analyzed toxicological data on all homicide offenders and victims in Sweden from 2007 to 2009. This included 273 victims and 257 perpetrators. They found that 57 percent of homicide victims and nearly 63 percent of homicide offenders tested positive for substances, the most common of which were ethanol (alcohol) and benzodiazepines. Those who committed homicide-suicide were about half as likely as other homicide offenders to be under the influence of a substance at the homicide event. Victims in unsolved homicide cases were nearly fivefold more likely to be intoxicated than victims in solved homicide cases.

Substance abuse severity has been shown to differentiate offenders who commit homicide from those who commit multiple homicides. In a comparative study of 84 offenders who killed one victim and 86 offenders who killed more than one victim, Cole, Plecas, Cohen, and Fortier (2010) reported significant differences in terms of their alcohol and drug use histories. Nearly half of the multiple homicide offenders had both drug and alcohol problems compared to nearly 27 percent of those who murdered one victim. Only 21 percent of multiple homicide offenders did not have a drug and alcohol problem, compared to nearly 46 percent of single murderers who did not have substance abuse problems. In multivariate analyses, they found that drug and alcohol problems increased the likelihood of committing an additional homicide by a factor of 6.5.

Substance abuse creates additional problems for homicide offenders. Dhingra, Boduszek, Hyland, and Shagufta (2015) studied 102 convicted murderers in prison in Pakistan and examined their psychiatric functioning and suicidal behavior during confinement. The murderers had an array of problems relating to drug use, feelings of loneliness and depression, feelings of isolation, difficulty in controlling their emotions, insomnia, nightmares, general anxiety, and mood liability. Greater drug abuse problems also were associated with attempting to commit suicide during prison.

The substance abuse-homicide linkage can also be seen at an aggregate level. Cities with more entrenched drug markets and drug distribution activity also have more homicides compared to cities where there is more limited drug activity and availability (Ousey & Lee, 2002). Indeed, there is evidence that the great declines in homicide across American cities since around 1993 are attributable in part to large-scale declines in drug activity and drug markets (Ousey & Lee, 2007).

The substance use-homicide link can also be understood as a function of the broader association between substance use and serious violent offending. Using data from the National Survey on Drug Use and Health between 2008 and 2012, a data collection effort that included nearly 300,000 participants, DeLisi, Vaughn, Salas-Wright, and Jennings (2015) found evidence of an acutely violent group of offenders who not only committed a range of violent acts, but also had severe drug problems. Although their study did not include a measure of homicide, these violent drug offenders were significantly more likely to commit robbery, burglary, arson, auto theft, and other crimes. They were nearly 20 times more likely to have arrests for possession or sale of narcotics. Just as they committed diverse crimes, they also abused multiple substances including alcohol, cocaine, heroin, inhalants, hallucinogens, sedatives, and tranquilizers. In this sense, drug using offenders are likely to engage in virtually any form of crime, and their total immersion in substance use and offending creates tremendous risks for homicide offending and victimization.

Finally, one of the most dangerous features of substance abuse is the effect it has on other psychological conditions in terms of escalating the risk for homicidal behavior. One of those conditions—Bipolar Disorder—is examined next.

CHAPTER 21

Homicide and the Bipolar Disorder Perspective

Persons with Bipolar Disorder are overrepresented among homicide offenders.

© veleknez/Shutterstock, Inc.

Conceptual Background

Robert Hansen was an apparently mild mannered baker who died in August 2014. Hansen died in prison while serving a life imprisonment without parole plus 461 year sentence for 17 abduction, rape, homicides that were perpetrated from the early 1970s to the early 1980s. Technically, he was convicted of four homicides and confessed to the author and assisted law enforcement in locating the bodies. Like nearly all serial killers, it is believed that Hansen murdered and raped many more victims. Also like many serial killers, Hansen was no stranger to the criminal justice system with numerous prior arrests and convictions for a bevy of offenses including arson, theft, and other crimes and multiple prior commitments to prison.

Also similar to other multiple homicide offenders, Hansen exhibited significant psychopathology including mood disturbances, poor behavioral and emotional regulation, speech pathology, and tremendous social anxiety and ineptitude. He harbored these grievances for most of his life and perversely used them as motivation and justification for raping, torturing, and murdering his victims.

Unlike other offenders was the manner in which Hansen killed his victims. Committing his crimes in the remote Alaskan wilderness, Hansen would release the women after abusing them, and then hunt them as if they were big game. They were shot often multiple times from long distance.

Rodrick Dantzler is less well known than Hansen. But in July 2011, Dantzler murdered seven victims including his estranged wife, daughter, former girlfriends, and various family members of these decedents. After a shootout with police, taking hostages, and barricading himself in a home, Dantzler committed suicide. Like Hansen, Dantzler had prior criminal history including multiple arrests and convictions for domestic violence, a gun assault in which he shot a victim after a road rage incident, and other crimes. Dantzler was a substance abuser and had lifelong problems with behavioral and emotional regulation.

In addition to the carnage of their homicides, Hansen and Dantzler also had Bipolar Disorder in common. This condition contributed to their mood disturbances, their oscillating feelings of mania and depression, and their difficulty with managing interpersonal relationships due to emotional and behavioral disturbances.

Bipolar disorder is one of the most important disorders of mood in psychiatry. Although the phrase bipolar disorder, or the more colloquial expression, manic depression has diffused into the popular culture, it is actually two conditions. **Bipolar I Disorder** is characterized by one or more manic or mixed episodes that are usually accompanied by major depressive episodes. Its prevalence in community samples ranges from 0.2 to 1.6 percent and the 12-month prevalence in the United States is 0.6 percent (American Psychiatric Association, 2013).

Bipolar II Disorder is characterized by one or more major depressive episodes that are accompanied by at least one hypomanic episode. The lifetime prevalence of Bipolar II Disorder is 0.5 percent and the 12-month prevalence in the United States is 0.8 percent (American Psychiatric Association, 2013). Thus Bipolar I is disproportionately manic and Bipolar II is disproportionately depressive.

These concepts introduce new vocabulary that warrants explanation. A **major depressive episode** is a change from previous functioning that lasts during a two-week period and includes five or more of the following symptoms with at least one of symptoms being depressed mood or loss of interest of pleasure. According to the American Psychiatric Association (2013), these symptoms are:

- Depressed mood most of the day nearly every day as indicated by subjective report or observation made by others.
- Markedly diminished interest or pleasure in all or almost all activities most of the day nearly every day.
- Significant weight loss not due to dieting or significant weight gain or major changes in appetite nearly every day.
- Insomnia or hypersomnia nearly every day.
- Psychomotor agitation or retardation nearly every day that is observable by others and not just subjectively reported.
- Fatigue or loss or energy nearly every day.
- Feelings of worthlessness or excessive or inappropriate guilt nearly every day.
- Diminished ability to think or concentrate or indecisiveness nearly every day.
- Recurrent thoughts of death, recurrent suicidal ideation without a specific plan, or a suicide attempt or a specific plan for committing suicide.

These symptoms must cause significant impairment in social, occupational, or other important areas of functioning and not be attributable to another medical condition or the effects of medication.

A **manic episode** is a one-week period of abnormally and persistently elevated, expansive, or irritable mood and abnormally and persistently increased goal-directed activity or energy. It lasts most of the day nearly every day. A manic episode represents a noticeable change from usual behavior and includes three or more of the following symptoms:

- Inflated self-esteem or grandiosity.
- Decreased need for sleep.
- More talkative than usual or pressure to keep talking.
- Flight of ideas or subjective experience that thoughts are racing.
- Distractibility as reported or observed.

- Increase in goal-directed activity or psychomotor agitation.
- Excessive involvement in activities that have a high potential for painful consequences, such as buying sprees, sexual indiscretions, or foolish business investments.

The manic mood disturbance is severe enough to cause marked impairment in social or occupational functioning or to necessitate hospitalization to prevent harm to self or others (American Psychiatric Association, 2013). A **hypomanic episode** is a less severe variant of a manic episode that lasts only four days.

Bipolar Disorders are a major health problem. A large-scale study of more than 50,000 participants in Sweden found that Bipolar Disorder was associated with a 15-fold increase in suicide risk for males and a 22-fold increase in suicide risk for females (Ösby, Brandt, Correia, Ekbom, & Sparén, 2001). In the Global Burden of Disease Study 2010, Bipolar Disorder caused 12,867,000 disability-adjusted life years which was a 41 percent increase from the 1990 study (Murray et al., 2012). This measure indicates the health gap between healthy persons and those with Bipolar Disorder. Bipolar Disorder is a major reason why mood disorders are so societally costly in terms of the social welfare burden of individuals with the condition (Vaughn, Fu, Beaver, DeLisi, Perron, & Howard, 2010).

Of course, these data only provide a descriptive and epidemiological snapshot of the condition. Bipolar Disorders are devastating in their day-to-day impact not only on the life of the person who has the condition, but also his or her family, friends, colleagues, and other acquaintances. The seismic shifts in mood from one extreme to the other create havoc for the ability to lead a structured, normal existence. Many patients with Bipolar Disorder attempt to come to grips with their condition by using alcohol and drugs, but these attempts at self-medication only exacerbate the condition, and significantly increase the likelihood of antisocial behavior, violence, and homicide. Empirical investigations are examined next.

Empirical Linkages to Homicide

A broad range of studies have found that persons with Bipolar I or II Disorder are at increased risk of criminal involvement, criminal violence, and even homicide (Arseneault, Moffitt, Caspi, Taylor, & Silva, 2000; Côté, & Hodgins, 1990; Nielssen, Malhi, & Large, 2012; Schanda, Knecht, Schreinzer, Stompe, Ortwein-Swoboda, & Waldhoer, 2004; Sher & Landers, 2014). Studies using data from Iceland (Pétursson, & Gudjónsson, 1981), Italy (Catanesi et al., 2011), Canada (Langevin, 2003), England and

Wales (Baxter, Duggan, Larkin, Cordess, & Page, 2001) report prevalence of bipolar disorders at between 2 to more than 4 percent among murderers which is significantly higher than the prevalence of the disorder in the general population. Like other disorders, the risk of homicide among persons with bipolar disorder is heightened when there is co-occurring alcoholism or substance abuse disorders (Gudjonsson, & Petursson, 1990).

The very nature of Bipolar Disorders are unfortunately conducive for criminal behavior and difficulty with the criminal justice system. In a study of nearly 4,000 patients with Bipolar Disorders including those with substance use problems, there was evidence of a significant risk for violent crimes including murder, rape, and others. In fact, those with Bipolar Disorder and Substance Use Disorders were six times more likely to be convicted of a serious violent felony including homicide (Large & Nielssen, 2011).

Although both poles of the disorder are associated with criminal offending and violence, research has indicated that manic phases are especially likely to result in violent confrontations and arrest in part because manic individuals are impulsive, irritable, and experience exalted mood which affects their judgment (Quanbeck, Frye, & Altshuler, 2003; Quanbeck, Stone, McDermott, Boone, Scott, & Frye, 2005). These conditions make criminal opportunities more available. For instance, case studies of manic criminal defendants indicate evidence of exceedingly frightening and unpredictable behavior in which serious violence is inflicted in part because of the agitated, frenetic state of the offender (Wulach, 1983).

The depressive side of the disorder is also linked with homicide. Stapleton (1979) reported that 21 of 25 homicides by bipolar defendants in Bulgaria committed their homicides during the depressed phase. Moreover, the homicides were of an altruistic variety in that the offender felt that committing the murder spared the victim of future suffering.

A recent systematic review indicated that the risk of violent criminal acts by persons with Bipolar Disorder is nearly threefold higher (odds ratio of 2.8). If persons with the condition also have a substance use disorder, the risk of violence is tenfold higher (Fovet, Geoffroy, Vaiva, Adins, Thomas, & Amad, 2015). Manic phases commonly produce behavioral and sexual disinhibition which can increase the likelihood of illicit sexual behavior, use of prostitutes, indiscriminant sexual behavior, and exhibitionistic displays. These behaviors significantly increase exposure to risky settings and high-risk populations and also encourage potentially for conflict (e.g., engaging in aggressive, seductive conduct that is unwanted or unsolicited).

These risks continue once placed in jail or prison custody. The impulsive features of Bipolar Disorder increase the risk of misconduct and violence especially if the impulsive behaviors are sexual in nature. Indeed, those with Bipolar Disorder are at increased risk of violent victimization in correctional facilities, homicide victimization, and suicide (Fovet et al., 2015).

In the United States, persons with bipolar disorder are overrepresented in correctional populations. A clinical study of 15 death row inmates (Lewis, Pincus, Feldman, Jackson, & Bard, 1986) indicated that two offenders had bipolar disorder (then referred to as manic depression) which is a prevalence of greater than 13 percent. In a study of 30 offenders who committed mass murder in the United States or Canada, Hempel, Meloy, and Richards (1999) found that 10 percent of the mass murderers were in a depressive phase or experiencing a major depressive episode prior to their homicides.

Other studies have focused on the two elements of Bipolar Disorder—mania and depression—to examine their linkages to homicide offending and victimization. In an epidemiological study of the relationship between depression and violence, Fazel and colleagues (2015) examined 47,158 persons with depressive disorders in Sweden and compared them to age and sex matched controls among nearly 900,000 people in the general population. After adjusting for sociodemographics, the odds of violent crime including homicide was three times higher among depressives. The absolute rates of violent offending were 3.7 percent for males and 0.5 percent for females (Fazel, Wolf, Chang, Larsson, Goodwin, & Lichtenstein, 2015).

© Christos Georghiou/Shutterstock, Inc.

Researchers have shown that both manic and depressive phases can be associated with homicide offending.

Research on filicide offenders indicated that nearly 40 percent of filicide offenders had mental illness at the time of their murder with a significant proportion experiencing depression when they decided to murder their child (Flynn, Shaw, & Abel, 2013). A related and larger study indicated that symptoms of depression and chronic mental illness are particularly salient among female relative to male homicide offenders (Flynn, Abel, While, Mehta, & Shaw, 2011).

The prevalence of Bipolar I Disorder is about six fold higher among prisoners than the general population suggesting a general association between the disorder and serious violence (Fovet et al., 2015; Latalova, 2009). A main reason is that the symptoms of mania that typify the disorder include impulsive behavior, psychosis, poor judgment, and grandiose feelings. Yoon and colleagues (2012) examined 219 patients with Bipolar I Disorder, 190 of whom were in a manic phase and 29 of whom were in a depressive phase of the disease. Of these, 90 percent of the depressed patients committed a homicide compared to 19 percent of manic patients. The ratio of planned homicides and homicides targeting family members were significantly higher in the depressive phase.

However, the rate of total offense was significantly higher in the manic (87 percent) compared to depressive (13 percent) phase. Since patients spend nearly four times more time with depressive symptoms, the overall risk of violent offending was nearly 24 times higher in the manic phase than the depression phase.

In their systematic review, Fazel, Lichenstein, Grann, Goodwin, and Långström (2010) found that persons with Bipolar Disorder were between two to nine times more likely than those without the disorder to commit violent crime including but not limited to homicide. The average effect was a fourfold increase in criminal violence among persons with the disorder. They also reported findings from a study of 3,743 persons with Bipolar I or II Disorder, more than 37,000 persons from the general population, and 4,059 unaffected full siblings of the individuals with Bipolar Disorder. They found that 8.4 percent of persons with Bipolar Disorder committed a violent crime that could include homicide for an odds ratio of 2.3. Persons with Bipolar Disorder and comorbid substance use disorders were 6.4 times more likely to commit criminal violence.

Bipolar Disorder is often comorbid with other psychopathology that itself is associated with aggression, violence, and potentially homicide. For example, Vaughn and colleagues (2010) analyzed data from the National Epidemiologic Survey on Alcohol and Related Conditions to examine the correlates of fire setting, a behavior that is importantly linked to homicide. They found that the prevalence of Bipolar Disorders among fire setters was nearly 27 percent. The prevalence among non-fire setters was 5.5 percent.

In addition, fire setters were significantly more likely to have Conduct Disorder and Antisocial Personality Disorder in addition to alcohol use and marijuana use disorders. They also significantly engaged in other criminal behaviors beyond fire setting, many of which also linked to homicide such as rape, physical fights, domestic violence, and assault with a deadly weapon, and many others (Vaughn, Fu, DeLisi, Wright, Beaver, et al., 2010).

Ballester and colleagues (2012) compared persons with Bipolar I and II Disorders and those without. They found that they prevalence of Conduct Disorder was 3.5 times higher among bipolar individuals. The prevalence of Oppositional Defiant Disorder was four times higher and the prevalence of ADHD was three times greater among persons with Bipolar Disorders. In addition, bipolar patients exhibited more total aggression, more physical aggression, more verbal aggression, greater anger, greater hostility, and greater indirect aggression than those without the condition.

These findings indicate that those with Bipolar Disorders have more raw material—anger and aggression—with which to engage in interpersonal disputes and have conflicts. These emotional raw materials often engender assaults and other problematic exchanges that can culminate in homicide.

An additional comorbidity—Borderline Personality Disorder—also figures prominently in the psychopathology of homicide offenders. For example, a study of 86 sexual homicide offenders incarcerated in high-security prisons in Canada revealed high prevalence of most personality disorders (Chan, Beauregard, & Myers, 2014). Specifically, nearly 47 percent of single-victim sexual homicide offenders presented with Borderline Personality Disorder and nearly 54 percent of serial sexual homicide offenders presented with Borderline Personality Disorder. The respective prevalence of Antisocial Personality Disorder was nearly 44 percent and 46 percent. In other words, Borderline Personality Disorder symptoms were more prevalent in an enriched sample of sexual homicide offenders.

One of the most infamous homicide offenders in American history is Aileen Wuornos who is believed to be the only case of a female who independently perpetrated serial sexual homicide. Based on a clinical interview and extensive review of her official records, Myers, Gooch, and Meloy (2005) asserted that Wuornos displayed Borderline Personality Disorder. Her life was characterized by a pervasive pattern of turmoil and instability in interpersonal relationships, was hampered by impulsivity, and was impaired by affective and self-image problems. Specifically, Wuornos avoided real or imagined abandonment by manipulative suicide attempts, engaged in unstable relationships that vacillated between extremes of idealization and devaluation, had identity disturbance with a persistently unstable self-image, was impulsive in terms of sexual promiscuity and substance use, was recurrently suicidal, had intense mood swings, and displayed extreme, and often inappropriate displays of anger.

As this author was completing this chapter, a major world event occurred that related to this chapter's content. Andreas Lubitz was the copilot of Germanwings Flight 9525 that crashed into the French Alps on March 24, 2015. After encouraging the pilot of the aircraft to go the restroom, Lubitz locked the cockpit door and set the plane on course to crash into the mountains. Voice recordings indicate that the pilot frantically tried to gain entry into the cockpit to save the plane, but to no avail. In the week (at this writing) since the event, there is tremendous speculation and investigation of Lubitz and his mental state prior to and during the crash. Thus far, there is psychiatric history including symptoms of depression, other mood problems, and suicidal ideation. It is not known thus far if Lubitz was bipolar, or if he suffered from Major Depressive Disorder. What is certain is that Lubitz planned and carried out a course of action that resulted in 149 other people losing their life. Lubitz murdered 149 victims in a matter of minutes.

The next chapter examines what is perhaps the most severe form of mental illness, and the one with perhaps the most extensive literature linking it to homicide: Schizophrenia.

CHAPTER 22

Homicide and the Schizophrenia Perspective

Many infamous homicide offenders including Howard Unruh, Richard Chase, David Berkowitz, and Herbert Mullin suffered from Schizophrenia.

Conceptual Background

Herbert Mullin was a successful young person in the 1960s who during high school was rated by his peers as most likely to succeed. However, beneath this successful exterior were two issues that distressed Mullin. One, he was a closeted homosexual who had difficulty coming to terms with his sexual orientation. Two, he experienced delusions, hallucinations, an often displayed erratic, bizarre, and disjointed behavior. In his late teens and early twenties, Mullin was briefly institutionalized in mental hospitals but never for an extended period. By the early 1970s, Mullin began to experience hallucinations that demanded that killing others was needed to forestall a major earthquake. Over a 4-month period from October 1972 to February 1973, Mullin murdered 13 people.

Mullin's homicides appeared completely random and the victimology included male and female victims and young children to elderly adults. Mullin knew some of his victims, while others were strangers. He murdered individual victims in addition to murdering multiple victims at one time. Some of his victims were shot, others shot and then repeatedly stabbed, others stabbed, and still others were bludgeoned. Mullin pleaded guilty to these murders and was sentenced to life imprisonment. He remains incarcerated in California at this writing. Mullin also has schizophrenia, paranoid subtype.

Schizophrenia is a major form of mental illness and is the most severe type of psychotic disorder. A **psychotic disorder** is an illness characterized by delusions and hallucinations in which the individual's ability to appreciate objective reality is compromised. In the criminal justice system, psychotic disorders are very important in the event that the individual is so impaired that he or she is unable to appreciate right from wrong in terms of conduct. Those who cannot understand that their criminal behavior is wrong cannot be held legally culpable or responsible. Such persons are deemed criminally insane and are placed in psychiatric facilities as patients as opposed to being placed in correctional facilities as inmates.

According to the American Psychiatric Association (2013, pp. 99–100), the following are criteria for schizophrenia. There must be two or more symptoms for a significant part during a one-month period. These are delusions, hallucinations, disorganized speech, such as frequent derailment or incoherence, grossly disorganized or catatonic behavior, and negative symptoms such as diminished emotional expression. These symptoms must cause significant impairment in multiple domains of life including interpersonal relationships, academic functioning, and occupational functioning.

A unique feature of schizophrenia is that it has positive and negative symptoms. **Positive symptoms** are symptoms of the disorder that are present but not present in unaffected persons. These include delusions, hallucinations, and disordered speech that are the hallmark of the illness. **Negative symptoms** are those that are absent in the affected person but present in unaffected persons. These include blunted or flattened affect, alogia which is limited talking or poverty of speech, and avolition which is the decline in goal-directed behavior.

For a schizophrenia diagnosis, there must be continuous signs of symptoms for six months. There are also specifications whether the patient is in their first episode or have had multiple episodes. Moreover, within these categories, the phase is characterized as currently in an acute episode, currently in partial remission, or currently in full remission. The prevalence of schizophrenia is about 1 percent but the toll it imposes is substantial.

Schizophrenia imposes a tremendous health burden. According to the Global Burden of Disease Study 2010, schizophrenia caused 198,000 deaths worldwide for an age-standardized death rate of 0.3 per 100,000. In addition, it caused 14,999,000 DALYs and 218 DALYs per 100,000 (Lozano et al., 2013; Murray et al., 2013). Schizophrenia also significantly increases the likelihood of homicide even though it is important to acknowledge that most individuals with schizophrenia are not violent, and never commit homicide. For example, a national clinical survey of all persons convicted of homicide in England and Wales between 1996 and 1999 found that just 85 of these homicide offenders had schizophrenia. This equals 5 percent of the population of homicide offenders (Meehan, Flynn, Hunt, Robinson, Bickley, et al., 2006). However, that prevalence is five times the prevalence of the disease. A conceptually similar study of all persons convicted of homicide and attempted homicide in Sweden from 1988 to 2001—which was 2,005 offenders—found that 20 percent had a psychotic illness most commonly being schizophrenia (Fazel & Grann, 2004). That prevalence is twenty times higher than the prevalence of the disease.

A reason for the increased likelihood of homicide among persons with schizophrenia is what is known as threat control override symptoms. **Threat control override symptoms** are positive symptoms in which the person perceives others as a threat, suffers from thought insertion (such as that displayed by Herbert Mullin at the beginning of this chapter), or perceives that outside forces controlled them (Link, Monahan, Stueve, & Cullen, 1999; Link, Stueve, & Phelan, 1998). Threat control symptoms cause the individual to believe that someone is a direct threat to harm them and/or intrude on their thoughts to such an extent that they override the person's ability to avoid violence. Threat control override symptoms can also be exacerbated by substance use and the abuse of some substances, such as cocaine and methamphetamine can itself contribute to psychosis.

Threat control override symptoms likely explain impulsive homicides and even the weapon used to perpetrate them. For instance, a study of 103 perpetrators of homicide and attempted homicide found that those with organic disorders and psychotic disorders (read schizophrenia) were more likely to use sharp weapons such as knives to murder their victims (Catanesi, Carabellese, Troccoli, Candelli, Grattagliano, et al., 2011). It could be that the threat control override symptoms become so intense that the individual uses a weapon of opportunity to respond to them. The sharp weapon attacks also often involved a high number of strikes or blows which is consistent with attempting to kill a persecutory delusion.

Several life circumstances and other factors have been shown to significantly increase the likelihood of homicidal behavior among individuals with schizophrenia. These include sudden onset of symptoms usually occurring at the onset of adulthood, change in the quality, intensity, and tone of delusional beliefs, alcohol use, drug use, changes in treatment, and termination of medication (Bennett, Ogloff, Mullen, Thomas, Wallace, & Short, 2011; Meehan et al., 2006; Nordström, Dahlgren, & Kullgren, 2006). For instance, a study of homicides by schizophrenia patients in Sweden found that although 79 percent had treatment programs in place, only 33 percent had ongoing or active treatment. In addition, 48 percent of the homicide offenders had been prescribed antipsychotic medication but a mere 4 percent of patients were actually taking their medication (Nordström et al., 2006). Moreover, some of the consequences of schizophrenia, such as social dysfunction and relationship problems themselves contribute to substance use and criminal offending (Bennett et al., 2011). This means that schizophrenia creates a cascade of effects that can culminate in homicidal behavior.

The treatment of patients with schizophrenia who also display violent and even homicidal behavior has historically varied from placement in asylums, psychiatric facilities, and prisons. For instance, in Norway patients with schizophrenia or dementia praecox were referred to asylums because of dangerous or violent behavior, and the referral was often made by immediate family members. Søndenaa, Gudde, and Thomassen (2015) found that more than 98 percent of persons referred to asylums—many with schizophrenia—displayed violent behavior; however, only about 5 percent of them had committed homicide.

Empirical Linkages to Homicide

A worldwide cast of researchers from several disciplinary fields have studied schizophrenia and its association with homicide. Schug and Fradella (2015) reviewed the homicide-schizophrenia literature and found 21 studies of homicide offenders that also examined mental health correlates. In these studies, the prevalence of schizophrenia among homicide offenders ranged from 2.7 to 57 percent. In studies of schizophrenia that also included crime prevalence, the prevalence of homicide among schizophrenia patients ranged from 3.4 to 62.1 percent. According to a meta-analysis and systematic review of the literature, about 6.5 percent of all homicide offenders had a diagnosis of schizophrenia (Large, Smith, & Nielssen, 2009). An international set of studies have examined the prevalence and relative risk of homicide among persons with schizophrenia. Although the estimates vary, the consistent theme is that schizophrenia imposes a significant and often substantial risk for homicide. In a 25-year study using Austrian homicide offender data, the risk of homicide increased twofold among men and six fold among women and this was entirely based on schizophrenia diagnoses (Schanda et al., 2004).

In a study of all homicides occurring in Victoria, Australia between 1997 and 2005, Bennett and colleagues (2011) found that persons with schizophrenia were 13.1 times more likely to commit homicide than those without the disease. They also found that the risk of homicide was highest among persons with schizophrenia who were also substance abuse problems. Those with schizophrenia were also more likely to accumulate more arrest charges including arrests for violent crimes including homicide (Wallace, Mullen, & Burgess, 2004).

In their study of Canadian prisoners including nearly 100 homicide offenders, Côté and Hodgins (1992) found that the prevalence of schizophrenia among homicide offenders was 12.6 percent whereas the prevalence among non-homicidal prisoners was 5.4 percent. Although not a large percentage, the prevalence of persons with schizophrenia among homicide offenders is nonetheless far higher than the prevalence of schizophrenia.

In their review of 204 studies using 66 independent data sets, Douglas, Guy, and Hart (2009) performed a meta-analysis that produced 885 effect sizes on the relationship between psychosis and violence. They found that psychosis was associated with a 49 to 68 percent increase in the risk for violence. They also offered several explanations for why psychosis is associated with violence. These include:

- Psychosis and other symptoms of schizophrenia can serve as a direct motivation for violence even if it is delusional. This is why many homicides perpetrated by schizophrenia patients appear complex, organized, and goal-oriented because the hallucination that drove the conduct was clear and organized.

- In other words, the positive symptoms of schizophrenia are what most likely cause violence.
- Psychosis and other symptoms of schizophrenia can interfere with the ability to manage interpersonal conflicts. For instance, thought disturbances, illogical speech, labile mood, and general agitation can be frustrating to the person with schizophrenia and those in their social network. These difficulties can serve as the situational causes of homicide.
- In other words, the negative symptoms of schizophrenia are what contribute to the interpersonal disputes that can escalate to a homicide.
- Psychosis and other symptoms of schizophrenia can be produced or exacerbated by involvement in violent offending.
- Psychosis and other symptoms of schizophrenia can be exacerbated by substance use and intoxication.
- Psychosis and other symptoms of schizophrenia can simply be correlates of violence in which both are worsened by some other condition.

Another recent meta-analysis examined 20 studies conducted between 1970 and 2009 that involved 18,423 individuals (Fazel, Gulati, Linsell, Geddes, & Grann, 2009). The study found that the odds of homicide among persons with schizophrenia and comorbid substance use disorders was three to 25 times higher than the risk of homicide in those without these conditions. Not including substance use disorders, persons with schizophrenia were nearly 20 times more likely to have committed homicide than people in the general population. However, only one in 300 people with schizophrenia had actually committed homicide which is a comparable risk as persons with substance abuse disorders.

Lewis and her colleagues (1985) conducted an interesting study of nine males who were clinically evaluated for psychiatric impairments during their adolescence and who subsequently perpetrated homicide. Their study examined the childhood neuropsychiatric and family characteristics of these homicidal youth. As children, 100 percent of these homicide offenders displayed psychotic symptoms, were hospitalized for their psychosis or had first-degree relatives with psychotic disorders, and engaged in serious violence as juveniles. All but one of the homicide offenders had major neurological impairments and were severely physically abused (Lewis, Moy, Jackson, Aaronson, Restifo, Serra, & Simos, 1985).

In addition, all of the boys' lives exemplified the major impairments posed by schizophrenia and the early warning signs of violence that predated their murders:

- Subject one set his bed on fire at age 4 years and beginning at age 12 perpetrated multiples rapes of younger boys. By age 19, he committed felony murder and assault with a dangerous weapon. He displayed paranoid ideation and often illogical thinking throughout his childhood and adolescence. Both his mother and maternal grandmother were hospitalized for psychosis.
- Subject two committed armed robberies and multiple assaults before fatally stabbing a bus driver after an argument about the fare. He displayed paranoid ideation, bizarre behaviors, loose and illogical thinking, and experienced auditory and visual hallucinations. His mother was hospitalized at age 14 years while pregnant with the defendant for psychosis.
- Subject three was expelled in the fifth grade for his repeated violent behavior that included armed robberies, assaults, and multiple weapons offenses. At age 24, he murdered his girlfriend and attempted to kill two of her relatives (they survived being shot). He engaged in bizarre behavior and paranoid ideation and behavior. Both of his parents were hospitalized for schizophrenia.
- Subject four committed armed robbery, kidnapping, and assault between the ages of 14 and 16 years. By age 20, he was charged with capital murder, kidnapping, armed robbery, and rape. He displayed paranoid behavior and both of his parents were hospitalized for psychotic episodes.
- Subject five committed several violent crimes during his early adolescence including assaulting an 85-year old woman, committing armed robbery, and beating one of his teachers with a hammer. At age 15, he murdered a butcher with whom he was no acquainted, and for which there was no apparent motive. He suffered from auditory hallucinations, paranoid ideation, and rambling and illogical thinking. Both his sister and father were hospitalized for psychosis.
- Subject six assaulted peers during elementary school and at age 20 murdered two young children. He displayed loose, illogical thinking and visual hallucinations. At age 8 years, he jumped out of a window in a suicide attempt. His father was a paranoid schizophrenic.
- Subject seven killed birds and dogs as early as age 2 years, and by early adolescence committed crimes such as rape and aggravated assault. At age 18 years, he raped and stabbed a woman 13 times resulting in her death. He had already been diagnosed with paranoid schizophrenia similar to his mother who was hospitalized for the disorder.

- Subject eight routinely attacked and threatened his teachers during elementary school and committed felony murder and arson at age 17 years. He had previously been hospitalized for attempting to burn himself and had paranoid ideation, auditory hallucinations, and loose, illogical thinking. His sister and maternal grandmother were hospitalized for psychosis.
- Subject nine committed a series of robberies and assaults during his childhood that culminated in the bludgeoning murder of another teenager at age 18 years. As a child, he was hospitalized for paranoid ideation and bizarre behaviors similar to his father who was psychotic.

Like homicide generally, which tends to occur among acquaintances, homicide of strangers is also rare among persons with a psychotic illness. For instance, a meta-analysis of 42 stranger homicides from offenders in Australia, Canada, Finland, and the Netherlands indicated that one stranger homicide by a person with a psychotic illness occurs per 14.3 million people per year. Among those who perpetrated these homicides, 64 percent had never previously received treatment with antipsychotic medication. They were also likely to be homeless and to have previously displayed anti-social conduct (Nielssen, Bourget, Laajasalo, Liem, Labelle, et al., 2011).

Some of the most impressive empirical findings stem from research of the 1966 Northern Finland Birth Cohort, a prospective study of 12,058 persons born in 1966 and followed over time through age 26. Tiihonen and colleagues (1997) focused on more than 5,000 males from the birth cohort and examined the association between schizophrenia and related mental disorders and various forms of crime which could include homicide. They found that males with schizophrenia were 7.2 times more likely to be registered for violent crime convictions and males with mood disorders with psychotic features (the core of schizophrenia) were 10.4 times more likely to be registered for a violent crime including homicide.

Drawing on data from Germany, Erb, Hodgins, Freese, Müller-Isberner, and Jöckel (2001) compared persons with schizophrenia who committed homicide in the German state of Hessen from 1992 to 1996 to all homicides in the Federal Republic of Germany from 1955 to 1964. They found that schizophrenia increased the relative risk of homicide 16.6 times in the recent cohort and 12.7 times in the older cohort. Interestingly, these prevalence estimates are not statistically different meaning that a policy of de-institutionalization of asylums did not result in an increased risk of homicide among schizophrenics.

In a study of all confirmed cases of homicide of mental illness patients in England and Wales from January 1, 2003 to December 31, 2005, patients with mental illness were about 2.6 times more likely to be murdered than persons without a mental illness in the general population (Rodway, Flynn, While, Rahman, Kapur, et al., 2014). Of the forms of mental illness, schizophrenia figured most prominently. Half of patient perpetrators and 19 percent of patient victims of homicide had a schizophrenia diagnosis. Moreover, 22 percent of offenders and 4 percent of victims were actively psychotic at their last contact with psychiatric personnel. A sizable number of perpetrators and victims also recently missed their last contact with treatment staff or refused treatment.

Using data from Finland, Tiihonen and colleagues (1996) studied the risk of homicide among 281 male forensic psychiatric patients who were released from custody between 1978 and 1991. Their findings were startling. Released patients were 300 times more likely to commit a homicide than males in the general population during the first year of release. During the average follow-up which was nearly eight years, schizophrenia patients were 53 times more likely to commit homicide. They also calculated that the odds ratio for committing a homicide among all Finnish schizophrenics over a 12-year period was 9.7 (Tiihonen et al., 1996).

Several factors have been shown to increase the risk for homicide among discharged schizophrenia patients. Based on data from Sweden from 1988 to 2001, Fazel and colleagues (2010) examined all homicides committed by patients with psychosis who killed within six months of their discharge. Those who were unemployed prior to admission were greater than three times more likely to commit homicide after discharge. Patients who had poor self-care were five times more likely to commit murder and those with substance abuse before admission were more than four times at risk. The greatest risk factor not unexpectedly was prior hospitalization for a violent crime which increased the risk of homicide post-release nearly six fold (Fazel, Buxrud, Ruchkin, & Grann, 2010).

A potent risk factor for homicide among persons with schizophrenia is comorbid alcoholism. Also relying on Finnish data, Eronen, Tiihonen, and Hakola (1996) found that for both men and women, the odds of committing a homicide were tenfold higher than those in the general population without the disorder. An important moderating factor was alcoholism. Those with schizophrenia who were not alcoholic were seven times more likely to commit murder. For those who were also alcoholic, the risk was 17 times higher in males.

A more recent study of 72 Finnish homicide offenders with schizophrenia and 72 without it showed significant differences in psychopathic personality across the groups (Laajasalo, Salenius, Linberg, Repo-Tiihonen, & Häkkänen-Nyholm, 2011). Among homicide offenders with schizophrenia there were significantly higher prevalence of the following psychopathic traits: proneness to boredom and stimulation seeking, pathological lying, conning and manipulation, shallow affect, parasitic lifestyle, poor behavioral controls, lack of realistic long term goals, impulsivity, irresponsibility, failure to accept responsibility, and varied criminal justice system involvement.

Box 22.1   Schizophrenia and Recidivist Homicide

The literature is clear that schizophrenia represents an increased likelihood of homicide perpetration. What about recidivist homicide perpetration? **Recidivist homicide** is a homicide committed after the conclusion (e.g., after conviction and serving a prison term) of a prior homicide offense (Bjørkly & Waage, 2005). Unlike spree, mass, or serial homicide offenders, a recidivist homicide offender commits a murder and then commits a separate murder often years later and the crimes are not connected in any ritualistic sense. Given that criminal offenders with schizophrenia are likely to spend considerable time in confinement settings, such as prison or a psychiatric hospital, it is possible that persons with schizophrenia are particularly likely to commit recidivist homicide because of lengthy spans of time removed from the community.

In a 30-year study of homicide offenders in the Chuvash Republic in Russia, Golenkov, Large, and Nielssen (2013) found that 149 offenders with schizophrenia had committed a homicide between January 1, 1981 and December 31, 2010. Of these, 16 or 10.7 percent had committed a previous homicide. Recently, Golenkov, Nielssen, and Large (2014) conducted a systematic review and meta-analysis of recidivist homicide among homicide offenders with schizophrenia among studies conducted from 1960 to 2013. These included studies of homicide offenders in Austria, Australia, Barbados, Finland, Germany, New Zealand, Netherlands, Nigeria, Russia, Saudi Arabia, Singapore, and Sweden. In most of these regions, zero patients with schizophrenia committed recidivist homicide. Among studies with incidence of recidivist homicide among schizophrenia patients, the prevalence estimates were 4.3 percent, 4.5 percent, and 10.7 percent. Overall, the pooled estimate of the proportion of homicide offenders with schizophrenia who had committed an earlier homicide was 2.3 percent. This suggests that long-term secure placement of homicide offenders with psychotic disorders and close supervision in the event of their release generally deter a subsequent murder.

Sources: Bjørkly, S., & Waage, L. (2005). Killing again: A review of research on recidivistic single-victim homicide. *International Journal of Forensic Mental Health, 4*(1), 99–106; Golenkov, A., Nielssen, O., & Large, M. (2014). Systematic review and meta-analysis of homicide recidivism and Schizophrenia. *BMC Psychiatry, 14*(1), 46; Golenkov, A., Large, M., & Nielssen, O. (2013). A 30-year study of homicide recidivism and schizophrenia. *Criminal Behaviour and Mental Health, 23*(5), 347–355.

Although alcoholism, substance use, and comorbid conditions, such as psychopathy play a role in homicidal behavior among persons with schizophrenia, it is important to note that the disease itself often gives rise to murder. For instance, Joyal, Putkonen, Paavola, and Tiihonen (2004) examined the circumstances that immediately preceded murders committed by offenders with schizophrenia. They found that psychotic symptoms were the primary cause, and that offenders usually murdered a family member or other person known to them at home or in a private residence.

The content and tone of hallucinations and delusions can have a significant effect on whether an individual with schizophrenia is homicidal or non-violent. A comparative study of violent and non-violent long-stay in patients with chronic schizophrenia found that violent persons were more likely to experience hallucinations with negative tone, negative emotions, and negative commands. Their delusions were more likely to be persecutory and to make the individual feel angry. Conversely, non-violent inpatients were more likely to manage or cope with their hallucinatory voices and to feel elated after experiencing them (Cheung, Schweitzer, Crowley, & Tuckwell, 1997).

© ostill/Shutterstock, Inc.

The content and tone of hallucinations and delusions can have a significant impact on whether an individual with Schizophrenia perpetrates homicide.

In sum, hallucinations that produced terror, irritation, sadness, anger, agitation, intrusion, and fright were more commonly seen in violent persons. In addition, the tone of hallucinations among violent inpatients were angry, bossy, malicious, sharp, and menacing and the tone was often abusive, derogatory, threatening, and critical.

Researchers have also disaggregated the schizophrenia-homicide link by examining specific types of homicide. In a study of parricide, Baxter, Duggan, Larkin, Cordess, and Page (2001) examined 98 individuals who killed their mother (58 percent of cases), their father (42 percent of cases) or both parents (there were six cases of double parricide). Nearly 80 percent of the parricide offenders had a diagnosis for schizophrenia. Compared to homicide offenders who had murdered a stranger, the parricide offenders were significantly less likely to have a criminal history and less likely to have a disrupted childhood. Nevertheless, 40 percent of the parricide offenders had previously attacked the parent whom they would one day murder.

In a comparative study of homicides involving family members as victims versus homicides involving other victims, Nordström, Dahlgren, and Kullgren (2006) examined all 48 homicides occurring in Sweden from 1992 to 2000 that were perpetrated by individuals with schizophrenia. They found that those who killed family members were more likely to kill female victims (usually matricides), more likely to kill in their home, less likely to be intoxicated, less likely for the victim to be intoxicated, and less likely to have a prior conviction for violence. Murderers of family victims were also significantly more likely to have obvious delusions and/or hallucinations at the time of the killing.

Finally, it is important to acknowledge that although schizophrenia is a major form of mental illness that does not mean it is necessarily a person's master status. Some persons who have schizophrenia *also* happen to be career criminals with a lifetime of antisocial acts including homicide. A study by Tengström, Hodgins, and Kullgren (2001) is illustrative. Drawing on data from 272 violent male offenders with schizophrenia in Sweden who underwent a pretrial psychiatric assessment between 1988 and 1995, Tengström and colleagues compared those with early starting criminal careers to those with later starting antisocial histories. Across the board, the early starters were dramatically worse in their offending and social risk profile. Early starters averaged more than 23 convictions including more than four for violent crimes and committed their first violence offense during adolescence. Late starters averaged about four convictions including one for violence and were not violent until nearly age 30.

Early starters were much more psychopathic and the prevalence of Antisocial Personality Disorder among this group was 13 times higher than the prevalence in the late starter group. The early starters were also much more likely to have drug problems, to abuse multiple drugs, to be chronically unemployed, to receive social welfare and to come from families where substance abuse and discord were common. Early starters displayed behavior problems in school, had major academic problems, and were prone to drop out of school. They also had earlier, more varied, and more extensive involvement in legal social agencies, foster care, and correctional institutions. In short, while the study contained homicide offenders who had schizophrenia, the most important status was that they were career criminals.

The next chapter examines another important source of interpersonal violence that is also overrepresented among homicide offenders: Antisocial Personality Disorder.

CHAPTER 23

Homicide and the Antisocial Personality Disorder Perspective

The prevalence of Antisocial Personality Disorder is dramatically higher among prisoners and homicide offenders than the general population.

Conceptual Background

Regrettably, there is coverage of a homicide in most local newspapers in the United States, and in large cities, there are entire sections of the paper dedicated to crime and violence that occurred the prior day. When presented with the behavioral history of most homicide offenders, several factors are common. There is usually an active criminal justice system status for the offender, such as parole, probation, on bond, escape status, or others. Similarly, it is frequently the case that the offender has a prior arrest history, and more often than not, the arrest record is extensive. What this record documents is a pervasive, stable pattern of misbehavior, noncompliance, and violence.

Many homicide offenders have engaged in violent conduct throughout their life, and if enough investigation is performed, and enough witnesses are interviewed, there emerges a similar story that typifies the offender in adulthood, in adolescence, and even in childhood. That continuity s what is seen in Antisocial Personality Disorder where anger, defiance, and rule breaking give way to assorted criminal acts and violence.

Antisocial Personality Disorder is preceded by two other similar conditions that reflect the basic nature of the disorder albeit in young, developmental form. These other conditions are Oppositional Defiant Disorder and Conduct Disorder, and are considered **prodromes**, or early symptoms of a disease, of Antisocial Personality Disorder.

Oppositional Defiant Disorder is a pattern of anger/irritable mood, argumentativeness, defiant behavior, or vindictiveness that lasts at least six months and is evidenced by at least four symptoms. The behavioral disturbance must be associated with distress in the child or others at home, school, and other settings such that the child's social, educational, or other functioning is negatively affected. In the DSM-5, the severity of Oppositional Defiant Disorder is specified. Mild pertains to symptoms that are limited to one setting. Moderate means that some symptoms are present in at least two settings and severe means that some symptoms are present in three or more settings (American Psychiatric Association, 2013, pp. 462–463).

The symptoms of Oppositional Defiant Disorder are:

Angry/Irritable mood

- Often loses temper
- Often touchy or easily annoyed
- Often angry and resentful

Argumentative/Defiant Behavior

- Often argues with authority figures such as adults
- Often actively defies or refuses to comply with requests from authority figures or with rules
- Often deliberately annoys others
- Often blames others for his or her mistakes or misbehavior

Vindictiveness

- Has been spiteful or vindictive at least twice in the prior six months

Conduct Disorder is a repetitive and pervasive pattern of behavior that involves the violation of the rights of others and the violation of age-appropriate norms or rules. According to the American Psychiatric Association (2013, pp. 469–471), there must be three of the following fifteen criteria present in the past 12 months with at least one of the criterion present in the past six months. In addition, the disorder must call significant impairment in multiple life domains such as family, school, work, or another area of functioning.

The criteria are organized into four categories:

Aggression to people and animals:

- often bullies, threatens or intimidates others
- often initiates physical fights
- has used a weapon that can cause serious physical harm to others
- has been physically cruel to people
- has been physically cruel to animals
- has stolen while confronting the victim (e.g., armed robbery)
- has forced someone into sexual activity

Destruction of property

- has deliberately engaged in fire setting with the intention of causing serious damage
- has deliberately destroyed others' property other than by fire setting

Deceitfulness or theft

- Has broken into someone's house or car
- Often lies to obtain goods or favors or to avoid obligations
- Has stolen items of nontrivial value without confronting the victim (e.g., shoplifting)

Serious violation of rules

- Often stays out at night despite parental prohibitions beginning before age 13 years
- Has run away from home at least twice
- Is often truant from school

Antisocial Personality Disorder is a pervasive, inflexible, and enduring pattern of disregarding and violating the rights of others occurring since age 15 years and included at least three diagnostic criteria. There must be evidence of Conduct Disorder with onset before age 15 years and the person must be at least 18 years of age. Moreover, the antisocial conduct in the disorder must be exclusive to schizophrenia or bipolar disorder (American Psychiatric Association, 2013, p. 659).

The criteria for Antisocial Personality Disorder are:

- Failure to conform to social norms with respect to lawful behaviors as indicated by repeatedly performing acts that are grounds for arrest.
- Deceitfulness as indicated by repeated lying, use of aliases, or conning others for personal profit or pleasure.
- Impulsivity or failure to plan ahead.
- Irritability and aggressiveness as indicated by repeated physical fights or assaults.
- Reckless disregard for safety of self or others.
- Consistent irresponsibility as indicated by repeated failure to sustain consistent work behavior or honor financial obligations.
- Lack of remorse as indicated by being indifferent to or rationalizing having hurt, mistreated, or stolen from another.

There is not perfect continuity across the three conditions, but severely antisocial adults have usually been antisocial for their entire life (DeLisi, 2005; Robins, 1979). This would theoretically be true for most homicide offenders as well, and empirical links between the concepts are examined next.

© Suzanne Tucker/Shutterstock, Inc.

For the most violent and antisocial offenders, Antisocial Personality Disorder represents the adult version of earlier conditions Conduct Disorder and Oppositional Defiant Disorder.

Empirical Linkages to Homicide

The evidence linking Antisocial Personality Disorder to homicide is indisputable. In their systematic review and meta-regression analysis, Yu, Geddes, and Fazel (2012) found that personality disorders generally increase the risk of violent criminal offending three fold. They also found that Antisocial Personality Disorder specifically increases the risk of violent offending which included homicide *thirteen fold*!

In their study, Eronen, Hakola, and Tiihonen (1996) found that the increased likelihood of committing homicide among those with Antisocial Personality Disorder was *ten fold* in men and a staggering *fifty fold* higher in women. Antisocial Personality Disorder is also perhaps the most common diagnostic condition of sexual homicide offenders and serial murderers (Geberth & Turco, 1997) and among female homicide offenders (Daniel & Harris, 1982; d'Orb, 1979).

Individuals with Antisocial Personality Disorder pay a heavy price in terms of increased mortality. A study of 250 criminal offenders from Finland compared them to men in the general population. Those with Antisocial Personality Disorder were five to ten times more likely to die by age 50. When non-natural causes of death such as homicide were considered, the risk of early death was increased by a factor of between 6 and 17 times (Repo-Tiihonen, Virkkunen, & Tiihonen, 2001). An examination of 500 outpatients from a psychiatric facility similarly found substantially higher mortality and early mortality among those with Antisocial Personality Disorder (Martin, Cloninger, Guze, & Clayton, 1985).

Yarvis (1990) examined 100 homicide offenders to assess their psychopathology and found that 38 percent of the sample had been diagnosed with Antisocial Personality Disorder. He then disaggregated their crimes to see the relative influence of the condition on various criminal outcomes. Antisocial Personality Disorder accounted for 24 percent of the cases where the offender was only convicted of homicide. In cases of armed robbery and homicide, the prevalence of Antisocial Personality Disorder was 90 percent. In cases of rape and homicide, the prevalence was also 90 percent. In other words, in the most violent, felonious cases, the offender had Antisocial Personality Disorder in nine out of ten cases.

Antisocial Personality Disorder often is comorbid in homicide offenders who have other major mental disorders. A study of 90 homicide offenders with psychotic disorders, for instance, found that 51 percent of them also had personality disorders (Putkonen, Kotilainen, Joyal, & Tiihonen, 2004). Of these, 47 percent were Antisocial Personality Disorder. Going further, 34 percent of those with Antisocial Personality

Disorder exclusively had that disorder. The remaining psychotic homicide offenders also had Borderline Personality Disorder, Obsessive Compulsive Personality Disorder, or all of these.

Most offenders with Antisocial Personality Disorder also had substance abuse disorders. Putkonen and colleagues (2004) also found that Antisocial Personality Disorder was a significant predictor of homicide among their psychotic sample. In addition, Antisocial Personality Disorder accounted for 61 percent of the total incidence of homicide in the sample.

There is worldwide evidence for the harm caused by homicide offenders with Antisocial Personality Disorder. Using data from 68 men with Antisocial Personality Disorder (15 that had attempted or completed homicide) and 65 healthy controls from Turkey, Basoglu, Oner, Ates, Algul, Bez, et al. (2011) reported significant life problems for those with the disorder. Compared to healthy controls, homicide offenders with Antisocial Personality Disorder were three times more likely to be divorced, nearly five times less likely to have long-term employment, four times more likely to have poor family relations, nearly 11 times more likely to engage in self-injurious behaviors, 15 times more likely to attempt suicide, and more than 31 times more likely to commit crime. Drawing on British prisoner data, Coid (2002) found that inmates with Antisocial Personality Disorder were significantly more violent during their confinement and more prone to break institutional rules.

One reason why Antisocial Personality Disorder is disproportionately associated with homicide is neurological. Persons with Antisocial Personality Disorder have difficulty maintaining cortical arousal or vigilance compared to persons without the disorder. As a result of this lower cortical arousal, persons with Antisocial Personality Disorder essentially are hungry for stimulation, which explains their sensation-seeking and risk-taking approach behaviors. Electroencephalographic studies of homicidal men with Antisocial Personality Disorder have shown reduced alpha power and increased theta and delta power in the occipital regions Lindberg, Tani, Virkkunen, Porkka-Heiskanen, Appelberg, Naukkarinen, & Salmi, 2005) which is consistent with the notion they are stimulus starved.

Similar research has shown that homicide offenders with Antisocial Personality Disorder also display **neurological soft signs**, which are motor, sensory, and executive abnormalities that are not localized to specific brain regions. Homicide offenders with Antisocial Personality Disorder display significantly more neurological soft signs than healthy controls and comparable brain dysfunction as persons with schizophrenia (Lindberg, Tani, Stenberg, Appelberg,

Porkka-Heiskanen, & Virkkunen, 2004). Moreover, neurological soft signs are caused by prenatal and perinatal insults, including malnutrition, prenatal tobacco and alcohol exposure, and birth complications—all causes of serious antisocial behavior.

Of course, murderers with Antisocial Personality Disorder also present with core structural and functional brain abnormalities compared to healthy controls. In a study of 26 persistently violent offenders with Antisocial Personality Disorder and matched healthy controls, Tiihonen and colleagues (2008) examined brain anatomy using magnetic resonance imaging volumetry and voxel-based morphometry. This method allows for much more refined analyses of brain volume.

Compared to controls, the violent offenders had significantly *larger* white matter volumes in the occipital and parietal lobes and in the left cerebellum. They also had larger gray matter volume in the right cerebellum. However, the brains of men with Antisocial Personality Disorder had small volume in the orbitofrontal cortex, frontopolar cortex, and postcentral gyri. These differences suggest atypical neurodevelopment that is involved in the initiation and maintenance of persistent violent behavior across the life-course. In addition, all of the violent men were alcohol dependent and 77 percent were polysubstance abusers.

© Jaimie Duplass/Shutterstock, Inc.

Neuropsychologists have shown that murderers with Antisocial Personality Disorder have neurological impairments in areas that affect emotional regulation, behavioral inhibition, and moral decision-making.

In their review of the literature, Glenn and Raine (2011) noted that brain imaging studies have revealed reduced blood flow in the prefrontal cortex, about 11 percent reduced gray matter volume in the prefrontal cortex, and reduced frontal functioning. Studies have also shown that murderers with Antisocial Personality Disorder also had reduced gray matter in the frontopolar and orbitofrontal cortex, a region that is involved in regulating emotion, inhibiting responses, and moral decision-making.

Box 23.1   Antisocial Personality Disorder in Deaf Murderers

This chapter makes clear that Antisocial Personality Disorder is a considerable risk factor for homicide. But do these effects hold among special populations of homicide offenders? Vernon, Steinberg, and Montoya (1999) conducted an interesting study of 28 deaf individuals who were convicted or awaiting trial for homicide offenses to examine their psychiatric profile.

The etiology of their deafness was diverse. Known causes included rubella, measles, encephalitis, Rh factor, prematurity, and various genetic disorders. In six of the cases, the cause of deafness was unknown. The offenders ranged in age from 17 to 43, and had IQs that ranged from 65 to 123. Their deafness imposed considerable education burden as 15 of the 28 were illiterate. Their English literacy grade equivalent ranged from 3.0 to 10.0. One of the murderers, with the highest IQ, was a graduate student at the time of his arrest.

The men (all of the killers were male) presented with an array of Axis I disorders including alcohol abuse, cannabis abuse, Post Traumatic Stress Disorder, Epilepsy, Intermittent Explosive Disorder, Dissociative Identity Disorder, Schizophrenia Paranoid Type, cocaine abuse, Pedophilia, exhibitionism, voyeurism, and Hyperbilirubinemia. They also presented with an assortment of Axis II disorders including Mixed Receptive-Expressive Language Disorder, Conduct Disorder, Dependent Personality Disorder, mild mental retardation, ADHD, and several who had no diagnoses.

But the most prevalent condition among the deaf murderers was Antisocial Personality Disorder. Indeed, 50 percent of the sample had an ASPD diagnosis. Consistent with this diagnosis, most of the deaf murderers had considerable criminal history and substance use problems. Their prior criminal acts included cruelty to animals, abduction and rape, assault, auto theft, burglary, drunk driving, arson, theft, indecent exposure, and attempted homicide. Some of the them had no prior criminal history; however, one without criminal history self-reported that he was always in trouble due to this erratic and antisocial behavior. One of the 28 had previously committed homicide. In that case, he murdered a prostitute and was held for one year until the court held that he was not competent to stand trial. Six months after his release, he murdered another prostitute, was convicted, and sentenced to 14 to 25 years in prison.

In sum, although deafness was a unique feature of the murderers in this sample, their behavioral history and the presence of Antisocial Personality Disorder was common and consistent with other clinical and forensic samples of homicide offenders.

Source: Vernon, M., Steinberg, A. G., & Montoya, L. A. (1999). Deaf murderers: Clinical and forensic issues. *Behavioral Sciences & the Law, 17*(4), 495–516.

Antisocial Personality Disorder is not just seen in multiple and sexual homicides, but also murders occurring in a more normal context. For example, Dutton and Kerry (1999) found high prevalence of the condition among men convicted of murdering their wife. Among cases where the murder was premeditated, 100 percent of the offenders had Antisocial Personality Disorder. Given the problematic set of symptoms that characterize Antisocial Personality Disorder, it is often implicated in virtually every type of homicide that has been covered in this book. Indeed, other than psychopathy—a condition that it is often incorrectly assumed to be the same condition—Antisocial Personality Disorder is the most pernicious condition in this text and the one with the most robust relation to homicide. The next chapter centers on the human brain, and the neuropsychological foundations of these disorders.

CHAPTER 24

Homicide and the Neuropsychological Perspective

© Lightspring/Shutterstock, Inc.

Neuroscientists have identified many unique features of the murderous brain, and have the potential to solve timeless philosophical and scientific questions.

Conceptual Background

The seat of all human behavior is the human brain, and ultimately the biosocial mechanisms that underlie all of the theoretical concepts covered in this book originate in the brain. Thus in a way, all theories of homicide are neuropsychological in that regard. The current chapter, however, focuses explicitly on this perspective to show the ways how neuroscientists are identifying the emotional and cognitive neural pathways that produce homicidal behavior.

Neuropsychology is a field of study that shows the ways that physiological development affects psychological functioning and behavior. It is understood that several biological systems (e.g., neurological, genetic, endocrine, and others) are themselves affected by environmental conditions, indeed this is the nature and nurture interplay that typifies the current biosocial paradigm for understanding not just crime, but all behavior. Several constructs, including temperament, autonomic functioning, and executive functioning can be generally subsumed under the rubric neuropsychology.

The epicenter of neuropsychology is the human brain, where more than half of human genes are expressed, and where the foundations of human behavior, emotion, and cognition are found. Before delving into neuropsychological models of antisocial behavior and crime, an overview of the most relevant brain regions is helpful.

The most advanced section of the brain, and the brain structures that separate humans from lower animals, is the **cerebral cortex** also known as the frontal lobe, frontal area, prefrontal cortex, or cortical area. This brain region is comprised of four important areas or cortices. The **orbitofrontal cortex (OFC)** which is located behind the orbit of the eyes (or eye sockets) is responsible for inhibitory control. Deficits in this area are associated with impulsive behavior. The **dorsolateral prefrontal cortex (DLPFC)** which is behind the OFC (anatomically behind the forehead) is responsible for executive functions, such as planning, decision-making, and other rational action. Located underneath the DLPFC is the **ventromedial prefrontal cortex (VMPFC)** is responsible for emotional cognition, which are sometimes referred to as the "hot" executive functions. The **anterior cingulate cortex (ACC)** which is close to the middle of the brain, near the limbic system, is responsible for attentional control.

The frontal regions of the brain function to control or modulate more primitive emotions that emanate from the midbrain, specifically the limbic system. The **limbic system**, also known as the visceral brain, subcortical region, emotional brain, or paleo mammalian brain (because it is phylogenetically younger than the reptilian brain stem, but older than the neomammalian cerebral cortex), contains the amygdala, hippocampus, septum, cingulate gyrus, hypothalamus, and thalamus.

Collectively, these brain structures are responsible for memory, learning, emotion, and fear conditioning. More importantly, behavioral regulation, and forms of dysregulation, such as crime, can be broadly understood as dysfunction in the connectivity between cortical and subcortical brain regions.

In the neurosciences and psychology, there are several conceptual models that point to the interplay between frontal and limbic structures as explanations for emotional and behavioral problems (e.g., Blair 2003; Damasio 1994; Davidson, Putnam, and Larson 2000). Neurological or brain development is central for understanding the emergence and developmental course of antisocial behavior including delinquency. For example, Steinberg (2010) advanced the **dual systems model** to show how psychophysiological development is critical for understanding how the brain affects antisocial behavior. Drawing on neuroscience findings based on neuroimaging studies, Steinberg suggests that the socioemotional, incentive-processing systems of the midbrain overwhelm the ability of frontal self-regulatory system. As a result, the adolescent brain is predisposed toward sensation-seeking, risk taking, approach behaviors, and impulsive acts. As the self-regulatory system develops into adulthood, it is able to control emotions and behaviors.

Steinberg's model is directly relevant to homicide because the logic of this theory was cited by the U.S. Supreme Court in their decisions to remove capital punishment and life imprisonment without parole as Constitutional punishments for adolescent murderers. At worst, a juvenile murderer can be sentenced to life imprisonment with the possibility of parole.

Importantly related to these neurophysiological factors are neuropsychological characteristics that often accompany antisocial and criminal behavior. Generally, neuropsychological functions broadly refer to cognitive and self-regulation processes, such as concentration, motor and cognitive planning, attention, goal formulation, self-awareness and self-monitoring of behavior, and perhaps most importantly, the suppression or modulation of cognitive and behavioral impulses (Beaver, Wright, & DeLisi, 2007).

Of particular importance for understanding neuropsychological functioning in antisocial or delinquent individuals are lower-order executive functions including behavioral impulsivity, cognitive impulsivity, and operant decision making. Individuals who have **neuropsychological deficits** present with a range of problems relating to verbal skills, receptive language, sustaining attention, memory, response inhibition, and self-control.

The U.S. Supreme Court cited neuropsychological theory and research when it invalidated capital punishment and life imprisonment without parole for juveniles convicited of homicide.

These deficits create a host of problems because the sociocognitive deficits and the maladaptive behavioral responses to those cognitive problems set into motion a dynamic, negative process whereby the youth becomes estranged from school and conventional peers. This unfolding set of negative interactions between the neuropsychological deficits and the responses to them also occur at home and in other social settings and contribute to aversive, often punitive responses from adults (Dodge, Bates, & Pettit, 1990; Crick & Dodge, 1994). Over the course of their antisocial development, an outcome of severe neuropsychological problems is homicide. Empirical studies on this association are examined next.

Empirical Linkages to Homicide

In cases histories of children and adolescents who perpetrate homicide, there is compelling evidence for the role of neurological problems as a potential cause of subsequent homicidal activity. A variety of head injuries resulting in loss of consciousness including falls from trees, car accidents, being hit in the head with a hammer, falling from a roller coaster, and other accidents are commonly seen in the backgrounds of juvenile homicide offenders (Lewis et al., 1988). In many case studies and biographies of notorious homicide offenders, there is often evidence of traumatic brain injuries resulting from their aberrant behavior, from their severe abuse histories, and often, from both causes.

Briken, Habermann, Berner, and Hill (2005) examined the prevalence of brain abnormalities in a sample of 166 sexual murderers and found that 30 percent of the homicide offenders had brain abnormalities. Many of these offenders also had severe psychiatric diagnoses. For instance, 50 percent of sexual murderers with brain abnormalities presented with sadistic personality disorder. Since the hallmark of sexual sadism is the infliction of pain and suffering for the gratification of the offender, it makes sense that amygdala dysfunction plays some role in aggravated homicide offending (Briken et al., 2005; Hill, Habermann, Berner, & Briken, 2007).

Zagar, Busch, Grove, and Hughes (2009) compared several groups at risk for homicide including 192 persons who were abused as infants, 181 persons who were abused as children, 127 homicidal youth, 425 juvenile assaulters, 223 rapists, and 223 child molesters. These groups were compared to matched non-offenders and non-violent offenders and followed into adulthood. One of the strongest areas that differentiated those who ultimately committed homicide were neurocognitive and neuropsychological features. Homicide offenders had reduced executive functioning, more head injuries, greater prevalence of epilepsy, more sensory, speech, and neurological disorders, and greater hospitalization for neuropsychological problems (also see, Gilligan & Lennings, 2011).

A study of 77 homicide defendants and/or death row inmates selected from Illinois and Missouri showcases the severe neuropsychological and cognitive deficits of homicide offenders. Hanlon, Rubin, Jensen, and Daoust (2010) found widespread evidence of neuropsychological harm among the murderers. Those who committed one homicide were characterized by executive dysfunction, lower intelligence, and slower information processing speed. Nearly 60 percent had developmental disorders and nearly half had a documented history of learning disorder and/or mental retardation. On a variety of tasks relating to intelligence, memory, and executive function, homicide offenders were anywhere from 0.5 to nearly 1.5 standard deviation units below average in their neuropsychological functioning.

A later study indicated that intelligent and cognitive functioning might separate homicide offenders who kill impulsively from those who kill for instrumental or predatory reasons. The average IQ of impulsive murderers was 79 whereas the average IQ for predatory murderers was 93 (Hanlon, Brook, Stratton, Jensen, & Rubin, 2013). Other research of murderers who were sentenced to death or life imprisonment indicated that low IQ and general cognitive deficits partially explained offenders' inability to deal with complications that arise in homicide events (Heilbrun, 1990).

A major reason for neurocognitive and neuropsychological effects among homicide offenders is there are structural and functional brain differences between violent individuals and non-violent individuals. **Structural brain imaging** measures anatomical features of brain regions of interest that are theorized to be associated with a particular behavior, trait, or condition. **Functional brain imaging** measures brain activity, such as glucose metabolism and cerebral blood flow, to see the processes involved in neurological functioning.

A variety of studies have conducted neuroimaging of homicide offenders to see if there are significant neurological differences between them, other violent criminals, other criminals, and non-criminal controls. In a study of 24 schizophrenia patients, 10 of whom had perpetrated murder or attempted murder, significant brain volume differences were found between them and controls. Homicidal patients had lower brain volume in the orbitofrontal, inferior frontal, middle frontal, superior frontal, temporal lobe, hippocampus, and amygdala (Kumari, Barkataki, Goswami, Flora, Das, & Taylor, 2009). They also found that homicidal patients displayed dysfunctional impulsivity, which they defined as recklessness without deliberation and evaluation of consequences.

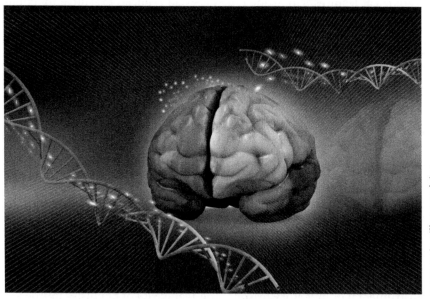

© ramcreations/Shutterstock, Inc.

More than half of human genes are expressed in the brain. Thus neurogeneticists are busily examining the genetic causes of brain products that relate to complex behaviors.

Several brain imaging studies have provided fascinating insights into the neuropsychological processes that underlie homicide. A fascinating study used fMRI to examine the neural correlates involved in justified killing and unjustified killing. Molenberghs, Ogilvie, Louis, Decety, Bagnall, and Bain (2015) had participants imagine being the perpetrator of a homicide while watching an animated video where they shot enemy soldiers. This condition was known as the justified killing condition. Next participants imagined themselves shooting civilians instead of the soldiers. This was the unjustified killing condition. When imaging unjustified homicide, participants had greater neural activation in the lateral orbitofrontal cortex. Moreover, the greater guilt that a person felt about shooting civilians was associated with a greater response in the lateral orbitofrontal cortex. There was also evidence of additional connectivity to the temporoparietal junction during the unjustified homicide condition. Thus there is less frontal activation in experimental conditions when an individual imagines themselves committing a justified homicide. But the neural mechanisms are different for unjustified homicides, at least among normally functioning persons.

Finally, Yang and Raine (2009) performed a meta-analysis of 43 studies of brain imaging of antisocial persons, several of which contained homicide offenders, and produced several key findings. Across studies, there are significant neural differences between violent persons such as murderers and normal controls. First, there are prefrontal abnormalities in the right orbitofrontal cortex (OFC), the left dorsolateral prefrontal cortex (DLPFC), and right anterior cingulate cortex (ACC) in terms of reduced volume and decreased functioning. Second, antisocial behavior including homicide is more associated with right-sided prefrontal pathology particularly in the OFC and ACC. Third, reductions in the right prefrontal cortex are associated with emotional deficits and poor decision-making in antisocial persons. Fourth, reductions in the left DLPFC are associated with impulsivity and poor behavioral control. Fifth, both structural and functional deficits in the left DLPFC also lead to impairments in attentional control and social information processing.

The next chapter contains critical concepts that have appeared throughout the book.

CHAPTER 25

Critical Concepts

Students should take some time to digest the data presented in Figure 25.1. Even in the most peaceful year, there were nearly 10,000 homicides in the United States, which prorates to more than 27 per day. That is an unbearable degree of violence. Moreover, homicide is not like cancer, or congenital heart disease, or type I diabetes, or other eventually fatal medical conditions because homicide is completely preventable. There is no justification for homicide even if we understand the distal and proximal causes of it, and even if we can identify with the basic emotions that preceded the homicide event.

Homicide never has to happen, but homicide has always happened. None of the topical areas in this book (although the victimology perspective comes closest) adequately capture the tragedy of homicide. There are no more fundamental human experiences than birth, life, and death. No one is spared death. But most people are able to live life to a relatively advanced age before passing. Homicide cuts that short, and homicide is

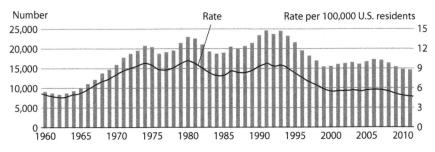

Figure 25.1 Number and Rate of Homicide in the United States, 1960–2011.

Source: Smith, E. L., & Cooper, A. (2013). *Homicide in the U.S. known to law enforcement, 2011.* Washington, DC: U. S. Department of Justice, Office of Justice Programs, Bureau of Justice Statistics.

most likely to cut life short among those who are generally young. It is for these heavy, philosophical, life-and-death reasons that homicide is so fascinating to us. It is why it is taken so seriously, and punished most harshly. The critical concepts in this chapter review major concepts from chapters 1–24, and provide a panoramic understanding of the topic.

Chapter 1

Homicide: the killing of a human being by another human being.

Justifiable homicide: the killing of a felon by a police officer or citizen during the commission of a serious crime.

Murder: the unlawful killing of a human being with malice aforethought.

Voluntary manslaughter: homicide committed with intention but in the immediate heat of passion.

Involuntary manslaughter: Homicide committed due to accident or negligence.

Vehicular homicide: Unplanned homicide caused by motor vehicle/traffic violation.

Mens rea: Criminal intent.

Filicide: The murder of a child by a parent.

Infanticide: The murder of a child in the first year of life.

Neonaticide: The killing of a child in the infant's first 24 hours of life.

Fatal child assault: The death of a child from acts of violence perpetrated by another person.

Parricide: The killing of one's father, mother, or another close relative.

Patricide: The killing of one's father.

Matricide: The killing of one's mother.

Fratricide: is the killing of one's brother or sister.

Uxoricide: commonly known as intimate partner homicide, domestic homicide, or spousal homicide, is the killing of an individual by their intimate partner usually a spouse.

Homicide-suicide: is the killing of one or more individuals followed by the suicide of the perpetrator. It is also known as murder-suicide or dyadic death.

Sexual homicide: is a homicide in which some form of sexual activity occurs with the victim prior to, during, or after the death of the victim.

Serial murder: Offenders who murder at least three victims with stoppages of cooling-off periods between.

Mass murder: Also known as multicide is the killing of multiple victims during a single event with roughly the same location or place and occurring at the same time.

Spree homicide: is a type of homicide that lies between mass murder and serial murder in terms of its temporal unfolding.

multiple homicide offenders: A criminal career approach with the hope of identifying risk factors for the perpetration of multiple homicides irrespective of serial, mass, or spree designation.

Adversary effect: An offender's tactical response to the threat posed by an adversary.

Chapter 2

Interactionist perspective: is a soft theory of human behavior that asserts that behavior emerges from social interaction and the subjective states relating to that interaction, and is not caused by objective characteristics of individuals.

Self-derogation theory: Self-derogation pertains to the set of negative feelings and low self-esteem regarding one's abilities, personal qualities, and behavior. Self-derogation is theorized to be the negative emotions that result from rejection by others.

Routine activities theory: Suggests that criminal behavior is produced by the coming together in time and space of three basic elements. The first is a motivated offender, the second is a suitable target, or potential victim, and the third is the absence of capable guardians, or simply, there are not police or others who could stop the crime.

Hot spots theory: Theory that attributes violence and homicide to the dynamics of a small number of crime-prone places.

Victim-precipitated homicide: Wolfgang's finding that many homicide victims initiated the confrontation that led to their murder.

Focused deterrence programs: Targeted law enforcement efforts to reduce gun homicides.

Chapter 3

Southern subculture of violence: Advances that an honor-based culture exists in the southern United States that is potentially conducive to violent provocation and retaliation.

Black subculture of violence thesis: Idea that blacks have a subcultural honor code that advocates the use of violence to defend status.

Herding/honor culture: A broad honor culture where one's reputation and self were built upon the steadfast use of violence to prove one's worth.

Lynching: An extra-legal trial (meaning that the trial was not formally conducted by the criminal justice system) and punishment of an alleged wrongdoer.

Chapter 4

Decent people: People who are generally prosocial and abide by the conventional norms of society.

Street people: People who are antisocial and tacitly or explicitly reject involvement in conventional social institutions.

Code of the street or street code: Subculture where blacks use violence as a means to achieve, maintain, and preserve status.

General altercation homicides: Public killings that occur between acquaintances because of an argument or fight.

Street efficacy: The perceived ability to avoid violent confrontations and be safe even in negative, violent environments.

Chapter 5

Lifestyle theory: Theory that criminal offenders and victims tend to "match" demographically because crime represents social interaction and social access among similarly situated people.

Homogamous interaction: Principle where people associate with others similar to them.

Lifestyle criminality: A life pattern of irresponsible, self-indulgent, interpersonally intrusive, and social rule-breaking behavior.

Disresponsibility: An intellectual effort or rationalization in which a person attributes his or her actions to other causes and other people.

Chapter 6

Self-control: The basic ability to regulate one's emotions and behaviors especially toward long-term consequences versus short-term benefits.

I³ theory: A self-control theory that identifies instigation, impellance, and inhibition as three conditions that lead to aggression and potentially lethal aggression

Intermittent Explosive Disorder: A disorder characterized by recurrent episodes of aggression involving violence or destruction of property that are out of proportion to provocation or precipitating stressors.

Self-control theory: Gottfredson and Hirschi's idea that self-control is the main cause of crime and other problem behaviors.

Sensation seeking: A tendency to seek novel experiences and excitement often in an impulsive way.

Disorganized sexual murderer: Killer whose offense was spontaneous, whose victim was known but depersonalized, and who engaged in minimal conservation during the attack.

Organized sexual murderer: Killer who committed a planned killing of a targeted stranger who was personalized.

Chapter 7

Containment theory: The idea that healthy self-concept is critical in the containment of delinquency.

Original Sin: Christian tradition which suggests that sin that typifies humanity because of Adam's succumbing to temptation in the Eden. From this perspective, humans are by definition flawed and prone to sinful behavior.

Social bond theory: Hirschi's idea which asserts that persons with weak or nonexistent bonds to others and society are more likely to engage in antisocial behavior.

Attachment: The affectional ties to family and friends that reflects the internalization of social and behavioral norms.

Commitment: The extent to which individuals invest in conventional, prosocial behavior.

Involvement: The engagement or participation in conventional activities.

Belief: The endorsement of social and legal mores such that norms and laws should be obeyed.

Disorganized attachment: The result of abuse, neglect, and poor parenting that impairs the ability of the child to form social bonds and contributes to a host of mental health and behavioral problems.

Multiple disadvantage model: A model which suggests that several negative statuses that blacks are more likely than whites to possess contributes to the former's greater likelihood of homicide victimization.

Chapter 8

Stratification: The informal hierarchy of a society divided into social classes that are based on educational attainment, income, and wealth. From one's socioeconomic status, power is derived.

Institutional anomie theory: A structural explanation which argues that cultural focus on achievement and wealth is a source of homicide in the United States

Achievement orientation: A fundamental marker of success in American society relates to the achievement of various milestones. Failure to achieve these milestones is consistent with failure.

Individualism: Individual autonomy, individual rights, and self-determination are fundamental values that drive the need to accomplish goals on one's own.

Universalism: This is the notion that all Americans should generally strive for achieving the same cultural goals.

Fetishism of money: The accumulation of wealth is an end goal in itself and is the primary metric on which people are evaluated.

Social support: Support that meets expressive needs (emotional connections to others that serve to bolster an individual's self-worth) and instrumental needs (material support, guidance and advice of an individual).

Chapter 9

Social learning theory: The idea that humans learn values, beliefs, and behaviors to produce behavior.

Differential coercion theory: Suggests that the blend of coercion and consistency of that coercion manifest in psychological and behavioral outcomes.

Differential association theory: Sutherland's idea that crime is learned from social learning processes based on interaction with others.

Differential association-reinforcement theory: Akers' idea which suggests that crime is produced by learned and reinforced according to operant conditioning principles.

Neutralization theory: Suggests that individuals are generally conventional but learn various forms of rationalization to morally free themselves to commit a misdeed.

Ecological-transactional model of community violence: Suggests that broad exposure to violence in the community stresses the ability of parents to protect their children from the pernicious effects of violence.

Catathymic process: Situation where an individual perceives that the only way to resolve an extraordinary inner conflict is to perpetrate murder.

Chapter 10

Anomie: A condition of normlessness where an individual is uncertain how to behave.

General strain theory: Agnew's idea that crime and violence are caused by actual or anticipated failure to achieve positively valued goals, actual or anticipated removal of positively valued stimuli, and actual or anticipated presentation of negatively valued stimuli.

Anticipated strains: Strains that are expected in the future and that can cause negative emotions currently.

Objective strains: Observed strains that create negative emotions and can result in problem behaviors.

Subjective strains: Perceived strains that create negative emotions and can result in problem behaviors.

Vicarious strains: Third-party strains where an individual observes another having strain and it negatively affects them emotionally or behaviorally.

Chapter 11

Structural perspective: Asserts that aggregate characteristics of neighborhoods, cities, states, or nations are associated with homicide rates occurring in those settings.

Poverty: Structural idea that there is generally a relationship where greater material disadvantage engenders greater involvement in antisocial behavior which increases the likelihood of conflict, and potentially homicide

Inequality or relative deprivation: Structural idea that although poverty can produce homicide in absolute terms, there is also the notion that one's economic position relative to another is also a motivating force for violence.

Family structure: Structural idea that several variables included percent married, percent divorced males, and percent female-headed households are associated with crime and homicide.

Population characteristics: Geographic areas or cities with populations that are disproportionately young, male, poor, and nonwhite are likely to experience more homicide than populations that are disproportionately older, female, more affluent, and white.

Concentrated disadvantage: Impoverished places where a high percentage of residents receive welfare, are unemployed, are disproportionately African American, are younger, and tend to live in female-headed households.

Social capital: Relationships with people and organizations that foster collective action and produce personal, social, and economic benefits.

Chapter 12

Social disorganization theory: Shaw and McKay's idea that neighborhoods characterized by high residential mobility, ethnic heterogeneity, and high poverty levels exhibit higher crime and delinquency rates.

Informal social control: The ability of family, friends, neighbors, and other acquaintances to monitor and regulate other's conduct through shared values and belief systems.

Broken windows theory: An ecological theory which asserts that physical disorder contributes to a breakdown in formal and informal social controls that give rise to social disorder, including crime.

Collective efficacy: The informal social control mechanisms in a neighborhood characterized by mutual trust and a neighborly willingness to intervene for the common good.

Concentric zone model: Burgess' model that divide the City of Chicago into five zones radiating out from the center based upon real estate values, level of disorganization, crime and violence, and others

Zone of transition: Zone II that contained the worst neighborhoods in terms of vice, delinquency, violence, and disorder and personified social disorganization theory

Chapter 13

Five Factor Model: A structural model of personality that contains five dimensions: openness to experience, conscientiousness, extraversion, agreeableness, and neuroticism.

Neuroticism: Refers to the chronic level of emotional adjustment and instability.

Extraversion: Refers to the quantity and intensity of preferred interpersonal interactions, activity level, need for stimulation, and capacity for joy.

Openness to experience: Involves the appreciation and seeking of experiences.

Agreeableness: Refers to the kinds of interactions a person has along a continuum from compassion to antagonism.

Conscientiousness: The degree of organization, persistence, control, and motivation in goal-directed behavior.

Personality disorder: An enduring pattern of inner experience and behavior that deviates markedly from the expectations of the individual's culture.

Cluster A Personality Disorders: Odd or eccentric personality disorders.

Cluster B Personality Disorders: Dramatic or emotional personality disorders.

Cluster C Personality Disorders: Anxious or fearful personality disorders.

Personality: A set of traits that generally typify the stable and relatively consistent ways that a person behaves, thinks, and feels.

PEN model: Eysenck's model that indicates three primary factors of personality: psychoticism, extraversion, and neuroticism.

Psychoticism: A personality factor that is comprised of nine lower-order traits. These are aggressiveness, coldness, egocentricity, impersonality, impulsivity, antisociality, unempathic, creativity, and tough-mindedness.

Extraversion: In Eysenck's PEN model, a personality factor that is comprised of nine lower-order traits. These are sociability, liveliness, activity, assertiveness, sensation-seeking, carefree, dominant, surgent, and venturesome.

Neuroticism: In Eysenck's PEN model, a personality factor that is comprised of nine lower-order traits. These are anxiousness, depressed, guilty feelings, low self-esteem, tension, irrationality, shyness, moodiness, and emotionality.

Stone's gradations of evil model: Personality model that assesses the level of inhumanity of evil of a homicide offender as a function of their behavior, sadism, and psychopathy.

Sadistic Personality Disorder: Personality disorder that is a pervasive pattern of cruel, demeaning, and aggressive behavior beginning in early adulthood.

Paraphilias: Sexual perversions or sexual deviations.

Chapter 14

Evolutionary psychology: A field of study that uses evolutionary biology principles—that humans have evolved over historical time—and their evolution reflects traits and behaviors that provided some adaptive function.

Homicide adaptation theory: A general evolutionary framework that suggests how and why homicide would have evolved as a behavioral option.

Conflict assay: An index of relationship-specific, demographic, and situational variations in the intensity of interpersonal conflict.

Evolved psychological mechanisms: Domain-specific information-processing mechanisms that relate to survival and reproduction.

Intrasexual competition: The competition between same sex rivals for access to mating opportunities.

Parental investment theory: The allocation of resources to offspring at the expense of other resources is a major difference between males and females.

Parental solicitude: Concern about the health and welfare of their biological child

Chapter 15

Epidemiology: A branch of medicine that deals with measuring how much of a particular problem, or disease, exists in a population.

Incidence: Measure of the quantity of a disease or condition in the population.

Prevalence: Measure of the proportion of a population that is affected by a disease or condition.

Supplementary Homicide Reports: Part of the Uniform Crime Reporting Program administered by the Federal Bureau of Investigation that measures homicide in the United States.

National Vital Statistics System, Fatal Injury Reports: Measure which includes data based on birth and death records at the state and local level.

Disability-adjusted life years (DALYs): A measure of the state of a population's health compared to normal life expectancy or some other normalized standard.

Years of life lost due to premature mortality (YLLs): A measure that is calculated by multiplying the number of deaths at each age by the standard life expectancy at each age.

Years lived with disability (YLDs): A measure of the loss of health associated with a disease state compared to those who are healthy.

Case-control design or case-control study: Design that compares two groups. One group has a particularly characteristic, disease, or condition and serves as the cases. The other group does not have the characteristic, disease, or condition and serves as the controls.

Proband: Affected person, such as homicide offender.

Population-attributable risk: The portion of homicide offenses that would be eliminated by a hypothetical intervention that reduced the offending risk of individuals with a record to the offending risk of those who lack a record.

Syndemic: The co-occurrence of two or more epidemics where social conditions and biological determinants interact synergistically to increase the burden of disease on the population.

Chapter 16

Biosocial criminology: The interdisciplinary study of crime using methods and data from multiple fields.

Behavioral genetics research: uses twin data to statistically model the relative effects of genes, similar environmental factors known as shared environment factors, and dissimilar environmental factors known as nonshared environmental factors.

Monozygotic (MZ) twins: Also known as identical twins, they share 100 percent of their DNA.

Dizygotic (DZ) twins: Also known as fraternal twins, they share 50 percent of their DNA.

Heritability: The amount of variance in a trait or behavior that is attributable to genetic factors.

Shared environmental factors: The amount of variance in a trait or behavior that is attributable to common factors between twins such as family environment.

Nonshared environmental factors: The amount of variance in a trait or behavior that is attributable to unique factors that differentiate twins such as peer associations.

Molecular genetic association studies: Studies that use measured genes to model their effects on observed outcomes (known as phenotypes)

Gene: A distinct section of DNA in a cell's chromosome that contains the codes for producing specific proteins involved in brain and bodily functions.

Polymorphism (or functional polymorphism): Genes that exist in various forms.

Alleles: variants of polymorphic genes.

Neurotransmission: Communication between neurons in the brain.

MAOA gene: Gene that encodes the MAOA enzyme that is responsible for metabolizing neurotransmitters in the brain such as norepinephrine, serotonin, and dopamine.

Catechol O-methyltransferase gene (COMT): An important candidate gene for antisocial and other problem behaviors due to the major role the enzyme plays in modulating dopamine levels in the prefrontal cortex, the area of the brain that controls executive cognitive functioning.

Chapter 17

Victimology: The study of victims of crime.

Sense-making: A restorative idea whereby victims create meaning to understand their loss and assist in their post-crime event self-identity.

Covictims of homicide: The family, friends, and acquaintances of murdered individuals.

Complicated grief: A debilitating, chronic sense of loss where an individual is not able to overcome the bereavement process.

Cold cases homicides: Open investigations in which there has not been judicial resolution. In many cold cases, there is never even an arrest.

Family liaison officers: Members of a police department who serve as a single point of contact between the police department handling a homicide case and the homicide victim's family and friends.

Victim liaison officers: Dedicated correctional staff who work with the family and friends of homicide victims to assist in relevant tasks, such as obtaining victims services and notification of release (if applicable) of the homicide offender.

Law Enforcement Officers Killed and Assaulted (LEOKA): A report produced by the Federal Bureau of Investigation that records the killing of law enforcement officers in the line of duty

Chapter 18

Criminal career: A measure of an individual's criminal activity across life.

Onset: The beginning of the criminal career.

Intermittency: Sporadic activity where an offender is arrested multiple times in a short-period of time, then has periods of time with little to no arrests.

Escalation: Increase in the severity of crimes committing in a criminal career.

Lambda: Measure of amount of crimes in a specific unit of time, such as one year.

Desistance: The declining of a criminal career.

Termination: The end of a criminal career.

Career criminals: The 5 percent of the offender population that commits the bulk of crimes and most homicides.

Developmental taxonomy: Moffitt's model that articulates three types of offenders: non-offenders (abstainers), minor offenders (adolescence-limited offenders), and severe offenders (life-course-persistent offenders.

Life-course-persistent offenders: Those that display antisocial conduct across life due to neuropsychological deficits, negative environmental contexts, and the interaction of those person- and environmental-deficits.

Recidivism: Subsequent offending following release from criminal justice system supervision among various types of homicide offenders.

Chapter 19

Psychopathy: A personality disorder that is characterized by a suite of interpersonal, affective, lifestyle, and behavioral characteristics that manifest in wide-ranging antisocial behaviors

Callous and unemotional traits: Lack of empathy and absence of guilt that are seen in young children at risk for psychopathy.

Moral disengagement: The tendency to engage in problem behaviors without feeling guilt, shame, or other self-conscious negative emotions.

Primary psychopathy: Psychopaths with the absence of conscience or superego where individuals experience no neurotic feelings or inner turmoil in terms of emotional response.

Secondary psychopaths: Psychopaths who display severe forms of antisocial behavior, but they also have comorbid psychiatric problems relating to what psychoanalysts called neuroses and what psychologists today call internalizing symptoms.

Malevolent psychopath: The most vicious, violent, and mean-spirited variant of psychopathy.

Elemental Psychopathy Assessment: A 178-item self-report measure designed to assess extreme personality variants from the Five Factor Model that relate to psychopathy.

Future dangerousness: A forecast of an offender's likely future violence that is made in capital sentencing.

Chapter 20

Substance use: The ingestion of a controlled substance for the purpose of causing intoxication or to experience the physiological effects of the substance.

Substance abuse: A pattern of substance use that leads to significant impairment or distress including at least one of the following four criteria in the prior 12 months: failure to fulfill major role obligations at work, school, or home, frequent use of substances when it is physically hazardous, frequent legal problems, and continued use despite recurrent social or interpersonal problems.

Substance dependence: Significant impairment or distress including at least three of the following criteria in the prior 12 months: Tolerance or markedly increased amounts of the substance to achieve intoxication or desired effect or markedly diminished effect with continued use of the same amount of substance, withdrawal symptoms or the use of certain substances to avoid withdrawal symptoms, use of a substance in larger amounts or over a longer period than was intended, persistent desire or unsuccessful efforts to cut down or control substance use, involvement in chronic behavior to obtain the substance, use the substance, or recover from its effects, reduction or abandonment of social, occupational or recreational activities because of substance use, use of substances even though there is a persistent or recurrent physical or psychological problem that is likely to have been caused or exacerbated by the substance

Chapter 21

Bipolar I Disorder: Disorder characterized by one or more manic or mixed episodes that is usually accompanied by major depressive episodes.

Bipolar II Disorder: Disorder characterized by one or more major depressive episodes that is accompanied by at least one hypomanic episode.

Major depressive episode: A change from previous functioning that lasts during a two-week period and includes five or more of the following symptoms with at least one of symptoms being depressed mood or loss of interest of pleasure.

Manic episode: A one-week period of abnormally and persistently elevated, expansive, or irritable mood and abnormally and persistently increased goal-directed activity or energy. It lasts most of the day nearly every day.

Hypomanic episode: A less severe variant of a manic episode that lasts only four days.

Chapter 22

Schizophrenia: A major form of mental illness and is the most severe type of psychotic disorder.

Psychotic disorder: An illness characterized by delusions and hallucinations in which the individual's ability to appreciate objective reality is compromised.

Positive symptoms: Symptoms of the disorder that are present but not present in unaffected persons. These include delusions, hallucinations, and disordered speech that are the hallmark of the illness.

Negative symptoms: Those that are absent in the affected person but present in unaffected persons. These include blunted or flattened affect, alogia which is limited talking or poverty of speech, and avolition which is the decline in goal-directed behavior.

Threat control override symptoms: Positive symptoms in which the person perceives others as a threat, suffers from thought insertion.

Recidivist homicide: A homicide committed after the conclusion (e.g., after conviction and serving a prison term) of a prior homicide offense.

Prodromes: Early symptoms of a disease.

Chapter 23

Oppositional Defiant Disorder: A pattern of anger/irritable mood, argumentativeness, defiant behavior, or vindictiveness that lasts at least six months and is evidenced by at least four symptoms. The behavioral disturbance must be associated with distress in the child or others at home, school, and other settings such that the child's social, educational, or other functioning is negatively affected.

Conduct Disorder: A repetitive and pervasive pattern of behavior that involves the violation of the rights of others and the violation of age-appropriate norms or rules.

Antisocial Personality Disorder: A pervasive, inflexible, and enduring pattern of disregarding and violating the rights of others occurring since age 15 years and included at least three diagnostic criteria.

Chapter 24

Neuropsychology: A field of study that shows the ways that physiological development affects psychological functioning and behavior.

Cerebral cortex: The prefrontal and frontal lobe sections of the brain that differentiate humans from animals based on the executive functioning that occurs within.

Orbitofrontal cortex (OFC): Located behind the orbit of the eyes (or eye sockets) is responsible for inhibitory control with deficits in this area are associated with impulsive behavior.

Dorsolateral prefrontal cortex (DLPFC): Located behind the OFC (anatomically behind the forehead) is responsible for executive functions, such as planning, decision-making, and other rational action.

Ventromedial prefrontal cortex (VMPFC): Located underneath the DLPFC, this region is responsible for emotional cognition, sometimes referred to as the "hot" executive functions.

Anterior cingulate cortex (ACC): Brain region close to the middle of the brain, near the limbic system, that is responsible for attentional control.

Limbic system: Area of brain involved in memory, learning, emotion, and fear induction

Dual systems model: Steinberg's theory which suggests that the socioemotional, incentive-processing systems of the midbrain overwhelm the ability of frontal self-regulatory system in the adolescent brain

Neuropsychological deficits: A range of problems relating to verbal skills, receptive language, sustaining attention, memory, response inhibition, and self-control.

Neurological soft signs: Motor, sensory, and executive abnormalities that are not localized to specific brain regions.

Structural brain imaging: Brain imaging that measures anatomical features of brain regions of interest that are theorized to be associated with a particular behavior, trait, or condition.

Functional brain imaging: Brain imaging that measures brain activity, such as glucose metabolism and cerebral blood flow, to see the processes involved in neurological functioning.

Adams, J. J., & Pizarro, J. M. (2014). Patterns of specialization and escalation in the criminal careers of gang and non-gang homicide offenders. *Criminal Justice and Behavior, 41*(2), 237–255.

Adinkrah, M. (2008). Spousal homicides in contemporary Ghana. *Journal of Criminal Justice, 36*(3), 209–216.

Adshead, G., Ferrito, M., & Bose, S. (2014). Recovery after homicide: Narrative shifts in therapy with homicide perpetrators. *Criminal Justice and Behavior, 42*(1), 70–81.

Agnew, R. (1985). A revised strain theory of delinquency. *Social Forces, 64*(1), 151–167.

Agnew, R. (1992). Foundation for a general strain theory of crime and delinquency. *Criminology, 30*(1), 47–88.

Agnew, R. (1999). A general strain theory of community differences in crime rates. *Journal of Research in Crime and Delinquency, 36*(2), 123–155.

Agnew, R. (2001). Building on the foundation of general strain theory: Specifying the types of strain most likely to lead to crime and delinquency. *Journal of Research in Crime and Delinquency, 38*(4), 319–361.

Agnew, R. (2007). Strain theory and violent behavior. In: D. Flannery, A. Vazsonyi, & I. D. Waldman (Eds.), *The Cambridge handbook of violent behavior and aggression* (pp. 519–532). New York: Cambridge University Press.

Agnew, R., Brezina, T., Wright, J. P., & Cullen, F. T. (2002). Strain, personality traits, and delinquency: Extending general strain theory. *Criminology, 40*(1), 43–72.

Akers, R. L. (1985). *Deviant behavior: A social learning approach*, 3rd edition. Belmont, CA: Wadsworth.

Akers, R. L. (1998). *Social learning and social structure: A general theory of crime and deviance*. Boston, MA: Northeastern University Press.

Altheimer, I. (2008). Social support, ethnic heterogeneity, and homicide: A cross-national approach. *Journal of Criminal Justice, 36*(2), 103–114.

Aluja, A., García, L. F., Blanch, A., & Fibla, J. (2011). Association of androgen receptor gene, CAG and GGN repeat length polymorphism and impulsive-disinhibited personality traits in inmates: The role of short–long haplotype. *Psychiatric Genetics, 21*(5), 229–239.

Alvarez, A., & Bachman, R. (2003). *Murder: American style*. Belmont, CA: Thomson.

American Psychiatric Association. (2013). *Diagnostic and statistical manual of mental disorders, fifth edition*. Washington, DC: Author.

Anderson, C. A., & Anderson, K. B. (1996). Violent crime rate studies in philosophical context: A destructive testing approach to heat and southern culture of violence effects. *Journal of Personality and Social Psychology, 70*(4), 740–756.

Arrigo, B. A., & Griffin, A. (2004). Serial murder and the case of Aileen Wuornos: Attachment theory, psychopathy, and predatory aggression. *Behavioral Sciences & The Law, 22*(3), 375–393.

Arrigo, B. A., & Purcell, C. E. (2001). Explaining paraphilias and lust murder: Toward an integrated model. *International Journal of Offender Therapy and Comparative Criminology, 45*(1), 6–31.

Arseneault, L., Moffitt, T. E., Caspi, A., Taylor, P. J., & Silva, P. A. (2000). Mental disorders and violence in a total birth cohort: Results from the Dunedin Study. *Archives of General Psychiatry, 57*(10), 979–986.

Assary, E., Salekin, R. T., & Barker, E. D. (2015). Big-Five and callous-unemotional traits in preschoolers. *Journal of Psychopathology and Behavioral Assessment,* in press.

Associated Press. (2013). Cancer killed Calif. Serial killer Richard Ramirez. Accessed April 1, 2015 from, http://www.usatoday.com/story/news/nation/2013/06/17/cancer-richard- ramirez/2432397/.

Associated Press. (2015). Missouri mother who encouraged boyfriend in baby's fatal sexual assault gets 25 years. Accessed January 12, 2015 from http://www.foxnews.com/us/2015/01/11/missouri-mother-who-encouraged-boyfriend-in-baby-fatal-sexual-assault-gets-25/?intcmp=ob_article_footer_text&intcmp=obnetwork.

Associated Press. (2015). Rap mogul Suge Knight charged with murder. Accessed January 30, 2015 from http://www.foxnews.com/entertainment/2015/01/30/rap-mogul-suge-knight-charged-with-murder/.

Atchison, A. J., & Heide, K. M. (2011). Charles Manson and the Family: The application of sociological theories to multiple murder. *International Journal of Offender Therapy and Comparative Criminology, 55*(5), 771–798.

Auxemery, Y. (2015). The mass murderer history: Modern classifications, sociodemographic and psychopathological characteristics, suicidal dimensions, and media contagion of mass murders. *Comprehensive Psychiatry, 56,* 149–154.

Baay, P., Liem, M., & Nieuwbeerta, P. (2012). "Ex-imprisoned homicide offenders: Once bitten, twice shy?" The effect of the length of imprisonment on recidivism for homicide offenders. *Homicide Studies, 16*(3), 259–279.

Bailey, J. E., Kellermann, A. L., Somes, G. W., Banton, J. G., Rivara, F. P., & Rushforth, N. P. (1997). Risk factors for violent death of women in the home. *Archives of Internal Medicine, 157*(7), 777–782.

Ballester, J., Goldstein, T., Goldstein, B., Obreja, M., Axelson, D., Monk, K.,... Birmaher, B. (2012). Is bipolar disorder specifically associated with aggression?. *Bipolar Disorders, 14*(3), 283–290.

Barak-Brandes, S., & Shaul, G. (2014). "The cameras were everywhere": Media conduct through the eyes of homicide victims' families: Switzerland, Italy, and Israel. *The Communication Review, 17*(4), 269–285.

Barker, T., & Human, K. M. (2009). Crimes of the big four motorcycle gangs. *Journal of Criminal Justice, 37*(2), 174–179.

Barry, P. B. (2013). *Evil and moral psychology.* New York, NY: Routledge.

Basoglu, C., Oner, O., Ates, A., Algul, A., Bez, Y., Ebrinc, S., & Cetin, M. (2011). Temperament traits and psychopathy in a group of patients with antisocial personality disorder. *Comprehensive Psychiatry, 52*(6), 607–612.

Batty, G. D., Deary, I. J., Tengstrom, A., & Rasmussen, F. (2008). IQ in early adulthood and later risk of death by homicide: cohort study of 1 million men. *The British Journal of Psychiatry, 193*(6), 461–465.

Baumeister, R. F., & Heatherton, T. F. (1996). Self-regulation failure: An overview. *Psychological Inquiry, 7*(1), 90–98.

Baxter, H., Duggan, C., Larkin, E., Cordess, C., & Page, K. (2001). Mentally disordered parricide and stranger killers admitted to high-security care. 1: A descriptive comparison. *Journal of Forensic Psychiatry, 12*(2), 287–299.

Beaulieu, M., & Messner, S. F. (2009). Assessing changes in the effect of divorce rates on homicide rates across large US cities, 1960–2000: Revisiting the Chicago school. *Homicide Studies, 14*(1), 25–51.

Beaver, K. M., Barnes, J. C., & Boutwell, B. B. (2014). The 2-repeat allele of the MAOA gene confers an increased risk for shooting and stabbing behaviors. *Psychiatric Quarterly, 85*(3), 257–265.

Beaver, K. M., DeLisi, M., Vaughn, M. G., & Barnes, J. C. (2010). Monoamine oxidase A genotype is associated with gang membership and weapon use. *Comprehensive Psychiatry, 51*(2), 130–134.

Beaver, K. M., DeLisi, M., Vaughn, M. G., & Wright, J. P. (2010). The intersection of genes and neuropsychological deficits in the prediction of adolescent delinquency and low self-control. *International Journal of Offender Therapy and Comparative Criminology, 54,* 22–42.

Beaver, K. M., Wright, J. P., & DeLisi, M. (2007). Self-Control as an executive function: Reformulating Gottfredson and Hirschi's parental socialization thesis. *Criminal Justice and Behavior, 34*(10), 1345–1361.

Beeghley, L. (2003). *Homicide: A sociological explanation.* Lanham, MD: Rowman & Littlefield.

Behnken, M. P., Caudill, J. W., Berg, M. T., Trulson, C. R., & DeLisi, M. (2011). Marked for death: An empirical criminal careers analysis of death sentences in a sample of convicted male homicide offenders. *Journal of Criminal Justice, 39*(6), 471–478.

Bennett, D. J., Ogloff, J. R., Mullen, P. E., Thomas, S. D. M., Wallace, C., & Short, T. (2011). Schizophrenia disorders, substance abuse and prior offending in a sequential series of 435 homicides. *Acta Psychiatrica Scandinavica, 124*(3), 226–233.

Berg, M. T., & Loeber, R. (2011). Examining the neighborhood context of the violent offending-victimization relationship: A prospective investigation. *Journal of Quantitative Criminology, 27*(4), 427–451.

Berk, R., Sherman, L., Barnes, G., Kurtz, E., & Ahlman, L. (2009). Forecasting murder within a population of probationers and parolees: A high stakes application of statistical learning. *Journal of the Royal Statistical Society: Series A (Statistics in Society), 172*(1), 191–211.

Bernstein, J. I. (1979). Premeditated murder by an eight-year old boy. *International Journal of Offender Therapy and Comparative Criminology, 23*(1), 47–56.

Binswanger, I., Stern, M. F., Deyo, R. A., Heagerty, P. J., Cheadle, A., Elmore, J. G., & Koepsell, T. D. (2007). Release from prison: A high risk of death for former inmates. *New England Journal of Medicine, 356,* 157–165.

Biro, M., Vuckovic, N., & Djuric, V. (1992). Towards a typology of homicides on the basis of personality. *British Journal of Criminology, 32*(3), 361–371.

Blackburn, R. (1971). Personality types among abnormal homicides. *British Journal of Criminology, 11*(1), 14–31.

Blair, R. J. R. (2003). Neurobiological basis of psychopathy. *The British Journal of Psychiatry, 182*(1), 5–7.

Blake, G. O. (2014). America's deadly export: Evidence from cross-country panel data of deportation and homicide rates. *International Review of Law and Economics, 37,* 156–168.

Blau, J. R., & Blau, P. M. (1982). The cost of inequality: Metropolitan structure and violent crime. *American Sociological Review, 47,* 114–129.

Blumstein, A. (1995). Youth violence, guns, and the illicit-drug industry. *Journal of Criminal Law and Criminology, 86*(1), 10–36.

Blumstein, A., & Rosenfeld, R. (1998). Explaining recent trends in US homicide rates. *Journal of Criminal Law and Criminology,* 1175–1216.

Bourget, D., & Bradford, J. M. (1990). Homicidal parents. *Canadian Journal of Psychiatry, 35,* 233–238.

Bowling, B. (1999). The rise and fall of New York murder: zero tolerance or crack's decline? *British Journal of Criminology, 39*(4), 531–554.

Braga, A. A. (2003). Serious youth gun offenders and the epidemic of youth violence in Boston. *Journal of Quantitative Criminology, 19*(1), 33–54.

Braga, A. A. (2008). Pulling levers focused deterrence strategies and the prevention of gun homicide. *Journal of Criminal Justice, 36*(4), 332–343.

Braga, A. A., & Weisburd, D. L. (2012). The effects of focused deterrence strategies on crime: A systematic review and meta-analysis of the empirical evidence. *Journal of Research in Crime and Delinquency, 49,* 323–358.

Brand, S., & Price, R. (2000). *The economic and social costs of crime.* London, England: Home Office Economics and Resource Analysis Unit.

Bratton, W., & Knobler, P. (2009). *The turnaround: How America's top cop reversed the crime epidemic.* Random House.

Brecht, M. L., & Herbeck, D. M. (2013). Methamphetamine use and violent behavior: User perceptions and predictors. *Journal of Drug Issues, 43*(4), 468–482.

Brenner, F. (1953). Impulsive murder and the degree device. *Fordham Law Review, 22,* 274–297.

Brewer, D. D., Dudek, J. A., Potterat, J. J., Muth, S. Q., Roberts, J. M., & Woodhouse, D. E. (2006). Extent, trends, and perpetrators of prostitution-related homicide in the United States. *Journal of Forensic Sciences, 51*(5), 1101–1108.

Brewer, D. D., Muth, S. Q., Dudek, J. A., Roberts, J. M., & Potterat, J. J. (2006). A comparative profile of violent clients of prostitute women. *Available at http://papers.ssrn.com/sol3/papers.cfm?abstract_id=2543592.*

Briken, P., Habermann, N., Berner, W., & Hill, A. (2005). The influence of brain abnormalities on psychosocial development, criminal history, and paraphilias in sexual murderers. *Journal of Forensic Sciences, 50,* 1204–1208.

Briken, P., Habermann, N., Berner, W., & Hill, A. (2006). XYY chromosome abnormality in sexual homicide perpetrators. *American Journal of Medical Genetics Part B: Neuropsychiatric Genetics, 141*(2), 198–200.

Briken, P., Habermann, N., Kafka, M. P., Berner, W., & Hill, A. (2006). The paraphilia-related disorders: An investigation of the relevance of the concept in sexual murderers. *Journal of Forensic Sciences, 51*(3), 683–688.

Broidy, L. M., Daday, J. K., Crandall, C. S., Sklar, D. P., & Jost, P. F. (2006). Exploring demographic, structural, and behavioral overlap among homicide offenders and victims. *Homicide Studies, 10*(3), 155–180.

Brookman, F. (2014). *Understanding homicide.* Thousand Oaks, CA: SAGE.

Brookman, F. (2015). Killer decisions: The role of cognition, affect and "expertise" in homicide. *Aggression and Violent Behavior, 20*(1), 42–52.

Brookman, F., Bennett, T., Hochstetler, A., & Copes, H. (2011). The 'code of the street'and the generation of street violence in the UK. *European Journal of Criminology, 8*(1), 17–31.

Brookman, F., Copes, H., & Hochstetler, A. (2011). Street codes as formula stories: How inmates recount violence. *Journal of Contemporary Ethnography, 40,* 397–424.

Brown, J., Hughes, N. S., McGlen, M. C., & Crichton, J. H. M. (2014). Misrepresentation of UK homicide characteristics in popular culture. *Journal of Forensic and Legal Medicine, 23,* 62–64.

Brown, R. P., Osterman, L. L., & Barnes, C. D. (2009). School violence and the culture of honor. *Psychological Science, 20*(11), 1400–1405.

Browning, C. R. (2002). The span of collective efficacy: Extending social disorganization theory to partner violence. *Journal of Marriage and Family, 64*(4), 833–850.

Buckholtz, J. W., & Meyer-Lindenberg, A. (2008). MAOA and the neurogenetic architecture of human aggression. *Trends in Neurosciences, 31*(3), 120–129.

Buker, H. (2011). Formation of self-control: Gottfredson and Hirschi's general theory of crime and beyond. *Aggression and Violent Behavior, 16,* 265–276.

Bullock, H. A. (1955). Urban homicide in theory and fact. *The Journal of Criminal Law, Criminology, and Police Science, 45*(5), 565–575.

Burgess, A. W., Hartman, C. R., Ressler, R. K., Douglas, J. E., & McCormack, A. (1986). Sexual homicide a motivational model. *Journal of Interpersonal Violence, 1*(3), 251–272.

Burgess, E. W. (1925). The growth of the city: An introduction to a research project. In R. E. Park, E. W. Burgess, & R. D. McKenzie (Eds.), *The city* (pp. 47–62). Chicago, IL: University of Chicago Press.

Burgess, R. L., & Akers, R. L. (1966). A differential association-reinforcement theory of criminal behavior. *Social Problems, 14,* 128–147.

Burman, S., & Allen-Meares, P. (1994). Neglected victims of murder: Children's witness to parental homicide. *Social Work, 39*(1), 28–34.

Bursik Jr, R. J., & Grasmick, H. G. (1999). *Neighborhoods and crime: The dimensions of effective community control.* Lanham, MD: Lexington Books.

Busch, N. B., Bell, H., Hotaling, N., & Monto, M. A. (2002). Male customers of prostituted women exploring perceptions of entitlement to power and control and implications for violent behavior toward women. *Violence Against Women, 8*(9), 1093–1112.

Buss, D. M. (2006). *The murderer next door: Why the mind is designed to kill*. New York, NY: Penguin.

Byrd, A. L., & Manuck, S. B. (2014). MAOA, childhood maltreatment, and anti-social behavior: Meta-analysis of a gene-environment interaction. *Biological Psychiatry, 75*(1), 9–17.

Cale, J., Plecas, D., Cohen, I. M., & Fortier, S. (2010). An exploratory analysis of factors associated with repeat homicide in Canada. *Homicide Studies, 14*(2), 159–180.

Camp, J. P., Skeem, J. L., Barchard, K., Lilienfeld, S. O., & Poythress, N. G. (2013). Psychopathic predators? Getting specific about the relation between psychopathy and violence. *Journal of Consulting and Clinical Psychology, 81*(3), 467.

Campbell, J. H., & DeNevi, D. (2004). *Profilers: Leading investigators take you inside the criminal mind*. Amherst, NY: Prometheus Books.

Catanesi, R., Carabellese, F., Troccoli, G., Candelli, C., Grattagliano, I., Solarino, B., & Fortunato, F. (2011). Psychopathology and weapon choice: A study of 103 perpetrators of homicide or attempted homicide. *Forensic Science International, 209*(1), 149–153.

Caywood, T. (1998). Routine Activities and Urban Homicides A Tale of Two Cities. *Homicide Studies, 2*(1), 64–82.

Centers for Disease Control and Prevention. (1994). Homicides among 15–19-year-old males-- United States, 1963–1991. *MMWR: Morbidity and Mortality Weekly Report, 43*(40), 725–727.

Cerdá, M., Tracy, M., Messner, S. F., Vlahov, D., Tardiff, K., & Galea, S. (2009). Misdemeanor policing, physical disorder, and gun-related homicide: a spatial analytic test of "broken-windows" theory. *Epidemiology, 20*(4), 533–541.

Chan, H. C. O., Beauregard, E., & Myers, W. C. (2015). Single-victim and serial sexual homicide offenders: Differences in crime, paraphilias and personality traits. *Criminal Behaviour and Mental Health, 25*(1), 66–78.

Chan, H. C. O., & Frei, A. (2013). Female sexual homicide offenders an examination of an underresearched offender population. *Homicide Studies, 17*(1), 96–118.

Chan, H. C. O., Frei, A. M., & Myers, W. C. (2013). Female sexual homicide offenders: An analysis of the offender racial profiles in offending process. *Forensic Science International, 233*(1), 265–272.

Chan, H. C. O., Heide, K. M., & Beauregard, E. (2010). What propels sexual murderers: A proposed integrated theory of social learning and routine activities theories. *International Journal of Offender Therapy and Comparative Criminology, 55*(2), 228–250.

Chassin, L., Piquero, A. R., Losoya, S. H., Mansion, A. D., & Schubert, C. A. (2013). Joint consideration of distal and proximal predictors of premature mortality among serious juvenile offenders. *Journal of Adolescent Health, 52*(6), 689–696.

Chauhan, P., Cerdá, M., Messner, S. F., Tracy, M., Tardiff, K., & Galea, S. (2011). Race/Ethnic-Specific Homicide Rates in New York City Evaluating the Impact of Broken Windows Policing and Crack Cocaine Markets. *Homicide Studies, 15*(3), 268–290.

Cheatwood, D. (1996). Interactional patterns in multiple-offender homicides. *Justice Quarterly, 13*(1), 107–128.

Cheung, P., Schweitzer, I., Crowley, K., & Tuckwell, V. (1997). Violence in schizophrenia: role of hallucinations and delusions. *Schizophrenia Research, 26*(2), 181–190.

Chilton, R., & Chambliss, W. J. (2014). Urban homicide in the United States, 1980–2010: The importance of disaggregated trends. *Homicide Studies*, doi: 10.1177/1088767914534241.

Cicchetti, D., & Lynch, M. (1993). Toward an ecological/transactional model of community violence and child maltreatment: Consequences for children's development. In D. Reiss, J. E. Richters, M. Radke-Yarrow, & D. Scharff (Eds.), *Children and violence* (pp. 96–118). New York: The Guilford Press.

Cima, M., & Raine, A. (2009). Distinct characteristics of psychopathy relate to different subtypes of aggression. *Personality and Individual Differences, 47*(8), 835–840.

Clark, R. D. (1995). Lone versus multiple offending in homicide: Differences in situational context. *Journal of Criminal Justice, 23*(5), 451–460.

Cleckley, H. (1941). *The mask of sanity*. Saint Louis, MO: Mosby.

Cloninger, C. R., & Guze, S. B. (1970). Psychiatric illness and female criminality: The role of sociopathy and hysteria in the antisocial woman. *American Journal of Psychiatry, 127*(3), 303–311.

Cloward, R. A., & Ohlin, L. E. (1960). *Delinquency and opportunity: A study of delinquent gangs*. Glencoe, IL: The Free Press.

Cohen, D., & Nisbett, R. E. (1994). Self-protection and the culture of honor: Explaining southern violence. *Personality and Social Psychology Bulletin, 20*(5), 551–567.

Cohen, J., Cork, D., Engberg, J., & Tita, G. (1998). The role of drug markets and gangs in local homicide rates. *Homicide Studies, 2*(3), 241–262.

Cohen, L. E., & Felson, M. (1979). Social change and crime rate trends: A routine activity approach. *American Sociological Review, 44*, 588–608.

Cohen, M. A. (1998). The monetary value of saving a high-risk youth. *Journal of Quantitative Criminology, 14*, 5–33.

Coid, J. W. (2002). Personality disorders in prisoners and their motivation for dangerous and disruptive behaviour. *Criminal Behaviour and Mental Health, 12*(3), 209–226.

Colvin, M. (2000). *Crime and coercion: An integrated approach to chronic criminality*. New York: St. Martin's Press.

Colvin, M., Cullen, F. T., & Vander Ven, T. (2002). Coercion, social support, and crime: An emerging theoretical consensus. *Criminology, 40*, 19–42.

Cook, P. J., Ludwig, J., & Braga, A. A. (2005). Criminal records of homicide offenders. *Journal of the American Medical Association, 294*(5), 598–601.

Cooper, A., & Smith, E. L. (2011). Homicide trends in the United States, 1980–2008. Washington, DC: U. S. Department of Justice, Office of Justice Programs, Bureau of Justice Statistics.

Cope, L. M., Ermer, E., Gaudet, L. M., Steele, V. R., Eckhardt, A. L., Arbabshirani, M. R.,...Kiehl, K. A. (2014). Abnormal brain structure in youth who commit homicide. *NeuroImage: Clinical, 4*, 800–807.

Copes, H., Kovandzic, T. V., Miller, J. M., & Williamson, L. (2014). The lost cause? Examining the southern culture of honor through defensive gun use. *Crime & Delinquency, 60*(3), 356–378.

Corradi, C., & Stöckl, H. (2014). Intimate partner homicide in 10 European countries: Statistical data and policy development in a cross-national perspective. *European Journal of Criminology, 11*(5), 601–618.

Corzine, J., Huff-Corzine, L., & Whitt, H. P. (1999). Cultural and subcultural theories of homicide. In M. D. Smith & M. A. Zahn (Eds.), *Homicide: A sourcebook of social research* (pp. 42–57). Thousand Oaks, CA: SAGE.

Costa, Jr., P. T., & McRae, R. R. (1985). *NEO Personality Inventory manual.* Odessa, FL: Psychological Assessment Resources.

Costa, Jr., P. T., & McRae, R. R. (1992). *Revised NEO Personality Inventory (NEO-PI-R) and NEO Five-Factor Inventory (NEO-FFI) professional manual.* Odessa, FL: Psychological Assessment Resources.

Costanza, S. E., & Helms, R. (2012). Street gangs and aggregate homicides: An analysis of effects during the 1990s violent crime peak. *Homicide Studies, 16*(3), 280–307.

Coston, C. T. M. (2014). Self-report justifications for serial sex murder: An exploratory study of neutralization techniques. *SAJ Forensic Science, 1*(1), 102.

Côté, G., & Hodgins, S. (1990). Co-occurring mental disorders among criminal offenders. *Journal of the American Academy of Psychiatry and the Law Online, 18*(3), 271–281.

Côté, G., & Hodgins, S. (1992). The prevalence of major mental disorders among homicide offenders. *International Journal of Law and Psychiatry, 15*(1), 89–99.

Coyne, M. A., Vaske, J. C., Boisvert, D. L., & Wright, J. P. (2015). Sex differences in the stability of self-regulation across childhood. *Journal of Developmental and Life Course Criminology, 1*(1), 4–20.

Crandall, C. S., Jost, P. F., Broidy, L. M., Daday, G., & Sklar, D. P. (2004). Previous emergency department use among homicide victims and offenders: A case-control study. *Annals of Emergency Medicine, 44*(6), 646–655.

Crick, N. R., & Dodge, K. A. (1994). A review and reformulation of social information-processing mechanisms in children's social adjustment. *Psychological Bulletin, 115*(1), 74–101.

Cullen, F. T. (1994). Social support as an organizing concept for criminology. Presidential address to the Academy of Criminal Justice Sciences. *Justice Quarterly, 11,* 527–559.

Cunningham, M. D., Sorensen, J. R., Vigen, M. P., & Woods, S. O. (2010). Inmate homicides: Killers, victims, motives, and circumstances. *Journal of Criminal Justice, 38*(4), 348–358.

Curry, G. D., & Spergel, I. A. (1988). Gang homicide, delinquency, and community. *Criminology, 26*(3), 381–406.

Cyr, C., Euser, E. M., Bakermanns-Kranenburg, M. J., & van IJzendoorn, M. H. (2010). Attachment security and disorganization in maltreating and high-risk families: A series of meta-analyses. *Development and Psychopathology, 22,* 87–108.

Daly, M., & Wilson, M. (1988a). Evolutionary social psychology and family homicide. *Science, 242*, 519–524.

Daly, M., & Wilson, M. (1988b). *Homicide*. Hawthorne, NY: Aldine de Gruyter.

Daly, M., & Wilson, M. (1999). An evolutionary psychological perspective on homicide. In M. D. Smith & M. A. Zahn (Eds.), *Homicide: A sourcebook of social research* (pp. 58–71). Thousand Oaks, CA: SAGE.

Damasio, A. R. (1994). *Descartes' error: Emotion, reason, and the human brain*. New York: Grosset/Putnam.

Daniel, A. E., & Harris, P. W. (1982). Female homicide offenders referred for pretrial psychiatric examination: A descriptive study. *Journal of the American Academy of Psychiatry and the Law, 10*(4), 261–269.

Darke, S. (2010). The toxicology of homicide offenders and victims: a review. *Drug and Alcohol Review, 29*(2), 202–215.

Davidson, R. J., Putnam, K. M., & Larson, C. L. (2000). Dysfunction in the neural circuitry of emotion regulation: A possible prelude to violence. *Science, 289*, 591–594.

Decker, S. H. (1995). Reconstructing homicide events: The role of witnesses in fatal encounters. *Journal of Criminal Justice, 23*(5), 439–450.

Decker, S. H. (1996). Collective and normative features of gang violence. *Justice Quarterly, 13*(2), 243–264.

Decker, S. H., & Curry, G. D. (2002). Gangs, gang homicides, and gang loyalty: Organized crimes or disorganized criminals? *Journal of Criminal Justice, 30*, 343–352.

Declercq, F., Willemsen, J., Audenaert, K., & Verhaeghe, P. (2012). Psychopathy and predatory violence in homicide, violent, and sexual offences: Factor and facet relations. *Legal and Criminological Psychology, 17*(1), 59–74.

DeJong, C., Pizarro, J. M., & McGarrell, E. F. (2011). Can situational and structural factors differentiate between intimate partner and "other" homicide? *Journal of Family Violence, 26*(5), 365–376.

DeLisi, M. (2001a). Extreme career criminals. *American Journal of Criminal Justice, 25*(2), 239–252.

DeLisi, M. (2001b). The affordable hypothesis: Punitive beliefs, violent beliefs, and race. *Journal of Criminal Justice, 29*(2), 101–106.

DeLisi, M. (2005). *Career criminals in society*. Thousand Oaks, CA: SAGE.

DeLisi, M. (2006). Zeroing in on early arrest onset: Results from a population of extreme career criminals. *Journal of Criminal Justice, 34*(1), 17–26.

DeLisi, M. (2009). Psychopathy is the unified theory of crime. *Youth Violence and Juvenile Justice, 7*(3), 256–273.

DeLisi, M. (2011). Self-control theory: The *Tyrannosaurus rex* of criminology is poised to devour criminal justice. *Journal of Criminal Justice, 39*, 103–105.

DeLisi, M. (2013). *Criminal psychology*. San Diego, CA: Bridgepoint Education.

DeLisi, M. (2014a). Antisocial traits murdered the code of the street in a battle for respect. *Journal of Criminal Justice, 42*, 431–432.

DeLisi, M. (2014b). An empirical study of rape in the context of multiple murder. *Journal of Forensic Sciences, 59*, 420–424.

DeLisi, M., & Gatling, J. M. (2003). Who pays for a life of crime? An empirical assessment of the assorted victimization costs posed by career criminals. *Criminal Justice Studies, 16*, 283–293.

DeLisi, M., Hochstetler, A., Jones-Johnson, G., Caudill, J. W., & Marquart, J. W. (2011). The road to murder: The enduring criminogenic effects of juvenile confinement among a sample of adult career criminals. *Youth Violence and Juvenile Justice, 9*(3), 207–221.

DeLisi, M., Hochstetler, A., Scherer, A. M., Purhmann, A., & Berg, M. T. (2008). The Starkweather Syndrome: Exploring criminal history antecedents of homicidal crime sprees. *Criminal Justice Studies, 21*(1), 37–47.

DeLisi, M., Kosloski, A., Sween, M., Hachmeister, E., Moore, M., & Drury, A. (2010). Murder by numbers: Monetary costs imposed by a sample of homicide offenders. *The Journal of Forensic Psychiatry & Psychology, 21*(4), 501–513.

DeLisi, M., Neppl, T. K., Lohman, B. J., Vaughn, M. G., & Shook, J. J. (2013). Early starters: Which type of criminal onset matters most for delinquent careers? *Journal of Criminal Justice, 41*(1), 12–17.

DeLisi, M., Piquero, A. R., & Cardwell, S. M. (2014). The unpredictability of murder: Juvenile homicide in the Pathways to Desistance Study. *Youth Violence and Juvenile Justice*, doi:10.1177/1541204014551805.

DeLisi, M., & Scherer, A. M. (2006). Multiple homicide offenders: Offense characteristics, social correlates, and criminal careers. *Criminal Justice and Behavior, 33*, 367–391.

DeLisi, M., Spruill, J. O., Peters, D. J., Caudill, J. W., & Trulson, C. R. (2013). "Half in, half out:" Gang families, gang affiliation, and gang misconduct. *American Journal of Criminal Justice, 38*(4), 602–615.

DeLisi, M., Spruill, J. O., Vaughn, M. G., & Trulson, C. R. (2014). Do gang members commit abnormal homicide? *American Journal of Criminal Justice, 39*(1), 125–138.

DeLisi, M., & Vaughn, M. G. (2008). The Gottfredson-Hirschi critiques revisited: Reconciling, self-control theory, criminal careers, and career criminals. *International Journal of Offender Therapy and Comparative Criminology, 52*, 520–537.

DeLisi, M., & Vaughn, M. G. (2014). Foundation for a temperament-based theory of antisocial behavior and criminal justice system involvement. *Journal of Criminal Justice, 42*(1), 10–25.

DeLisi, M., Vaughn, M. G., Salas-Wright, C. P., & Jennings, W. G. (2015). Drugged and dangerous: Prevalence and variants of substance use comorbidity among seriously violent offenders in the United States. *Journal of Drug Issues*, doi:10.1177/0022042615557237.

DeLisi, M., & Walters, G. D. (2011). Multiple homicide as a function of prisonization and concurrent instrumental violence: Testing an interactive model—a research note. *Crime & Delinquency, 57*, 147–161.

de Pádua Serafim, A., de Barros, D. M., Castellana, G. B., & Gorenstein, C. (2014). Personality traits and violent behavior: A comparison between psychopathic and non-psychopathic male murderers. *Psychiatry Research, 219*(3), 604–608.

de Ridder, D. T. D., Lensvelt-Mulders, G., Finkenauer, C., Stok, M., & Baumeister, R. F. (2012). Taking stock of self-control: A meta-analysis of how trait self-control relates to a wide range of behaviors. *Personality and Social Psychology Review,* 16, 76–99.

DeWall, C. N., Finkel, E. J., & Denson, T. F. (2011). Self-control inhibits aggression. *Social and Personality Psychology Compass,* 5(7), 458–472.

Dhingra, K., Boduszek, D., Hyland, P., & Shagufta, S. (2015). Suicide attempts among incarcerated homicide offenders. *Suicidology Online,* in press.

Diem, C., & Pizarro, J. M. (2010). Social structure and family homicides. *Journal of Family Violence,* 25(5), 521–532.

Dietz, P. E. (1986). Mass, serial and sensational homicides. *Bulletin of the New York Academy of Medicine,* 62(5), 477.

Digman, J. M. (2002). Historical antecedents of the Five-Factor Model. In P. T. Costa, Jr., & T. A. Widiger (Eds.), *Personality disorders and the five-factor model of personality,* second edition (pp. 17–22). Washington, DC: American Psychological Association.

Dinitz, S., Scarpitti, F. R., & Reckless, W. C. (1962). Delinquency vulnerability: A cross group and longitudinal analysis. *American Sociological Review,* 27, 515–517.

Dixon, J., & Lizotte, A. J. (1987). Gun ownership and the "southern subculture of violence." *American Journal of Sociology,* 93(2), 383–405.

Dobash, R. E., Dobash, R. P., Cavanagh, K., & Lewis, R. (2004). Not an ordinary killer—Just an ordinary guy: When men murder an intimate woman partner. *Violence against Women,* 10(6), 577–605.

Dobrin, A. (2001). The risk of offending on homicide victimization: A case control study. *Journal of Research in Crime and Delinquency,* 38(2), 154–173.

Dobrin, A., & Brusk, J. J. (2003). The risk of offending on homicide victimization: A public health concern. *American Journal of Health Behavior,* 27(6), 603–612.

Dobrin, A., Lee, D., & Price, J. (2005). Neighborhood structure differences between homicide victims and non-victims. *Journal of Criminal Justice,* 33(2), 137–143.

Dodge, K. A., Bates, J. E., & Pettit, G. S. (1990). Mechanisms in the cycle of violence. *Science,* 250, 1678–1683.

Doerner, W. G. (1975). A regional analysis of homicide rates in the United States. *Criminology,* 13(1), 90–101.

Doerner, W. G. (1978). The index of Southernness revisited: The influence of wherefrom upon whodunnit. *Criminology,* 16(1), 47–56.

Doerner, W. G. (1979). The violent world of Johnny Reb: An attitudinal analysis of the 'Regional Culture of Violence' thesis. *Sociological Forum,* 2, 61–71.

Doerner, W. G. (1983). Why does Johnny Reb die when shot? The impact of medical resources upon lethality. *Sociological Inquiry,* 53(1), 1–15.

Doerner, W. G. (1988). The impact of medical resources on criminally induced lethality: A further examination. *Criminology,* 26(1), 171–180.

Doerner, W. G., & Speir, J. C. (1986). Stitch and sew: The impact of medical resources upon criminally induced lethality. *Criminology,* 24(2), 319–330.

Dolan, M., & Smith, C. (2001). Juvenile homicide offenders: 10 years' experience of an adolescent forensic psychiatry service. *Journal of Forensic Psychiatry, 12*(2), 313–329.

d'Orb, P. T. (1979). Women who kill their children. *The British Journal of Psychiatry, 134*(6), 560–571.

Doucet, J. M., D'Antonio-Del Rio, J. M., & Chauvin, C. D. (2014). GRITS: The southern subculture of violence and homicide offenses by girls raised in the south. *Journal of Interpersonal Violence, 29*(5), 806–823.

Douglas, K. S., Guy, L. S., & Hart, S. D. (2009). Psychosis as a risk factor for violence to others: A meta-analysis. *Psychological Bulletin, 135*(5), 679–706.

Drummond, H., Bolland, J. M., & Ann Harris, W. (2011). Becoming violent: Evaluating the mediating effect of hopelessness on the code of the street thesis. *Deviant Behavior, 32*(3), 191–223.

Duncan, J. W., & Duncan, G. M. (1971). Murder in the family: A study of some homicidal. *American Journal of Psychiatry, 127*(11), 1498–1502.

Duncan, G. M., Frazier, S. H., Litin, E. M., Johnson, A. M., & Barron, A. J. (1958). Etiological factors in first-degree murder. *Journal of the American Medical Association, 168*(13), 1755–1758.

Duntley, J. D. (2005). Adaptations to dangers from humans. In D. M. Buss (Ed.), *The handbook of evolutionary psychology* (pp. 224–255). Hoboken, NJ: John Wiley and Sons.

Duntley, J. (2012). Homicide. *Encyclopedia of human behavior* (pp. 334–341). New York: Elsevier.

Duntley, J. D., & Buss, D. M. (2008). The origins of homicide. In J. D. Duntley & T. K. Shackelford (Eds.), *Evolutionary forensic psychology: Darwinian foundations of crime and law* (pp. 41–64). New York, NY: Oxford University Press.

Duntley, J. D., & Buss, D. M. (2011). Homicide adaptations. *Aggression and Violent Behavior, 16*(5), 399–410.

Durkheim, É. (1897 [1951]). *Suicide: A study in sociology*. New York, NY: The Free Press.

Durrant, R. (2009). Born to kill? A critical evaluation of homicide adaptation theory. *Aggression and Violent Behavior, 14*(5), 374–381.

Dutton, D. G., & Kerry, G. (1999). Modus operandi and personality disorder in incarcerated spousal killers. *International Journal of Law and Psychiatry, 22*(3), 287–299.

Eaves, L., Eysenck, H. J., & Martin, N. (1989). *Genes, culture, and personality*. New York, NJ: Academic Press.

Eckhardt, K., & Pridemore, W. A. (2009). Differences in female and male involvement in lethal violence in Russia. *Journal of Criminal Justice, 37*(1), 55–64.

Edens, J. F., Davis, K. M., Fernandez Smith, K., & Guy, L. S. (2013). No sympathy for the devil: Attributing psychopathic traits to capital murderers also predicts support for executing them. *Personality Disorders: Theory, Research, and Treatment, 4*(2), 175.

Eisner, M. (2001). Modernization, self-control and lethal violence: The long-term dynamics of European homicide rates in theoretical perspective. *British Journal of Criminology, 41*(4), 618–638.

Eisner, M. (2014). From swords to words: Does macro-level change in self-control predict long-term variation in levels of homicide? *Crime and Justice*, 43(1), 1–75.

Eisner, M., & Nivette, A. (2012). How to reduce the global homicide rate to 2 per 100,000 by 2060. In R. Loeber & B. C. Welsh (Eds.), *The future of criminology* (pp. 219–225). New York, NY: Oxford University Press.

Ellinwood, E. H. (1971). Assault and homicide associated with amphetamine abuse. *American Journal of Psychiatry*, 127(9), 1170–1175.

Ellison, C. G. (1991). An eye for an eye? A note on the southern subculture of violence thesis. *Social Forces*, 69(4), 1223–1239.

Ellison, C. G., Burr, J. A., & McCall, P. L. (2003). The Enduring Puzzle of Southern Homicide Is Regional Religious Culture the Missing Piece? *Homicide Studies*, 7(4), 326–352.

Emerick, N. A., Curry, T. R., Collins, T. W., & Fernando Rodriguez, S. (2014). Homicide and Social Disorganization on the Border: Implications for Latino and Immigrant Populations. *Social Science Quarterly*, 95(2), 360–379.

Erb, M., Hodgins, S., Freese, R., Müller-Isberner, R., & Jöckel, D. (2001). Homicide and schizophrenia: Maybe treatment does have a preventive effect. *Criminal Behaviour and Mental Health*, 11(1), 6–26.

Erik Mouridsen, S., & Tolstrup, K. (1988). Children who kill: A case study of matricide. *Journal of Child Psychology and Psychiatry*, 29(4), 511–515.

Eriksson, L., & Mazerolle, P. (2013). A general strain theory of intimate partner homicide. *Aggression and Violent Behavior*, 18(5), 462–470.

Eronen, M., Hakola, P., & Tiihonen, J. (1996). Mental disorders and homicidal behavior in Finland. *Archives of General Psychiatry*, 53(6), 497.

Eronen, M., Tiihonen, J., & Hakola, P. (1996). Schizophrenia and homicidal behavior. *Schizophrenia Bulletin*, 22(1), 83–89.

Esmail, A. (2005). Physician as serial killer–the Shipman case. *New England Journal of Medicine*, 352(18), 1843–1844.

Esposito, D. (2006). Case study: Andrew Cunanan. In J. E. Douglas, A. W. Burgess, A. G. Burgess, & R. K. Ressler (Eds.), *Crime classification manual: A standard system for investigating and classifying violent crimes* (pp. 448–452). San Francisco, CA: Jossey Bass.

Eysenck, H. J. (1967). *The biological basis of personality*. Springfield, IL: Charles C. Thomas.

Eysenck, H. J. (1977). *Crime and personality*. London, England: Routledge & Keegan Paul.

Eysenck, H. J. (2003). Personality and crime. In T. Millon, E. Simonsen, M. Birket-Smith, & R. D. Davis (Eds.), *Psychopathy: Antisocial, criminal, and violent behavior* (pp. 40–49). New York, NY: The Guilford Press.

Eysenck, H. J., & Eysenck, M. W. (1985). *Personality and individual differences*. New York, NY: Plenum Press.

Ezell, M. E., & Tanner-Smith, E. E. (2009). Examining the role of lifestyle and criminal history variables on the risk of homicide victimization. *Homicide Studies*, 13(2), 144–173.

Falk, Ö., Wallinius, M., Lundström, S., Frisell, T., Anckarsäter, H., & Kerekes, N. (2013). The 1% of the population accountable for 63% of all violent crime convictions. *Social Psychiatry and Psychiatric Epidemiology*, epub, 1–13.

Farrell, A. L., Keppel, R. D., & Titterington, V. B. (2011). Lethal ladies: Revisiting what we know about female serial murderers. *Homicide Studies*, 15(3), 228–252.

Farrington, D. P., & Loeber, R. (2011). Early risk factors for convicted homicide offenders and homicide arrestees. In R. Loeber & D. P. Farrington (Eds.), *Young homicide offenders and victims: Risk factors, prediction, and prevention from childhood* (pp. 57–78). New York: Springer.

Farrington, D. P., Loeber, R., & Berg, M. T. (2012). Young men who kill: A prospective longitudinal examination from childhood. *Homicide Studies*, 16(2), 99–128.

Farrington, D.P., Loeber, R., Stallings, R., & Homish, D.L. (2012). Early risk factors for young homicide offenders and victims. In M. DeLisi and P.J. Conis (Eds.), *Violent offenders: theory, research, policy, and practice* (second edition) (pp. 143–159). Burlington, MA: Jones & Bartlett Learning.

Fazel, S., Buxrud, P., Ruchkin, V., & Grann, M. (2010). Homicide in discharged patients with schizophrenia and other psychoses: A national case-control study. *Schizophrenia Research*, 123(2), 263–269.

Fazel, S., & Grann, M. (2004). Psychiatric morbidity among homicide offenders: A Swedish population study. *American Journal of Psychiatry*, 161(11), 2129–2131.

Fazel, S., Gulati, G., Linsell, L., Geddes, J. R., & Grann, M. (2009). Schizophrenia and violence: systematic review and meta-analysis. *PLoS Medicine*, 6(8), e1000120.

Fazel, S., Lichtenstein, P., Grann, M., Goodwin, G. M., & Långström, N. (2010). Bipolar disorder and violent crime: New evidence from population-based longitudinal studies and systematic review. *Archives of General Psychiatry*, 67(9), 931–938.

Fazel, S., Wolf, A., Chang, Z., Larsson, H., Goodwin, G. M., & Lichtenstein, P. (2015). Depression and violence: A Swedish population study. *The Lancet Psychiatry*, 2(3), 224– 232.

Feldmeyer, B., & Steffensmeier, D. (2013). Patterns and trends in elder homicide across race and ethnicity, 1985–2009. *Homicide Studies*, 17(2), 204–223.

Felson, R. B., & Messner, S. F. (1996). To kill or not to kill? Lethal outcomes in injurious attacks. *Criminology*, 34(4), 519–545.

Felson, R. B., & Painter-Davis, N. (2012). Another cost of being a young black male: Race, weaponry, and lethal outcomes in assaults. *Social Science Research*, 41(5), 1241–1253.

Felson, R. B., & Pare, P-P. (2010). Firearms and fisticuffs: Region, race, and adversary effects on homicide and assault. *Social Science Research*, 39, 272–284.

Ferguson, C. J. (2010). Genetic contributions to antisocial personality and behavior: A meta- analytic review from an evolutionary perspective. *The Journal of Social Psychology*, 150(2), 160–180.

Ferracuti, F., & Wolfgang, M. E. (1962). Design for a proposed study of violence: A socio-psychological study of a subculture of violence. *British Journal of Criminology*, 3, 377–380.

Firestone, P., Bradford, J. M., Greenberg, D. M., Larose, M. R., & Curry, S. (1998). Homicidal and nonhomicidal child molesters: Psychological, phallometric, and criminal features. *Sexual Abuse: A Journal of Research and Treatment, 10*(4), 305–323.

Flynn, S., Abel, K. M., While, D., Mehta, H., & Shaw, J. (2011). Mental illness, gender and homicide: A population-based descriptive study. *Psychiatry Research, 185*(3), 368–375.

Flynn, S. M., Shaw, J. J., & Abel, K. M. (2013). Filicide: mental illness in those who kill their children. *PLoS ONE, 8*(4), e58981.

Forsyth, C. J. (2015). Posing: The sociological routine of a serial killer. *American Journal of Criminal Justice,* doi: 10.1007/s12103-014-9287-x.

Fovet, T., Geoffroy, P. A., Vaiva, G., Adins, C., Thomas, P., & Amad, A. (2015). Individuals with bipolar disorder and their relationship with the criminal justice system: A critical review. *Psychiatric Services in Advance,* doi:10.1176/appi.ps.201400104.

Fox, B. H., Perez, N., Cass, E., Baglivio, M. T., & Epps, N. (2015). Trauma changes everything: Examining the relationship between adverse childhood experiences and serious, violent and chronic juvenile offenders. *Child Abuse & Neglect,* in press.

Fox, J. A., & Zawitz, M. W. (2006). *Homicide trends in the United States.* Washington, DC: U.S. Department of Justice, Office of Justice Programs, Bureau of Justice Statistics.

Fox, K. A., & Allen, T. (2014). Examining the instrumental–expressive continuum of homicides: Incorporating the effects of gender, victim–offender relationships, and weapon choice. *Homicide Studies, 18*(3), 298–317.

Franklin, C. A. (2011). An investigation of the relationship between self-control and alcohol-induced sexual assault victimization. *Criminal Justice and Behavior, 38*(3), 263–285.

Franklin, C. A., Franklin, T. W., Nobles, M. R., & Kercher, G. A. (2012). Assessing the effect of routine activity theory and self-control on property, personal, and sexual assault victimization. *Criminal Justice and Behavior, 39*(10), 1296–1315.

Freudenberg, N., Fahs, M., Galea, S., & Greenberg, A. (2006). The impact of New York City's 1975 fiscal crisis on the tuberculosis, HIV, and homicide syndemic. *American Journal of Public Health, 96*(3), 424–434.

Friedman, L. M. (1993). *Crime and punishment in American history.* New York, NY: Basic Books.

Friedman, S. H., Cavney, J., & Resnick, P. J. (2012a). Child murder by parents and evolutionary psychology. *Psychiatric Clinics of North America, 35*(4), 781–795.

Friedman, S. H., Cavney, J., & Resnick, P. J. (2012b). Mothers who kill: Evolutionary underpinnings and infanticide law. *Behavioral Sciences & the Law, 30*(5), 585–597.

Fukuyama, F. (1999). *The great disruption: Human nature and the reconstitution of the social order.* New York, NY: Simon and Schuster.

Gallagher, C. A., & Dobrin, A. (2006). Deaths in juvenile justice residential facilities. *Journal of Adolescent Health, 38*(6), 662–668.

Ganpat, S. M., Liem, M., van der Leun, J., & Nieuwbeerta, P. (2012). The influence of criminal history on the likelihood of committing lethal versus nonlethal violence. *Homicide Studies, 18*(2), 221–240.

Ganpat, S. M., van der Leun, J., & Nieuwbeerta, P. (2013). The influence of event characteristics and actors' behaviour on the outcome of violent events comparing lethal with non-lethal events. *British Journal of Criminology, 53*, 685–704.

Garlicki, D. (1994). Robinson's father convicted of murder, too. The Morning Call, accessed at http://articles.mcall.com/1994–11-27/news/3003993_1_father-and-son-robinson-s-son- elder.

Gastil, R. D. (1971). Homicide and a regional culture of violence. *American Sociological Review, 36*, 412–427.

Geberth, V. J., & Turco, R. N. (1997). Antisocial personality disorder, sexual sadism, malignant narcissism, and serial murder. *Journal of Forensic Sciences, 42*(1), 49–60.

Gilligan, D. G., & Lennings, C. J. (2011). An examination of the divergent general, specific, and other criminogenic risk/needs across neuropathic and psychopathic pathways to homicide. *International Journal of Offender Therapy and Comparative Criminology, 55*(5), 693–715.

Glenn, A. L., & Raine, A. (2011). Antisocial personality disorders. In J. Decety & J. Cacioppo (Eds.), *The Oxford handbook of social neuroscience* (pp. 885–894). New York, NY: Oxford University Press.

Godwin, M., & Canter, D. (1997). Encounter and death: The spatial behavior of US serial killers. *Policing: An International Journal of Police Strategies & Management, 20*(1), 24–38.

Goldstein, R. (2009). Howard Unruh, 88, Dies: Killed 13 of his Neighbors in Camden in 1949. Accessed December 18, 2014 from http://www.nytimes.com/2009/10/20/nyregion/20unruh.html?pagewanted=all&_r=0.

Golenkov, A., Large, M., & Nielssen, O. (2013). A 30-year study of homicide recidivism and schizophrenia. *Criminal Behaviour and Mental Health, 23*(5), 347–355.

Golenkov, A., Nielssen, O., & Large, M. (2014). Systematic review and meta-analysis of homicide recidivism and Schizophrenia. *BMC Psychiatry, 14*(1), 46.

Gottfredson, M. R., & Hirschi, T. (1990). *A general theory of crime.* Stanford, CA: Stanford University Press.

Graeber, C. (2013). *The good nurse: A true story of medicine, madness, and murder.* New York, NY: Twelve.

Graif, C., & Sampson, R. J. (2009). Spatial heterogeneity in the effects of immigration and diversity on neighborhood homicide rates. *Homicide Studies, 13*(3), 242–260.

Green, E., & Wakefield, R. P. (1979). Patterns of middle and upper class homicide. *Journal of Criminal Law & Criminology, 70*, 172–181.

Gresswell, D. M., & Hollin, C. R. (1994). Multiple murder: A review. *British Journal of Criminology, 34*(1), 1–14.

Griffiths, E., & Tita, G. (2009). Homicide in and around public housing: Is public housing a hotbed, a magnet, or a generator of violence for the surrounding community? *Social Problems, 56*, 474–493.

Gudjonsson, G. H., & Petursson, H. (1990). Homicide in the Nordic countries. *Acta Psychiatrica Scandinavica, 82*(1), 49–54.

Hagan, M. (1997). An analysis of adolescent perpetrators of homicide and attempted homicide upon return to the community. *International Journal of Offender Therapy and Comparative Criminology, 41,* 250–259.

Hagedorn, J., & Rauch, B. (2007). Housing, gangs, and homicide: What we can learn from Chicago. *Urban Affairs Review, 42*(4), 435–456.

Hall, R. E., & Pizarro, J. M. (2010). Cool pose: Black male homicide and the social implications of manhood. *Journal of Social Service Research, 37*(1), 86–98.

Hanlon, R. E., Brook, M., Stratton, J., Jensen, M., & Rubin, L. H. (2013). Neuropsychological and Intellectual Differences Between Types of Murderers Affective/Impulsive Versus Predatory/Instrumental (Premeditated) Homicide. *Criminal Justice and Behavior, 40*(8), 933–948.

Hanlon, R. E., Rubin, L. H., Jensen, M., & Daoust, S. (2010). Neuropsychological features of indigent murder defendants and death row inmates in relation to homicidal aspects of their crimes. *Archives of Clinical Neuropsychology, 25*(1), 1–13.

Hanna, J. (2014). Hernandez prosecutors: Bump, spilled drink led to double homicide. Accessed December 18, 2014 from http://www.cnn.com/2014/05/28/justice/aaron-hernadez-double-homicde-arraignment/index.html.

Hare, R. D. (1991). *The Hare Psychopathy Checklist-Revised*. Toronto, Canada: Multi-Health Systems.

Hare, R. D. (2003). *The Hare Psychopathy Checklist-Revised, second edition*. Toronto, Canada: Multi-Health Systems.

Hare, R. D., & Neumann, C. S. (2008). Psychopathy as a clinical and empirical construct. *Annual Review of Clinical Psychology, 4,* 217–246.

Hartley, D., Biddle, E. A., & Jenkins, E. L. (2005). Societal cost of workplace homicides in the United States, 1992–2001. *American Journal of Industrial Medicine, 47*(6), 518–527.

Hawk, S. R., & Dabney, D. A. (2014). Are all cases treated equal?: Using Goffman's frame analysis to understand how homicide detectives orient to their work. *British Journal of Criminology, 54*(6), 1129–1147.

Hawkins, D. F. (1983). Black and white homicide differentials: Alternatives to an inadequate theory. *Criminal Justice and Behavior, 10*(4), 407–440.

Hawkins, D. F. (1985). Black homicide: The adequacy of existing research for devising prevention strategies. *Crime & Delinquency, 31*(1), 83–103.

Hawkins, D. F. (1999). What can we learn from data disaggregation? The case of homicide and African Americans. In M. D. Smith & M. A. Zahn (Eds.), *Homicide: A sourcebook of social research* (pp. 195–210). Thousand Oaks, CA: SAGE.

Hayes, T. C., & Lee, M. R. (2005). The southern culture of honor and violent attitudes. *Sociological Spectrum, 25*(5), 593–617.

Hazelwood, R. R., & Douglas, J. E. (1980). The lust murderer. *FBI Law Enforcement Bulletin, 49*(4), 18–22.

Hedlund, J., Ahlner, J., Kristiansson, M., & Sturup, J. (2014). A population-based study on toxicological findings in Swedish homicide victims and offenders from 2007 to 2009. *Forensic Science International, 244,* 25–29.

Heide, K. M. (1993a). Parents who get killed and the children who kill them. *Journal of Interpersonal Violence, 8*(4), 531–544.

Heide, K. M. (1993b). Juvenile involvement in multiple offender and multiple victim parricides. *Journal of Police and Criminal Psychology, 9*(2), 53–64.

Heide, K. M. (1994). Evidence of child maltreatment among adolescent parricide offenders. *International Journal of Offender Therapy and Comparative Criminology, 38*(2), 151- 162.

Heide, K. M. (1995). *Why kids kill parents: Child abuse and adolescent homicide.* Thousand Oaks, CA: SAGE.

Heide, K. M., Roe-Sepowitz, D., Solomon, E. P., & Chan, H. C. O. (2012). Male and female juveniles arrested for murder: A comprehensive analysis of US data by offender gender. *International Journal of Offender Therapy and Comparative Criminology, 56*(3), 356–384.

Heide, K. M., & Solomon, E. P. (2009). Female juvenile murderers: Biological and psychological dynamics leading to homicide. *International Journal of Law and Psychiatry, 32*(4), 244–252.

Heide, K. M., Spencer, E., Thompson, A., & Solomon, E. P. (2001). Who's in, who's out, and who's back: Follow-up data on 59 juveniles incarcerated ion adult prison for murder or attempted murder in the early 1980s. *Behavioral Sciences and the Law, 19,* 97–108.

Heilbrun Jr, A. B. (1990). Differentiation of death-row murderers and life-sentence murderers by antisociality and intelligence measures. *Journal of Personality Assessment, 54*(3–4), 617- 627.

Heilbrun, A. B., Heilbrun, L. C., & Heilbrun, K. L. (1978). Impulsive and premeditated homicide: An analysis of subsequent parole risk of the murderer. *Journal of Criminal Law and Criminology, 69,* 108–114.

Hempel, A. G., & Richards, T. C. (1999). Offender and offense characteristics of a nonrandom sample of mass murderers. *Journal of the American Academy of Psychiatry and the Law, 27*(2), 213–225.

Herrenkohl, T. I. (2013). Who dies? Disparities in mortality risk among juvenile offenders. *Journal of Adolescent Health, 52,* 668–669.

Hilal, S. M., Densley, J. A., Li, S. D., & Ma, Y. (2014). The routine of mass murder in China. *Homicide Studies, 18*(1), 83–104.

Hill, A., Habermann, N., Berner, W., & Briken, P. (2006). Sexual sadism and sadistic personality disorder in sexual homicide. *Journal of Personality Disorders, 20*(6), 671–684.

Hill, A., Habermann, N., Berner, W., & Briken, P. (2007). Psychiatric disorders in single and multiple sexual murderers. *Psychopathology, 40,* 22–28.

Hill, A., Habermann, N., Klusman, D., Berner, W., & Briken, P. (2008). Criminal recidivism in sexual homicide perpetrators. *International Journal of Offender Therapy and Comparative Criminology, 52*(1), 5–20.

Hill-Smith, A. J., Hugo, P., Hughes, P., Fonagy, P., & Hartman, D. (2002). Adolescents murderers: Abuse and adversity in childhood. *Journal of Adolescence, 25*(2), 221–230.

Hindelang, M. J., Gottfredson, M. R., & Garofalo, J. (1978). *Victims of personal crime: An empirical foundation for a theory of personal victimization.* Cambridge, MA: Ballinger.

Hiroeh, U., Appleby, L., Mortensen, P. B., & Dunn, G. (2001). Death by homicide, suicide, and other unnatural causes in people with mental illness: A population-based study. *The Lancet, 358*(9299), 2110–2112.

Hirschi, T. (1969). *Causes of delinquency.* Berkeley, CA: University of California Press.

Hochstetler, A., Copes, H., & Williams, J. P. (2010). "That's not who I am" How offenders commit violent acts and reject authentically violent selves. *Justice Quarterly, 27*(4), 492–516.

Holcomb, W. R., Adams, N. A., & Ponder, H. M. (1985). The development and cross-validation of an MMPI typology of murderers. *Journal of Personality Assessment, 49*(3), 240–244.

Holland, N. R., & DeLisi, M. (2015). The warrior gene: MAOA genotype and anti-social behavior in males. In M. DeLisi & M. G. Vaughn (Eds.), *The Routledge international handbook of biosocial criminology* (pp. 179–189). New York, NY: Routledge.

Holmes, R. M., & DeBurger, J. (1988). *Serial murder.* Newbury Park, CA: SAGE.

Holmes, R. M., & Holmes, S. (2001). *Mass murder in the United States.* Upper Saddle River, NJ: Prentice Hall.

Howard, R. C., Hepburn, E., & Khalifa, N. (2015). Is delusional ideation a critical link in the nexus between personality disorder and violent offending? *The Journal of Forensic Psychiatry & Psychology,* doi: 10.1080/14789949.2015.1017594.

Hu, G., Webster, D., & Baker, S. P. (2008). Hidden homicide increases in the USA, 1999–2005. *Journal of Urban Health, 85*(4), 597–606.

Huebner, B. M., Martin, K., Moule Jr, R. K., Pyrooz, D., & Decker, S. H. (2014). Dangerous places: Gang members and neighborhood levels of gun assault. *Justice Quarterly,* (ahead- of-print), 1–27.

Huff-Corzine, L., Corzine, J., & Moore, D. C. (1986). Southern exposure: Deciphering the South's influence on homicide rates. *Social Forces, 64*(4), 906–924.

Hughes, L. A., Schaible, L. M., & Gibbs, B. R. (2015). Economic dominance, the "American Dream," and homicide: A cross-national test of institutional anomie theory. *Sociological Inquiry, 85*(1), 100–128.

Israel, S., Caspi, A., Belsky, D. W., Harrington, H., Hogan, S., Houts, R., ... & Moffitt, T. E. (2014). Credit scores, cardiovascular disease risk, and human capital. *Proceedings of the National Academy of Sciences of the United States of America, 111*(48), 17087–17092.

Jenkins, P. (1990). Sharing murder: Understanding group serial homicide. *Journal of Crime and Justice, 13*(2), 125–147.

Jennings, W. G., & Piquero, A. R. (2008). Trajectories of non-intimate partner and intimate partner homicides, 1980–1999: The importance of rurality. *Journal of Criminal Justice, 36*(5), 435–443.

Johnson, B. R., & Becker, J. V. (1997). Natural born killers?: the development of the sexually sadistic serial killer. *Journal of the American Academy of Psychiatry and the Law, 25*(3), 335–348.

Joireman, J., Anderson, J., & Strathman, A. (2003). The aggression paradox: understanding links among aggression, sensation seeking, and the consideration of future consequences. *Journal of Personality and social Psychology, 84*(6), 1287.

Jolliffe, D., Loeber, R., Farrington, D. P., & Cotter, R. B. (2011). Homicide offenders speak. In R. Loeber & D. P. Farrington (Eds.), *Young homicide offenders and victims: Risk factors, prediction, and prevention from childhood* (pp. 115–122). New York: Springer.

Jones, S. E., Miller, J. D., & Lynam, D. R. (2011). Personality, antisocial behavior, and aggression: A meta-analytic review. *Journal of Criminal Justice, 39,* 329–337.

Joyal, C. C., Putkonen, A., Paavola, P., & Tiihonen, J. (2004). Characteristics and circumstances of homicidal acts committed by offenders with schizophrenia. *Psychological Medicine, 34*(03), 433–442.

Juodis, M., Woodworth, M., Porter, S., & Ten Brinke, L. (2009). Partners in crime: A comparison of individual and multi-perpetrator homicides. *Criminal Justice and Behavior, 36*(8), 824–839.

Kaplan, H. B. (1967). Toward a general theory of psychosocial deviance: The case of aggressive behavior. *Social Science & Medicine, 6*(5), 593–617.

Kaplan, H. B. (1970). Self-derogation and adjustment to recent life experiences. *Archives of General Psychiatry, 22,* 324–331.

Kaplan, H. B., & Pokorny, A. D. (1969). Self-derogation and psychosocial adjustment. *Journal of Nervous and Mental Disease, 149,* 421–434.

Karpman, B. (1930). Criminality, the superego, and the sense of guilt. *Psychoanalytic Review, 17,* 280–296.

Karpman, B. (1947). Passive parasitic psychopathy: Toward the personality structure and psychogenesis of idiopathic psychopathy (anethopathy). *Psychoanalytic Review, 34,* 198–222.

Katz, J. (2010). Seductions of crime: Moral and sensual attractions in doing evil. In H. Copes & V. Topalli (Eds.), *Criminological theory: Readings and retrospectives* (pp. 351–357). New York: McGraw-Hill.

Kellermann, A. L., Rivara, F. P., Rushforth, N. B., Banton, J. G., Reay, D. T., Francisco, J. T.,...& Somes, G. (1993). Gun ownership as a risk factor for homicide in the home. *New England Journal of Medicine, 329*(15), 1084–1091.

Khachatryan, N., Heide, K. M., Hummel, E. V., & Chan, H. C. O. (2014). Juvenile sexual homicide offenders: Thirty-year follow-up investigation. *International Journal of Offender Therapy and Comparative Criminology,* doi: 10.1177/0306624X14552062.

Kim, S. W., & Pridemore, W. A. (2005). Poverty, socioeconomic change, institutional anomie, and homicide. *Social Science Quarterly, 86*(s1), 1377–1398.

Kim, S. W., & Pridemore, W. A. (2005). Social support and homicide in transitional Russia. *Journal of Criminal Justice, 33*(6), 561–572.

Kim-Cohen, J., Caspi, A., Taylor, A., Williams, B., Newcombe, R., Craig, I. W., & Moffitt, T. E. (2006). MAOA, maltreatment, and gene–environment interaction predicting children's mental health: new evidence and a meta-analysis. *Molecular Psychiatry, 11*(10), 903–913.

King, R. D., Messner, S. F., & Baller, R. D. (2009). Contemporary hate crimes, law enforcement, and the legacy of racial violence. *American Sociological Review, 74*(2), 291–315.

Kirk, D. S., & Papachristos, A. V. (2011). Cultural mechanisms and the persistence of neighborhood violence. *American Journal of Sociology, 116*(4), 1190–1233.

Kizer, K. W., & Yorker, B. C. (2010). Health care serial murder: a patient safety orphan. *Joint Commission journal on quality and patient safety/Joint Commission Resources, 36*(4), 186–191.

Koch, J., Berner, W., Hill, A., & Briken, P. (2011). Sociodemographic and diagnostic characteristics of homicidal and nonhomicidal sexual offenders. *Journal of Forensic Sciences, 56*(6), 1626–1631.

Konstantin, D. N. (1984). Homicides of American law enforcement officers, 1978–1980. *Justice Quarterly, 1*(1), 29–45.

Kort-Butler, L. A. (2010). Experienced and vicarious victimization: Do social support and self- esteem prevent delinquent responses? *Journal of Criminal Justice, 38*(4), 496–505.

Kotler, M., Barak, P., Cohen, H., Averbuch, I. E., Grinshpoon, A., Gritsenko, I.,... Ebstein, R. P. (1999). Homicidal behavior in schizophrenia associated with a genetic polymorphism determining low catechol O-methyltransferase (COMT) activity. *American Journal of Medical Genetics (Neuropsychiatric Genetics), 88*(6), 628–633.

Kozma, C., & Zuckerman, M. (1983). An investigation of some hypotheses concerning rape and murder. *Personality and Individual Differences, 4*(1), 23–29.

Krivo, L. J., & Peterson, R. D. (1996). Extremely disadvantaged neighborhoods and urban crime. *Social Forces, 75*(2), 619–648.

Krivo, L. J., & Peterson, R. D. (2000). The structural context of homicide: Accounting for racial differences in process. *American Sociological Review, 65,* 547–559.

Kubrin, C. (2005). Gangstas, thugs, and hustlas: Identity and the code of the street in rap music. *Social Problems, 52,* 360–378.

Kubrin, C. E. (2003). Structural covariates of homicide rates: Does type of homicide matter? *Journal of Research in Crime and Delinquency, 40*(2), 139–170.

Kubrin, C. E. (2006). "I see death around the corner": Nihilism in rap music. *Sociological Perspectives, 48*(4), 433–459.

Kubrin, C. E., & Herting, J. R. (2003). Neighborhood correlates of homicide trends. *The Sociological Quarterly, 44*(3), 329–355.

Kubrin, C. E., & Weitzer, R. (2003). Retaliatory homicide: Concentrated disadvantage and neighborhood culture. *Social Problems, 50*(2), 157–180.

Kuhns, J. B., Exum, M. L., Clodfelter, T. A., & Bottia, M. C. (2014). The prevalence of alcohol-involved homicide offending: A meta-analytic review. *Homicide Studies, 18*(3), 251–270.

Kumari, V., Barkataki, I., Goswami, S., Flora, S., Das, M., & Taylor, P. (2009). Dysfunctional, but not functional, impulsivity is associated with a history of seriously violent behaviour and reduced orbitofrontal and hippocampal volumes in schizophrenia. *Psychiatry Research: Neuroimaging, 173*(1), 39–44.

Laajasalo, T., Salenius, S., Lindberg, N., Repo-Tiihonen, E., & Häkkänen-Nyholm, H. (2011). Psychopathic traits in Finnish homicide offenders with schizophrenia. *International Journal of Law and Psychiatry, 34*(5), 324–330.

Land, K. C., McCall, P. L., & Cohen, L. E. (1990). Structural covariates of homicide rates: Are there any invariances across time and social space? *American Journal of Sociology, 95,* 922–963.

Langan, P. A., & Levin, D. J. (2002). Recidivism of prisoners released in 1994. *Federal Sentencing Reporter, 15*(1), 58–65.

Langevin, R. (2003). A study of the psychosexual characteristics of sex killers: can we identify them before it is too late?. *International Journal of Offender Therapy and Comparative Criminology, 47*(4), 366–382.

Langevin, R., & Handy, L. (1987). Stranger homicide in Canada: A national sample and a psychiatric sample. *Journal of Criminal Law and Criminology, 78*(2), 398–429.

Large, M. M., & Nielssen, O. (2011). People with bipolar disorder and comorbid substance abuse are six times more likely to be convicted of violent crime than the general population. *Evidence Based Mental Health, 14*(1), 17–17.

Large, M., Smith, G., & Nielssen, O. (2009). The relationship between the rate of homicide by those with schizophrenia and the overall homicide rate: a systematic review and meta- analysis. *Schizophrenia Research, 112*(1), 123–129.

Larson, M., Vaughn, M. G., Salas-Wright, C. P., & Delisi, M. (2014). Narcissism, low self-control, and violence among a nationally representative sample. *Criminal Justice and Behavior,* doi: 10.1177/0093854814553097.

Latalova, K. (2009). Bipolar disorder and aggression. *International journal of clinical practice, 63*(6), 889–899.

Laurell, J., & Dåderman, A. M. (2007). Psychopathy (PCL-R) in a forensic psychiatric sample of homicide offenders: Some reliability issues. *International Journal of Law and Psychiatry, 30,* 127–135.

Lawrence, R. (2004). Understanding fatal assault of children: A typology and explanatory theory. *Children and Youth Services Review, 26*(9), 837–852.

Lederman, D., Loayza, N., & Menendez, A. M. (2002). Violent crime: Does social capital matter? *Economic Development and Cultural Change, 50*(3), 509–539.

Lee, A. Y., & Pridmore, S. (2014). Emerging correlations between measures of population well-being, suicide and homicide: a look at global and Australian data. *Australasian Psychiatry, 22*(2), 112–117.

Lee, M. R. (2000). Concentrated poverty, race, and homicide. *The Sociological Quarterly, 41*(2), 189–206.

Lee, M. R. (2011). Reconsidering culture and homicide. *Homicide Studies, 15*(4), 319–340.

Lee, M. R., Bankston, W. B., Hayes, T. C., & Thomas, S. A. (2007). Revisiting the Southern culture of violence. *The Sociological Quarterly, 48*(2), 253–275.

Lee, M. R., & Bartkowski, J. P. (2004). Civic Participation, Regional Subcultures, and Violence The Differential Effects of Secular and Religious Participation on Adult and Juvenile Homicide. *Homicide Studies, 8*(1), 5–39.

Lee, M. R., & DeHart, E. (2007). The influence of a serial killer on changes in fear of crime and the use of protective measures: a survey-based case study of Baton Rouge. *Deviant Behavior, 28*(1), 1–28.

Lee, M. R., & Ousey, G. C. (2005). Institutional access, residential segregation, and urban black homicide. *Sociological Inquiry, 75*(1), 31–54.

Lee, M. R., & Ousey, G. C. (2011). Reconsidering the culture and violence connection: strategies of action in the rural south. *Journal of Interpersonal Violence, 26*, 899–929.

Lee, M. R., & Shihadeh, E. S. (2009). The spatial concentration of Southern whites and argument-based lethal violence. *Social Forces, 87*(3), 1671–1694.

Lee, M. R., Thomas, S. A., & Ousey, G. C. (2009). Southern culture and homicide: examining the cracker culture/Black rednecks thesis. *Deviant Behavior, 31*(1), 60–96.

Lester, D., & White, J. (2012). Which serial killers commit suicide? An exploratory study. *Forensic Science International, 223*(1), e56–e59.

Lester, D., & White, J. (2014). A Study of African American Serial Killers. *Journal of Ethnicity in Criminal Justice, 12*(4), 308–316.

Levchak, P. J. (2014). Extending the anomie tradition an assessment of the impact of trade measures on cross-national homicide rates. *Homicide Studies*, doi: 1088767914551169.

Levi-Minzi, M., & Shields, M. (2007). Serial sexual murderers and prostitutes as their victims: Difficulty profiling perpetrators and victim vulnerability as illustrated by the Green River case. *Brief Treatment and Crisis Intervention, 7*(1), 77–89.

Levin, J., & Madfis, E. (2009). Mass murder at school and cumulative strain: A sequential model. *American Behavioral Scientist, 52*(9), 1227–1245.

Lewandowski, L. A., McFarlane, J., Campbell, J. C., Gary, F., & Barenski, C. (2004). "He killed my mommy!" Murder or attempted murder of a child's mother. *Journal of Family Violence, 19*(4), 211–220.

Lewis, D. O., Lovely, R., Yeager, C., Ferguson, G., Friedman, M., Sloane, G.,... Pincus, J. H. (1988). Intrinsic and environmental characteristics of juvenile murderers. *Journal of the American Academy of Child & Adolescent Psychiatry, 27*(5), 582–587.

Lewis, D. O., Moy, E., Jackson, L. D., Aaronson, R., Restifo, N., Serra, S., & Simos, A. (1985). Biopsychosocial characteristics of children who later murder: A prospective study. *American Journal of Psychiatry, 142*(10), 1161–1167.

Lewis, D. O., Pincus, J. H., Feldman, M., Jackson, L., & Bard, B. (1986). Psychiatric, neurological, and psychoeducational characteristics of 15 death row inmates in the United States. *American Journal of Psychiatry, 143*(7), 838–845.

Liddle, J. R., Shackelford, T. K., & Weekes–Shackelford, V. A. (2012). Why can't we all just get along? Evolutionary perspectives on violence, homicide, and war. *Review of General Psychology, 16*(1), 24.

Liem, M. (2013). Homicide offender recidivism: A review of the literature. *Aggression and Violent Behavior, 18*(1), 19–25.

Liem, M., Barber, C., Markwalder, N., Killias, M., & Nieuwbeerta, P. (2011). Homicide–suicide and other violent deaths: An international comparison. *Forensic Science International, 207*(1), 70–76.

Liem, M., & Koenraadt, F. (2008). Filicide: A comparative study of maternal versus paternal child homicide. *Criminal Behaviour and Mental Health, 18*(3), 166–176.

Lim, S., Seligson, A. L., Parvez, F. M., Luther, C. W., Mavinkurve, M. P., Binswanger, I. A., & Kerker, B. D. (2012). Risks of drug-related death, suicide, and homicide during the immediate post-release period among people released from New York City jails, 2001–2005. *American Journal of Epidemiology, 175*(6), 519–526.

Lindberg, N., Laajasalo, T., Holi, M., Putkonen, H., Weizmann-Henelius, G., & Häkkänen- Nyholm, H. (2009). Psychopathic traits and offender character-istics–a nationwide consecutive sample of homicidal male adolescents. *BMC Psychiatry, 9*(1), 18.

Lindberg, N., Tani, P., Stenberg, J. H., Appelberg, B., Porkka-Heiskanen, T., & Virkkunen, M. (2004). Neurological soft signs in homicidal men with antiso-cial personality disorder. *European Psychiatry, 19*(7), 433–437.

Lindberg, N., Tani, P., Virkkunen, M., Porkka-Heiskanen, T., Appelberg, B., Naukkarinen, H., & Salmi, T. (2005). Quantitative electroencephalographic measures in homicidal men with antisocial personality disorder. *Psychiatry Research, 136*(1), 7–15.

Lindqvist, P. (1986). Criminal homicide in Northern Sweden 1970–1981: Alcohol intoxication, alcohol abuse and mental disease. *International Journal of Law and Psychiatry, 8*(1), 19–37.

Link, B. G., Monahan, J., Stueve, A., & Cullen, F. T. (1999). Real in their conse-quences: A sociological approach to understanding the association between psychotic symptoms and violence. *American Sociological Review, 64*, 316–332.

Link, B. G., Stueve, A., & Phelan, J. (1998). Psychotic symptoms and violent behav-iors: Probing the components of "threat/control-override" symptoms. *Social Psychiatry and Psychiatric Epidemiology, 33*(1), S55–S60.

Lo, C. C., Howell, R. J., & Cheng, T. C. (2013). Explaining black–white differences in homicide victimization. *Aggression and Violent Behavior, 18*(1), 125–134.

Lo, C. C., Howell, R. J., & Cheng, T. C. (2015). Racial disparities in age at time of homicide victimization: A test of the multiple disadvantage model. *Journal of Interpersonal Violence, 30*, 152–167.

Loeber, R., & Ahonen, L. (2013). Invited address: Street killings: Prediction of homicide offenders and their victims. *Journal of Youth and Adolescence, 42*(11), 1640–1650.

Loeber, R., & Farrington, D. P. (2011). *Young homicide offenders and victims: Risk factors, prediction, and prevention from childhood.* New York, NY: Springer.

Loeber, R., Pardini, D., Homish, D. L., Wei, E. H., Crawford, A. M., Farrington, D. P., Stouthamer-Loeber, M., Creemers, J., Koehler, S. A., & Rosenfeld, R. (2005). The prediction of violence and homicide in young men. *Journal of Consulting and Clinical Psychology, 73*, 1074–1088.

Loftin, C., & Hill, R. H. (1974). Regional subculture and homicide: An examina-tion of the Gastil-Hackney thesis. *American Sociological Review*, 714–724.

Loftin, C., Kindley, K., Norris, S. L., & Wiersema, B. (1987). An attribute approach to relationships between offenders and victims in homicide. *Journal of Criminal Law and Criminology, 78*(2), 259–271.

Loftin, C., Wiersema, B., McDowall, D., & Dobrin, A. (2003). Underreporting of justifiable homicides committed by police officers in the United States, 1976–1998. *American Journal of Public Health, 93*(7), 1117–1121.

Logan, J., Hill, H. A., Black, M. L., Crosby, A. E., Karch, D. L., Barnes, J. D., & Lubell, K. M. (2008). Characteristics of perpetrators in homicide-followed-by-suicide incidents: National Violent Death Reporting System—17 US states, 2003–2005. *American Journal of Epidemiology, 168*(9), 1056–1064.

Lozano, R., Naghavi, M., Foreman, K., Lim, S., Shibuya, K., Aboyans, V.,... Cross, M. (2013). Global and regional mortality from 235 causes of death for 20 age groups in 1990 and 2010: a systematic analysis for the Global Burden of Disease Study 2010. *The Lancet, 380*(9859), 2095–2128.

Luckenbill, D. F. (1977). Criminal homicide as a situated transaction. *Social Problems, 25,* 176–186.

Lundrigan, S., & Canter, D. (2001). Spatial patterns of serial murder: An analysis of disposal site location choice. *Behavioral Sciences & the Law, 19*(4), 595–610.

Lynam, D. R., & Widiger, T. A. (2007). Using a general model of personality to identify the basic elements of psychopathy. *Journal of Personality Disorders, 21,* 160–178.

Lysell, H., Runeson, B., Lichtenstein, P., & Långström, N. (2014). Risk factors for filicide and homicide: 36-year national matched cohort study. *The Journal of Clinical Psychiatry, 75,* 127–132.

Mac Donald, H. (2003). *Are cops racist? How the war against the police harms black Americans*. Chicago, IL: Ivan R. Dee.

MacDonald, J. M., & Gover, A. R. (2005). Concentrated disadvantage and youth-on-youth Homicide: Assessing the structural covariates over time. *Homicide Studies, 9*(1), 30–54.

Maier-Katkin, D., Mears, D. P., & Bernard, T. J. (2009). Towards a criminology of crimes against humanity. *Theoretical Criminology, 13*(2), 227–255.

Makhlouf, F., & Rambaud, C. (2014). Child homicide and neglect in France: 1991–2008. *Child Abuse & Neglect, 38,* 37–41.

Malmquist, C. P. (2006). *Homicide: A psychiatric perspective*, second edition. Washington, DC: American Psychiatric Publishing.

Malone, L. (2007). In the aftermath: Listening to people bereaved by homicide. *Probation Journal, 54*(4), 383–393.

Maniglio, R. (2012). The role of parent–child bonding, attachment, and interpersonal problems in the development of deviant sexual fantasies in sexual offenders. *Trauma, Violence, & Abuse, 13*(2), 83–96.

Mann, C. R. (1988). Getting even? Women who kill in domestic encounters. *Justice Quarterly, 5*(1), 33–51.

Manning, J. (2014). The Social Structure of Homicide-Suicide. *Homicide Studies,* doi: 10.1177/1088767914547819.

Mares, D. (2010). Social Disorganization and gang homicides in Chicago A neighborhood level comparison of disaggregated homicides. *Youth Violence and Juvenile Justice, 8*(1), 38–57.

Markey, P. M., French, J. E., & Markey, C. N. (2014). Violent movies and severe acts of violence: Sensationalism versus science. *Human Communication Research,* doi:10.1111/hcre.12046.

Mariano, T. Y., Chan, H. C. O., & Myers, W. C. (2014). Toward a More Holistic Understanding of Filicide: A Multidisciplinary Analysis of 32 Years of US Arrest Data. *Forensic Science International, 236,*46–53.

Mason, D. A., & Frick, P. J. (1994). The heritability of antisocial behavior: A meta-analysis of twin and adoption studies. *Journal of Psychopathology and Behavioral Assessment, 16*(4), 301–323.

Massey, C. R., & McKean, J. (1985). The social ecology of homicide: A modified life-style/routine activities perspective. *Journal of Criminal Justice, 13*(5), 417–428.

Massey, D. S. (1995). Getting away with murder: Segregation and violent crime in urban America. *University of Pennsylvania Law Review, 143*(5), 1203–1232.

Mastrocinque, J. M., Metzger, J. W., Madeira, J., Lang, K., Pruss, H., Navratil, P. K.,... Cerulli, C. (2014). I'm still left here with the pain: Exploring the health consequences of homicide on families and friends. *Homicide Studies*, doi: 10.1177/1088767914537494.

Maume, M. O., & Lee, M. R. (2003). Social institutions and violence: a sub-national test of institutional anomie theory. *Criminology, 41*(4), 1137–1172.

Marzuk, P. M., Tardiff, K., & Hirsch, C. S. (1992). The epidemiology of murder-suicide. *Journal of the American Medical Association, 267*(23), 3179–3183.

Mayhew, P. (2003). *Counting the costs of crime in Australia.* Canberra, Australia: Australian Institute of Criminology.

McCall, P. L., Land, K. C., & Parker, K. F. (2010). An empirical assessment of what we know about structural covariates of homicide rates: a return to a classic 20 years later. *Homicide Studies, 14*, 219–243.

McCall, P. L., Nieuwbeerta, P., Engen, R. L., & Thames, K. M. (2012). Explaining variation in homicide rates across Eastern and Western European cities: The effects of social, political, and Economic Forces. In M. C. A. Liem & W. A. Pridemore (Eds.), *Handbook of European homicide research: Patterns, explanations, and country studies* (pp. 137–154). New York, NY: Springer.

McCall, P. L., Parker, K. F., & MacDonald, J. M. (2008). The dynamic relationship between homicide rates and social, economic, and political factors from 1970 to 2000. *Social Science Research, 37*(3), 721–735.

McCollister, K. E., French, M. T., & Fang, H. (2010). The cost of crime to society: New crime-specific estimates for policy and program evaluation. *Drug and Alcohol Dependence, 108*(1), 98–109.

McCrae, R. R., & Costa Jr, P. T. (1997). Personality trait structure as a human universal. *American Psychologist, 52*(5), 509–516.

McCuish, E. C., Bouchard, M., & Corrado, R. (2014). The search for suitable homicide Co-offenders among gang members. *Journal of Contemporary Criminal Justice*, doi: 10.1177/1043986214553375.

McGurk, B. J. (1981). The validity and utility of a typology of homicides based on Megargee's theory of control. *Personality and Individual Differences, 2*(2), 129–136.

McLaughlin, C. R., Daniel, J., & Joost, T. F. (2000). The relationship between substance use, drug selling, and lethal violence in 25 juvenile murderers. *Journal of Forensic Sciences, 45*(2), 349–353.

McLaughlin, K. A., Green, J. G., Hwang, I., Sampson, N. A., Zaslavsky, A. M., & Kessler, R. C. (2012). Intermittent explosive disorder in the National Comorbidity Survey Replication Adolescent Supplement. *Archives of General Psychiatry, 69*(11), 1131–1139.

Megargee, E. I. (1966). Undercontrolled and overcontrolled personality types in extreme antisocial aggression. *Psychological Monographs: General and Applied, 80*(3), 1–29.

Meehan, J., Flynn, S., Hunt, I. M., Robinson, J., Bickley, H., Parsons, R., ... & Shaw, J. (2006). Perpetrators of homicide with schizophrenia: a national clinical survey in England and Wales. *Psychiatric Services, 57*(11), 1648–1651.

Merton, R. K. (1938). Social structure and anomie. *American Sociological Review, 3*(5), 672–682.

Messing, J. T., & Heeren, J. W. (2004). Another side of multiple murder: Women killers in the domestic context. *Homicide Studies, 8*(2), 123–158.

Messner, S. F. (1983). Regional and racial effects on the urban homicide rate: The subculture of violence revisited. *American Journal of Sociology, 88*(5), 997–1007.

Messner, S. F., Baller, R. D., & Zevenbergen, M. P. (2005). The legacy of lynching and southern homicide. *American Sociological Review, 70*(4), 633–655.

Messner, S. F., Baumer, E. P., & Rosenfeld, R. (2004). Dimensions of social capital and rates of criminal homicide. *American Sociological Review, 69*(6), 882–903.

Messner, S. F., Galea, S., Tardiff, K. J., Tracy, M., Bucciarelli, A., Piper, T., M. Frye, V., & Vlahov, D. (2007). Policing, drugs, and the homicide decline in New York City in the 1990s. *Criminology, 45*(2), 385–414.

Messner, S. F., & Rosenfeld, R. (1994). *Crime and the American dream.* Belmont, CA: Wadsworth.

Messner, S. F., & Rosenfeld, R. (1997). Political restraint of the market and levels of criminal homicide: A cross-national application of institutional-anomie theory. *Social Forces, 75*(4), 1393–1416.

Messner, S. F., & Rosenfeld, R. (1999). Social structure and homicide. In M. D. Smith & M. A. Zahn (Ed.), *Homicide: A sourcebook of social research* (pp. 27–41). Thousand Oaks, CA: SAGE.

Messner, S. F., Rosenfeld, R., & Karstedt, S. (2013). Social institutions and crime. In F. T. Cullen & P. Wilcox (Eds.), *The Oxford handbook of criminological theory* (pp. 405–423). New York, NY: Oxford University Press.

Messner, S. F., & Tardiff, K. (1985). The social ecology of urban homicide: An application of the "routine activities" approach. *Criminology, 23*(2), 241–267.

Messner, S. F., & Tardiff, K. (1986). Economic inequality and levels of homicide: An analysis of urban neighborhoods. *Criminology, 24*(2), 297–316.

Miles, D. R., & Carey, G. (1997). Genetic and environmental architecture on human aggression. *Journal of Personality and Social Psychology, 72*(1), 207–217.

Miller, J. D., & Lynam, D. R. (2001). Structural models of personality and their relation to antisocial behavior: A meta-analytic review. *Criminology, 39,* 765–798.

Miller, T. R., Fisher, D. A., & Cohen, M. A. (2001). Costs of juvenile violence: Policy implications. *Pediatrics, 107,* 1–7.

Millon, T., & Davis, R. D. (1998). Ten subtypes of psychopathy. In T. Millon, E. Simonsen, M. Birket-Smith, & R. D. Davis (Eds.), *Psychopathy* (pp. 161–170). New York: Guilford Press.

Moffitt, T. E. (1993). Adolescence-limited and life-course-persistent antisocial behavior: a developmental taxonomy. *Psychological Review, 100*(4), 674–701.

Moffitt, T. E. (2007). A review of research on the taxonomy of life-course-persistent versus adolescence-limited antisocial behavior. In D. J. Flannery, A. T. Vazsonyi, & I. D. Waldman (Eds.), *The Cambridge handbook of violent behavior and aggression* (pp. 49–74). New York: Cambridge University Press.

Moffitt, T. E., Arsenault, L., Belsky, D., Dickson, N., Hancox, R. J., Harrington, H., Houts, R., Poulton, R., Roberts, B. W., Ross, S., Sears, M. R., Thomson, W. M., & Caspi, A. (2011). A gradient of childhood self-control predicts health, wealth, and public safety. *Proceedings of the National Academy of Sciences of the United States of America, 108,* 2693–2698.

Molenberghs, P., Ogilvie, C., Louis, W. R., Decety, J., Bagnall, J., & Bain, P. (2015). The neural correlates of justified and unjustified killing: An fMRI study. *Social Cognitive and Affective Neuroscience,* nsv027.

Moran, L. (2013). Rapper charged with homicide after bragging about murder in one of his songs. New York Daily News, August 1, 2013, accessed from http://www.nydailynews.com/news/national/rapper-song-arrested-homicide-article-1.1414493.

Morenoff, J. D., Sampson, R. J., & Raudenbush, S. W. (2001). Neighborhood inequality, collective efficacy, and the spatial dynamics of urban violence. *Criminology, 39*(3), 517–558.

Murray, C. J., Vos, T., Lozano, R., Naghavi, M., Flaxman, A. D., Michaud, C.,... Bridgett, L. (2013). Disability-adjusted life years (DALYs) for 291 diseases and injuries in 21 regions, 1990–2010: A systematic analysis for the Global Burden of Disease Study 2010. *The Lancet, 380*(9859), 2197–2223.

Myers, W. C., & Blashfield, R. (1997). Psychopathology and personality in juvenile sexual homicide offenders. *Journal of the American Academy of Psychiatry and the Law, 25*(4), 497–508.

Myers, W. C., Chan, H. C. O., Vo, E. J., & Lazarou, E. (2010). Sexual sadism, psychopathy, and recidivism in juvenile sexual murderers. *Journal of Investigative Psychology and Offender Profiling, 7*(1), 49–58.

Myers, W. C., Gooch, E., & Meloy, J. R. (2005). The role of psychopathy and sexuality in a female serial killer. *Journal of Forensic Sciences, 50*(3), 652–657.

Myers, W. C., & Monaco, L. (2000). Anger experience, styles of anger expression, sadistic personality disorder, and psychopathy in juvenile sexual homicide offenders. *Journal of Forensic Sciences, 45*(3), 698–701.

Nelsen, C., & Huff-Corzine, L. (1998). Strangers in the night: An application of the lifestyle-routine activities approach to elderly homicide victimization. *Homicide Studies, 2*(2), 130–159.

Nielsen, A. L., Lee, M. T., & Martinez, R. (2005). Integrating race, place and motive in social disorganization theory: Lessons from a comparison of Black and Latino homicide types in two immigrant destination cities. *Criminology, 43*(3), 837–872.

Nielssen, O. B., Malhi, G. S., & Large, M. M. (2012). Mania, homicide and severe violence. *Australian and New Zealand Journal of Psychiatry, 46*(4), 357–363.

Nielssen, O., Bourget, D., Laajasalo, T., Liem, M., Labelle, A., Hakkanen-Nyholm, H., Koenraadt, F., & Large, M. M. (2011). Homicide by strangers by people with a psychotic illness. *Schizophrenia Bulletin, 37*(3), 572–579.

Nieuwbeerta, P., McCall, P. L., Elffers, H., & Wittebrood, K. (2008). Neighborhood characteristics and individual homicide risks effects of social cohesion, confidence in the police, and socioeconomic disadvantage. *Homicide Studies, 12*(1), 90–116.

Nisbett, R. E. (1993). Violence and US regional culture. *American Psychologist, 48*(4), 441–449.

Nisbett, R. E., & Cohen, D. (1996). *Culture of honor: The psychology of violence in the South.* Boulder, CO: Westview Press.

Nivette, A. E. (2011). Cross-national predictors of crime: A meta-analysis. *Homicide Studies, 15*(2), 103–131.

Nivette, A. E., & Eisner, M. (2013). Do legitimate polities have fewer homicides? A cross-national analysis. *Homicide Studies, 17*(1), 3–26.

Nordström, A., Dahlgren, L., & Kullgren, G. (2006). Victim relations and factors triggering homicides committed by offenders with schizophrenia. *The Journal of Forensic Psychiatry & Psychology, 17*(2), 192–203.

Nye, F. I. (1958). *Family relationships and delinquent behavior.* New York, NY: John Wiley & Sons.

Odgers, C. L., Moffitt, T. E., Tach, L. M., Sampson, R. J., Taylor, A., Matthews, C. L., & Caspi, A. (2009). The protective effects of neighborhood collective efficacy on British children growing up in deprivation: a developmental analysis. *Developmental Psychology, 45*(4), 942.

O'Flaherty, B., & Sethi, R. (2010). Homicide in black and white. *Journal of Urban Economics, 68*(3), 215–230.

Ogilvie, C. A., Newman, E., Todd, L., & Peck, D. (2014). Attachment & violent offending: A meta-analysis. *Aggression and Violent Behavior, 19*(4), 322–339.

Ogle, R. S., Maier-Katkin, D., & Bernard, T. J. (1995). A theory of homicidal behavior among women. *Criminology, 33*(2), 173–193.

Ösby, U., Brandt, L., Correia, N., Ekbom, A., & Sparén, P. (2001). Excess mortality in bipolar and unipolar disorder in Sweden. *Archives of General Psychiatry, 58*(9), 844–850.

Ousey, G. C. (1999). Homicide, structural factors, and the racial invariance assumption. *Criminology, 37*(2), 405–426.

Ousey, G. C., & Augustine, M. C. (2001). Young guns: Examining alternative explanations of juvenile firearm homicide rates. *Criminology, 39*(4), 933–968.

Ousey, G. C., & Lee, M. R. (2002). Examining the conditional nature of the illicit drug market-homicide relationship: A partial test of the theory of contingent causation. *Criminology, 40*(1), 73–102.

Ousey, G. C., & Lee, M. R. (2007). Homicide trends and illicit drug markets: exploring differences across time. *Justice Quarterly, 24*(1), 48–79.

Overpeck, M. D., Brenner, R. A., Trumble, A. C., Trifiletti, L. B., & Berendes, H. W. (1998). Risk factors for infant homicide in the United States. *New England Journal of Medicine, 339*(17), 1211–1216.

Paciello, M., Fida, R., Tramontano, C., Lupinetti, C., & Caprara, G. V. (2008). Stability and change of moral disengagement and its impact on aggression and violence in late adolescence. *Child Development, 79*(5), 1288–1309.

Palermo, G. B. (2014). A moral tragedy: Patricide and step-patricide. *International Journal of Offender Therapy and Comparative Criminology, 58*(11), 1259–1260.

Paluszny, M., & McNabb, M. (1975). Therapy of a 6-year-old who committed fratricide. *Journal of the American Academy of Child Psychiatry, 14*(2), 319–336.

Panczak, R., Geissbühler, M., Zwahlen, M., Killias, M., Tal, K., & Egger, M. (2013). Homicide-suicides compared to homicides and suicides: Systematic review and meta-analysis. *Forensic Science International, 233*(1), 28–36.

Papachristos, A. V. (2009). Murder by structure: Dominance relations and the social structure of gang homicide. *American Journal of Sociology, 115*(1), 74–128.

Papachristos, A. V., Braga, A. A., & Hureau, D. M. (2012). Social networks and the risk of gunshot injury. *Journal of Urban Health, 89*(6), 992–1003.

Papachristos, A. V., Hureau, D. M., & Braga, A. A. (2013). The corner and the crew: The influence of geography and social networks on gang violence. *American Sociological Review, 78*(3), 417–447.

Papachristos, A. V., & Wildeman, C. (2014). Network exposure and homicide victimization in an African American community. *American Journal of Public Health, 104*(1), 143–150.

Pare, P. P., & Korosec, L. (2014). Regional variations in self-protection in Canada. *Violence and Victims, 29*(5), 828–842.

Parker, B., Steeves, R., Anderson, S., & Moran, B. (2004). Uxoricide: A phenomenological study of adult survivors. *Issues in Mental Health Nursing, 25*(2), 133–145.

Parker, K. F., & Pruitt, M. V. (2000a). Poverty, poverty concentration, and homicide. *Social Science Quarterly, 81*(2), 555–570.

Parker, K. F., & Pruitt, M. V. (2000b). How the West was one: Explaining the similarities in race-specific homicide rates in the West and South. *Social Forces, 78*(4), 1483–1508.

Parker, R. N. (1995a). Bringing "booze" back in: The relationship between alcohol and homicide. *Journal of Research in Crime and Delinquency, 32*(1), 3–38.

Parker, R. N. (1995b). *Alcohol and homicide: A deadly combination of two American traditions*. Albany, NY: SUNY Press.

Peltz, J. (2012). Convicted serial killer pleads not guilty in 2 NYC murders. Accessed January 30, 2015 from http://www.nbcnewyork.com/news/local/Serial-Killer-Rodney-Alcala-California-New-York-Murder-Dating-Game-Killer-159848035.html.

Perdue, W. C., & Lester, D. (1974). Temperamentally suited to kill: The personality of murderers. *Corrective & Social Psychiatry & Journal of Behavior Technology, Methods & Therapy, 20*(1), 13–15.

Petee, T. A., Padgett, K. G., & York, T. S. (1997). Debunking the stereotype: An examination of mass murder in public places. *Homicide Studies, 1*, 317–337.

Peterson, R. D., & Krivo, L. J. (1993). Racial segregation and black urban homicide. *Social Forces, 71*(4), 1001–1026.

Peterson, R. D., & Krivo, L. J. (2005). Macrostructural analyses of race, ethnicity, and violent crime: Recent lessons and new directions for research. *Annual Review of Sociology, 31*, 331–356.

Pettigrew, T. F., & Spier, R. B. (1962). The ecological structure of Negro homicide. *American Journal of Sociology*, 621–629.

Pétursson, H., & Gudjónsson, G. H. (1981). Psychiatric aspects of homicide. *Acta Psychiatrica Scandinavica*, 64(5), 363–372.

Phillips, J. A. (2002). White, Black, and Latino homicide rates: Why the difference? *Social Problems*, 49(3), 349–373.

Pinker, S. (2011). *The better angels of our nature: Why violence has declined.* New York, NY: Viking.

Piquero, A. R., MacDonald, J., Dobrin, A., Daigle, L. E., & Cullen, F. T. (2005). Self-control, violent offending, and homicide victimization: Assessing the general theory of crime. *Journal of Quantitative Criminology*, 21(1), 55–71.

Pizarro, J. M., Corsaro, N., & Yu, S. S. V. (2007). Journey to crime and victimization: An application of routine activities theory and environmental criminology to homicide. *Victims and Offenders*, 2(4), 375–394.

Pizarro, J. M., & McGloin, J. M. (2006). Explaining gang homicides in Newark, New Jersey: Collective behavior or social disorganization? *Journal of Criminal Justice*, 34(2), 195–207.

Pizarro, J. M., Zgoba, K. M., & Jennings, W. G. (2011). Assessing the interaction between offender and victim criminal lifestyles & homicide type. *Journal of Criminal Justice*, 39(5), 367–377.

Pokorny, A. D. (1965). A comparison of homicides in two cities. *The Journal of Criminal Law, Criminology, and Police Science*, 56(4), 479–487.

Pontius, A. A. (1997). Homicide linked to moderate repetitive stresses kindling limbic seizures in 14 cases of limbic psychotic trigger reaction. *Aggression and Violent Behavior*, 2, 125–141.

Porter, S., & Woodworth, M. (2007). "I'm sorry I did it... but he started it": a comparison of the official and self-reported homicide descriptions of psychopaths and non-psychopaths. *Law and Human Behavior*, 31(1), 91–107.

Porter, S., Woodworth, M., Earle, J., Drugge, J., & Boer, D. (2003). Characteristics of sexual homicide committed by psychopathic and non-psychopathic offenders. *Law and Human Behavior*, 27, 459–470.

Porter, T., & Gavin, H. (2010). Infanticide and neonaticide: a review of 40 years of research literature on incidence and causes. *Trauma, Violence, & Abuse*, 11(3), 99–112.

Potterat, J. J., Brewer, D. D., Muth, S. Q., Rothenberg, R. B., Woodhouse, D. E., Muth, J. B.,...Brody, S. (2004). Mortality in a long-term open cohort of prostitute women. *American Journal of Epidemiology*, 159(8), 778–785.

Pratt, T. C., & Godsey, T. W. (2002). Social support and homicide: A cross-national test of an emerging criminological theory. *Journal of Criminal Justice*, 30(6), 589–601.

Pratt, T. C., & Godsey, T. W. (2003). Social support, inequality, and homicide: A cross-national test of an integrated theoretical model. *Criminology*, 41(3), 611–644.

Pridemore, W. A. (2002). What we know about social structure and homicide: A review of the theoretical and empirical literature. *Violence and Victims*, 17(2), 127–156.

Pridemore, W. A., & Trent, C. L. (2010). Do the invariant findings of Land, McCall, and Cohen generalize to cross-national studies of social structure and homicide? *Homicide Studies, 14*(3), 296–335.

Putkonen, A., Kotilainen, I., Joyal, C. C., & Tiihonen, J. (2004). Comorbid personality disorders and substance use disorders of mentally ill homicide offenders: A structured clinical study on dual and triple diagnoses. *Schizophrenia Bulletin, 30*(1), 59–72.

Putkonen, A., Ryynänen, O. P., Eronen, M., & Tiihonen, J. (2002). The quantitative risk of violent crime and criminal offending: A case-control study among the offspring of recidivistic Finnish homicide offenders. *Acta Psychiatrica Scandinavica, 106*(s412), 54–57.

Putkonen, H., Komulainen, E., Virkkunen, M., & Lönnqvist, J. (2001). Female homicide offenders have greatly increased mortality from unnatural deaths. *Forensic Science International, 119*(2), 221–224.

Pyrooz, D. C. (2012). Structural covariates of gang homicide in large US cities. *Journal of Research in Crime and Delinquency, 49*(4), 489–518.

Quanbeck, C., Frye, M., & Altshuler, L. (2003). Mania and the law in California: understanding the criminalization of the mentally ill. *Mania, 160*(7).

Quanbeck, C. D., Stone, D. C., McDermott, B. E., Boone, K., Scott, C. L., & Frye, M. A. (2005). Relationship between criminal arrest and community treatment history among patients with bipolar disorder. *Psychiatric Services, 56*(7), 847–852.

Quinet, K. (2011). Prostitutes as victims of serial homicide: Trends and case characteristics, 1970–2009. *Homicide Studies, 15*(1), 74–100.

Quinet, K., & Nunn, S. (2013). Establishing the victim–offender relationship of initially unsolved homicides: Partner, family, acquaintance or stranger? *Homicide Studies, 18*(3), 271–297.

Raine, A. (2013). *The anatomy of violence: The biological roots of crime.* New York, NY: Pantheon.

Raine, A., Buchsbaum, M., & LaCasse, L. (1997). Brain abnormalities in murderers indicated by positron emission tomography. *Biological Psychiatry, 42*, 495–508.

Raine, A., Buchsbaum, M. S., Stanley, J., Lottenberg, S., Abel, L., & Stoddard, J. (1994). Selective reductions in prefrontal glucose metabolism in murderers. *Biological Psychiatry, 36*(6), 365–373.

Raine, A., Meloy, J. R., Bihrle, S., Stoddard, J., LaCasse, L., et al. (1998). Reduced prefrontal and increased subcortical brain functioning assessed using positron emission tomography in predatory and affective murderers. *Behavioral Sciences and the Law, 16*, 319–332.

Ramsland, K. (2012). Youngest serial killer on death row. Psychology Today, accessed at http://www.psychologytoday.com/blog/shadow-boxing/201207/youngest-serial-killer- death-row.

Ratcliffe, J. H., & Rengert, G. F. (2008). Near-repeat patterns in Philadelphia shootings. *Security Journal, 21*(1), 58–76.

Reckless, W. C. (1967). *The crime problem,* 4th edition. New York, NY: Meredith.

Reckless, W. C., & Dinitz, S. (1967). Pioneering with self-concept as a vulnerability factor in delinquency. *Journal of Criminal Law, Criminology, and Police Science, 58*, 515–523.

Reckless, W. C., Dinitz, S., & Kay, B. (1957). The self-component in potential delinquency and potential non-delinquency. *American Sociological Review, 22,* 566–570.

Reckless, W. C., Dinitz, S., & Murray, E. (1956). Self-concept as an insulator against delinquency. *American Sociological Review, 21,* 744–746.

Redfield, H. V. (1880/2000). *Homicide, north and south: Being a comparative view of crime against person in several parts of the United States.* Columbus, OH: The Ohio University Press.

Regoeczi, W., Banks, D., Planty, M., Langton, L., & Warner, M. (2014). *The nation's two measures of homicide.* Washington, DC: U.S. Department of Justice, Office of Justice Programs, Bureau of Justice Statistics.

Regoeczi, W. C., & Jarvis, J. P. (2013). Beyond the social production of homicide rates: Extending social disorganization theory to explain homicide case outcomes. *Justice Quarterly, 30*(6), 983–1014.

Reisinger Walker, E., McGee, R. E., & Druss, B. G. (2015). Mortality in mental disorders and global disease burden implications: A systematic review and meta-analysis. *JAMA Psychiatry,* doi:10.1001/jamapsychiatry.2014.2502.

Reiss, Jr., A. J. (1951). Delinquency as the failure of personal and social controls. *American Sociological Review, 16,* 196–207.

Relkin, N., Plum, F., Mattis, S., Eidelberg, D., & Tranel, D. (1996). Impulsive homicide associated with an arachnoid cyst and unilateral frontotemporal cerebral dysfunction. *Seminars in Clinical Neuropsychiatry, 1*(3), 172–183.

Repo-Tiihonen, E., Virkkunen, M., & Tiihonen, J. (2001). Mortality of antisocial male criminals. *The Journal of Forensic Psychiatry, 12*(3), 677–683.

Resnick, P. J. (1969). Child murder by parents: a psychiatric review of filicide. *American Journal of Psychiatry, 126*(3), 325–334.

Resnick, P. J. (1970). Murder of the newborn: a psychiatric review of neonaticide. *American Journal of Psychiatry, 126*(10), 1414–1420.

Ressler, R., & Burgess, A. W. (1985). The men who murdered. *FBI Law Enforcement Bulletin, 54*(8), 2–6.

Ressler, R. K., Burgess, A. W., & Douglas, J. E. (Eds.). (1988). *Sexual homicide: Patterns and motives.* Lexington, MA: Lexington Books.

Rhee, S. H., & Waldman, I. D. (2002). Genetic and environmental influences on antisocial behavior: a meta-analysis of twin and adoption studies. *Psychological Bulletin, 128*(3), 490–529.

Ribeiro da Silva, D., Rijo, D., & Salekin, R. T. (2012). Child and adolescent psychopathy: A state-of-the-art reflection on the construct and etiological theories. *Journal of Criminal Justice, 40*(4), 269–277.

Rice, T. W., & Goldman, C. R. (1994). Another look at the subculture of violence thesis: Who murders whom and under what circumstances. *Sociological Spectrum, 14*(4), 371–384.

Riley, K. J. (1998). Homicide and Drugs A Tale of Six Cities. *Homicide Studies, 2*(2), 176–205.

Rivara, F. P., Mueller, B. A., Somes, G., Mendoza, C. T., Rushforth, N. B., & Kellermann, A. L. (1997). Alcohol and illicit drug abuse and the risk of violent death in the home. *Journal of the American Medical Association, 278*(7), 569–575.

Robbins, B., & Pettinicchio, D. (2012). Social capital, economic development, and homicide: A cross-national investigation. *Social Indicators Research, 105*(3), 519–540.

Roberts, A., & Willits, D. (2011). Lifestyle, routine activities, and felony-related eldercide. *Homicide Studies,* 17(2), 184–203.

Robins, L. N. (1978). Sturdy childhood predictors of adult antisocial behaviour: Replications from longitudinal studies. *Psychological Medicine,* 8(04), 611–622.

Robinson, P. L., Boscardin, W. J., George, S. M., Teklehaimanot, S., Heslin, K. C., & Bluthenthal, R. N. (2009). The effect of urban street gang densities on small area homicide incidence in a large metropolitan county, 1994–2002. *Journal of Urban Health,* 86(4), 511–523.

Robinson, W. (2015). Newborn baby dies after mother 'douses it in flammable liquid and sets it on fire in the middle of the road.' Accessed January 18, 2015 from http://www.dailymail.co.uk/news/article-2914684/Newborn-baby-dies-woman-douses- flammable-liquid-sets-fire-middle-road.html.

Rocque, M., Posick, C., & Felix, S. (2015). The role of the brain in urban violent offending: integrating biology with structural theories of 'the streets'. *Criminal Justice Studies,* 28(1), 84–103.

Rodway, C., Flynn, S., While, D., Rahman, M. S., Kapur, N., Appleby, L., & Shaw, J. (2014). Patients with mental illness as victims of homicide: a national consecutive case series. *The Lancet Psychiatry,* 1(2), 129–134.

Rodway, C., Norrington-Moore, V., While, D., Hunt, I. M., Flynn, S., Swinson, N.,... Shaw, J. (2011). A population-based study of juvenile perpetrators of homicide in England and Wales. *Journal of Adolescence,* 34(1), 19–28.

Rogers, R., Salekin, R. T., Sewell, K. W., & Cruise, K. R. (2000). Prototypical analysis of antisocial personality disorder: A study of inmate samples. *Criminal Justice and Behavior, 27,* 234–255.

Roper v. Simmons, 543 U.S. 551 (2005).

Rosenfeld, R., Baumer, E. P., & Messner, S. F. (2001). Social capital and homicide. *Social Forces,* 80(1), 283–310.

Rosenfeld, R., Fornango, R., & Rengifo, A. F. (2007). The impact of order-maintenance policing on New York City homicide and robbery rates: 1988-2001. *Criminology,* 45(2), 355–384.

Roth, R. (2011). Biology and the deep history of homicide. *British Journal of Criminology,* 51(3), 535–555.

Rountree, M. M. (2012). "I'll make them shoot me": Accounts of death row prisoners advocating for execution. *Law & Society Review,* 46(3), 589–622.

Rowhani-Rahbar, A., Zatzick, D., Wang, J., Mills, B. M., Simonetti, J. A., Fan, M. D., & Rivara, F. P. (2015). Firearm-related hospitalization and risk for subsequent violent injury, death, or crime perpetration. *Annals of Internal Medicine,* doi: 10.7326/M14-2362.

Rudegeair, P. (2013). "Dating Game" killer sentenced for 1970s murders. Accessed January 30, 2015 from http://www.reuters.com/article/2013/01/07 /us-usa-crime-serialkiller-idUSBRE9060S020130107.

Russell, D. H. (1979). Ingredients of juvenile murder. *International Journal of Offender Therapy and Comparative Criminology, 23,* 65–72.

Rydberg, J., & Pizarro, J. M. (2014). Victim lifestyle as a correlate of homicide clearance. *Homicide Studies*, doi: 10.1177/1088767914521813.

Sack, K. (1999). Shootings in Atlanta: The overview; killer confessed in a letter spiked with rage. *The New York Times*, accessed March 30, 2015, from http://www.nytimes.com/1999/07/31/us/shootings-in-atlanta-the-overview-killer-confessed-in-a-letter-spiked-with-rage.html.

Salfati, C. G., Labuschagne, G. N., Horning, A. M., Sorochinski, M., & De Wet, J. (2015). South African serial homicide: Offender and victim demographics and crime scene actions. *Journal of Investigative Psychology and Offender Profiling*, *12*(1), 18–43.

Sampson, R. J., Raudenbush, S. W., & Earls, F. (1997). Neighborhoods and violent crime: A multilevel study of collective efficacy. *Science*, *277*(5328), 918–924.

Samuel, D. B., & Widiger, T. A. (2008). A meta-analytic review of the relationships between the five-factor model and DSM-IV-TR personality disorders: A facet level analysis. *Clinical Psychology Review*, *28*, 1326–1342.

Savage, J. (2014). The association between attachment, parental bonds and physically aggressive and violent behavior: A comprehensive review. *Aggression and Violent Behavior*, *19*(2), 164–178.

Savolainen, J. (2000). Inequality, welfare state, and homicide: Further support for the institutional anomie theory. *Criminology*, *38*(4), 1021–1042.

Savolainen, J., Lehti, M., & Kivivuori, J. (2008). Historical origins of a cross-national puzzle: Homicide in Finland, 1750 to 2000. *Homicide Studies*, *12*(1), 67–89.

Scarpitti, F. R., Murray, E., Dinitz, S., & Reckless, W. C. (1960). The "good" boy in a high delinquency area: Four years later. *American Sociological Review*, *25*, 555–558.

Schanda, H., Knecht, G., Schreinzer, D., Stompe, T. H., Ortwein-Swoboda, G., & Waldhoer, T. H. (2004). Homicide and major mental disorders: A 25-year study. *Acta Psychiatrica Scandinavica*, *110*(2), 98–107.

Schechter, H. (2000). *Fiend: The shocking true story of America's youngest serial killer*. New York, NY: Pocket True Crime/Simon and Schuster.

Schechter, H. (2003). *The serial killer files*. New York, NY: Ballantine Books.

Schechter, H. (2004). *Bestial: The savage trail of a true American monster*. New York, NY: Pocket Star Books.

Scheyett, A. M., Morgan, C., Lize, S. E., Proescholdbell, S., Norwood, T., & Edwards, D. (2013). Violent death among recently released prison inmates: Stories behind the numbers. *Journal of Forensic Social Work*, *3*(1), 69–86.

Schlesinger, L. B. (1998). Pathological narcissism and serial homicide: Review and case study. *Current Psychology*, *17*(2–3), 212–221.

Schlesinger, L. B. (2002). Stalking, homicide, and catathymic process: A case study. *International Journal of Offender Therapy and Comparative Criminology*, *46*(1), 64–74.

Schug, R. A., & Fradella, H. F. (2015). *Mental illness and crime*. Thousand Oaks, CA: SAGE.

Schwaner, S. L., & Keil, T. J. (2003). Internal colonization, folk justice, and murder in Appalachia: The case of Kentucky. *Journal of Criminal Justice*, *31*(3), 279–286.

Sewall, L. A., Krupp, D. B., & Lalumière, M. L. (2013). A test of two typologies of sexual homicide. *Sexual Abuse: A Journal of Research and Treatment*, 25(1), 82–100.

Sharkey, P. T. (2006). Navigating dangerous streets: The sources and consequences of street efficacy. *American Sociological Review*, 71(5), 826–846.

Sharkey, P. (2010). The acute effect of local homicides on children's cognitive performance. *Proceedings of the National Academy of Sciences of the United States of America*, 107(26), 11733–11738.

Sharpe, T. L. (2014). Understanding the sociocultural context of coping for African American family members of homicide victims: A conceptual model. *Trauma, Violence, & Abuse*, doi: 10.1177/1524838013515760.

Shaw, C. R., & McKay, H. D. (1929). *Delinquency areas*. Chicago: University of Chicago Press.

Shaw, C. R., & McKay, H. D. (1942). *Juvenile delinquency and urban areas*. Chicago, IL: University of Chicago Press.

Shaw, C. R., & McKay, H. D. (1971). Social disorganization. In L. Radzinowicz & M. E. Wolfgang (Eds.), *Crime and justice, volume I: The criminal in society* (pp. 406–419). New York, NY: Basic Books.

Shaw, J., Appleby, L., Amos, T., McDonnell, R., Harris, C., McCann, K.,... Parsons, R. (1999). Mental disorder and clinical care in people convicted of homicide: national clinical survey. *British Medical Journal*, 318(7193), 1240–1244.

Shedlock, J., & Burke, J. (2014). Joshua Wade admits to 3 additional killings. Accessed February 5, 2015 from http://www.adn.com/print/article/20140620/authorities-joshua-wade-admits-3-additional-killings-0.

Shelton, J. L. E., Muirhead, Y., & Canning, K. E. (2010). Ambivalence toward mothers who kill: An examination of 45 US cases of maternal neonaticide. *Behavioral Sciences & the Law*, 28(6), 812–831.

Sher, L., & Landers, S. (2014). Bipolar disorder, testosterone administration, and homicide: A case report. *International Journal of Psychiatry in Clinical Practice*, 18(3), 215–216.

Sherman, L. W. (1995). Hot spots of crime and criminal careers of places. *Crime and Place*, 4, 35–52.

Sherman, L. W., & Rogan, D. P. (1995). Effects of gun seizures on gun violence: "Hot spots" patrol in Kansas City. *Justice Quarterly*, 12(4), 673–693.

Shon, P. C. H., & Roberts, M. A. (2010). An archival exploration of homicide-suicide and mass murder in the context of 19th-century American parricides. *International JOURNAL of Offender Therapy and Comparative Criminology*, 54(1), 43–60.

Shook, J. J., Vaughn, M. G., & Salas-Wright, C. P. (2013). Exploring the variation in drug selling among adolescents in the United States. *Journal of Criminal Justice*, 41(6), 365–374.

Short, J. F., & Strodtbeck, F. L. (1965). *Group process and gang delinquency*. Chicago: University of Chicago Press.

Shultz, J. M., Thoresen, S., Flynn, B. W., Muschert, G. W., Shaw, J. A., Espinel, Z.,... Cohen, A. M. (2014). Multiple vantage points on the mental health effects of mass shootings. *Current Psychiatry Reports*, 16(9), 469–487.

Shumaker, D. M., & Prinz, R. J. (2000). Children who murder: a review. *Clinical Child and Family Psychology Review, 3*(2), 97–115.

Siegel, M., Ross, C. S., & King III, C. (2013). The relationship between gun ownership and firearm homicide rates in the United States, 1981–2010. *American Journal of Public Health, 103*(11), 2098–2105.

Søndenaa, E., Gudde, C., & Thomassen, Ø. (2015). Patients with intellectual disabilities in the forensic asylums 1915–1982: before admission. *Scandinavian Journal of Disability Research, 17*(1), 14–25.

Sonderman, J. S., Munro, H. M., Blot, W. J., Tarone, R. E., & McLaughlin, J. K. (2014). Suicides, homicides, accidents, and other external causes of death among Blacks and Whites in the Southern Community Cohort Study. *PLoS One, 9*(12), e114852.

Sorensen, J. R., Marquart, J. W., & Brock, D. E. (1993). Factors related to killings of felons by police officers: A test of the community violence and conflict hypotheses. *Justice Quarterly, 10*(3), 417–440.

Sorrells, J. (1977). Kids who kill. *Crime and Delinquency, 23,* 312–320.

Spano, R., Rivera, C., & Bolland, J. M. (2010). Are chronic exposure to violence and chronic violent behavior closely related developmental processes during adolescence? *Criminal Justice and Behavior, 37*(10), 1160–1179.

Spano, R., Rivera, C., Vazsonyi, A., & Bolland, J. (2008). Does exposure to violence undermine parental monitoring over time? A partial test of the ecological-transactional model of community violence. *Criminal Justice and Behavior, 35,* 1411–1428.

Spinelli, M. G. (2001). A systematic investigation of 16 cases of neonaticide. *American Journal of Psychiatry, 158*(5), 811–813.

Stack, S. (1997). Homicide followed by suicide: An analysis of Chicago data. *Criminology, 35*(3), 435–453.

Stamatel, J. P. (2014). Explaining variations in female homicide victimization rates across Europe. *European Journal of Criminology, 11*(5), 578–600.

Stansfield, R., & Parker, K. F. (2013). Teasing out the effects of macro-conditions on race-specific male homicide rates: Do distinct predictors vary by racial group and over time?. *Social Science Research, 42*(3), 633–649.

Stapleton, T. R. (1979). Mania in criminal populations. *Western Journal of Medicine, 131*(2), 165.

Starr, D. (2010). *The killer of little shepherds.* New York, NY: Vintage.

Steeves, R., Laughon, K., Parker, B., & Weierbach, F. (2007). Talking about talk: The experiences of boys who survived intraparental homicide. *Issues in Mental Health Nursing, 28,* 899–912.

Stefanska, E. B., Carter, A. J., Higgs, T., Bishopp, D., & Beech, A. R. (2015). Offense pathways of non-serial sexual killers. *Journal of Criminal Justice, 43*(2), 99–107.

Steinberg, L. (2010). A dual systems model of adolescent risk-taking. *Developmental Psychobiology, 52*(3), 216–224.

Stöckl, H., Devries, K., Rotstein, A., Abrahams, N., Campbell, J., Watts, C., & Moreno, C. G. (2013). The global prevalence of intimate partner homicide: a systematic review. *The Lancet, 382*(9895), 859–865.

Stoddard-Dare, P., Tedor, M. F., Quinn, L., & Mallett, C. (2014). An assessment of risk factors for early death among a sample of previously incarcerated youth. *Criminal Justice Studies, 27*(2), 191–209.

Stone, M. H. (1993). *Abnormalities of personality: Within and beyond the realm of treatment.* New York, NY: Norton.

Stone, M. H. (1998). Sadistic personality in murderers. In T. Millon, E. Simonsen, M. Birket-Smith, & R. D. Davis (Eds.), *Psychopathy: Antisocial, criminal, and violent behavior* (pp. 346–355). New York, NY: The Guilford Press.

Stone, M. H., Butler, J. R., & Young, K. M. (2009). Sadistic personality disorder. In P. H. Blaney & T. Millon (Eds.), *Oxford textbook of psychopathology,* second edition (pp. 651–670). New York, NY: Oxford University Press.

Stretesky, P. B., Shelley, T. O. C., Hogan, M. J., & Unnithan, N. P. (2010). Sense-making and secondary victimization among unsolved homicide co-victims. *Journal of Criminal Justice, 38*(5), 880–888.

Sturup, J., & Lindqvist, P. (2013). Homicide offenders 32 years later–A Swedish population-based study on recidivism. *Criminal Behaviour and Mental Health.* doi:10.1002/cbm.1896.

Sutherland, E. H. (1947). *Principles of criminology,* 4th edition. Philadelphia, PA: Lippincott.

Sykes, G. M., & Matza, D. (1957). Techniques of neutralization: A theory of delinquency. *American Sociological Review,* 22, 664–670.

Tardiff, K., Gross, E., Wu, J., Stajic, M., & Millman, R. (1989). Analysis of cocaine-positive fatalities. *Journal of Forensic Sciences, 34*(1), 53–63.

Tengström, A., Hodgins, S., & Kullgren, G. (2001). Men with schizophrenia who behave violently: The usefulness of an early- versus late-start offenders typology. *Schizophrenia Bulletin, 27*(2), 205–218.

Teplin, L. A., Jakubowski, J. A., Abram, K. M., Olson, N. D., Stokes, M. L., & Welty, L. J. (2014). Firearm homicide and other causes of death in delinquents: A 16-year prospective study. *Pediatrics, 134*(1), 63–73.

Tiihonen, J., Hakola, P., Eronen, M., Vartiainen, H., & Ryynänen, O. P. (1996). Risk of homicidal behavior among discharged forensic psychiatric patients. *Forensic Science International, 79*(2), 123–129.

Tiihonen, J., Hakola, P., Nevalainen, A., & Eronen, M. (1995). Risk of homicidal behaviour among persons convicted of homicide. *Forensic Science International, 72*(1), 43–48.

Tiihonen, J., Isohanni, M., Rasanen, P., Koiranen, M., & Moring, J. (1997). Specific major mental disorders and criminality: A 26-year prospective study of the 1966 northern Finland birth cohort. *American Journal of Psychiatry, 154*(6), 840–845.

Tiihonen, J., Kuikka, J. T., Bergström, K. A., Karhu, J., Viinamäki, H., Lehtonen, J.,... Hakola, P. (1997). Single-photon emission tomography imaging of monoamine transporters in impulsive violent behaviour. *European Journal of Nuclear Medicine, 24*(10), 1253–1260.

Tiihonen, J., Räsänen, P., & Hakko, H. (1997). Seasonal variation in the occurrence of homicide in Finland. *American Journal of Psychiatry, 154*(12), 1711–1714.

Tiihonen, J., Rautiainen, M. R., Ollila, H. M., Repo-Tiihonen, E., Virkkunen, M., Palotie, A.,...Paunio, T. (2014). Genetic background of extreme violent behavior. *Molecular Psychiatry*, doi: 10.1038/mp.2014.130.

Tiihonen, J., Rossi, R., Laakso, M. P., Hodgins, S., Testa, C., Perez, J.,...Frisoni, G. B. (2008). Brain anatomy of persistent violent offenders: more rather than less. *Psychiatry Research: Neuroimaging, 163*(3), 201–212.

Toby, J. (1957). Social disorganization and stake in conformity: Complementary factors in the predatory behavior of hoodlums. *Journal of Criminal Law, Criminology & Police Science, 48*, 12–17.

Torok, M., Darke, S., & Kaye, S. (2012). Predisposed violent drug users versus drug users who commit violence: Does the order of onset translate to differences in the severity of violent offending?. *Drug and Alcohol Review, 31*(4), 558–565.

Tracy, P. E., Wolfgang, M. E., & Figlio, R. M. (1990). *Delinquency careers in two birth cohorts.* York, NY: Springer.

Trivers, R. L. (1972). Parental investment and sexual selection. In B. Campbell (Ed.), *Sexual selection and the descent of man 1871–1971* (pp. 136–179). Chicago, IL: Aldine.

Turanovic, J. J., & Pratt, T. C. (2014). "Can't stop, won't stop": Self-control, risky lifestyles, and repeat victimization. *Journal of Quantitative Criminology, 30*(1), 29–56.

Twemlow, S. W. (2003). A crucible for murder: The social context of violent children and adolescents. *The Psychoanalytic Quarterly, 72*(3), 659–698.

van Denderen, M., de Keijser, J., Gerlsma, C., Huisman, M., & Boelen, P. A. (2014). Revenge and psychological adjustment after homicidal loss. *Aggressive Behavior, in press.*

van Denderen, M., de Keijser, J., Huisman, M., & Boelen, P. A. (2014). Prevalence and correlates of self-rated posttraumatic stress disorder and complicated grief in a community-based sample of homicidally bereaved individuals. *Journal of Interpersonal Violence*, doi: 10.1177/0886260514555368.

van Denderen, M., de Keijser, J., Kleen, M., & Boelen, P. A. (2014). Psychopathology among homicidally bereaved individuals: A systematic review. *Trauma, Violence, & Abuse*, doi: 10.1177/1524838013515757.

van IJzendoorn, M. H., Schuengel, C., & Bakermanns-Kranenburg, M. J. (1999). Disorganized attachment in early childhood: Meta-analysis of precursors, concomitants, and sequelae. *Development and Psychopathology, 11*, 225–249.

Vandiver, M., & Giacopassi, D. (1997). One million and counting: Students' estimates of the annual number of homicides in the US. *Journal of Criminal Justice Education, 8*(2), 135–143.

Vaughn, M. G., Beaver, K. M., & DeLisi, M. (2009). A general biosocial paradigm of antisocial behavior: A preliminary test in a sample of adolescents. *Youth Violence and Juvenile Justice, 7*, 279–298.

Vaughn, M. G., DeLisi, M., Beaver, K. M., & Howard, M. O. (2009). Multiple murder and criminal careers: A latent class analysis of multiple homicide offenders. *Forensic Science International, 183*(1), 67–73.

Vaughn, M. G., DeLisi, M., Beaver, K. M., & Wright, J. P. (2009). Identifying latent classes of behavioral risk based on early childhood manifestations of self-control. *Youth Violence and Juvenile Justice, 7,* 16–31.

Vaughn, M. G., DeLisi, M., Gunter, T., Fu, Q., Beaver, K. M., Perron, B. E., & Howard, M. O. (2011). The severe 5%: A latent class analysis of the externalizing behavior spectrum in the United States. *Journal of Criminal Justice, 39*(1), 75–80.

Vaughn, M. G., Fu, Q., Beaver, D., DeLisi, M., Perron, B., & Howard, M. (2010). Are personality disorders associated with social welfare burden in the United States? *Journal of Personality Disorders, 24*(6), 709–720.

Vaughn, M. G., Fu, Q., DeLisi, M., Wright, J. P., Beaver, K. M., Perron, B. E., & Howard, M. O. (2010). Prevalence and correlates of fire-setting in the United States: results from the National Epidemiological Survey on Alcohol and Related Conditions. *Comprehensive Psychiatry, 51*(3), 217–223.

Vaughn, M. G., Fu, Q., Wernet, S. J., DeLisi, M., Beaver, K. M., Perron, B. E., & Howard, M. O. (2011). Characteristics of abstainers from substance use and anti-social behavior in the United States. *Journal of Criminal Justice, 39*(3), 212–217.

Vaughn, M. G., Salas-Wright, C. P., DeLisi, M., & Maynard, B. R. (2014). Violence and externalizing behavior among youth in the United States: Is there a severe 5%? *Youth Violence and Juvenile Justice, 12*(1), 3–21.

Vélez, M. B. (2009). Contextualizing the immigration and crime effect an analysis of homicide in Chicago neighborhoods. *Homicide Studies, 13*(3), 325–335.

Vernon, M., Steinberg, A. G., & Montoya, L. A. (1999). Deaf murderers: Clinical and forensic issues. *Behavioral Sciences & the Law, 17*(4), 495–516.

Vilalta, C., & Muggah, R. (2012). Violent disorder in Ciudad Juarez: a spatial analysis of homicide. *Trends in Organized Crime,* doi: 10.1007/s12117-014-9213-0.

Wallace, C., Mullen, P. E., & Burgess, P. (2014). Criminal offending in schizophrenia over a 25-year period marked by deinstitutionalization and increasing prevalence of comorbid substance use disorders *American Journal of Psychiatry, 161,* 716–727.

Walters, G. D. (1990). *The criminal lifestyle: Patterns of serious criminal conduct.* Thousand Oaks, CA: SAGE.

Walters, G. D. (1994). *Drugs and crime in lifestyle perspective* (Vol. 1). Thousand Oaks, CA: SAGE.

Walters, G. D. (2012). *Crime in a psychological context: From career criminals to criminal careers.* Thousand Oaks, CA: SAGE.

Ward, J. T., Fox, K. A., Tillyer, M. S., & Lane, J. (2015). Gender, low self-control, and violent victimization. *Deviant Behavior, 36*(2), 113–129.

Weizmann-Henelius, G., Putkonen, H., Grönroos, M., Lindberg, N., Eronen, M., & Häkkänen- Nyholm, H. (2010). Examination of psychopathy in female homicide offenders: Confirmatory factor analysis of the PCL-R. *International Journal of Law and Psychiatry, 33*(3), 177–183.

Wells, W., Wu, L., & Ye, X. (2012). Patterns of near-repeat gun assaults in Houston. *Journal of Research in Crime and Delinquency, 49*(2), 186–212.

Wellman, A. P. (2014). Grief in comparison: Use of social comparion among cold case homicide survivors. *Journal of Loss and Trauma, 19,* 462–473.

Wertham, F. (1937). The catathymic crisis: A clinical entity. *Archives of Neurology & Psychiatry, 37*(4), 974–978.

White, T. W., & Walters, G. D. (1989). Lifestyle criminality and the psychology of disresponsibility. *International Journal of Offender Therapy and Comparative Criminology, 33*(3), 257–263.

Wieczorek, W. F., Welte, J. W., & Abel, E. L. (1990). Alcohol, drugs and murder: A study of convicted homicide offenders. *Journal of Criminal Justice, 18*(3), 217–227.

Williams, K. R. (1984). Economic sources of homicide: Reestimating the effects of poverty and inequality. *American Sociological Review, 49*, 283–289.

Williams, K. R., & Flewelling, R. L. (1988). The social production of criminal homicide: A comparative study of disaggregated rates in American cities. *American Sociological Review, 53*, 421–431.

Wilson, J. Q. (1983). *Thinking about crime*, revised edition. New York, NY: Vintage.

Wilson, J. Q., & Kelling, G. L. (1982). Broken windows. *Atlantic Monthly, 249*(3), 29–38.

Wilson, M. I., & Daly, M. (1992). Who kills whom in spouse killings? On the exceptional sex ratio of spousal homicides in the United States. *Criminology, 30*(2), 189–216.

Wilson, M., & Daly, M. (1993). Spousal homicide risk and estrangement. *Violence and Victims, 8*, 3–16.

Wirth, L. (1938). Urbanism as a way of life. *American Journal of Sociology, 44*, 1–24.

Wolfgang, M. E. (1957). Victim precipitated criminal homicide. *Journal of Criminal Law, Criminology, and Police Science, 48*, 1–11.

Wolfgang, M. E. (1958). *Patters in criminal homicide*. Philadelphia, PA: University of Pennsylvania Press.

Wolfgang, M. E., & Ferracuti, F. (1967). *The subculture of violence: Toward an integrated theory in criminology*. London, England: Tavistock Publications.

Wolfgang, M. E., Figlio, R. M., & Sellin, T. (1972). *Delinquency in a birth cohort*. Chicago, IL: University of Chicago Press.

Woodworth, M., Agar, A. D., & Coupland, R. B. (2013). Characteristics of Canadian youth-perpetrated homicides. *Criminal Justice and Behavior, 40*(9), 1009–1026.

Woodworth, M., & Porter, S. (2002). In cold blood: Characteristics of criminal homicides as a function of psychopathy. *Journal of Abnormal Psychology, 111*, 436–445.

Wright, J., & Hensley, C. (2003). From animal cruelty to serial murder: Applying the graduation hypothesis. *International Journal of Offender Therapy and Comparative Criminology, 47*(1), 71–88.

Wright, K. A., Pratt, T. C., & DeLisi, M. (2008). Examining offending specialization in a sample of male multiple homicide offenders. *Homicide Studies, 12*(4), 381–398.

Wulach, J. S. (1983). Mania and crime: A study of 100 manic defendants. *Journal of the American Academy of Psychiatry and the Law, 11*(1), 69–75.

Wyant, B. R., Taylor, R. B., Ratcliffe, J. H., & Wood, J. (2012). Deterrence, firearm arrests, and subsequent shootings: A micro-level spatio-temporal analysis. *Justice Quarterly, 29*(4), 524–545.

Yang, Y., & Raine, A. (2009). Prefrontal structural and functional brain imaging findings in antisocial, violent, and psychopathic individuals: a meta-analysis. *Psychiatry Research: Neuroimaging, 174*(2), 81–88.

Yang, Y., Raine, A., Han, C-B., Schug, R. A., Toga, A. W., et al. (2010). Reduced hippocampal and parahippocampal volumes in murderers with schizophrenia. *Psychiatry Research: Neuroimaging, 182,* 9–13.

Yarvis, R. M. (1990). Axis I and Axis II diagnostic parameters of homicide. *Journal of the American Academy of Psychiatry and the Law, 18*(3), 249–269.

Yoon, J. H., Kim, J. H., Choi, S. S., Lyu, M. K., Kwon, J. H., Jang, Y. I., & Park, G. T. (2012). Homicide and bipolar I disorder: A 22-year study. *Forensic Science International, 217*(1), 113–118.

Yorker, B. C., Kizer, K. W., Lampe, P., Forrest, A. R. W., Lannan, J. M., & Russell, D. A. (2006). Serial murder by healthcare professionals. *Journal of Forensic Sciences, 51*(6), 1362–1371.

Yu, R., Geddes, J. R., & Fazel, S. (2012). Personality disorders, violence, and antisocial behavior: A systematic review and meta-regression analysis. *Journal of Personality Disorders, 26*(5), 775–792.

Zagar, R. J., Grove, W. M., Busch, K. G., & Hughes, J. R. (2009). Summary of studies of abused infants and children later homicidal, and homicidal, assaulting later homicidal, and sexual homicidal youth and adults. *Psychological Reports, 104*(1), 17–45.

Zeoli, A. M., Pizarro, J. M., Grady, S. C., & Melde, C. (2012). Homicide as infectious disease: Using public health methods to investigate the diffusion of homicide. *Justice Quarterly, 31,* 609–632.

Zuckerman, M. (2007). *Sensation seeking and risky behavior.* Washington, DC: American Psychological Association.

INDEX

A

abnormal homicide offenders, 143
abuse, 9–13, 105, 128–132, 137
ACC. *See* anterior cingulate cortex
achievement orientation, 111
acquaintance murders, 139
active criminal justice system status, 292
acute strain, 142
adenine, 214
ADHD, prevalence of, 274
adolescent murderers, psychopathic, 254
adversary effect, 18
affective-cognitive processes, 29
African American community, 58
African Americans, homicide, 152
aggression, 131–132, 179
Agnew, Robert, 135–138
agreeableness, 175
alcohol
    substance use-homicide, 261
    use disorders, 262
alleles, 214
altruism, 10
altruistic filicides, 9
altruistic homicide, 13
American Psychiatric Association, 269,
    278, 293
American social institutions, 119
amphetamines, 263
Anderson's assessment, 63
Anderson's theory, 57
anomie, 136, 137
antagonism, 175, 183, 251
anterior cingulate cortex (ACC), 302
anticipated strains, 136
antisocial behaviors, 122, 123, 179, 248,
    249, 307
antisocial bonds, salience of, 102
antisocial cognitive schemas, 31
antisocial personality disorder (ASPD),
    179, 208, 274, 288, 292–296

conceptual background, 291–294
condition, 299
in deaf murderers, 298–299
empirical linkages to homicide, 295–299
murderers with, 297–298
offenders with, 296
prevalence of, 291
Aristotle, 96
ASPD. *See* antisocial personality disorder
asylums, 280, 284
attachment, social bond theory, 99–100
avoidant personality disorder, 178, 183

B

barroom interactions, 2
Barton, Mark, 109–112, 119
behavioral disturbance, 292
behavioral genetics research, 212, 213
belief, social bond theory, 100
benzodiazepines, 265
*Better Angels of Our Nature: Why Violence
    Has Declined, The,* 86
biosocial criminology, 212, 213
biosocial paradigm, 221
biosocial perspective
    conceptual background, 211–215
    empirical linkages to homicide, 215–221
bipolar disorder, 268–270
    conceptual background, 267–270
    empirical linkages to homicide, 270–275
    impulsive features of, 271
Bipolar I Disorder, 268–270, 273
Bipolar II Disorder, 268–270
Bittaker, Lawrence, 121–122
black female homicide
    offending by age, 20
    victimization by age, 18
black gun-homicide, 166
black male homicide
    offending by age, 19
    victimization by age, 17

black offenders, 18
black subculture of violence thesis, 41
black to white homicide ratios, 107
black-white homicide differentials, 18
Borderline Personality Disorder,
    178, 183, 274
bourgeois civilizing offensive, 87
broken windows policing, 168–169
broken windows theory, 162, 163, 169

C

California Youth Authority, 72, 88
callous and unemotional traits, 249
Canadian General Social Surveys, 50
career criminals, 235
case-control design, 201, 205
case-control study, 201
catathymic process, 130
catechol O-methyltransferase (COMT)
    gene, 219
Centers for Disease Control and
    Prevention, 203
    Web-Based Injury Statistics Query and
    Reporting Systems database, 49
cerebral cortex, 302
children
    homicide by, 2
    infanticides of, 10, 11
    uxoricide effects on, 13
Christianity, doctrine of Original Sin,
    95–96
chronic strains, 142
chronic violence, developmental patterns
    in, 127
Cicchetti and Lynch's theory, 126–127
Cincinnati Initiative to
    Reduce Violence, 38
civilizing process, 86–87
cluster analyses, 106
Cluster A Personality Disorders, 177
Cluster B Personality Disorders, 178
Cluster C Personality Disorders, 178
cocaine, 280
cocaine intoxication, 263
code of the street, 56, 57, 61
    conceptual background, 51–57
    empirical linkages to homicide, 57–64
coercive interactions, 114
cognitive schemas, 31

cold cases homicides, 230
collective efficacy, 167
collective identification of threat, 73
commitment, social bond theory, 100
communication, verbal and nonverbal, 122
community-level factors, differential social
    organization, 124
community organizations, 162
community violence, 126–127
comorbidity, substance use-homicide, 261
comorbid substance use, disorders of, 282
complicated grief, 227
COMT gene. *See* catechol
    O-methyltransferase gene
concentrated disadvantage, 149, 154
concentric zone model, 161
conceptual model, 48
condemnation, 126
Conduct Disorder, 274, 292–294
conflict assay, 193
conflict subculture, 110–111
conscientiousness, 175, 251
containment theory, 97
conventional society, standards of, 27
conventional standards, 27
coping mechanisms, 20, 21
courtization of warriors era, 87
covictims of homicide, 226, 229
*Crime and Coercion: An Integrated
    Approach to Chronic Criminality*
    (Colvin), 113
Crime and the American Dream (1994)
    (Messner and Rosenfeld), 111
crime-inducing mechanisms, 161
crime in nonsocial situations, 123
crime victims, 224, 226
criminal behavior, 123, 124, 126, 189, 197
criminal career, 233–235
    conceptual background, 234–237
    empirical linkages to homicide, 237–246
criminal career paradigm, 245
criminal careers literature, 208
criminal justice system, 2, 13, 224, 234,
    268, 271, 278
criminal lifestyle, 70
criminal offenders, 138, 173, 204
criminal subcultures, 110
criminal violence, 138
criminological theories, testing of, 237

criminology, 224
  epidemiological research in, 200
  social control theory, 96
cross-national predictors of homicide, 116
cross-sectional designs, homicide
  offenders, 104
cultural trauma, legacy of, 226
Cunanan, Andrew, 118–119

D

DALYs. *See* disability-adjusted life years
Dantzler, Rodrick, 268
Dating Game, The, 66
deaf murderers, antisocial personality
  disorder in, 298–299
decent people, 55
defensive violence, 29
delinquency/problem behaviors, 123, 136
  containment of, 97
  risk factor for, 96
DeLisi, Matt, 243
delusions, 278, 279, 287
denial of injury, 126
denial of responsibility, 126
denial of victim, 126
deoxyribonucleic acid (DNA), 213–214
dependent personality disorder, 178
depression, 272, 273
  mood, 269
desistance, 235
developmental psychopathology, 101
developmental taxonomy, 236
*Diagnostic and Statistical Manual of Mental
  Disorders,* 177
Diagnostic Interview for Children and
  Adolescents (DICA-R), 252
Diagnostic Statistical Manual for Mental
  Disorders, 83
DICA-R. *See* Diagnostic Interview for
  Children and Adolescents
differential association-reinforcement
  theory, 123
differential coercion theory, 113
differential location, 124
differential social location, 124
differential social organization, 124
diminished emotional expression, 278
direct controls, social control, 98
disability-adjusted life years (DALYs), 200

disorganized attachment, 101
disorganized sexual murderer, 90–91
dispute homicides, 37
disresponsibility, 69
Divine Comedy, The, 83
divorce rate, 150, 152
dizygotic (DZ) twins, 212
DLPFC. *See* dorsolateral prefrontal cortex
DNA. *See* deoxyribonucleic acid
DNDR. *See* Do Not Delay Retaliation
domestic homicides, 188
Do Not Delay Retaliation (DNDR), 66
dorsolateral prefrontal cortex
  (DLPFC), 302
double helix, 214
drugs
  abuse, 266
  in home, 261
  homicides, 37
  selling, 148, 260
  use disorders, 262
dual systems model, 303
Durkhei, Émile, 145
Dutch Homicide Monitor, 166
dyadic death. *See* homicide-suicide
DZ twins. *See* dizygotic twins

E

early absolutist state, 87
ecological-transactional model of
  community violence, 126–127
economic dominance in United States,
  116–117
economic inequality on homicide, 115–117
'effectively polygynous' mating system, 193
eldercide, 13
electroencephalographic studies, 296
Elemental Psychopathy Assessment, 251
epicenter of neuropsychology, 302
epidemiological approach, 203
epidemiological criminology, data source
  for, 208
epidemiological perspective
  conceptual background, 197–201
  empirical linkages to homicide, 201–209
epidemiological research, 202, 205,
  207, 209
epidemiology, 197
erratic coercion, 114

erratic noncoercion, 113–114
escalation, 235
ethanol (alcohol), 265
ethnic groups, 160
evil scale, gradations of, 176
evolutionary perspective
  conceptual background, 188–192
  empirical linkages to homicide, 192–195
evolutionary psychology, 188, 190, 192
  filicide and, 194
evolutionary theories, 187
evolved psychological mechanisms, 188
expressive homicides, 165
expressive needs, social support, 113
externalizing behaviors, 208
extraversion, 175, 176, 251
Eysenck's PEN model, 176, 179

F

factor analyses, 106
family income inequality, 115–116
family liaison officers, 229–230
family structure, homicide, 149
fatal child assault, 10–11
fatalism, 56
Federal Bureau of Investigation, 45, 48,
  226, 231
  Supplementary Homicide Reports, 21
federal law, 6
female homicide offender, 257
female juvenile homicide offender, 21
female multiple homicide offender, 193
female serial sexual homicide offender,
  255–256
fetishism of money, 111
fictional homicide, 5
filicide, 7–9, 194
Finland, homicide in, 156
Finnish welfare state, 156
firearm homicides
  data for, 54
  mortality rate, 54–55
  rates, 227–228
firearm-related hospitalization, 203
first-degree murder, 7
Five Factor Model of Personality,
  174, 179, 251
five-stage sequential model, 142
focused deterrence programs, 37

formal social controls, 163
fratricide, 12
Freudian psychoanalytic theory, 97
frustration tolerance, 97
functional brain imaging, 306
future dangerousness, assessments of, 257

G

Gacy, John Wayne, 108
gang activity, substance use-homicide, 260
gang dynamics, 34
gang homicides, 37
gang-related homicides, 165
gene, 214
general altercation homicides, 57–58
General Social Survey, 45, 46
general strain theory, 135, 136
  conceptual background, 136–138
  empirical linkages to homicide, 138–143
  negative emotions in, 141
General Theory of Crime, A, 84
genocide, 143
Girls Raised in the South (G.R.I.T.S.), 46
Global Burden of Disease Study,
  201, 262, 279
globalization in worldwide economy, 116
Gorilla Man, 101
gratification delay, 84
G.R.I.T.S. *See* Girls Raised in the South
gun-related homicides, 169, 170
guns, substance use-homicide, 260

H

hallucinations, 278, 279, 287–288
Hansen, Robert, 267–268
healthcare serial murder, epidemiology of,
  206–207
hedonistic killers, 15
Heide, Kathleen, 11
herding/honor culture, 42
heritability, 212
Hernandez, Aaron, 51–52
high activity-level/physicality, 84
high self-centeredness, 85
Hillside Strangler case, 124–125
Hispanics, homicide, 18, 107, 152, 166
histrionic personality disorder, 178
homicidal behavior, 11, 287
homicidal child molesters, 238

homicide, 1, 6
  age and multiple offender, 128
  characteristics of, 151
  correlates of, 16–22
  costs of, 4–5
  cross-national predictors of, 116
  economic inequality on, 115
  empirical linkages to homicide, 86–93
  experiences in, 105
  in Finland, 156
  motivations for, 2
  multiple offenders and victims in, 127
  offending rates, 148
  research purpose, 22
  types of, 6–16, 131
  victims, 224–226, 228–230
  visualization of places, 145–146
homicide adaptation theory, 190
homicide detectives approach, 35
homicide—intimate-partner homicide, 192
Homicide, North and South: Being a
    Comparative View of Crime Against
    Person in Several Parts of the United
    States, 40
homicide offenders, 2, 3, 6, 16, 78, 101,
    127–128, 230–231, 254, 305
  from broken home, 103
  features of, 137
  social bonds, 102
  and victim, 32, 225
homicide rates, 117, 119
  structural conditions, race, and serial
    killers, 153
  in United States, 152–154
homicide ratios, black to white, 107
homicide-suicide, 13–14, 104, 151
homogamous interaction, 67
homophily, principle of, 181
honor-based violence, 29
hopelessness, 56
hot spots theory, 30
human behavior, determinants of, 162
Human Development Index, 117
hypomanic episode, 268, 270

I

immigrants, 160
impellance, 83
impulsive homicide offenders, 92

impulsive murderers, 92
impulsivity, 81
incidence, 197
Indianapolis Violence Reduction
    Partnership, 38
indirect controls, social control, 98
individualism, 111
industrialization of United States, 146
inequality, homicide, 148–149
infanticide, 9–10
informal social control, 161, 163
  mechanisms, 167
inhibition, 84
inner containment, containment theory, 97
instigation, 83
institutional anomie theory, 111
  American culture, 111
  American Dream, money obsession, and
    murder, 118–119
  conceptual background, 109–115
  criminologists, 115
  empirical linkages to homicide, 115–119
  social institutions, 112
institutional imbalance, 112
institutional legitimacy, 116
instrumental homicides, 165
instrumental needs, social support, 113
interactionist dynamics of homicides, 33
interactionist-oriented theory of crime, 28
interactionist perspective
  conceptual background, 25–31
  empirical linkages to homicide, 31–38
interactionist-routine activities approach,
    37
interactionist themes, 43
interactionist theory, 26
intermittency, 235
Intermittent Explosive Disorder, 83
internal controls, social control, 98
"internalizing symptoms," 249
interpersonal intrusiveness, 68
interpersonal violence, 201
intersubjective behavior, 29
intersubjective homicide, 43
intimate groups, 122
intimate partner homicide, 12, 13
intimate partner murders, 36
intrasexual competition, 189
intrasexual violence, sex difference in, 193

introverts, 175
involuntary manslaughter, 7
involvement, social bond theory, 100
I³ theory, 83

J

James, Jesse, 233
Jones, Genene, 245
justifiable homicide, 6
justified killing condition, 307
juvenile drug markets, 154
juvenile homicide, 38
    offenders, 21
juvenile offenders, 18
juvenile sexual homicide offenders, 183,
    241–243

K

Killer of Little Shepherds, The, 40
"kill or be killed" culture, 56
Klimek, Tillie, 245
Kraft, Randy, 220–221

L

lambda, 235
lateral orbitofrontal cortex, 307
Law Enforcement Officers Killed and
    Assaulted (LEOKA), 231
Lee's theory, 43
legal cynicism, 61
LEOKA. *See* Law Enforcement Officers
    Killed and Assaulted
life-course-persistent offenders, 236
lifestyle criminality, 67–68
lifestyle criminological theory, 69
lifestyle factors, 77
lifestyle perspective
    conceptual background, 65–70
    empirical linkages to homicide, 70–79
lifestyle theory, 67, 68, 70, 73, 77, 78
Limbic Psychotic Trigger Reaction, 217
limbic system, 302
low-activity versions of gene, 214
low cognitive/verbal skills, 85
low gratification delay, 84
low persistence, 84
lust killers, 15
lynching, 47, 48

M

Major Depressive Disorder, 275
major depressive episode, 268, 269
male homicide, large component of, 188
male-homicide link, 188
male juvenile homicide offenders, 21
malevolent psychopath, 250
maltreating parents, 101
mania, 272, 273
manic depression, 272
manic episode, 269–270
manic mood disturbance, 270
Manson, Charles, 130–131, 140–141
MAOA gene. *See* monoamine oxidase A
    gene
massacre, 142
mass homicides, 2
mass media outlets, 5
mass murders, 15, 105–106, 110, 142,
    227–228, 272
matricide, 11
media coverage, public scrutiny, 225
mens rea of perpetrator, 6
mental disorders, 230
    research on, 202
mental health services, 3
mental illness patients, homicide of,
    284–285
mercy-killing suicide, 13
meriticide, 12
meta-analysis, 282, 284
methamphetamine, 264, 280
"Midsomer Murders," 5
mission-oriented killers, 15
Mobile Youth Survey, 127
Moffitt's developmental taxonomy, 237
Moffitt's theory, 244
molecular genetic association studies, 213
monoamine oxidase A (MAOA) gene,
    214, 218
monozygotic (MZ) twins, 212
mood disorders, 202
moral disengagement, 249
Mullin, Herbert, 278, 279
multicide. *See* mass murders
multiple disadvantage model, 107
multiple homicides, 142
    offenders, 16, 250, 265, 268

multiple meta-analyses, 214
multiple-offender homicides, 34
multivariate models, 205
mundane homicides, 81
murderers
   with antisocial personality disorder,
      297–298
   personality functioning of, 140
   personality types of, 180
Murder in Britain Study, 98–99
murders, 6, 61, 71, 224, 283–284
   of family victims, 288
   victims of, 225
murder-suicide. See homicide-suicide
MZ twins. See monozygotic twins

N

narcissism, 85, 88
narcissistic personality disorder, 88, 178
National Center for
   Education Statistics, 45
National Center for Health Statistics, 48,
   52, 199
National Crime Victimization Survey, 47
National Epidemiologic Survey on Alcohol
   and Related Conditions
   (NESARC), 208
National Incident-Based Reporting System
   (NIBRS), 18
national-level measuring systems, 198
National Longitudinal Study of Adolescent
   Health, 218
National Mortality Followback Survey, 107
national sample of homicides, 139
National Survey on Drug Use and Health,
   208, 266
National Violent Death Reporting
   System, 104
National Vital Statistics System
   Fatal Injury Reports, 199, 200
   mortality data, 6
negative emotions in general
   strain theory, 141
negative symptoms, 279
   of schizophrenia, 282
Nelson, Leonard, 100–101
neonaticide, 10
   offenders, 231

NESARC. See National Epidemiologic
   Survey on Alcohol and Related
   Conditions
neurogeneticists, 306
neurological soft signs, 296
neuropsychological deficits, 303
neuropsychological perspective, 301
   conceptual background, 302–304
   empirical linkages to homicide,
      304–307
neuropsychology, 302
neuroticism, 175, 176, 179, 251
neurotransmission process, 214
neutralization techniques, 132
neutralization theory, 126
Nicomachean Ethics (Aristotle), 96
nonpsychopathic murderers, 253
nonserial sexual homicide offenders,
   offense pathways, 106
nonshared environmental factors, 212
"normal" homicides, 5
normal personality traits, 185
norm retention, inner containment, 97
Norris, Roy, 121–122
North Carolina Department of Corrections
   and North Carolina Violent Death
   Reporting System, 71
Northwestern Juvenile Project, 204
nucleotides, 214

O

objective strains, 136
obsessive-compulsive personality
   disorder, 178
OFC. See orbitofrontal cortex
offense-specific effects, 103
onset, 234–235
openness to experience, 175
Operation Ceasefire, 37, 38
Operation Peacekeeper, 37
opportunity, substance use-homicide, 260
Oppositional Defiant Disorder, 274, 294
   symptoms of, 292
orbitofrontal cortex (OFC), 302
organic disorders, 280
organized sexual murderer, 91
Original Sin, 95–96
overcontrolled individuals, 89

P

Panzram, Carl, 173
paranoid personality disorder, 177, 183
paraphilias, 184
paraphilic behaviors, 184
paraphilic-related disorders, 184
parental investment theory, 189
parental solicitude, 192
parricide, 11
  offenders, 288
patricide, 11
PCL-R. *See* Psychopathy Checklist-Revised
PCL-SV. *See* Psychopathy Checklist
  Screening Version
pedophilia, 184
PEN model, 176
performative behavior, 29
personality, 173
  conceptual background, 173–179
  empirical linkages to homicide, 179–185
  and homicide, interrelationship
    between, 179
  model, 176
personality disorders, 3, 177, 178, 181,
    183–185
  prevalence of, 183
physical violence, 188
Pittsburgh Youth Study (PYS),
    102–103, 240
planning stage, 142
polygynous mating system, 195
polymorphisms, 214
population-attributable risk, 207
population characteristics, homicide, 149
population growth in United States, 146
pornography, 132
positive symptoms, 279
  of schizophrenia, 282
positivist criminology, 28
positron emission tomography study, 216
poverty, homicide, 148, 150
poverty-homicide linkage, 150
power/control-oriented killers, 15
prefrontal abnormalities, 307
prevalence, 197
primary psychopathy, 249
private social control, 162
proband, 202
prodromes, 292

Project on Human Development in
    Chicago Neighborhoods, 62, 63
Project Safe Neighborhoods, 38
prostitutes, homicides of, 205
prostitution, 75
psychiatric diagnosis, prevalence of, 205
psychiatric disorders, 183–184
psychiatric disturbance, 7
psychiatric sample of homicides, 139
psychopathic interpersonal style, 248
psychopathic traits, 285–286
psychopathy
  adolescent murderers, 254
  conceptual background, 248–252
  empirical linkages to homicide,
    252–257
  homicide offenders, 253
  murderers, 248, 253, 257
  personality, 248
  taxonomy of, 249
Psychopathy Checklist-Revised (PCL-R),
    251, 252, 255
Psychopathy Checklist Screening Version
    (PCL-SV), 255
psychosis, 10, 281–282
psychotic disorders, 202, 278, 280
psychotic filicides, 9
psychotic illness, 284
psychoticism, 176
PTSD symptoms, 227, 228
public health research, 77
public housing developments, 165
PYS. *See* Pittsburgh Youth Study

Q

qualitative research, 60

R

racial groups, 160
Ramirez, Richard, 259–260
rape, 195
recidivism, 245
recidivist homicide, 286
Redfield, 40–41
regional arguments for homicide, 50
regional explanation of homicide, 180
regional perspective
  conceptual background, 39–43
  empirical linkages to homicide, 43–50

relative deprivation, homicide, 148–149
resource deprivation, 152
retreatist subculture, 111
retrospective cohort study design, 203
robbery homicides, victims of, 37
Robinson, Harvey, 216
routine activities theory, 28
    ample empirical support for, 36
rule of thumb, 263

S

sadistic personality disorder, 178, 184
sadistic sexual homicide offenders, 184
Schedule for Nonadaptive and Adaptive
    Personality (SNAP), 252
Schizoid Personality Disorder, 177, 178
schizophrenia, 230, 278
    conceptual background, 278–280
    and recidivist homicide, 286
    unique feature of, 279
schizotypal personality disorder, 183
school bonding, 103
schools, mass murders, 142
secondary psychopaths, 249
securitization and new culture of control
    spans, 87
self-concept, inner containment, 97
self-control, 82–83
    conceptual background, 81–86
    empirical linkages to homicide, 86–93
self-control theory, 84, 88
self-defense outcomes, 33
self-derogation theory, 27
self-fulfilling prophecy, 29
self-regulatory system, 303
sensational homicides, 2
sensation seeking, 83
sense-making, 226
serial homicides, 2
    offenders, 14, 183
    prostitutes as victims of, 75–76
serial killers, 36
serial murder, 14–15, 131–132
serious offenders, 231
service-oriented establishments, 146
sex chromosome abnormalities, 219
sex differences
    in homicide, 19
    in intrasexual violence, 193

sexual abuse victimization, 10
sexual dysfunction, 195
sexual homicide, 14, 131, 132, 195
    offenders, 106, 184
    psychopaths, 252, 253
sexual masochism, 184
sexual murderer, 132
sexual sadism, 184
shared environmental factors, 212
sharp weapons attacks, 280
sheer sex differences in homicide, 20, 21
simulation models, 3
single-photon emission tomography
    (SPET), 221
Skinner, B. F., 123
slums, 161
SMSAs. *See* standard metropolitan
    statistical areas
SNAP. *See* Schedule for Nonadaptive and
    Adaptive Personality
social activism, 156
social bonds
    disorganized attachment, 101
    individuals with stronger, 107
    parts of, 99–100
    salience of, 102
social bond theory, 99
social capital, 155–156
Social Capital Benchmark Survey, 156
social control
    forms of, 98
    prosocial type of, 113
social control theory, 96
    conceptual background, 95–100
    elements of, 106
    empirical linkages to homicide,
        100–108
    to homicide, relevance of, 105–106
    importance of, 104
    Murder in Britain Study, 98–99
    relevance of, 105–106
social disciplining revolution, 87
social disorder, zero-tolerance
    policies for, 163
social disorganization, 163, 170
    factors, 164
    perspective, conceptual background,
        159–164
    variables, 166

social disorganization theorists, 162, 166
social disorganization theory, 159, 160, 162, 164, 166
social disorganized neighborhood, negative features of, 163
social institutions, 112, 115
social learning perspective
  conceptual background, 121–127
  differential association-reinforcement theory, 123
  ecological-transactional model of community violence, 126–127
  empirical linkages to homicide, 127–133
  forensic-oriented constructs, 130
  Hillside Strangler case, 125
  network analyses, 133
  neutralization theory, 126
  theory of differential association (Sutherland), 122, 123
  violent movies, 133
social learning principles, illustration of, 129
social learning processes, 127
social learning theory, 122
  Hillside Strangler case, 125
social networks, homicide, 133
social organization theory, 164
social structural theory, 124
Social Structure and Social Learning (SSSL) model, 124
social support, 113, 116–117, 119
  theory, 117, 118
  violent offenders, 138
social ties, homicide suicides, 104
societal-level strain, 143
society, physical and social structure changes of, 146–147
sociology, 145
sociopathy, 257
southern effect, 39, 41, 44
  regional argument for, 46
southern homicide, 47
southern subculture of violence, 40
SPET. See single-photon emission tomography
spousal homicides, 12
spree killing, 15
spree murder, 15–16
SSSL model. See Social Structure and Social Learning model

'stages of grief' model, 224
standard metropolitan statistical areas (SMSAs), 149, 150
Steinberg's model, 303
Stone's gradations of evil model, 176, 177
strains, 143
  concept of, 136
  and motivations, 139
  scope of, 137
  types of, 136–137
stranger homicides, 284
stratification system, 110
street code, 56, 57, 61
street efficacy, 62
street people, 55
structural brain imaging, 306
structural perspective, 147
  approaches, 151
  concentrated disadvantage, 149
  conceptual background of, 145–149
  empirical linkages to homicide, 149–157
  offending rates, 148
  predictors of, 154
  research, 154–155
  risk factors, 150
  structural variables, 148–149
  theories, 154
  victimization rates, 147
subcultural street codes, 62
subjective strains, 136
substance abuse
  conceptual perspectives, 259–262
  in criminal carrier, role of, 260
  dangerous features of, 266
  disorders of, 271
  empirical linkages to homicide, 263–266
  and homicide, relationship between, 262
substance abuse-homicide linkage, 266
substance dependence, 262
substance use, 260, 262
  disorders of, 3, 282
substance use-homicide linkage, 266
substance use-homicide relationship, 260–261
Supplementary Homicide Reports, 47, 48, 150, 198–200, 203
  for 454 U.S. urban counties, 115
  of Uniform Crime Reporting program, 6

Sutherland's (1947) theory of differential
    association, 122–124, 126
symbolic interactionism, 28
syndemic, 209

T

taxonomy of psychopathy, 249
temper, 84–85
termination, 235
theory of differential association
    (Sutherland), 122–124, 126
threat control override symptoms,
    279–280
thrill killers, 15
Toppan, Jane, 245
traffic behavior, 43
2-repeat allele of MAOA gene, 218

U

UCR. *See* Uniform Crime Reporting
    Program
uncontrolled strain, 142
undercontrolled individuals, 89
unemployment, homicide, 105
uneven distribution of homicide, 52, 53
Uniform Crime Reporting Program
    (UCR), 198
Uniform Crime Reports, 19
United States
    economic dominance in, 116–117
    education in, 137
    homicide rates in, 152–154, 200
    population growth and industrialization
        of, 146
    standard metropolitan statistical areas
        in, 149, 150
    structural predictors of
        homicides in, 154
universal emotional motivations, 191
universalism, 111
unjustified killing condition, 307
Unruh, Howard, 65–66
urban segregation, basic ecological process
    of, 164
U.S. Centers for Disease Control and
    Prevention, 45
U.S. Supreme Court, 304
"us *vs.* them" primary groups, 143
uxoricide, 12–13, 225

V

Vacher, Joseph, 40
Vann, Darren, 159
Vaughn, Michael, 243, 244
vehicular homicide, 7
ventromedial prefrontal cortex
    (VMPFC), 302
vicarious strains, 137
victimization, 188
    homicide, 207–208
victim liaison officers, 230
victim offender relationship in homicides, 21
victimology, 223, 224
    conceptual background, 224–226
    empirical linkages to homicide, 226–232
victim-precipitated homicide, 32
victims *vs.* homicides, 288
violence, 281, 288
    exposure to, 126
    warning signs of, 283–284
violent behaviors, 201, 208, 209
violent offenders, social support, 138
violent youths, 140
visionary murderers, 15
VMPFC. *See* ventromedial prefrontal
    cortex
voluntary manslaughter, 7

W

Wade, Joshua, 234
white female homicide, 19
    offending by age, 20
    victimization by age, 18
white male homicide
    offending by age, 19
    victimization by age, 17
willingness-to-pay concept, 4
witnessing murder, 264
Wolfgang, Marvin, 31–32
work-life balance, 114

Y

years lived with disability (YLDs), 200
years of life lost due to premature mortality
    (YLLs), 200
YLDs. *See* years lived with disability
YLLs. *See* years of life lost due to premature
    mortality

young offenders, 73
Youth Risk Behavior Surveillance System, 45
youths
   convicted of murder, 128
   homicide, 103

Z

zero-tolerance policies for social
   disorder, 163
zone of transition, 161

CPSIA information can be obtained at www.ICGtesting.com
Printed in the USA
LVOW02s0046230615

443176LV00006B/15/P